THE ENCLOSURE OF KNOWLEDGE

The rise of agrarian capitalism in Britain is usually told as a story about markets, land and wages. *The Enclosure of Knowledge* reveals that it was also about books, knowledge and expertise. It argues that during the early modern period, farming books were a key tool in the appropriation of the traditional art of husbandry possessed by farm workers of all kinds. It challenges the dominant narrative of an agricultural 'enlightenment', in which books merely spread useful knowledge, by showing how codified knowledge was used to assert greater managerial control over land and labour. The proliferation of printed books helped divide mental and manual labour to facilitate emerging social divisions between labourers, managers and landowners. The cumulative effect was the slow enclosure of customary knowledge. By synthesising diverse theoretical insights, this study opens up a new social history of agricultural knowledge and reinvigorates long-term histories of knowledge under capitalism.

JAMES D. FISHER is a historian of early modern Britain. He is a postdoctoral research fellow at the University of Exeter (2020–23) and has previously taught history at King's College London, Royal Holloway, and the University of East London. James is trained in disciplines across the humanities and sciences, including political philosophy and physics.

T0382278

CAMBRIDGE STUDIES IN EARLY MODERN BRITISH HISTORY

SERIES EDITORS

MICHAEL BRADDICK
Professor of History, University of Sheffield

KRISTA KESSELRING
Professor of History, Dalhousie University

ALEXANDRA WALSHAM
*Professor of Modern History, University of Cambridge,
and Fellow of Emmanuel College*

This is a series of monographs and studies covering many aspects of the history of the British Isles between the late fifteenth century and the early eighteenth century. It includes the work of established scholars and pioneering work by a new generation of scholars. It includes both reviews and revisions of major topics and books, which open up new historical terrain or which reveal startling new perspectives on familiar subjects. All the volumes set detailed research within broader perspectives, and the books are intended for the use of students as well as for their teachers.

For a list of titles in the series go to
www.cambridge.org/earlymodernbritishhistory

THE ENCLOSURE
OF KNOWLEDGE

*Books, Power and Agrarian Capitalism
in Britain, 1660–1800*

JAMES D. FISHER

University of Exeter

CAMBRIDGE
UNIVERSITY PRESS

Shaftesbury Road, Cambridge CB2 8EA, United Kingdom

One Liberty Plaza, 20th Floor, New York, NY 10006, USA

477 Williamstown Road, Port Melbourne, VIC 3207, Australia

314–321, 3rd Floor, Plot 3, Splendor Forum, Jasola District Centre, New Delhi – 110025, India

103 Penang Road, #05–06/07, Visioncrest Commercial, Singapore 238467

Cambridge University Press is part of Cambridge University Press & Assessment, a department of the University of Cambridge.

We share the University's mission to contribute to society through the pursuit of education, learning and research at the highest international levels of excellence.

www.cambridge.org
Information on this title: www.cambridge.org/9781009048736

DOI: 10.1017/9781009049283

First published 2022
First paperback edition 2024

A catalogue record for this publication is available from the British Library

ISBN   978-1-316-51798-7   Hardback
ISBN   978-1-009-04873-6   Paperback

Cambridge University Press & Assessment has no responsibility for the persistence or accuracy of URLs for external or third-party internet websites referred to in this publication and does not guarantee that any content on such websites is, or will remain, accurate or appropriate.

For my parents

Contents

Figures

Tables

Acknowledgements

The single name of an author always disguises a collective effort. When I reflect on the processes culminating in this book, acts of generosity flash up in my memory. I remember the reassuring response to a hopeful email, for which I owe Carolyn Steedman more than she can possibly be aware. I remember how Jane Whittle kindly gave her time and expertise when I was shaping my ideas on rural labour at the start of the project. She has continued to play a key intellectual and supportive role, providing invaluable comments on an earlier version of this text and recently helping me find an institutional home at the University of Exeter. I remember, too, the joyful shock of being offered a PhD scholarship years ago while sitting by the Old Street roundabout on my lunch break. I can say with complete sincerity that the research in this book was only possible with funding from the Arts and Humanities Research Council through the London Arts and Humanities Partnership (LAHP).

I owe my greatest thanks to my supervisors Arthur Burns and Alex Sapoznik at King's College London, who not only refined my research but also patiently cultivated my historical sensibilities. This book benefitted immeasurably from having two excellent historians – so different as scholars both from myself and each other – interrogate multiple drafts. I recall with equal gratitude the demanding conversations that forced me to rethink, to start again and to pursue unfamiliar paths, as I do the day when I finally felt I had reached the standard towards which they had steered me. As a whole, the King's Department of History provided a nourishing environment, and I look back with gratitude for every small chat in a hallway, office or pub with brilliant scholars such as Laura Gowing, Hannah Dawson, Abigail Woods, David Edgerton, Adam Sutcliffe and Richard Vinen, to name only a few.

I was sustained most of all by my fellow-suffering PhD students. The excitement and urgency I felt while doing history were fuelled by my friends in our nomadic 'Radical History' reading group, especially Laura Forster,

Prerna Agarwal, Christian Melby, Zhang Lifei, Grace Redhead, Lenny Hodges, Theo Williams, Molly Corlett and Agnes Arnold-Forster. My imaginative soul was nurtured by my co-editors of *The Still Point Journal*, clustered in the English Department, particularly Francesca Brooks, James Morland, Briony Wickes, Charlotte Rudman and Fran Allfrey. I was also fortunate to be surrounded by many wonderful early modernists who offered friendly feedback on a draft chapter; my thanks to William Tullett, Alice Marples, Philip Abraham, Tom Colville, Rebecca Simon and Philippa Hellawell.

My arguments were tested among various audiences, especially at the British Society for Eighteenth-Century Studies (BSECS) conference, the Social History Society (SHS) conference and the Society, Culture and Belief, 1500–1800 seminar at the Institute for Historical Research (IHR). Of most value has been my participation over many years in the British History in the Long 18th Century seminar (IHR), which consistently generates lively and rigorous debate. A few individuals stand out again at vital moments. The invigorating advice and backing of Penny Corfield preserved my morale during tough periods. The thoughtful reading, questioning and comments of James Raven, as an examiner, raised the quality of this study. Finally, my appreciation to Sarah Toulalan for a nudge in the right direction at the right time. The final set of scholarly acknowledgements are crammed into hundreds of footnotes; this volume is a mosaic of historical research spanning many decades, mostly by people I will never meet.

On a more personal note, a warm thanks to everyone close to me who lifted me up countless times with an enthusiastic word or sympathetic smile, especially my bemused housemates during intense bouts of writing: Laura Rodrigues, Eirwen-Jane Pierrot, Simon Wingrove and Ian. And for being there alongside me, Suzane Muhereza, Mai Vu, Mona Ahmed and Andreea Pintea.

Finally, I dedicate this book to my loving family and my extraordinary parents, who accepted every peculiar decision I have made and gave me the confidence to pursue what felt right.

This study began loosely as a history of work, took a tangent into a narrower history of books, before expanding into a broader history of knowledge, which enabled me to eventually tell a new story about work that I could not have conceived at the beginning. It is a story that remains startlingly relevant in the present 'knowledge economy'.

Notes

In the interests of accessibility, some early modern spellings (instances of i, u, v and vv) have been silently modernised.

Abbreviations

AgHR	Agricultural History Review
AHEW	Agrarian History of England and Wales
EcHR	Economic History Review
ODNB	*Oxford Dictionary of National Biography*
OED	*Oxford English Dictionary*

Introduction
Pen over Plough

It was the goddess Ceres who first gifted the secrets of agriculture to humankind, according to classical mythology as told by Virgil and Ovid.[1] In one story borrowed from Greek myth, Ceres (originally Demeter) gave Triptolemus her chariot drawn by winged dragons to spread the knowledge of agriculture among men and women, symbolised in art as the handing over of sheaves of corn.[2] This ancient tale of the origins of cultivation was given a striking new twist in the frontispiece to the agricultural treatise *The Compleat Body of Husbandry* in 1756, captioned 'The Goddess Ceres in her Chariot drawn by Dragons, Teaching Mankind the Art of Husbandry' (see Figure 0.1). It depicted Ceres presenting a scroll with the book's title to a ploughman, and thereby symbolised the transfer of knowledge as flowing through the written word. In doing so, the treatise harnessed the potency of classical myth to declare that writing was the primary vehicle for agricultural knowledge. While the engraving was in part self-aggrandisement, it was a rare illustration of the emerging idea that the practical knowledge to grow crops and raise livestock was best acquired from books.

This was a controversial idea in early modern Britain. Consider the following words of a countryman in dialogue with a courtier, imagined by a court poet in 1618.

> What more learning have we need of, but that experience will teach us without booke? We can learne to plough and harrow, sow and reape, plant and prune, thrash and fanne, winnow and grinde, brue and bake, and all without booke, and these are our chiefe businesse in the Country …[3]

The countryman further explains that the only motive he has for 'learning' is to be able to engage in activities directly requiring reading and

---

[1] 'It was Ceres who first taught to men the use of iron ploughs' (line 148): Virgil, *Georgics*, trans. Peter Fallon (Oxford World Classics; Oxford, 2006), 10. See also Ovid's *Fasti: Book IV* (lines 401–5).
[2] Barbette Stanley Spaeth, *The Roman goddess Ceres* (Austin, 1996), 17, 37.
[3] Nicholas Breton, *The court and country* (London, 1618), fo. 11.

The Goddess CERES *in her* Chariot *drawn by* Dragons, *Teaching* MANKIND *the* Art *of* Husbandry.

Figure 0.1   'The Goddess Ceres in her Chariot drawn by Dragons, Teaching Mankind the Art of Husbandry', engraving printed as frontispiece in Thomas Hale, *The Compleat Body of Husbandry* (1756), by Samuel Wale (painter/draughtsman) and Benjamin Cole (printmaker).

writing, such as making wills. The pen and the plough seem to belong to different worlds. Husbandry does not deal in words, so what help is a book? If the labours of husbandry are learned through experience, then an instruction manual is superfluous.

These two fragments, and the gaps in time and perspective between them, prompt a series of questions about agricultural books in the seventeenth and eighteenth centuries. Who valued books as a source of knowledge about farming; when and why did they come to do so; and what historical processes drove such transformations? While agricultural historians have been willing to criticise the value of individual agricultural books, their general value as a medium for transmitting farming knowledge is rarely questioned. This is despite the frequent recognition that for centuries most farmers have been deeply sceptical about what they could learn from farming books. Such scepticism continued even with the expansion of literacy into the nineteenth and twentieth centuries – although it has been suggested that by 1850 all English farmers were 'aware that they could no longer ignore written information on agriculture, whatever their continued misgivings about "book-farming"'.[4] Such misgivings are taken seriously in this book. It offers a new history of why, how and for whom books became a key source of knowledge about farming in Britain over the early modern period.

It is a history that links knowledge, power and capitalism. The formation of agrarian capitalism in Britain is usually told as a story about markets, land and wages, but it was also about knowledge, books and expertise. Up to the sixteenth century, men and women had learned to farm through their labour, acquiring the customary knowledge passed down from generation to generation, mostly without the aid of the written word. Writing and farming were predominantly distinct skills possessed by distinct classes. Yet between the sixteenth and the nineteenth century, agriculture was transformed through a polarisation in landholdings, evolving from a landscape dominated by small family farms to one dominated by large capitalist farms using hired wage labour. This demanded a reorganisation and redistribution of agricultural knowledge among rural society, as the people making decisions about how to farm were less likely to be the same people executing those decisions.

---

[4] Nicholas Goddard, 'Agricultural literature and societies', in G. E. Mingay (ed.), *AHEW: 1750–1850 Vol 6* (Cambridge, 1989), 370. See also: '[f]ew Scottish farmers in 1700 would have been likely to admit that they could learn anything about their business from books'. G. E. Fussell and H. Fyrth, 'Eighteenth-century Scottish agricultural writings', *History*, 35 (1950), 49.

However, this profound social transformation has been obscured by the dominant historical narratives of agricultural 'improvement', 'revolution' and 'enlightenment', which all present a linear progression of knowledge. In these narratives, agricultural books are understood solely as drivers of technological change by disseminating useful knowledge leading to increases in productivity, with only occasional hints about the social conditions or effects. Yet when we examine these satisfied tales about new flows of knowledge we invariably find they rest upon an implied social hierarchy. This is explicit in one triumphalist account of how the enlightenment stimulated economic growth in agriculture and industry, described as an elite-driven phenomenon: 'what the large majority of workers knew mattered little as long as they did what they were told by those who knew more'.[5] But how were such hierarchies of knowledge established, both practically and ideologically, such that historians could later investigate how knowledge 'trickled-down' the social order? And what if, in the case of early modern agriculture, we tend to find workers who knew more than their social superiors?

To answer these questions, this study adopts a new sociological approach to early modern agricultural knowledge and literature. It examines how books disrupted and reordered the social system of agricultural knowledge – how knowledge was produced, stored, transferred, acquired, exercised and legitimated – subordinating a communal, labour-based system to an individual, book-based system. It argues that the printing of agricultural knowledge was both stimulated by and a contribution to a reorganisation of knowledge aligned with the emerging social relations of agrarian capitalism. Printed agricultural treatises and manuals were in part a tool in the appropriation and codification of the customary art of husbandry possessed by practitioners in the interests of those in managerial positions such as landowners, estate stewards and large tenant farmers. The proliferation of agricultural books, especially in the eighteenth century, facilitated the growing separation of intellectual and manual labour as part of a process by which an educated and mostly landowning elite gained greater control over cultivation. Since women performed around a third of all agricultural work in the sixteenth and seventeenth centuries, the control exercised by male authors necessarily entailed the masculinisation of customary knowledge, which assisted the increasing exclusion and marginalisation of women in farming.[6]

---

[5] Joel Mokyr, 'The intellectual origins of modern economic growth', *Journal of Economic History*, 65 (2005), 301.

[6] For recent evidence on women's work: Jane Whittle and Mark Hailwood, 'The gender division of labour in early modern England', *EcHR*, 73 (2020).

Together these processes can be characterised metaphorically as the 'enclosure' of customary knowledge. While it is not meant in a strict sense, the choice of metaphor is intended as a serious provocation.[7] It forms the title of this book for three reasons. Firstly, it provides a stimulating analogy. The enclosure of land took many different forms, for different reasons and through different mechanisms, which varied greatly between regions and across centuries.[8] But it typically involved a physical process of creating a boundary around an area of land, and more importantly a legal process of switching from multiple rights of use to exclusive rights of ownership. Enclosure meant the transformation of land from a communally managed resource requiring some collective decision-making to a privately managed resource allowing individual control.[9] Similarly, agricultural books facilitated a shift away from a communal to an individualised system of knowledge, as custom – the accumulated resource of a community – was packaged into a private resource for the individual cultivator. The analogy evoked here is not with the quasi-mythologised version of enclosure as a singular event that severed a past rural idyll from industrialised modernity, but instead as a set of gradual processes through which the management of land was transformed and contested, and as a synecdoche for the structural shifts in landownership, which concentrated land in fewer hands.[10] Similarly, the enclosure of customary knowledge in agricultural books gradually transformed the management of knowledge, and printed books were only the most conspicuous (and inherently best documented) of diverse trends that concentrated knowledge and expertise in fewer heads. Since books are usually presumed to be natural liberators of knowledge, the enclosure analogy purposefully re-frames books as devices that can help to control knowledge.

---

[7] For a more direct study of the link between enclosure and knowledge, see Elly Robson, 'Improvement and epistemologies of landscape in seventeenth-century English forest enclosure', *Historical Journal*, 60 (2016).

[8] Tom Williamson, 'Understanding enclosure', *Landscapes*, 1 (2000).

[9] For the best holistic account of enclosure, see Jeanette M. Neeson, *Commoners: common right, enclosure and social change in England, 1700–1820* (Cambridge, 1996). For a critique of Neeson, see Leigh Shaw-Taylor, 'Parliamentary enclosure and the emergence of an English agricultural proletariat', *The Journal of Economic History*, 61 (2001); Leigh Shaw-Taylor, 'Labourers, cows, common rights and parliamentary enclosure: The evidence of contemporary comment c.1760–1810', *Past & Present*, (2001). See also J. R. Wordie, 'The chronology of English enclosure, 1500–1914', *EcHR*, 36 (1983); Robert C. Allen, *Enclosure and the yeoman: The agricultural development of the south midlands 1450–1850* (Oxford, 1992).

[10] Briony McDonagh and Stephen Daniels, 'Enclosure stories: Narratives from Northamptonshire', *Cultural Geographies*, 19 (2012).

Secondly, however, these processes are not merely analogous, but linked symbiotically in the formation of a capitalist mode of agriculture. The social reorganisation of the land and the social reorganisation of knowledge were necessary corollaries. The campaigns for 'improvement' encompassed reform of both land and knowledge: its initial sixteenth-century meaning covered ways for landlords to maximise estate revenues, including enclosure, before expanding in the seventeenth century to mean the application of better ideas to intensify farming methods. Improvement, therefore, constituted a twin challenge to both customary rights and customary knowledge. Indeed, a key justification for enclosure was to allow improving landlords and entrepreneurial farmers to implement new farming techniques; cooperative field management using customary methods was to be replaced by private field management using improved methods. The shift from custom to improvement required both land and knowledge to be consolidated and packaged accordingly.[11] Farming books were highly conducive to a competitive system of farming, as individual market-oriented cultivators with full control over their fields could both acquire and apply knowledge independently from custom.

The role of knowledge has been neglected in the old 'transition' debates about the long-term development in Europe from a peasant to a capitalist economy.[12] Yet knowledge can be viewed as a factor of agricultural production alongside land and labour – in fact, this study traces how knowledge was extracted and controlled separately from labour. To exert full control over agricultural production, it is advantageous to control knowledge of cultivation. Knowledge must, therefore, be included in narratives of capitalist development. Rural proletarianisation was a process in which commoners not only lost access to land but in which over generations their knowledge itself was increasingly transferred to and exercised by those for whom they were forced to work for wages – or, perhaps more accurately, in which knowledge was controlled and exercised by a shrinking minority as rural communities became increasingly polarised. In this light, it is only a slight simplification to describe the gathering of knowledge collectively

---

[11] In a virtuous feedback loop, enclosed fields provided the basis for the rationalisation and experimentation in which new knowledge could be developed: '[f]arms had to be changed to make them knowable'. Simon Schaffer, 'Enlightenment brought down to earth', *History of Science*, 41 (2003), 260.

[12] For a comprehensive discussion of this debate, see Ch. 1 in Jane Whittle, *The development of agrarian capitalism: Land and labour in Norfolk 1440–1580* (Oxford, 2000).

produced by past generations in texts predominantly for large tenant farmers and landowners as a hidden form of 'primitive accumulation'.

Thirdly, the analogy indicates the scale and significance of the historical change described here. The social reorganisation of knowledge was a centuries-long process that fundamentally altered rural relations and merits equal attention to landownership from historians of early modern Britain. It also links to a modern phenomenon subject to fierce debate: the phrase 'enclosure of knowledge' usually refers to the growth of intellectual property rights in the knowledge economy, seen as comparable to earlier enclosures of common land.[13] Specifically, it resonates with debates about the enclosure of indigenous agricultural knowledge around the world by corporations.[14] The story here is not about legal rights over knowledge, but a broader story in which the codification of customary knowledge and its deracination from labour was a preliminary step that made the commodification of agricultural knowledge possible. We do not need to sentimentalise the lost wisdom of past generations to recognise the profound change that occurred.[15]

By explicitly connecting questions of knowledge to questions of economic power, this book contributes to – and challenges – the rapidly growing number of histories that explore the nexus of early modern books, knowledge and expertise. The complex negotiations between theory and practice, between head and hand, are a common theme in studies of early how-to books.[16] However, too often these are abstracted from the material interests of the actors and inattentive to their place in the social and occupational hierarchy. The organisation of knowledge cannot be understood separately from the distribution of power in early modern society. It is not simply that knowledge bestows power, but that power demands knowledge. In this case, those with the greatest power over the land sought to monopolise knowledge of how to use it in order to fully exercise and extend that power.[17] In this way, the history of early modern

---

[13] For example, Ugo Pagano, 'The crisis of intellectual monopoly capitalism', *Cambridge Journal of Economics*, 38 (2014).

[14] Laurie Anne Whitt, 'Biocolonialism and the commodification of knowledge', *Science as Culture*, 7 (1998).

[15] As cautioned recently in Francis Dolan, *Digging the past: How and why to imagine seventeenth-century agriculture* (Philadelphia, 2019), 2.

[16] For example, Matteo Valleriani (ed.), *The structures of practical knowledge* (Switzerland, 2017).

[17] On how a similar dynamic linking natural knowledge and political authority in colonial expansion, the 'imperialism of "improvement"', see Richard Drayton, *Nature's government: Science, imperial Britain, and the 'improvement' of the world* (London, 2000), xv.

agricultural knowledge parallels histories of early modern medicine. Just as a professionalised and scientific medicine challenged folk medicine and vernacular knowledge, so a professionalised and scientific agriculture challenged 'folk husbandry'.[18]

The intervention made here can be summarised by a small revision to an important essay by Joan Thirsk, titled 'Pen and Plough', which painted a harmonious picture: 'the plough is placed alongside the pen, for, in fact, most writers handled the tools of both trades'. Thirsk cautioned us not to impose our expectation of specialisation and divide the writers from the farmers.[19] While she is correct that these were not exclusive activities, it is a fundamental mischaracterisation to imply that writing and farming were in some way socially equivalent. Writing was not simply added to farming practice; instead, the agricultural author sought to displace and subordinate the common farmer as the acknowledged expert. This book, therefore, tells the story of how the pen mastered the plough.

The rest of this introduction lays the groundwork for a new interpretation of the history of agricultural books and knowledge in early modern Britain. First, it offers a critique of the standard research paradigm, which is termed the *enlightenment model*. It argues that the enlightenment model only evaluates the role of books with respect to technological change and is insensitive to early modern social relations. The model is unable to explain many features of agricultural books in its own terms and thus provides an inadequate theoretical framework. At best it offers a partial account and thus unwittingly distorts our understanding, but at worst it is actively complicit in rehearsing the polemical creations of eighteenth-century propagandists. Hence the need is established for a new approach to explore the cumulative social impact of printed agricultural knowledge. Second, it explains the research method and scope, focused on British agricultural books printed between 1660 and 1800. Since the structure of the book is thematic, it presents a broad survey of agricultural books and authors to serve as a reference for the analysis in specific chapters. Finally, it ends with a summary of how the core argument is developed over seven chapters.

---

[18] Mary Fissell and Roger Cooter, 'Exploring natural knowledge: Science and the popular', in Roy Porter (ed.), *Cambridge history of science: Vol 4: Eighteenth century science* (Cambridge, 2003), 146–51; Andrew Wear, *Knowledge and practice in English medicine, 1550–1680* (Cambridge, 2000), 65.

[19] Joan Thirsk, 'Plough and pen: Agricultural writers in the seventeenth century', in T. H. Aston et al. (eds), *Social relations and ideas: Essays in honour of R.H. Hilton* (Cambridge, 1983), 299.

Agricultural Enlightenment: A Critique

A full understanding of the history of agricultural literature has been hindered by the broader research paradigm of the 'agricultural revolution'. The classic idea of the agricultural revolution refers to a rapid increase in productivity and output over a few decades, sometime in the seventeenth or eighteenth century, accompanied by sweeping transformations in the organisation of farming.[20] The fundamental question driving almost all studies of agricultural literature has been: what contribution did books make to the 'agricultural revolution', meaning what contribution did books make to the dissemination of knowledge leading to increases in agricultural productivity?

The notion that an increase in agricultural publishing was advancing the art of agriculture was itself claimed by agricultural authors themselves in the eighteenth century, which became widely accepted in the nineteenth century.[21] In 1854, an agricultural bibliography aimed to show how the progress of agriculture was assisted by 'the writings of theoretical and practical men'.[22] A successor bibliography in 1908 declared that 'books and journals promoted the advancement of the art more than any other means'.[23] The assertion of a causal link between the publication of books, the spread of knowledge and technological improvements solidified into a truism. Twentieth- and twenty-first-century studies have offered variations on this theme, producing increasingly critical and sophisticated studies within the same general framework. Historians have been examining the contours of the self-image constructed by agricultural writers in the eighteenth century rather than subjecting that self-image to critical analysis. Our view of agricultural literature has been shaped by the agenda of its advocates, even when some of their specific propositions are challenged, in a similar way that many early histories of enclosure were shaped by the views of the enclosers.[24]

G. E. Fussell, who dominated studies of early modern agricultural literature between the 1930s and 1970s, did not dwell on the wider social impact, but continued to connect 'advance in practice' with the 'large increase in

---

[20] Mark Overton, *Agricultural revolution in England: The transformation of the agrarian economy, 1500–1850* (Cambridge, 1996).

[21] For example, see John Sinclair, *Code of agriculture* (2nd edn; London, 1819), iii; John Loudon, *An encyclopædia of agriculture* (London, 1825), 41.

[22] John Donaldson, *Agricultural biography* (London, 1854), 1.

[23] Donald McDonald, *Agricultural writers, from Sir Walter of Henley to Arthur Young, 1200–1800* (London, 1908), 4.

[24] Neeson, *Commoners*, 7.

the number of books'.[25] The first extended assessments came in the 1980s.[26] Pamela Horn posed the question of 'how far did [literature] assist the spread of agricultural improvement?'[27] Joan Thirsk's essay on seventeenth-century writers attempted to 'understand the role of books of husbandry in advancing agricultural improvement', while her essay entitled 'Agricultural Innovations and their Diffusion', covering 1640–1750, was largely concerned with the development of agricultural literature.[28] Similarly, Nicholas Goddard's essays assessed how successful literature had been in advancing scientific methods in late eighteenth- and early nineteenth-century farming.[29] The approach was taken to the extreme by Richard Sullivan who used the number of agricultural publications as a measure of technological development.[30] More recently, Heather Holmes' sophisticated analysis of the eighteenth-century circulation of Scottish agricultural books aimed to facilitate the assessment of 'the role of print in spreading innovation and good practice'.[31] Elsewhere, she analysed publications explicitly as one channel for the dissemination of agricultural knowledge in Scotland.[32] All these studies focus on the question of how agricultural books were motivated by, and contributed to, technical 'improvements' in agricultural production, and thus situate books within debates about knowledge diffusion.

This approach has significant theoretical and empirical weaknesses. The theoretical failings will be explored in Chapter 1, but fundamentally

[25] G. E. Fussell, *More Old English farming books from Tull to the Board of Agriculture, 1731 to 1793* (London, 1950), iii. See also G. E. Fussell, *The Old English farming books from Fitzherbert to Tull 1523 to 1730* (London, 1947); G. E. Fussell, *The Old English farming books, Vol III 1793–1839* (London, 1983).
[26] For a study of the diffusion of agricultural knowledge throughout sixteenth-century Europe by surveying the distribution of treatises, see Corinne Beutler, 'Un chapitre de la sensibilité collective: la littérature agricole en Europe continentale au XVIe siècle', *Annales*, 28 (1973).
[27] Pamela Horn, 'The contribution of the propagandist to eighteenth-century agricultural improvement', *Historical Journal*, 25 (1982), 320.
[28] Thirsk, 'Plough and pen', 295. Joan Thirsk, 'Agricultural innovations and their diffusion', in Joan Thirsk (ed.), *AHEW: 1640–1750 Vol 5 / 2. Agrarian change* (Cambridge, 1985). Same framing later in Joan Thirsk, 'The world-wide farming web, 1500–1800', in John Broad (ed.), *A common agricultural heritage? Revising French and British rural divergence* (Exeter, 2009).
[29] Nicholas Goddard, 'The development and influence of agricultural periodicals and newspapers, 1780–1880', *AgHR*, 31 (1983); Goddard, 'Agricultural literature'. See also Nicholas Goddard, '"Not a reading class": The development of the Victorian agricultural textbook', *Paradigm*, 1 (1997).
[30] Richard J. Sullivan, 'Measurement of English farming technological change, 1523–1900', *Explorations in Economic History*, 21 (1984).
[31] Heather Holmes, 'The circulation of Scottish agricultural books during the eighteenth century', *AgHR*, 54 (2006), 45.
[32] Heather Holmes, 'The dissemination of agricultural knowledge 1700–1850', in Alexander Fenton and Kenneth Veitch (eds), *Scottish life and society: A compendium of Scottish ethnology: Vol 2 Farming and the land* (Edinburgh, 2011). Similarly, see T. C. Smout, 'A new look at the Scottish improvers', *Scottish Historical Review*, 91 (2012), 146.

arise from treating both 'knowledge' and 'books' as socially neutral entities that exist in a single form of equal value to all levels of society; as if knowledge naturally diffuses through a homogenous social body unless it meets obstacles, and as if books are inert vehicles that merely increase the efficiency for such knowledge diffusion. Recent histories of knowledge, however, highlight that knowledge exists in multiple forms; that it serves particular social purposes; and that it is transformed when it moves between contexts. Similarly, that writing and print are better at storing certain kinds of knowledge than others; that to articulate knowledge in writing is to transform it; and that as a medium of knowledge books have varying value depending on recipient and context.

The empirical problem is that when subjected to any sustained scrutiny, the books produced during the early modern period appear to have been rather poor transmitters of useful knowledge to practising farmers. Many agricultural books did not contain knowledge that was especially new or useful, but plagiarised earlier texts.[33] Agricultural writers were often amateurs, who lacked practical farming experience and filled their books with speculative theories.[34] Moreover, some publications were clearly produced for short-term commercial gain rather than to disseminate useful knowledge, including what were essentially extended adverts to promote agricultural products for sale.[35]

The increase of publications of agricultural books from the sixteenth to the eighteenth century does at least indicate a demand. Their ownership and use by gentlemen have been easiest to demonstrate.[36] Indeed, it has been argued that sixteenth-century French manuals were explicitly written for nobility and landowners in order to instruct unlettered peasants.[37] Multiple studies have shown that seventeenth-century English gentlemen's

[33] Fussell, *Farming Books 1731–1793*, 152; Fussell, *Farming books 1793–1839*, 110.

[34] Fussell, *Farming books 1523–1730*, 2; Fussell, *Farming books 1793–1839*, 63; Horn, 'Contribution of the propagandist', 319; Goddard, '"Not a reading class"'. Thirsk defended the best authors against the charge of being hacks and plagiarists in Thirsk, 'Plough and pen', 300.

[35] For example, see the case of Gervase Markham in Lynette Hunter, 'Books for daily life: Household, husbandry, behaviour', in John Barnard and D. F. McKenzie (eds), *Cambridge history of the book in Britain vol 4: 1557–1695* (Cambridge, 2002), 517–18. For example, Horn notes the example of Kirkpatrick using his book on the cultivation of potatoes to advertise his own seed potatoes at 5s./ lb. See Horn, 'Contribution of the propagandist', 319.

[36] There are numerous individual case studies, such as Elizabeth Griffiths, '"A country life": Sir Hamon Le Strange of Hunstanton in Norfolk, 1583–1654', in R. W. Hoyle (ed.), *Custom, improvement and the landscape in early modern Britain* (Farnham, 2011).

[37] Discussed in Natalie Zemon Davis, 'Printing and the people', *Society and culture in early modern France: Eight essays* (Cambridge, 1975), 206. Supported by Beutler, 'La littérature agricole en Europe'.

libraries were full of well-used agricultural books.[38] Yet there is a lack of evidence that the books penetrated to a substantial readership below gentlemen and professionals. A study of subscription lists for agricultural and horticultural books published in Dublin from 1727 to 1732 found most subscribers were landowners, clergy, or medical and military professionals.[39] Goddard concluded that the circulation of late eighteenth-century books was still mostly restricted to a leisured elite.[40] Even influential publications such as the long-running periodical *Annals of Agriculture* (1784– 1804) suffered from poor sales.[41] Indeed, the low rates of literacy among the rural population in the eighteenth century, the high costs of books and the manifestly impractical design of many large multi-volume treatises, would all appear to have been significant barriers to the widespread dissemination of books among small and middling farmers.[42] It has been commonly observed that, in the words of Lord Summerville (president of the Board of Agriculture, 1798–1800), in general farmers were 'not a reading class of people'.[43] Agricultural authors were fully aware of their limited audience. The most prominent author of his age, Arthur Young, introduced an early work with the recognition that he did not 'expect too much from the common farmer's reading this, or indeed any book: I am sensible that not one *farmer* in five thousand reads at all'. Instead, he targeted his book at the small but growing number of gentlemen farmers.[44]

Were some agricultural books owned and read by yeomen and tenant farmers? There are a few clear examples such as Henry Best, a prosperous yeoman well known for his surviving farming memorandum books from the early seventeenth century, who clearly read and applied Thomas Tusser's sixteenth-century husbandry manual.[45] Yet the absence of evidence is equally informative.[46] There is little sign of books of husbandry

---

[38] Thirsk, 'Agricultural innovations', 572. Survey of private libraries in Mauro Ambrosoli, *The wild and the sown: Botany and agriculture in Western Europe, 1350–1850* (Cambridge, 1997).

[39] Máire Kennedy, 'Botany in print: Books and their readers in eighteenth century Dublin', *Dublin Historical Record,* 68 (2015).

[40] Goddard, 'Agricultural literature', 366.

[41] Horn, 'Contribution of the propagandist', 320–21.

[42] In an Irish context, Adams makes a plausible case that some printed agricultural information *could* have spread to ordinary farmers in the eighteenth century, but mostly in newspaper articles: J. R. R. Adams, 'Agricultural literature for the common reader in eighteenth-century Ulster', *Folk Life,* 26 (1987).

[43] Goddard, 'Agricultural literature', 366; Goddard, '"Not a reading class"'.

[44] Arthur Young, *A six weeks tour, through the southern counties of England and Wales* (2nd edn; London, 1769), viii–ix.

[45] Donald Woodward (ed.), *The farming and memorandum books of Henry Best of Elmswell, 1642* (Oxford, 1984), 10, 16, 23.

[46] A useful sceptical summary: G. E. Fussell, 'Rural reading in old time England', *Library Review,* 19 (1964).

in the libraries of most sixteenth- and seventeenth-century yeomen.[47] A study of three literate, innovative farmers of the late eighteenth and early nineteenth centuries found that they did not have much use for farming books.[48] The detailed accounts and diaries of middling farmers such as Richard Latham (1724–67) and Peter Walkden (1733–34) show no sign that they bought, borrowed or read farming books, although they purchased newspapers and almanacs.[49] A study of literate farming families who valued reading, writing and book-keeping show no indication of an interest in farming books.[50] The most systematic research has been conducted in regard to Scotland, which does find signs of a widening readership, including tenant farmers, but only around the turn of the nineteenth century.[51]

The question of whether ideas in books were applied in practice has been difficult to answer. The annotations found in surviving copies of sixteenth- and seventeenth-century books have been used to suggest that some readers were extracting information for practical purposes.[52] There are some indications in estate accounts about the application of advice from books.[53] Yet after fifty years of scholarship on the topic Fussell was a 'confirmed agnostic' on the question of whether the publications of early agricultural scientists actually reached working farmers.[54] Paul Warde recently expressed similar caution about 'the precise contribution of literature' to higher crop yields.[55] Others have struggled to find signs of the application of scientific theory.[56] Commenting on late eighteenth-century Scotland, Ian Adams judged that 'the publications themselves had little influence in

---

[47] Mildred Campbell, *The English yeomen under Elizabeth and the Stuarts* (London, 1942), 170.

[48] John Broad, 'Farmers and improvement, 1780–1840', in Richard W. Hoyle (ed.), *The farmer in England, 1650–1980* (Farnham, 2013), 190.

[49] Lorna Weatherill (ed.), *Account book of Richard Latham, 1724–1767* (Oxford, 1990); *A diary, from January 1733 to March 1734, written by the Reverend Peter Walkden* (Smith Settle, Otley, West Yorkshire, 2000).

[50] Susan Whyman, *The pen and the people: English letter writers 1660–1800* (Oxford, 2009), 75–111.

[51] Holmes, 'Circulation', 71; Mark Towsey, '"Store their minds with much valuable knowledge": Agricultural improvement at the Selkirk Subscription Library, 1799–1814', *Journal for Eighteenth-Century Studies*, 38 (2015). For context: R. A. Houston, *Scottish literacy and the Scottish identity: Illiteracy and society in Scotland and Northern England, 1600–1800* (Cambridge, 1985).

[52] A few examples are given in Ambrosoli, *Wild and the Sown*, 235. See also account of book by Gervase Markham in Thirsk, 'Plough and pen', 305.

[53] Thirsk, 'Agricultural innovations', 366.

[54] G. E. Fussell, 'Agricultural science and experiment in the eighteenth century: An attempt at a definition', *AgHR*, 24 (1976), 47.

[55] Paul Warde, *The invention of sustainability: Nature, human action, and destiny, 1500–1870* (Cambridge, 2018), 143.

[56] Sarah Wilmot, *'The business of improvement': Agriculture and scientific culture in Britain, c.1770–c.1870* (Bristol, 1990), 12.

promoting agrarian change'.[57] Even the most optimistic accounts are often forced to speculate about indirect influence, through gentlemen passing on books to their tenants, or instructing or 'bullying' their stewards and bailiffs.[58] With underwhelming evidence for a direct causal link to innovations in methods, books have largely been reduced to a symbolic role, as evidence for an enthusiasm for agricultural progress on the part of a small group of writers and readers. Horn suggested that the influence of eighteenth-century writers on practising farmers lay chiefly in their general encouragement, rather than spreading new methods.[59]

Scholars have, therefore, begun to abandon the effort to demonstrate that books influenced agricultural methods directly and settled for the lesser claim that they at least indicate an increasing desire for knowledge. This reframes the study of agricultural literature as part of a history of 'agricultural enlightenment', a step removed from the 'agricultural revolution', as seen in the ambitious argument of Joel Mokyr about the impact of the Enlightenment on the British economy through the growth and spread of useful knowledge.[60] Mokyr readily admits that the apparent growth in useful farming knowledge had little discernible effect on output and productivity.[61] Therefore, he shifts the argument to claim that the 'true significance of the "Agricultural Enlightenment"' was that there 'was a thirst for this kind of knowledge among many British farmers'.[62]

Peter Jones builds on Mokyr's framework in his comprehensive work titled *Agricultural Enlightenment*.[63] Jones defines the agricultural enlightenment as the period 'characterised by the widespread diffusion and take-up of new farming techniques and technologies', driven by supply-side factors including the production and diffusion of knowledge.[64] He declares that

---

[57] Ian H. Adams, 'The agents of agricultural change', in M. L. Parry and T. R. Slater (eds), *The making of the Scottish countryside* (London, 1980), 172.

[58] Goddard, 'Agricultural literature', 366; Thirsk, 'Agricultural innovations', 553, 557.

[59] Horn, 'Contribution of the propagandist', 326.

[60] Joel Mokyr, *The enlightened economy: Britain and the industrial revolution 1700–1850* (London, 2009), 9.

[61] Ibid., 171.

[62] Ibid., 186–87.

[63] In a German context, see Marcus Popplow, 'Economizing agricultural resources in the German economic enlightenment', in Ursula Klein and Emma C. Spary (eds), *Materials and expertise in early modern Europe: Between market and laboratory* (Chicago, 2010).

[64] Peter M. Jones, *Agricultural enlightenment: Knowledge, technology, and nature, 1750–1840* (Oxford, 2016), 83. The same approach is found in Janken Myrdal, 'Agricultural literature in Eurasia circa 200 BCE–1500 CE', *Stockholm Papers in Economic History*, 15 (2014); Janken Myrdal, 'Agricultural literature in Scandinavia and Anglo-Saxon countries, 1700–1800 as indicator of changed mentality', University of Leuven, Belgium (27–29 August 2014). In the latter, Myrdal accepts at the outset that agricultural literature had little influence on 'technological change and increased production', and hence focuses on the significance of 'a new mentality' in the countryside (14).

published literature was a key vector of agricultural enlightenment, yet he is sceptical of its impact before 1800.[65] He dismisses treatises of the 1750s and 1760s as a 'branch of belles-lettres', but argues that the end of the eighteenth century saw new efforts to produce practical manuals for farmers.[66] Even then, in his final assessment, he concedes that the evidence indicates 'that the mechanics of innovation and adoption were … unconnected, or only very loosely connected, to the written word'.[67] Jones is ultimately only able to repeat the hopeful speculation that knowledge in printed form trickled down through rural society. In summary, the enlightenment model of agricultural books as disseminators of useful knowledge that spread innovations and increased productivity has encountered a number of challenges, leading to increasingly weak conclusions resting heavily on theoretical assumptions about books as tools of knowledge diffusion.

While the enlightenment model has only recently been explicitly articulated and theorised, the language of enlightenment has been key to shaping perceptions of agricultural books for much longer.[68] However, if we look at how agricultural writers in the eighteenth century used the adjective 'enlightened', we find that the motive to disseminate knowledge was inextricably tied to a wider social project. Consider this oft-quoted passage from the most influential English agricultural writer of the day, Arthur Young, from 1770:

> It is the business of the nobility and gentry who practice agriculture, and of authors, who practice and write on it, to help forward the age… to spread the knowledge of them as much as possible; to endeavour to quicken the motions of the vast but unwieldy body, the common farmers. But to omit this … is to reduce themselves to the level of those whom they ought to instruct; and to submit to that ignorance and backwardness, which left to themselves, cloud any country, in an enlightened age, with the darkness of many preceding centuries. Common farmers love to grope in the dark: it is the business of superior minds … [to] shine forth to dissipate the night that involves them.[69]

The abstract model of knowledge diffusion is incapable of fully explaining such passages, which are fundamentally and irreducibly an articulation of a socio-political programme for rural reform. The notion of spreading knowledge cannot be neatly separated from the notion that it must

---

[65] Jones, *Agricultural enlightenment*, 60.
[66] Ibid., 6, 62–64.
[67] Ibid., 100.
[68] For example, Thirsk wrote that 'the first enlightenment dawned in the sixteenth century with the publication of an entirely new class of books of husbandry'. Thirsk, 'Agricultural innovations', 534.
[69] Arthur Young, *Rural economy: Or, essays on the practical parts of husbandry* (London, 1770), 20–21.

spread from the nobility and gentry ('superior minds') to common farmers ('the ignorant'). The light of knowledge and the darkness of ignorance
are mapped onto a fundamental class division. Hence the notion of an
'enlightened' agriculture was first used in a context that assumed and reaf-
firmed a social hierarchy of knowledge. For educated gentlemen such as
Young, agriculture would be 'enlightened' when it was under the control
of the gentry; even if indirectly through various layers of supervision at
a local and national level. Agricultural enlightenment cannot be used to
describe a purely abstract campaign for the application of reason to cultivation, for it was originally connected to a campaign for self-proclaimed
'men of reason' to manage or supervise cultivation.[70]

Remarkably few attempts have been made to link agricultural writing
to socio-economic change. In a rare exception, Thirsk suggested that a
'managerial revolution' around 1200, in which lords began to take lands
into their own hands, prompted the compiling of the first English treatises on estate management.[71] This process was repeated in reverse in the
sixteenth century, as the printing of classical agricultural treatises inspired
gentlemen to turn their attention back to farm management after over a
century of leasing land to others.[72] Hence it was claimed that writing could
be both stimulated by and contribute to shifts in behaviour of a particular
social group, regardless of whether or how the knowledge gleaned from
books was applied in practice. Yet this analysis has not been extended
to the crucial expansion in publishing in the seventeenth and eighteenth
centuries.

By focusing on books as disseminators of knowledge, the enlightenment model ignores two general problems. Firstly, the epistemological
problem: the technical difficulties in the development and use of written
knowledge, requiring the translation from practice to text, then back into

---

[70] Schaffer recognises this broad connection between improvement and the social order in two
refreshing essays: Simon Schaffer, 'The earth's fertility as a social fact in early modern England',
in Mikulas Teich et al. (eds), *Nature and society in historical context* (Cambridge, 1997); Schaffer,
'Enlightenment brought down to earth'. Warde shows some awareness of this point, remarking on
the 'association of progress with particular social strata', noting that 'the majority of tillers of the soil
were seen as targets for propaganda rather than participants in debate'. Warde, *Invention of sustainability*, 162–63.

[71] See Edward Miller and John Hatcher, *Medieval England: Rural society and economic change 1086–
1348* (Abingdon, 1978). Also Christopher Dyer, *Making a living in the middle ages: The people of
Britain 850–1520* (New Haven, 2002). Treatises available in Dorothea Oschinsky, *Walter of Henley
and other treatises on estate management and accounting* (Oxford, 1971).

[72] Joan Thirsk, 'Making a fresh start: Sixteenth-century agriculture and the classical inspiration', in
Michael Leslie and Timothy Raylor (eds), *Culture and cultivation in early modern England: Writing
and the land* (Leicester, 1992), 16.

practice; both the codification of a practical art and the decoding of written instructions. Secondly, the social problem: the class division between the majority of those working the land and the majority of those writing and reading about it. This book seeks to address both problems, but focuses on the latter.

We can only fully understand the role of early modern agricultural books by being attentive to the relations between writing, knowledge and power. To do so we need to shift away from concerns with technical innovation and productivity and focus on social change. We can build a new interpretation by reorientating our study away from the grand narrative of the 'agricultural revolution' and towards that of the distinctive social relations that emerged with the rise of agrarian capitalism. The case for this interpretation is made in Chapter 1, which draws together a series of sociological insights into the relation between books, knowledge and labour, and sets out a new theoretical framework for understanding agricultural books in terms of the social structure of knowledge rather than the diffusion of knowledge.

Agricultural Books

The research in this study sits at the intersection of the history of knowledge and the history of the book. Agricultural books are both the primary unit of analysis and chief source base. Book history combines 'textual criticism, bibliography, and cultural history' – the linguistic analysis of texts, the history of the physical objects bearing texts and the study of the practices that produce meanings using these texts or objects.[73] The approach here is rooted in textual criticism rather than bibliography, while maintaining a holistic view of the book as simultaneously written text, material object and cultural transaction.[74] This approach is justified by the rich layers of self-reference within the texts themselves. As books both represent and act within the world, we can gain insights into books as causal agents by fully contextualising how they represent their own cultural role. 'Role' is used as shorthand for all the ways books interacted with their social context, both the factors leading to their production (general trends and motivations of individual authors) and the effects arising from their

---

[73] Roger Chartier, *The order of books: Readers, authors, and libraries in Europe between the fourteenth and eighteenth centuries* (Cambridge, 1994), 2–3.

[74] For a discussion of different disciplinary approaches, see Leslie Howsam, *Old books and new histories: An orientation to studies in book and print culture* (London, 2006), ch. 1.

circulation (general influences and uses in particular contexts). This focus on books as causal agents distinguishes the approach here from studies of representations within husbandry books, such as Andrew McRae on the preceding period 1500–1660.[75]

The core research is based on a systematic survey of printed agricultural books, pamphlets and periodicals, supplemented by select evidence from book reviews, diaries, correspondence, commonplace notebooks, manuscript drafts, poetry, novels and newspapers. Although a number of new sources are introduced, the primary approach consists of the close re-reading and re-contextualisation of known printed sources. A broad timeframe is adopted to cover the long-term development of agricultural print as a whole. The analysis focuses on agricultural writing rather than reading, partly because evidence for reading habits is still too fragmentary.[76] Similarly, it is limited to the role of agricultural authors in the production of books, rather than the wider set of actors within the book trade.[77] The linguistic analysis is qualitative rather than quantitative. While the online databases Early English Books Online (EEBO) and Eighteenth Century Collections Online (ECCO) enable surveys and comparisons over large volumes of text, they do not enable meaningful quantitative analysis.[78] Beyond print, a few agricultural manuscripts are discussed, although primarily with respect to planned publication.

The questions of terminology and chronology are linked by the argument. During this period, the terms 'husbandry', 'agriculture' and 'farming' were all used to describe the activity of growing crops and keeping livestock, but each with a distinct meaning, scope and set of associations. *Husbandry* was used to mean 'management of the household' from

---

[75] Andrew McRae, *God speed the plough: The representation of agrarian England, 1500–1660* (Cambridge, 1996).

[76] For an example study on agricultural reading, see Towsey, 'Store their minds'. On methods, see James Raven, 'New reading histories, print culture and the identification of change: The case of eighteenth-century England', *Social History*, 23 (1998); I. A. N. Jackson, 'Approaches to the history of readers and reading in eighteenth-century Britain', *Historical Journal*, 47 (2004); Stephen Colclough, *Consuming texts: Readers and reading communities, 1695–1870* (London, 2007).

[77] James Raven, *The business of books: Booksellers and the English book trade 1450–1850* (London, 2007).

[78] EEBO contains digital facsimiles of over 130,000 titles printed in England, Ireland, Scotland, Wales and British North America (http://eebo.chadwyck.com/home). ECCO contains digital facsimiles of over 180,000 titles from the eighteenth century (http://find.galegroup.com/ecco/). Considering the errors arising from optical character recognition (OCR) and the poor quality of microfilmed texts, as well as the methodological limits of key-word searches in texts with multiple spellings and multiple context-dependent meanings. See Patrick Spedding, '"The new machine": Discovering the limits of ECCO', *Eighteenth-Century Studies*, 44 (2011).

the thirteenth century, including cultivation. *Agriculture* as 'cultivation of the soil' or field was in occasional use from the late sixteenth century. *Farming* in the sixteenth century described the 'action or system of farming (out) or letting out to farm', and only acquired its meaning as 'business of cultivating land' in the eighteenth century.[79] 'Husbandry' was the primary term in the sixteenth century, gradually joined by 'agriculture' in the seventeenth century, which became the more frequent term from the mid-eighteenth century. 'Farmer' gradually replaced 'yeoman' and 'husbandman' as the favoured occupational term over the eighteenth century.[80]

The chosen period from 1660 to 1800 is due to a number of factors, including the striking growth of agricultural literature, the cultural dominance of 'improvement' discourse, and the favoured timing for the emergence of agrarian capitalism.[81] But it links to the above terminology, because in a strict sense the mid-seventeenth century marked the invention of agriculture, as it was only from the 1660s that an explicitly 'agricultural' literature emerged in English, since previous books were on the topic of 'husbandry'. Following the radical shift in the discourse of husbandry manuals in the 1640s and 1650s and the establishment of the language of 'improvement', the first English agricultural treatise was John Worlidge's *Systema Agriculturæ* (1669). This marked the beginning of a conscious effort to establish books as the primary source of knowledge about farming and the creation of a new system of agricultural knowledge. The end of the period is marked by the formation of the Board of Agriculture in 1793, a quasi-state body, once described as the 'culmination' of the agricultural enlightenment.[82] The Board of Agriculture was the first centralised body for collecting and distributing agricultural knowledge in Britain, which introduced a new phase of agricultural literature by initially commissioning and publishing ninety short county reports for England, Scotland and Wales, followed by longer 'revised' or 'corrected' reports

---

[79] 'agriculture, n.', *OED Online*, www.oed.com/view/Entry/4181 (8 February 2018); 'husbandry, n.', *OED Online*, www.oed.com/view/Entry/89667 (8 February 2018); 'farming, n.', *OED Online*, www.oed.com/view/Entry/68262 (8 February 2018).

[80] Using *Gale Artemis* function to search term frequency (number of documents) in *Eighteenth Century Collections Online* (ECCO).

[81] On chronology of improvement, see Paul Warde, 'The idea of improvement, c.1520–1700', in R. W. Hoyle (ed.), *Custom, improvement and the landscape in early modern Britain* (Farnham, 2011). See chapter 1 for the chronology of agrarian capitalism.

[82] Mokyr, *Enlightened economy*, 184.

until 1817.[83] Therefore, the period from the mid-seventeenth to the end of the eighteenth century, or more precisely 1669–1792, covers the construction and establishment of an agricultural genre and body of knowledge. This genre established a new relationship between writing and farming, as the science of agriculture was abstracted from the household context of the moralised art of husbandry.

The corpus under examination is presented chronologically in Appendix A. It includes all books intended to inform or instruct on the practice of farming, defined as the cultivation of crops (arable husbandry) and keeping of domestic livestock (animal husbandry).[84] It excludes books wholly on gardening or horticulture as they formed a distinct, albeit overlapping, genre.[85] The selected corpus from 1669 to 1792 amounts to 131 distinct books and pamphlets printed in England or Scotland, with an additional 13 periodicals (12 from 1669 to 1700, 34 from 1700 to 1750, 85 from 1750 to 1792).[86] Dublin publications are excluded due to the distinct social and economic conditions of Ireland, although these were mostly reprints of English books first published in London.[87] As only a single agricultural author originated from Wales, it is not given independent attention. Imported foreign books constituted an important part of the agricultural book market in England, especially in the sixteenth and seventeenth centuries.[88] However, as a distinct English and Scottish tradition developed over the long eighteenth

[83] Heather Holmes, 'Sir John Sinclair, the county agricultural surveys, and the collection and dissemination of knowledge 1793–1817, with a bibliography of the surveys: Part 1', *Journal of the Edinburgh Bibliographical Society*, 7 (2012); Heather Holmes, 'Sir John Sinclair, the county agricultural surveys, and the collection and dissemination of knowledge 1793–1817, with a bibliography of the surveys: Part 2', *Journal of the Edinburgh Bibliographical Society*, 8 (2013).

[84] Based on similar criteria to W. Frank Perkins, who simply asked: is this 'a book of instruction in the Practice of Farming?' W. Frank Perkins, *British and Irish writers on agriculture* (3rd edn; Lymington, 1939). Similarly, G. E. Fussell (1947, 1950) included those he considered a 'farming text-book' or 'practical treatise on farming'. Fussell, *Farming Books 1523–1730*, 1–4. It includes specific methods of agricultural improvement and books on estate management, but excludes publications solely on the associated topics of forestry, gardening and plantations; the supplementary topics of land surveying and measurement, farm architecture and veterinary medicine; any general scientific works on natural history, botany or chemistry; the specialist topics of farriery (horses), cider, fruit-trees and bee-keeping; and political or economic topics such as enclosures, tithes or employment for the rural poor.

[85] Blanche Henrey, *British botanical and horticultural literature before 1800*, 3 vols (London, 1975).

[86] Pamphlets have not been explicitly separated. Holmes identified 88 Scottish pamphlets between 1696 and 1800, double the number of books. Heather Holmes, 'Agricultural pamphlets', in Stephen W. Brown and Warren McDougall (eds), *Enlightenment and expansion 1707–1800* (The Edinburgh history of the book in Scotland, 2; Edinburgh, 2012), 399.

[87] The main exception is work by John Wynn Baker, an Englishman who moved to Ireland and published on agriculture in the 1760s and 1770s. G. E. Fussell, 'John Wynn Baker: An "improver" in eighteenth century Ireland', *Agricultural History*, 5 (1931).

[88] See continental books in English private libraries 1500–1640, Ambrosoli, *Wild and the Sown*, 423.

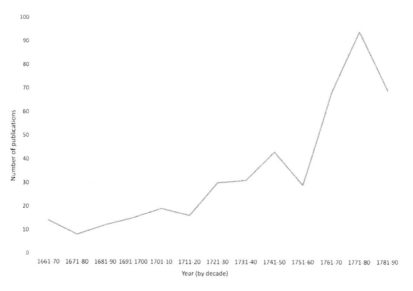

Figure 0.2   A graph of the total number of titles published in England each decade
between 1661 and 1790.

century, the influence of non-English texts declined.[89] Over the following
chapters, greater attention is given to the more prolific authors and most
popular books, partly guided by the numbers of reprints and new editions, but mostly guided by qualitative indications such as references by
later authors and anecdotal accounts of ownership or reading.

The rough chronological trend of agricultural publishing is shown in
Figures 0.2 and 0.3.[90] In England, there was a steady increase in titles from
the 1670s with a significant surge in the decades from 1760 to 1790. In

[89] The lines of influence were reversed, as Britain became an exporter of agricultural literature. For
example, Jethro Tull's book inspired a new generation of French writing on agronomy, led by
Henri Louis Duhamel du Monceau (1700–1782). Laura B. Sayre, 'The pre-history of soil science:
Jethro Tull, the invention of the seed drill, and the foundations of modern agriculture', *Physics and
Chemistry of the Earth*, 35 (2010), 854.

[90] The *English Short Title Catalogue* (ESTC) records over 500 titles under the subject 'agriculture'
published in England and Scotland between 1669 and 1792, but this includes political and economic commentary, and around of these were reprints or new editions. Including: 445 printed in
England, 69 in Scotland, 119 in Ireland, and 41 in North America. Note the ESTC is an unstable
and incomplete bibliography: Michael Suarez, 'Towards a bibliometric analysis of the surviving
record, 1701–1800', in Michael F. Suarez and Michael L. Turner (eds), *Cambridge history of the book
in Britain Vol 5: 1695–1830* (Cambridge, 2014). Heather Holmes has identified a higher figure of 123
Scottish publications between 1683 and 1790 by applying broader criteria and including periodicals:
Holmes, 'Agricultural publishing', 503–4.

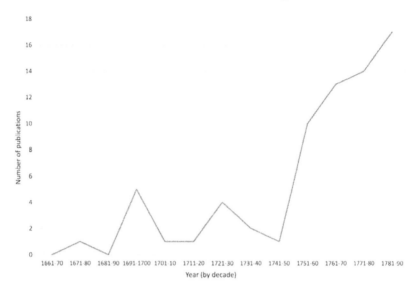

Figure 0.3   A graph of the total number of titles published in Scotland each decade between 1661 and 1790.

Scotland, there were no agricultural publications before 1697, and then only a few before a rapid rise from the 1750s. This broadly mirrors the general trend of increasing publications across all genres as the whole book trade expanded.[91] A previous analysis of eighteenth-century genres suggests that books in the category of 'agriculture, almanacs and other practical matters' remained stable as a proportion of total output, hovering around 2–3 per cent.[92] However, Mokyr estimated that books categorised as 'Science, Technology and Medicine' (using ECCO) increased from 5.5 to 9 per cent of the total over the eighteenth century.[93] A similar analysis for publications on 'agriculture' indicates a proportional as well as a numerical increase, especially in the 1760s, 1770s and 1790s (Table 0.1).[94]

This simple analysis supports the impression of both contemporaries and historians that there was an increase in the range of available agricultural literature in the second half of the eighteenth century, even exceeding the underlying expansion of publishing.

[91] See graph in Raven, *Business of books*, 9.
[92] Suarez, 'Towards a bibliometric analysis', 46.
[93] Mokyr, *Enlightened economy*, 46.
[94] Data from ECCO. The numbers of results for searches for all items under subject 'agriculture' were compared with number of results for total items across all subjects, for each decade.

Table 0.1 *Number and proportion of titles catalogued as subject 'agriculture', based on ECCO searches*

Decade	Number of Titles	Percentages of Total (%)
1701–1710	14	0.1
1711–1720	16	0.1
1721–1730	53	0.4
1731–1740	45	0.3
1741–1750	51	0.3
1751–1760	67	0.4
1761–1770	145	0.7
1771–1780	153	0.6
1781–1790	97	0.3
1791–1800	345	0.9

Periodicals play a central role as vectors of knowledge diffusion in the enlightenment model. However, periodicals did not become a significant form of agricultural publishing until the nineteenth century, when they were stimulated by the proliferation of farmers' clubs and agricultural societies.[95] As such they are not prominent in the following analysis. If we examine the list of twenty-two British periodicals covering agriculture published before 1793, we find that most were extremely short lived (only seven lasted more than three years), only eight primarily concerned agriculture (others covered art, manufacture and commerce generally) and three were essentially single works published in parts.[96] The first English periodical on agriculture was John Houghton's weekly *Collection for the Improvement of Husbandry and Trade* (1681–82, then 1692–1702), but the first successful specialist venture was Arthur Young's *Annals of Agriculture* (1784–1808).[97] The first agricultural newspaper in England was not launched until 1807.[98] Before 1800 there were only three short-lived agricultural journals in Scotland, and the first Scottish newspapers were not founded until the 1840s.[99]

---

[95] Goddard, 'Agricultural periodicals', 129. See also Goddard, '"Not a reading class"'.

[96] F. A. Buttress, *Agricultural periodicals of the British Isles, 1681–1900, and their location* (Cambridge, 1950). Fussell discussed ten periodicals before 1800 in G. E. Fussell, 'Early farming journals', *EcHR*, 3 (1932).

[97] Goddard, 'Agricultural periodicals', 120. The significance of the *Annals* was less as a means of mass communication among farmers and more as a forum for an elite group of agriculturists.

[98] Goddard, 'Agricultural literature', 372.

[99] Heather Holmes, 'Scottish agricultural newspapers and journals and the industrialisation of agriculture, 1800–1880', *Folk Life*, 40 (2001).

Agricultural Authors

The sociological approach adopted in the following chapters requires a clear sense of the socio-economic profile of agricultural authors. The current consensus is that most of the men who wrote farming books in the seventeenth and eighteenth centuries were not farmers by occupation. The majority of agricultural authors are described as gentlemen, although the degree of their engagement in farming is debated.[100] Fussell's more flexible characterisation is that they were 'men of education', and therefore a social constellation that expanded over time and stretched beyond the gentry.[101] In John Donaldson's 1854 collective biography of agricultural writers, he suggested that the most valuable contributions came from 'persons of alien professions'.[102] This is unsurprising as clergymen and physicians constituted a significant proportion of the rural educated class.[103] This prevalence of professional backgrounds outside agriculture was noted in a survey of Scottish authors from 1697 to 1790.[104] An analysis of the periodical *Annals of Agriculture* (1784–1815) found that country gentlemen or clergymen wrote the majority of articles, although a significant minority were by substantial tenant farmers.[105]

To test and build on these impressions, the available biographical information of eighty-seven British agricultural authors has been systematically collated to approximate a prosopographical study. Appendix B presents all known authors whose first book on agriculture was published in England or Scotland between 1669 and 1792 (see Table B.1). Basic information is available for over half of these authors concerning their social background, education and occupation (there are Oxford DNB entries for forty-seven out of eighty-seven, and a further twenty-two have partial information available elsewhere).[106] A brief survey of

---

[100] For example, Thirsk emphasises the engagement of gentlemen managing estates and younger sons of gentlemen who were forced to farm for a living. Thirsk, 'Agricultural innovations', 534.

[101] G. E. Fussell, *The classical tradition in West European farming* (Fairleigh, 1972), 138.

[102] Donaldson, *Agricultural biography*, 43. See also Fussell, *Farming Books 1523–1730*, 105.

[103] Fussell, *Classical tradition*, 39. On the role of rural clergy, see Jones, *Agricultural enlightenment*, 74.

[104] Heather Holmes, 'Scottish agricultural writers and the creation of their personal identities between 1697 and 1790', *Folk Life*, 44 (2005), 90–91.

[105] Horn, 'Contribution of the propagandist', 321.

[106] Compiled using Oxford DNB; Donaldson, *Agricultural biography*; McDonald, *Agricultural writers*; Perkins, *British and Irish writers*; Fussell, *Farming Books 1523–1730*; Fussell, *Farming Books 1731–1793*; Holmes, 'Scottish agricultural writers'. Many authors listed by Donaldson (1854) were erroneous, by repetition or mistaken attribution, while others were anonymous or wrote on tangential topics (e.g. highway maintenance). Holmes' survey included anonymous and institutional

this biographical information allows for a broad characterisation of agricultural authorship in the long eighteenth century and the relation between authorship and the practice of farming, from which we can compile a composite portrait (note that all quantities refer to the number of instances an author is linked to the relevant category, such that individuals are often double-counted). It is first worth noting the chronological trend: a handful of new authors in each decade between the 1670s and 1720s, with small increases in the 1730s and 1750s, before a sharp rise in the 1760s and 1770s, dropping slightly in the 1780s.[107] Most of the authors (twenty-nine of the forty) we know least about were first published between 1760 and 1790, often with a single publication, which indicates a widening of the social pool.

The broad characterisation that most authors were not farmers by occupation is accurate; however, we can add greater nuance and identify significant trends that have been previously overlooked. The typical agricultural author was neither a labouring husbandman nor a leisured landowner. The majority of authors came from and moved within that increasingly fluid strata of British society that encompassed the minor gentry and the upper middling sort, where the country gentleman who kept a farm and the prosperous freeholder or tenant overlapped, and which embraced the respectable professions and genteel trades.[108] This was the era in which the 'gentleman farmer' emerged fully in social commentaries and the realms of land, trade and industry were increasingly intertwined.[109] Using a father's occupation or status as an indicator for thirty-six authors, four fathers can be identified as noblemen, six as landowning gentry, ten as farmers (of which at least four were freeholders or yeomen), six as clergymen (some of whom may have kept a farm), six as other professionals and six as tradesmen. For those we know least about, at least nine of the title pages of their books designate the author as 'Gentleman' or 'Esquire'. Using education as a further indicator of status, we find that twenty-one (out of information for thirty-six) went to university, the Inns of Court or a 'private Civil

publications, plus a further ten authors on topics not strictly didactic, based on J. A. S. Watson and G. D. Amery, 'Early Scottish agricultural writers', *Transactions of the Highland and Agricultural Society of Scotland*, 43 (1931).

[107] Trend broadly in line with table by Pamela Horn for the 1730s–1790s, but corrects previous errors and adopts a narrower criterion. Horn, 'Contribution of the propagandist', 318.

[108] On the defining a 'gentleman' in the eighteenth century, see Penelope J. Corfield, 'Class by name and number in eighteenth-century Britain', *History*, 72 (1987), 43, 61; William Stafford, 'Representations of the social order in The Gentleman's Magazine, 1785–1815', *Eighteenth-Century Life*, 33 (2009), 68, 87.

[109] G. E. Mingay, *English landed society in the eighteenth century* (London, 1963), 105–6.

Law College'. Hence agricultural authors came from a wide enough social spectrum that many were required to earn their living and took up writing as a route to prosperity as much as filling their leisure hours, and there are signs that the social base widened over time to include professionals and large tenant farmers.[110]

Our main concern is the prevalence of agricultural occupations and experience. The claim that agricultural authors were completely inexperienced or ignorant of farming is unfair. However, they tended to share *a particular kind* of agricultural experience that was fundamentally different from a youth 'bred to husbandry' (in the common saying) who learned local customs through direct instruction and laborious practice. If an author had farming experience, it was most likely limited to managerial roles as landowner, steward, agent, or large tenant farmer, hence primarily as an observer and organiser rather than a performer of farm labour. We know that forty-one authors were occupied in or held a position directly related to agriculture in some way at some point in their lives, although often tenuous. Only fourteen were occupied as farmers at some point, mostly as tenants, but four as landowners personally engaged in management. Of those who held a farm, most were substantial farmers, managing large tracts of land, often considerably greater than 100 acres.[111] It is also probable that some clergymen had experience cultivating their glebe. Ten authors are known to have been owners of estates or farms, but the extent of their involvement in management is variable and uncertain. Nine were at some point employed in specialist service roles as stewards, agents, surveyors and land valuers, or enclosure commissioners. At least three were engaged in ancillary trades.[112] Various authors were hired as advisors or consultants at certain points, often as a result of their publications. A couple of authors patented new machine designs. Two authors we know little about (George Cooke

---

[110] A point already made about Scottish agricultural authors. Smout, 'Scottish improvers', 134.

[111] Young divided 'common' and 'gentlemen' farmers as below or above 60–80 acres. Arthur Young, *The farmer's guide in hiring and stocking farms* (London, 1770), 247. Jethro Tull farmed a total of around 200 acres; Robert Maxwell leased an arable farm of 130 acres near Edinburgh in 1723; Arthur Young first took tenancy of 80 acres of farm in Suffolk in 1763, but soon added 300 acres; William Marshall first managed 300 acres near Croydon from 1774 to 1778; James Anderson took a lease of a 1,300-acre farm in Aberdeenshire in the 1770s; Thomas Stone also farmed 1,300 acres in Shropshire around the year 1780; George Culley began on a 200-acre farm with his brother Matthew in 1767, then gradually expanded their holdings to 4,000 acres by 1800. On Tull's farm, Cuthbert William Johnson, *The farmer's encyclopædia, and dictionary of rural affairs* (London, 1842), 1182.

[112] James Small (1740–1793) was a farmer but also a plough- and cartwright; William Ellis (1700–1758) sold implements and seeds; and Josiah Twamley was a cheese factor (dealer).

and Robert Billing) adopted the title of 'Farmer' on their title pages. Besides direct experience in farm management, a few took notes on agricultural methods while travelling through Europe before publishing their books.

Additional geographical information about the place of origin and known areas of residence or location of farms (not shown in the table) reveals little correlation with areas traditionally considered the most progressive in terms of agricultural improvements, such as the eastern counties of Norfolk and Suffolk. Over half the authors were raised in southern England, primarily London, or Scotland.[113] But the recorded residences (for at least some part of their lives) have a much wider and more balanced geographical spread, and a few authors lived in many different counties for at least a short period, often employed in agricultural work as a land steward or landscape gardener, and were, therefore, able to accumulate experience of diverse parts of the country. While regional differences in agriculture were hugely significant, the following analysis does not address them in detail, primarily because agricultural books were generally attempts to transcend local and regional practices in order to establish national or universal agriculture. However, the prevalence of Scottish authors – eighteen out of all forty-eight known origins and almost half (sixteen out of thirty-three) of new authors from 1732 to 92 – is particularly striking.[114] The combination of post-1745 economic reforms and enlightenment thought produced many of the most important agricultural authors of the second half of the eighteenth century who embraced and accelerated the programme of English improvement and land reform.[115] Edinburgh became of equal importance to London as a centre of agricultural publishing, and books circulated between both nations.[116]

---

[113] Using the 'agricultural departments' defined by William Marshall as natural agricultural units in the early nineteenth century (with Scotland and Wales added for completeness), the origins of forty-eight authors can be divided as follows: eighteen from Scotland; fourteen from the southern department; six from the northern; five from the midland; two from the western; two from the eastern; only one from Wales. No authors came from the south-western peninsula.

[114] For more detail, see Holmes, 'Scottish agricultural writers'.

[115] Schaffer, 'The earth's fertility', 138.

[116] For example, students at Glasgow University were borrowing English authors such as Mortimer, Bradley and Tull in the 1760s. Sangster, Matthew, Karen Baston and Brian Aitken, *Eighteenth-Century Borrowing from the University of Glasgow* (Glasgow, 2020) https://18c-borrowing.glasgow.ac.uk. Similarly, Alexander Hunter's book was borrowed regularly from the Bristol Library in the 1770s. Paul Kaufman, *Borrowings from the Bristol Library, 1773–1784, a unique record of reading vogues* (Charlottesville, 1960).

Beyond the prevalence of managerial experience in agriculture, authors shared considerable (perhaps greater) experience in non-agricultural areas, which meant they brought new perspectives when they turned to farming, especially from commerce, horticulture and the learned professions. Indeed, those with direct agricultural experience usually only turned to farming as an adult after training or experience in another occupation. Aside from attending schools and universities, a significant number of authors (ten) were apprenticed to a trade or were trained for a commercial occupation. It is clear why men who lacked practical training from a young age, who then engaged with farming primarily as a problem of management, would have taken an interest in learning about agriculture from books. When Arthur Young took up farming aged twenty-two on the advice of his mother, after abandoning his apprenticeship to wine merchants, he admitted that he 'had no more idea of farming than of physic or divinity', and so collected books on the subject.[117]

In adulthood, at least fifty-three authors held non-agricultural occupations for a period in their life. While farmers had long gained experience in other trades through by-employments (for example, as a blacksmith, weaver or shoemaker), the eighteenth century saw significant numbers of merchants and tradesmen entering the business of farming.[118] At least twelve authors had experience in a trade (as an apothecary, carpenter, architect, astrologer, printer or thread-hosier) or in the commercial world of insurance, brewing and fishing. For example, John Mortimer was born in London around 1656, received a commercial education and became a wealthy merchant on Tower Hill, before buying an estate in 1693 in Essex, and later authoring *The Whole Art of Husbandry* (1707). When these men applied their minds to agriculture, they inevitably projected the assumptions and values gained by their participation in commerce onto farming.

In a more subtle way, initial or ongoing interest and experience of gardening influenced the way many writers approached and re-imagined agriculture. Nine authors were for a time occupied in the closely related area of horticulture, as gardeners, landscape designers, market-gardeners or nurserymen. While gardening and agriculture overlapped, books on growing fruits, flowers and vegetables were framed in terms of beauty and

---

[117] Matilda Betham-Edwards (ed.), *The autobiography of Arthur Young with selections from his correspondence* (London, 1898), 29.

[118] The extent of by-employments has been the subject of debate, see S. A. J. Keibek and Leigh Shaw-Taylor, 'Early modern rural by-employments: A re-examination of the probate inventory evidence', *AgHR*, 61 (2013).

pleasure, rather than food production.[119] The influence was a conscious one: in 1776, Richard Weston contrasted agriculture by 'the mere peasant' with gardening by 'a skillful artist' and argued that the advance of agriculture would only be achieved by 'uniting the garden-culture with farming'.[120]

The prevalence of the professions among author occupations is especially striking: not only the three great learned professions of law, physic and divinity but also occupations in the armed forces or education, and others that could broadly be termed 'skilled tertiary-sector occupations'.[121] Eleven authors were clergymen; seven were engaged in educational professions and services, including as a university professor, a private tutor, a public lecturer and a schoolmaster; six were trained or practising physicians; four had experience in the legal profession; five had experience in politics or diplomatic service; and three had military experience.[122] In some cases, these roles could be combined with agricultural interests with relative ease: a vicar tending his garden, an out-of-favour politician attending to his estate, or an educated farmer who found employment as a tutor. The unique occupational culture of professionals – built upon the mastery of specialist knowledge and increasingly formalised processes of training and qualification – was consequently a significant influence upon agricultural writing.

We can also consider the theme of professionalisation from the reverse perspective, as many writers were employed in the role of professional agricultural service, as land stewards, agents, surveyors and valuers – part of the 'pseudo gentry' of late-eighteenth-century rural society.[123] In many cases, they were employed on the basis of their publications.[124] A series of mutually reinforcing processes were at play linking books with the professionalisation of agriculture: members of the learned professions wrote books about agriculture; some writers acquired professional roles

---

[119] On this point, see Rebecca Bushnell, *Green desire: Imagining early modern English gardens* (London, 2003).

[120] Richard Weston, *Tracts on practical agriculture and gardening. Particularly addressed to the gentlemen-farmers in Great-Britain* (2nd edn; London, 1773), 2 & iii.

[121] Penelope J. Corfield, *Power and the professions in Britain 1700–1850* (London, 1995), 25.

[122] These last two categories include the Scottish noblemen John Hamilton, second Lord Belhaven and Stenton (1656–1708), Sir Archibald Grant of Monymusk, second baronet (1696–1778), and Sir John Dalrymple, the second earl of Stair (1673–1747).

[123] J. H. Porter, 'The development of rural society', in G. E. Mingay (ed.), *AHEW: 1750–1850 Vol 6* (Cambridge, 1989), 844.

[124] In 1783, William Marshall was offered the role of estate steward by Samuel Pipe-Wolferstan (1751–1820) in Staffordshire after the latter had read his earlier books about managing a farm in Surrey. Pamela Horn, *William Marshall (1745–1818) and the Georgian countryside* (Abingdon, 1982), 20.

in agriculture by virtue of their literary repute; while those (often lawyers) employed as stewards acquired specialist agricultural knowledge which could form the basis of further books.

Finally, an authorial identity often preceded an agricultural one; many were writers first and farmers second. At least thirty-nine are known to have also published books on non-agricultural topics. Ten authors published on the associated topics of gardening or botany; six on medicine; five on political economy or trade; five on religion; four on natural philosophy or mathematics; three on the law; and three published poetry or fiction; with some further writings on history, architecture and education. Indeed, some writers are better known for their contributions to other subjects: Giles Jacob (1686–1744) and Lord Kames (1696–1782) on the law, and the Rev. John Trusler (1735–1820) is notorious for his diverse publications on medicine, history, law, theology, travel and gardening. Hence agriculture was only one of many topics that engaged the pen of these authors; even Arthur Young wrote novels in the 1760s before writing on agriculture.[125]

Were any agricultural writers bred to husbandry? Only a handful could claim to have gained practical experience of farming from a young age, but even these often combined a rural upbringing with other experiences. James Small (1740–93) was the son of a farmer in Berwickshire and apprenticed to a carpenter and plough-maker. William Marshall (1745–1818), the son of a yeomen farmer in North Riding, Yorkshire, declared he was '*born a Farmer*' and could 'trace his blood through the veins of AGRICULTURALISTS, for upwards of four hundred years'.[126] But he was apprenticed in the linen trade at fifteen and then tried his luck for a number of years in insurance and commercial activities in the West Indies, before returning to London and taking up farming due to illness. If we trust the autobiographical sketch of Charles Varlo (or Varley) (c.1725–95), he spent his childhood helping out on his father's farm, in between brief periods at school, before gaining experience as a servant for neighbouring farmers and learning all the labours on a farm.[127] George Culley (1735–1813) was born in County Durham, the youngest son of a freehold farmer, and

---

[125]　Ruth Perry, *Novel relations: The transformation of kinship in English literature and culture, 1748–1818* (Cambridge, 2009), 290–91.

[126]　William Marshall, *Experiments and observations concerning agriculture* (London, 1779), 1.

[127]　Reprinted with commentary: Desmond Clarke and Charles Varlo, *The unfortunate husbandman: An account of the life and travels of a real farmer in Ireland, Scotland, England and America* (London, 1964); G. E. Fussell, '"A real farmer" of eighteenth-century England and his book, "The modern farmers guide"', *Agricultural History*, 17 (1943), 211.

perhaps worked on his father's farm until he was sent to learn from the famous sheep-breeder Robert Bakewell in Leicestershire.

In summary, it is clear that collectively agricultural authors had a set of perspectives that were rather alien to the majority of husbandmen, housewives, servants and labourers who learned about farming from a young age from their elders and through their own labour – even if there were some who could more successfully bridge the divide. It was precisely this situation that led a pamphleteer in 1785 to lament that it was 'unfortunate for agriculture, that lawyers, physicians, private gentlemen, clergymen … should write and publish in abundance; yet very few, if any… who have been regularly brought up from their youth in the employment'.[128]

Argument

This book has two overall aims. The first is a general theoretical intervention, seeking to demonstrate both the necessity and usefulness of a sociological approach to agricultural knowledge and books. It does so partly by showing how it can better explain the known, and illuminate the unknown, features of early modern agricultural books, and partly by highlighting broader changes in the social history of agricultural knowledge. The second is to advance specific historical arguments about the social role of agricultural books in Britain 1660–1800, in particular their contribution to the development of agrarian capitalism. These historical arguments form the substance of the book, but reinforce the underlying theoretical and methodological claims.

The central argument is that the printing of agricultural instructions over the long eighteenth century was both stimulated by and a contribution to significant changes in the social system of agricultural knowledge. The structure is thematic, but the chapters have a logical sequence that approximates a loose narrative. Chapter 1 sets out a new theoretical model, building on the critique (above) of the standard interpretive framework, the enlightenment model. It argues that early modern agriculture saw a concentration in managerial control over the land and therefore required a reorganisation of knowledge. It then explores recent sociological approaches to books, knowledge and labour in order to identify alternative theoretical tools to analyse and interpret the role of printed books in

---

[128] *A political enquiry into the consequences of enclosing waste lands, and the causes of the present high price of butchers meat* (London, 1785), vi.

this process. This sets up the key research question: how did book knowledge relate to changes in the division of labour? Chapter 2 establishes the context usually neglected by histories of agricultural literature: how farming was learned without books in the prevailing system of knowledge in the sixteenth and seventeenth centuries. It examines the discourse on the 'mystery of husbandry', a term denoting the knowledge and skill acquired by experienced practitioners that was inaccessible to amateurs, to both elucidate contemporary beliefs about learning through labour and to indicate the ways in which the publication of husbandry manuals disrupted existing notions of expertise. Chapter 3 sets out the book's core argument and consciously inverts existing historiography. It argues that agricultural books were in part used as a tool to appropriate the practical art of husbandry by learned culture, enabling a 'bottom-up' transfer of knowledge as much as a 'top-down' diffusion of knowledge from expert to practitioner. It shows how from the 1660s educated gentlemen collected into writing the knowledge of husbandry stored in customary practice and oral tradition, with the aim of transforming a low practical art into a high literary science. This was simultaneously a process of the masculinisation of farming knowledge, accompanying the progressive marginalisation of women in farming practice. Chapter 4 examines this process of transforming practical knowledge into written knowledge. It argues that the art of husbandry was codified in accordance with the cultural preferences and managerial interests of landowners, professionals and large farmers. Crucially, codification was shaped by the need to establish the supremacy of written knowledge and subordinate customary knowledge and labour. While agricultural authors embraced a new empiricism, it was an empiricism in which the recorded observations and experiments made by managers had primacy over the experience and customs of their workers.

The final three chapters shift to consider the social effects of the appropriation and codification of the art of husbandry by examining the impact on new divisions of labour. Chapter 5 argues that agricultural books facilitated the increasing separation between intellectual and manual labour and used codified knowledge to create a new model of managerial expertise in agriculture. This was manifested in the figure of the gentleman farmer who farmed with a pen, but further developed by the appearance of the 'agriculturist' at the end of the eighteenth century, whose contribution to farming was primarily theoretical. Chapter 6 explores the efforts to institutionalise the new book-based expertise by establishing agriculture as a profession analogous to medicine, seen most clearly in the increasing professionalisation of estate stewards who claimed to possess superior theoretical knowledge to common farmers. It charts the various educational schemes that did not come to fruition until the following century, but which nonetheless reveal the scope of ambition of agricultural authors seeking to establish a new system of knowledge. Finally, Chapter 7 details both the internal problems generated by this reorganisation of agricultural knowledge and the signs of resistance by those who sought to defend the customary, labour-based system of knowledge. It re-examines the 'book-farming' controversy of the late eighteenth century, identifying the social problems arising from the codification of agricultural knowledge, including struggles over expertise between master and servant, and landowner and tenant.

The chronological focus shifts between the chapters. Chapter 2 takes a broad look at the seventeenth and eighteenth century; the arguments of Chapter 3, 4, 5 and 6 cover the period 1660–1800; Chapter 7 is a more focused study of the decades from 1760s to 1790s. Over these chapters, a chronological pattern emerges, such that agricultural literature can be roughly divided before and after 1750, which maps onto the pattern of economic and social change: from the 1650s to the 1740s there was a depression in agricultural prices and falling rents, but from the 1750s, prices and rents soared. Between the 1650s and 1740s, the landowning gentry were the driving force behind improvement and agricultural literature, but from 1750 onwards the improvers included increasing numbers of professionals (especially physicians), land stewards and capitalist farmers. This loosely maps onto the pattern of enclosure; the state was explicitly anti-enclosure before 1660; almost all authors after 1660 were strong proponents; but the distinctive phase of widespread enclosure by Act of Parliament began around 1760.

The analysis is less about farming knowledge itself and more about the social conditions in which it exists. The intention is to re-balance our account and correct the mischaracterisations resulting from a focus solely on technological progress. Hence, it does not directly address the role of books in disseminating useful knowledge and spreading innovations, as this has already been considered at length elsewhere. Nor does this study attempt the additional and immensely complex task of weaving together how books contributed to both technological and social changes. Nonetheless, it does address a question neglected in the enlightenment model: how and why did books become an important form of knowledge for a minority of cultivators in England and Scotland by the nineteenth century? Previous interpretations usually proceed as if the growth of books was simply a matter of removing obstacles to the natural flow of written knowledge. Yet sixteenth-century conditions were manifestly unsuited for printed books to function as the primary tool of knowledge transmission between practitioners in agriculture. This only changed gradually. The decline of small owner-occupiers and the emergence of large tenants, gentlemen farmers and a cohort of agricultural professionals, created a substantial stratum of educated men who were directly involved in farm management. Whereas peasant farmers had minimal use for written instructions, this managerial class found print a highly useful technology. Books were poor tools for teaching the whole practical art of husbandry, but highly effective for constructing a managerial knowledge to be applied to expanding estates, projects of improvement and large-scale commercial farming. In particular, the master of enclosed fields operating in a competitive market was an ideal reader, as they had the motive and scope to implement new methods that deviated from local custom. At the same time, wider trends all encouraged the use of books for transferring knowledge, as increases in literacy, education and income transformed books from elite luxuries to popular commodities. The sudden burst of Scottish agricultural writers from the 1750s, when the imposition of English landholding structures stimulated commercial farming, shows the close association between social reform and agricultural publishing. While new channels of information such as the growth in agricultural societies have been credited with creating the necessary infrastructure for books to be a vector of useful knowledge among a section of the agricultural community, this was only possible due to the long-term social reorganisation of agricultural production.[129] However, books were not simply a response to the demands of a changing economy, but causal agents themselves that assisted these social changes by creating new ways for agricultural knowledge to be produced, acquired, stored, transferred, legitimated and exercised.

Overall, this book presents a new perspective on the development of agrarian capitalism. The capitalist structure of landlord, tenant and labourer required a corresponding structure of knowledge, whereby mental labour was largely extracted from those performing manual labour and concentrated in managerial positions. Printed books were a key part of this transition. This study, therefore, overturns the existing historiography on the impact of printed agricultural literature and opens up new paths

---

[129] Smout, 'Scottish improvers', 145; Holmes, 'Dissemination', 874.

for research into the social history of agricultural knowledge. While the long-term trend from self-organising peasants to supervised labourers is a familiar narrative, we are yet to fully investigate what happened to the knowledge and skills of husbandry during this transformation. We can begin by examining why and how customary knowledge was enclosed within books.

CHAPTER I

Rethinking Agricultural Books, Knowledge and Labour

What stimulated the writing, printing and reading of farming books, and what impact did they have on farming practice in early modern Britain? This is a social question, not merely a technological one. Books changed the relationship between people working in agriculture, regardless of the degree to which they contributed to innovations in methods and increased productivity. This chapter makes the case for a sociological interpretation of the role of agricultural books, building on the critique of the standard enlightenment model made in the Introduction. It primarily takes inspiration from sociologies of knowledge rather than the 'sociology of texts' specifically.[1] The first section argues that the well-known major social and institutional trends in early modern agriculture necessarily involved significant redistributions of knowledge within rural society. Hence, the circulation of books needs to be placed in this context, namely the rise of capitalist farming. The second section explores recent sociological approaches to books, knowledge and labour in order to identify alternative theoretical tools. It concludes by summarising how these sociological insights can be applied to early modern agriculture to develop a new framework for understanding the cumulative social impact of printed information and advice. This retelling of the socio-economic story of agriculture and synthesis of the theoretical links between books, knowledge and labour serves as the foundation for the following six chapters.

Divisions of Early Modern Agricultural Labour and Knowledge

The social or institutional trends in early modern English and Scottish agriculture are well established in outline, but their extent and timing are still subject to debate. The two grand narratives that have shaped histories

---

[1] Donald Francis McKenzie, *Bibliography and the sociology of texts* (Cambridge, 1999).

of agrarian change in this period are the 'agricultural revolution' and the 'rise of agrarian capitalism'. The classic idea of the agricultural revolution refers to a rapid increase in productivity and output over a few decades, accompanied by sweeping transformations in the organisation of farming.[2] But after decades of scholarship, there is no consensus on when such a revolution took place and of what exactly it consisted.[3] While revisionists argued for the significance of innovations in the sixteenth and seventeenth centuries, Mark Overton defended the case for unprecedented increases in output from the mid-eighteenth century through rising land and labour productivity.[4] Overton identified the crucial advance as the integration of grass and grain through convertible husbandry and new crop rotations (based on the principle of Norfolk four-course rotation) using clover and turnips that increased nitrogen availability.[5] Yet long-term estimates indicate incremental improvements in output from the sixteenth to nineteenth centuries whose effects were cumulative rather than revolutionary.[6] In any case, the 'revolution' framing has tended to concentrate on technological changes (in crops, methods or tools), often reducing social changes to factors that either encouraged or discouraged technical innovations. To the extent that it does emphasise social change, it also foregrounds the growth of the market and increasing commercial orientation of farmers.[7]

The narrative frame of agrarian capitalism emphasises social change rather than technological advances, without the obligation to identify a short-term transformation. However, similar problems of definition, chronology and causation beset this tradition, running from Marx through R. H. Tawney, Maurice Dobb and Robert Brenner, with important recent contributions from Jane Whittle, Rob Albritton and Leigh

[2] J. D. Chambers and G. E. Mingay, *The agricultural revolution, 1750–1880* (New York, 1966).
[3] For useful summary of the debate, see M. E. Turner et al., *Farm production in England, 1700–1914* (Oxford, 2001), ch. 1.
[4] Eric Kerridge, *The agricultural revolution* (New York, 1967); E. L. Jones, 'Agriculture and economic growth in England, 1660–1750: Agricultural change', *Journal of Economic History*, 25:1 (1965); Allen, *Enclosure and the yeoman*.
[5] Overton, *Agricultural revolution*. See also Bruce Campbell and Mark Overton, 'A new perspective on medieval and early modern agriculture: Six centuries of Norfolk farming c.1250–c.1850', *Past & Present*, 141 (1993). See critique: Robert C. Allen, 'Tracking the agricultural revolution in England', *EcHR*, 52 (1999).
[6] Stephen Broadberry et al., *British economic growth, 1270–1870* (Cambridge, 2015), 129; Joyce Burnette, 'Agriculture, 1700–1870', in Roderick Floud et al. (eds), *The Cambridge economic history of modern Britain: Volume I: 1700–1870* (Cambridge, 2014).
[7] Overton, *Agricultural revolution*, 133–49, 207.

Shaw-Taylor.[8] In Whittle's account, the development of agrarian capitalism concerns the long-term transition from a peasant society, of small
subsistence-oriented producers in possession of the land, to a capitalist
society, defined by a market dependence for goods and labour, landless
wage labourers and the means of production concentrated in the hands
of a minority, who employ wage labour and sell to the market for profit.[9]
It is crucial to recognise that this is not merely commercial farming,
which simply designates production for the market. Arguments have
been presented for the critical developments occurring at various times
between 1500 and 1800.[10] Whittle suggests that while there was an active
land market in sixteenth-century England and the beginning of differentiation within peasant society, the critical shift to capitalist relations probably took place in the eighteenth century.[11] Shaw-Taylor uses
occupational data and a crude measure of the prevalence of wage labour
to argue that 'the decisive shift to agrarian capitalism took place before
1700'.[12] However, considering the limited extent to which agricultural
labour power was commodified, Albritton argues that British agriculture was only minimally capitalist by 1700 and only became substan-
tially capitalist in the late nineteenth century.[13] In general, while recent
research has emphasised long-term developments, the 'tipping point' is
most often identified in the seventeenth century.[14] For the present study,
the exact chronology is less important than the broad dynamics and
direction of change, but it will be argued that agricultural literature
made a distinctive contribution to the development of agrarian capitalist
relations between 1660 and 1800.

In Scotland, the picture is a little clearer, as the transition from peasant to capitalist social relations in the eighteenth century was both rapid

---

[8] See summary of the 'transition debate' in David Ormrod, 'Agrarian capitalism and merchant
capitalism: Tawney, Dobb, Brenner and beyond', in Jane Whittle (ed.), *Landlords and tenants in
Britain, 1440–1660: Tawney's agrarian problem revisited* (Woodbridge, 2013); T. H. Aston and C.
H. E. Philpin (eds), *The Brenner debate: Agrarian class structure and economic development in pre-
industrial Europe* (Cambridge, 1985); Henry French and R. W. Hoyle, *The character of English rural
society: Earls Colne, 1550–1750* (Manchester, 2007), ch. 1.

[9] Whittle, *The development of agrarian capitalism*, 8–11.

[10] Leigh Shaw-Taylor, 'The rise of agrarian capitalism and the decline of family farming in England',
EcHR, 65 (2012), 27.

[11] Whittle, *The development of agrarian capitalism*, 24.

[12] Shaw-Taylor, 'Rise of agrarian capitalism', 58.

[13] Robert Albritton, 'Did agrarian capitalism exist?', *The Journal of Peasant Studies*, 20 (1993), 424.

[14] Jane Whittle, 'Land and people', in Keith Wrightson (ed.), *A social history of England, 1500–1750*
(Cambridge, 2017), 165.

and partially planned.[15] While the critical decades in the transformation are generally identified as between 1760 and 1815, there were earlier signs of reformist energy after the catastrophic harvest failure of 1695, which stimulated gradual changes in the structure of tenure in the first half of the eighteenth century.[16] After the Jacobite defeat in 1746 and the loss of their traditional feudal powers, Scottish landlords transformed themselves into capitalists with the wholesale adoption of the English model of agricultural production, rapidly reorganising estates and commercialising Scottish farming from the 1760s and 1770s.[17]

There are at least four interrelated trends in the rise of agrarian capitalism that have implications for the distribution and exercise of agricultural knowledge: the concentration of land ownership, the increase in average farm size, the polarisation in occupational structure and increasing managerial control over methods of production. Further consideration could be given to the growth and integration of markets, but the focus here is on the social relations of production rather than exchange. The general context was a dramatic reduction in the proportion of the English population engaged in farming. While precise estimates vary, recent studies on male occupational data all position the critical structural shift from agriculture to manufacturing and services in the seventeenth century. A recent estimate suggests a decline from around 60 per cent to less than 40 per cent of the labour force engaged in agriculture (rather than industry or services) from around the 1550s to 1700s, then a further reduction to around 30 per cent by early 1800s.[18] These estimates oversimplify the early modern economy, especially since by-employments were common, but cultivation was certainly shifting from a majority capacity to a minority skill.[19]

---

[15] E. J. Hobsbawm, 'Scottish reformers of the eighteenth century and capitalist agriculture', in E. J. Hobsbawm et al. (eds), *Peasants in history: Essays in honour of Daniel Thorner* (Oxford, 1980).

[16] Tom Devine, *The transformation of rural Scotland: Social change and the agrarian economy, 1660–1815* (Edinburgh, 1994).

[17] See Neil Davidson, 'The Scottish path to capitalist agriculture 1: From the crisis of feudalism to the origins of agrarian transformation (1688–1746)', *Journal of Agrarian Change*, 4 (2004); Neil Davidson, 'The Scottish path to capitalist agriculture 2: The capitalist offensive (1747–1815)', *Journal of Agrarian Change*, 4 (2004).

[18] Broadberry et al., *British economic growth*, 346–63. See also Patrick Wallis et al., 'Structural change and economic growth in the British economy before the Industrial Revolution, 1500–1800', *Journal of Economic History*, 78 (2018); Leigh Shaw-Taylor and E. A. Wrigley, 'Occupational structure and population change', in Roderick Floud et al. (eds), *The Cambridge economic history of modern Britain: Volume I: 1700–1870* (Cambridge, 2014); S. A. J. Keibek, 'The male occupational structure of England and Wales, 1600–1850', PhD thesis (University of Cambridge, 2017).

[19] For argument that by-employments are insignificant for calculating male occupations, see S. A. J. Keibek, 'By-employments in early modern England and their significance for estimating historical male occupational structures', *Cambridge Working Papers in Economic and Social History*, 29 (2017).

The concentration of land ownership is a clear trend, but the causes and chronology are contested, with enclosure being only one of the more visible mechanisms.[20] Early sixteenth-century England was recognisably a peasant society with land ownership still widely distributed, but there was an active land market and growing differentiation among peasant proprietors, or yeomanry, who were able to accumulate more land in the early seventeenth century.[21] Landownership estimates over the eighteenth century show a decreasing proportion for yeomen or freeholders and an increase for the gentry and owners of great estates.[22] The century after the Restoration was long seen as the critical period for the concentration of landownership.[23] However, others stress a gradual polarisation of land-holdings over many centuries, with markedly different regional trends and diverse underlying mechanisms, and periods of stasis or even reversal.[24] Similarly, it has been argued that the decline in the number of small farmers and owner-occupiers has been exaggerated, although the decline itself is not disputed.[25] Nonetheless, the period from the late seventeenth century to the late eighteenth century is consistently viewed as a critical period for the consolidation of landholdings, especially in the south and east of England.

Another trend closely linked to the gradual concentration of landownership was an increase in average farm size, perhaps driven by the need for larger production units and better economies of scale.[26] The issue has been confused by the lack of clear definition for categories of 'small' or 'large' farms, which vary from the sixteenth to eighteenth centuries,

[20] Alexandra Sapoznik, 'Britain, 1000–1750', in Erik Thoen and Tim Soens (eds), *Struggling with the environment: Land use and productivity* (Rural Economy and Society in North-western Europe, 500–2000; Turnhout, 2016), 76.

[21] Alan Everitt, 'Farm labourers', in Joan Thirsk (ed.), *AHEW: 1500–1640 Vol 4* (Cambridge, 1967), 400–1; Whittle, *The development of agrarian capitalism*, ch. 4; Allen, *Enclosure and the yeoman*, 14.

[22] It is estimated that yeomen owned around 25–33 per cent of land in 1690, declining to 15 per cent in 1790, while ownership by gentry and great landowners increased: Overton, *Agricultural revolution*, 168.

[23] Argument for 'landlords' revolution' in Allen, *Enclosure and the yeoman*, 78.

[24] F. M. L. Thompson, 'The social distribution of landed property in England since the sixteenth century', *EcHR*, 19 (1966); Christopher Clay, 'Landlords and estate management in England', in Joan Thirsk (ed.), *AHEW: 1640–1750 Vol 5 / 2. Agrarian change* (Cambridge, 1985), 163, 182; J. V. Beckett, 'The pattern of landownership in England and Wales, 1660–1880', *EcHR*, 37 (1984); Stephen Hipkin, 'The structure of landownership and land occupation in the Romney Marsh region, 1646–1834', *AgHR*, 51 (2003).

[25] J. V. Beckett, 'The decline of the small landowner in England and Wales 1660–1900', in F. M. L. Thompson (ed.), *Landowners, capitalists and entrepreneurs: Essays for Sir John Habakkuk* (Oxford, 1994); Michael Turner, 'The demise of the yeoman, c.1750–1940', in John Broad (ed.), *A common agricultural heritage? Revising French and British rural divergence* (Exeter, 2009).

[26] French and Hoyle, *Character of English rural society*, 30–31.

depending on the type of farming and broader economic context.[27] Further, the apparent prevalence of subtenancies undermines data from manorial records, which rely on units of ownership to measure units of farming.[28] Various case studies using alternative records of parish rates or taxes demonstrate the significant discrepancy between structures of land ownership and occupation. Nor is there a simple correlation between the two, as subtenancy could result in units of farming being either smaller or larger than units of ownership.[29] However, Stephen Hipkin's study of the almost unique records of Romney Marsh in Kent shows that the farm size (or land occupied) increased significantly over the seventeenth century.[30] Hence, the precise changes in the structures of land occupation and farm size remain unclear, but the general claim that the average farm size increased has not been refuted.

Changes in occupational structure were in part a consequence of these shifts in landownership. The main trend was a polarisation within the labouring population, mirroring the polarisation in landholding. In the sixteenth century, the social roles of labourer, husbandman and yeomen existed along a continuous spectrum that became increasingly clustered around a few positions in the eighteenth century.[31] With the decline of the small farmer or owner-occupier and the expansion of the large estate, the three-tiered structure of landowners, large-scale tenant farmers and landless wage labourers began to dominate English rural society.[32] Evidence of male occupations has been used to estimate a ratio of 2.5 farm workers to farmers across south-eastern England by 1700, yet family farming remained dominant across northern England for much of the eighteenth century.[33] Similar estimates of a ratio of 0.8 workers per farmer in sixteenth-century Norfolk and 0.6 in Gloucestershire around 1608 also

---

[27] Whittle, *The development of agrarian capitalism*, 195–96. Allen calculated that the average open-field farm increased from 65 to 145 acres over the eighteenth century. Allen, *Enclosure and the yeoman*, 79–80.

[28] Shaw-Taylor, 'Rise of agrarian capitalism', 39–44. Joseph Barker, 'The emergence of agrarian capitalism in early modern England: A reconsideration of farm sizes', PhD thesis (University of Cambridge, 2013).

[29] A recent case study mapping subletting practices found that the average farm size was larger than the average property size. Joshua Rhodes, 'Subletting in eighteenth-century England: A new methodological approach', *AgHR*, 66 (2018), 90.

[30] Stephen Hipkin, 'Tenant farming and short-term leasing on Romney Marsh, 1587–1705', *EcHR*, 53 (2000).

[31] Everitt, 'Farm labourers', 418.

[32] Proportion of landless families rose from 12 per cent c.1550 to 66 per cent c.1688 to 73 per cent in 1851. Overton, *Agricultural revolution*, 178.

[33] Shaw-Taylor, 'Rise of agrarian capitalism', 53.

suggest a seventeenth-century shift from family labour to hired labour.[34] However, a simple ratio of workers to farmers neglects the nature of employment. Servants constituted between a third and a half of all hired labour throughout much of the early modern period, only declining from the mid-eighteenth century.[35] In Shaw-Taylor's analysis, farm servants and day labourers are grouped together as 'farm workers', and servants are alternately included or excluded from the data. While he suggests that his method undercounts the labour force and therefore understates the extent of capitalist relations, the inclusion of service has the opposite effect of overstating the case for the critical transition to capitalist agriculture by 1700.[36] Service was primarily a life-cycle employment for young unmarried people, strictly regulated by labour laws, in which labour was not fully commodified. The paternalistic master–servant relation cannot be reduced to a purely contractual wage relation.[37] The difference between service and day labour is particularly pertinent for understanding the structure of knowledge, as service functioned as a period of informal training, in which knowledge and skills were acquired for adult independence. Proletarianisation – the expansion of a class of lifelong, landless wage labourers – was therefore a more gradual process.

The overall picture suggests that, from the early sixteenth century to the late eighteenth century, the typical conditions of labour changed significantly from families farming their own land primarily for subsistence to waged workers farming the land of a large tenant or wealthy landowner.[38] The small husbandman who, in partnership with the housewife, performed a whole variety of tasks, with support from children and perhaps a young servant, was progressively replaced in the occupational order by the hired labourer, performing a narrower range of tasks, and the large tenant farmer, who managed the labourers.[39] More farms began to approximate the capitalist division of labour in which the farmer was primarily engaged in management or mental labour.[40] By 1850, three-quarters of the male

---

[34] Whittle, 'Land and people', 158.
[35] Ann Kussmaul, *Servants in husbandry in early modern England* (Cambridge, 1981); Craig Muldrew, *Food, energy and the creation of industriousness: Work and material culture in agrarian England, 1550–1780* (Cambridge, 2011), 222.
[36] Muldrew estimated 1.7 servants per labourer in village censuses from 1688 to 1750, as discussed in Whittle, 'Land and people', 164. A. J. Gritt, 'The "survival" of service in the English agricultural labour force: Lessons from Lancashire, c.1650–1851', *AgHR*, 50 (2002).
[37] Albritton, 'Did agrarian capitalism exist?', 431; Whittle, *The development of agrarian capitalism*, 256.
[38] Sapoznik, 'Britain, 1000–1750', 76.
[39] On large tenant farmers as managers, see Susanna Wade-Martins, *Farmers, landlords and landscapes: Rural Britain, 1720 to 1870* (Macclesfield, 2004), 124.
[40] Albritton, 'Did agrarian capitalism exist?', 426–27.

agricultural labour force worked for wages.[41] Over time, therefore, the distribution of knowledge changed: the lower end of the rural population went through a process which pessimists call 'deskilling' and optimists call 'specialisation'.[42] A recent study concluded that there was a significant rise in the share of unskilled workers in early modern English agriculture linked to the concentration of land, albeit on the basis of occupational titles that can misrepresent the actual work performed.[43] A bleak vision of the consequences was summed up by a comment about the south-west in an 1849–51 survey, which described the average farm worker as a kind of 'machine': 'His daily task assigned to him, and he performs it, but the work is the work merely of his hands, and is scarcely ever directed by the mind'.[44]

As waged work became the norm, women's work was marginalised. Recent evidence demonstrates that over a third of agricultural work was performed by women in the sixteenth and seventeenth centuries, especially in dairying, but also a range of field work, including weeding, hoeing, reaping and haymaking. Further, although specific tasks were gendered (winnowing not threshing, sowing not ploughing), there was significant flexibility and overlap between men's and women's agricultural labour.[45] Women performed farm work not only as housewives (or farmer's wives) and servants in husbandry but also as widows who took over management of a farm or estate (perhaps for a short time until a male heir) or elite women who managed their husband's estate while he was absent in London. The work of the eighteenth-century farmer's wife was oriented around three spaces: the kitchen garden (growing fruits, vegetables and herbs), the dairy (making cheese and butter) and the farmyard (rearing of pigs, hens and other poultry).[46] Yet, the range of women's farming activities was increasingly circumscribed by the nineteenth century with the cumulative loss of common rights and restricted opportunities for waged work, primarily because larger farms preferred to employ male day labourers.[47]

---

[41] Burnette, 'Agriculture, 1700–1870', 92–93.
[42] Allen, *Enclosure and the yeoman*, 219–20.
[43] Alexandra M. de Pleijt and Jacob L. Weisdorf, 'Human capital formation from occupations: The "deskilling hypothesis" revisited', *Cliometrica,* 11 (2017).
[44] From the *Morning Chronicle*, quoted in Nicola Verdon, *Working the land: A history of the farmworker in England from 1850 to the present day* (London, 2017), 2.
[45] Whittle and Hailwood, 'Gender division of labour'.
[46] Nicola Verdon, '"... Subjects deserving of the highest praise": Farmers' wives and the farm economy in England, c.1700–1850', *AgHR,* 51 (2003), 27.
[47] Jane Humphries, 'Enclosures, common rights, and women: The proletarianization of families in the late eighteenth and early nineteenth centuries', *The Journal of Economic History,* 50 (1990); Peter King, 'Customary rights and women's earnings: The importance of gleaning to the rural labouring poor, 1750–1850', *EcHR,* 44 (1991); Deborah Valenze, *The first industrial woman* (Oxford, 1995), ch. 2.

The last trend is subtler and concerns the management rather than ownership of land. We can consider the management at two general levels: the estate (by the landowner) and the farm (by the farmer). First, there were four main ways in which a landlord or steward could exert influence over the cultivation methods of tenants: direct instruction, bargaining, prescriptions in leases and setting an example on the home farm.[48] Formally, the general shift from customary to leasehold tenure increased the ability of landlords to control tenants' farming, as copyhold gave tenants a great deal of freedom to manage their lands according to the local custom.[49] The century before 1650 actually saw many farmers convert customary tenancies to freeholds, but later circumstances allowed landlords to reduce freeholds and increase leaseholds.[50] As late as 1688, the combination of small-scale freeholders and copyholders (or life leaseholds) meant that around two-thirds of England was 'farmed by a virtually independent group'.[51] But the increasing use of leasehold allowed for the stipulation of conditions or 'covenants' dictating what a tenant could and could not do.[52] The number and complexity of these covenants increased during the eighteenth century, with more prescriptions for 'improved' methods and financial penalties regulating tenants' behaviour.[53] Yet, the extent to which covenants enforced improvements or were adhered to in practice is debated.[54] Informally, the landlord or steward could exercise close supervision, offering casual advice or more forceful directions under threat of eviction.[55] In fact, the increasing role of professional land stewards is a key indicator of more active estate management in the late eighteenth century. In general, management strategies shifted from treating the estate as a source of revenue to be maintained through efficient administration of rents to seeing it as an investment whose returns depended on increases in agricultural productivity.[56] For example, a Midland case study shows how

[48] Discussed in J. Ross Wordie, *Estate management in eighteenth-century England: The building of the Leveson-Gower fortune* (London, 1982), 179.
[49] Clay, 'Landlords', 205–6.
[50] R. W. Hoyle, 'Tenure and the land market in early modern England: Or a late contribution to the Brenner debate', *EcHR*, 43 (1990), 17.
[51] Wade-Martins, *Farmers, landlords*, 18.
[52] Clay, 'Landlords', 208–12. Overton, *Agricultural revolution*, 184; Ormrod, 'Agrarian capitalism', 213.
[53] Clay, 'Landlords', 204, 216–18.
[54] Wade-Martins suggests these mostly concerned long-term structural improvements. Wade-Martins, *Farmers, landlords*, 6, 120.
[55] Clay, 'Landlords', 228–29. Tenants-at-will were especially susceptible to such control. Wordie, *Estate management*, 49.
[56] J. V. Beckett, 'Landownership and estate management', in G. E. Mingay (ed.), *AHEW: 1750–1850 Vol 6* (Cambridge, 1989), 590–92.

in 1691 the landlord had no influence on the farming practice of tenants, but over 130 years, they became progressively more involved in regulating practice through changes in leasing policy and the role of the chief agent.[57] Further, rack-renting incentivised landowners to take a greater interest and to exert a greater degree of control over the methods of tenants.[58]

Second, the management of farms as units of production changed over the early modern period. The classic agricultural revolution can be seen as a 'managerial revolution' from the tenants' perspective, in the sense that new methods required a change in the management of resources to maximise rewards.[59] This is usually understood as a process of commercialisation, in which farming was increasingly pursued as a profit-making enterprise in response to market opportunities, encouraging innovations in farm management and the adoption of improved methods.[60] In this narrative, the market is the primary driver of change, rather than changes in the social relations of production.[61] However, Rob Bryer draws attention to how market-oriented and profit-seeking farming was based on a reorganisation of labour in farm production. The key shift in the creation of a capitalist farmer was not simply the employment of wage labour but the reorganisation of the labour process itself in the pursuit of increased labour productivity and a higher rate of return on capital.[62] This latter framework more usefully focuses analysis on labour management, but both approaches agree broadly that there was a trend towards more active and innovative management of farm labour to increase productivity and profits.[63]

The same general points apply to post-1746 Scotland, as a series of reforms rapidly commercialised Scottish farming, including the introduction of long leases, the transition to rents in cash, the abolition of communal land and the consolidation of farming units.[64] But whereas in England the class structure of agrarian capitalism emerged through a two-way process driven simultaneously by landlords and commercially minded tenants, in Scotland the social and institutional transformation

[57] Wordie, *Estate management*, 23.
[58] M. E. Turner et al., *Agricultural rent in England, 1690–1914* (Cambridge, 2004), 14–15.
[59] F. M. L. Thompson, 'The second agricultural revolution, 1815–1880', *EcHR*, 21 (1968), 63.
[60] Overton, *Agricultural revolution*, 128, 206–7.
[61] Ibid., 121–22, 132. Also French and Hoyle, *Character of English rural society*, 37–38.
[62] Rob Bryer, 'The genesis of the capitalist farmer: Towards a Marxist accounting history of the origins of the English agricultural revolution', *Critical Perspectives on Accounting*, 17 (2006), 370–71.
[63] On the eighteenth-century tenant farm as a capitalist enterprise requiring new kinds of management, see Keith Tribe, *Genealogies of capitalism* (Atlantic Highlands, NJ, 1981), 85, 94.
[64] Davidson, 'Scottish path 2', 431.

was much closer to a 'revolution from above'.[65] This initiative 'from above' came not only from landlords but also from professional managers and often required the willing participation of enterprising tenants.[66]

All these trends together point to a general conclusion: over time, there was a concentration of managerial control over cultivation. While it is difficult to identify the decision-makers in diverse contexts with precision, it is clear that control over cultivation was gradually concentrated into a smaller section both of the population as a whole and of the agricultural sector specifically. Moreover, the commercialisation of farming and system of competitive rents drove efforts to intensify control over the labour process in order to increase labour productivity. Even if the chronology of these changes remains uncertain in the case of England, the direction of social change during the period of growth in agricultural literature is apparent. Since management over the labour process in farm production correlates to the possession of some knowledge, we can infer a significant change in the distribution of knowledge – that is, the positions in the occupational structure where knowledge was held and exercised. New divisions of labour necessitated new divisions of knowledge. The changes were likely most acute in the areas with widespread common rights that were enclosed during the eighteenth century, extinguishing the commoners' way of life based around the shared use of resources and a degree of communal decision-making.[67] This is the context in which the creation and distribution of agricultural books must be explored. First, however, we need to equip ourselves with sociological insights into the relation between books, knowledge and labour.

Knowledge

The enlightenment interpretation, as most recently articulated by Peter Jones, is explicitly based on the model of 'knowledge diffusion'.[68] There are two general problems with this view of knowledge and a further problem when applied to books. The first problem is that the concept of 'diffusion' itself obscures social relations. The basic term describes a substance moving uniformly through a homogenous substrate. Hence, knowledge diffusion is a model of how knowledge flows through a homogenous

[65] Ibid., 414–17. See also Adams, 'Agents'.
[66] Davidson, 'Scottish path 2', 441; Jones, *Agricultural enlightenment*, 156.
[67] Neeson, *Commoners*.
[68] Jones, *Agricultural enlightenment*, 83.

social body, from the centre to the periphery; implicitly a top-down process from experts (an area of high concentration) to practitioners (an area of low concentration). This is of course an untenable view of the complex social hierarchies of early modern Britain, and consequently the model always requires correction after application. But this treats major features of early modern society as anomalies or deviations from the model. A core mistake is viewing knowledge (or information) as an independent force that will naturally spread until it meets an obstacle. For example, agricultural 'information' is described as having had to 'cross a number of social boundaries between landlords and tenants, and tenants and farm servants'.[69] Even the vocabulary adopted (of 'networks' and 'nodes', of 'agents' and 'vectors') has the peculiar effect of flattening out the social structure, as if we are examining an idealised network of equals engaged in peer-to-peer exchange. This is a false picture of the highly stratified early modern social order, which cannot be resolved with a few qualifications.

The second problem is that it assumes the existence of a pure knowledge abstracted from its social conditions. It is therefore treated as socially neutral, with a purely technical relation to labour and production: useful knowledge is simply fed into the labour process to improve productivity. In contrast, all recent social histories of knowledge begin with the recognition that there is no singular and pure 'knowledge', but multiple types of knowledge constructed in different social contexts that can compete, conflict and combine with each other.[70] Crucially, different types of knowledge serve different functions to the advantage or disadvantage of different social groups. The dominant knowledge categories for the early modern period embodied the ancient opposition between *epistēmē* (theoretical knowledge) and *technē* (craft skill), which can be variously translated as the distinction between 'knowing that' and 'knowing how', or the metonymic dualism of head and hand. This distinction was mapped onto the social order in various ways, most crudely in the opposition between scholar and artisan, although recent scholarship has problematised this hierarchical distinction by exploring the hybrid nature of knowledge-making.[71] Similarly, the primacy of textual knowledge has

---

[69] Holmes, 'Dissemination', 867.

[70] Peter Burke, *What is the history of knowledge?* (Cambridge, 2016); Peter Burke, *Social history of knowledge: From Gutenberg to Diderot* (Cambridge, 2000), 14.

[71] Lissa Roberts et al. (eds), *The mindful hand: Inquiry and invention from the late renaissance to industrialization* (Chicago, 2007); Ursula Klein and Emma C. Spary, 'Introduction', in Ursula Klein and Emma C. Spary (eds), *Materials and expertise in early modern Europe: Between market and laboratory* (Chicago, 2010), 2.

been challenged by renewed attention to the role of material objects and practices.[72] Indeed, a significant tradition in the history of science argues that the new experimental science of the seventeenth century was based on the unwritten knowledge of practitioners in mechanical arts.[73] Knowledge is now understood to be produced in a 'moral field', such that credible knowledge is based on trust and social authority (e.g. codes of gentility in seventeenth-century science).[74] By attending to the social construction of knowledge, historians have therefore explored how particular kinds of expertise were established and maintained in the early modern period.[75]

To go beyond the diffusion model, we need to identify and examine the types of agricultural knowledge in the early modern period. Here we can look for resources in the growing interest in the nature and history of 'knowing how', variously described as 'practical', 'artisanal', 'craft', 'technical', 'experiential', 'tacit', 'empirical' or 'embodied' knowledge, all of which try to capture the nature of the knowledge and skills learned and exercised through practice.[76] A recent collection of essays has sought to develop a general theory for studying the social structure of practical knowledge, meaning the division of knowledge and expertise created by the division of labour within an occupational hierarchy.[77] However, the farmer is invariably absent from these histories of practical, artisanal or craft knowledge.[78] Farmers are widely acknowledged as carrying out complex practical tasks, but rarely viewed as skilled artisans.[79] They do not

---

[72] See Sachiko Kusukawa and Ian Maclean, *Transmitting knowledge: Words, images, and instruments in early modern Europe* (Oxford, 2006); Pamela H. Smith and Benjamin Schmidt (eds), *Making knowledge in early modern Europe: Practices, objects, and texts, 1400–1800* (Chicago, 2007); P. H. Smith et al. (eds), *Ways of making and knowing: The material culture of empirical knowledge* (Ann Arbor, 2014).

[73] Pamela O. Long, *Artisans/practitioners and the rise of the new sciences 1400–1600* (Oregon, 2011), ch. 1. See overview in Catharina Lis and Hugo Soly, *Worthy efforts: Attitudes to work and workers in pre-industrial Europe* (Leiden, 2012), ch. 6. For example, Bert De Munck, 'Corpses, live models, and nature: Assessing skills and knowledge before the industrial revolution (Case: Antwerp)', *Technology and Culture*, 51 (2010).

[74] Steven Shapin, *A social history of truth: Civility and science in seventeenth-century England* (Chicago, 1994), xxvi.

[75] Summarised in Eric H. Ash, 'Introduction: Expertise and the early modern state', *Osiris*, 25 (2010). See also Christelle Rabier (ed.), *Fields of expertise: A comparative history of expert procedures in Paris and London, 1600 to present* (Newcastle, 2007).

[76] A seminal study of artisanal knowledge was Pamela H. Smith, *The body of the artisan: Art and experience in the scientific revolution* (Chicago, 2004).

[77] Valleriani (ed.), *Structures*.

[78] A legacy of the ambiguous status long-held by agriculture. Elspeth Whitney, 'Paradise restored. The mechanical arts from antiquity through the thirteenth century', *Transactions of the American Philosophical Society*, 80 (1990).

[79] See distinction in Long, *Artisans/practitioners*, 4. See similar point about fishermen in Didi van Trijp, 'Fresh fish: Observation up close in late seventeenth-century England', *Notes Rec.*, (2020).

make things as craftsmen do, and hence do not fit easily into the 'maker's knowledge tradition'.[80] Seamen suffer from the same classificatory gap, prompting Philippa Hellawell to suggest that skilled practitioners such as seamen and husbandmen are better understood as engaged in Aristotle's third form of activity, *praxis* (action), rather than *poesis* (production), with the corresponding virtue of *phronesis* (practical wisdom).[81]

Agriculture has consequently been neglected in social histories of practical knowledge, with notable exceptions in arguments advanced by Stephen Marglin and James Scott. Both contrast two kinds of agricultural logic or systems of knowledge, distinguishing the peasant or farmer's knowledge from the scientific knowledge of modern hi-tech agriculture. Marglin loosely applies the *epistemē / technē* distinction to the systems of knowledge belonging to the 'expert' and the 'farmer'. He argues that agriculture is fundamentally based on *technē*, a knowledge exercised in the inherent uncertainties of weather and climate.[82] Similarly, mostly in an East African colonial context, Scott argues that peasant farming was a matter of practical judgements in response to a unique and changing environment, in contrast to the standardisation and the reduction to universal principles of scientific agriculture.[83] Scott prefers the Greek term *mētis* (often translated as 'cunning') rather than *technē* or *phronesis,* arguing that the former better captures practical skills and experiential knowledge. *Mētis* refers to contextual knowledge that is irreducible to a set of fixed rules, and therefore fundamentally resistant to book learning.[84] While adopting slightly different concepts, both Marglin and Scott map these contrasting epistemologies onto social struggles between farmers and experts or state institutions.[85] These analyses offer a fruitful way of thinking about the development of eighteenth-century agricultural knowledge in the context of a polarising rural society.

In an eighteenth-century context, the only existing sociological analysis of agricultural knowledge forms part of a wider treatment of knowledge

---

[80] Long, *Artisans/practitioners*, 37.
[81] Philippa Hellawell, '"The best and most practical philosophers": Seamen and the authority of experience in early modern science', *History of Science,* 58 (2019), 34. On agriculture as praxis, see also Pamela O. Long, *Openness, secrecy, authorship: Technical arts and the culture of knowledge from antiquity to the renaissance* (Baltimore, 2001), 16, 22.
[82] Stephen A. Marglin, 'Farmers, seedsmen, and scientists: Systems of agriculture and systems of knowledge', in Frédérique Apffel-Marglin and Stephen A. Marglin (eds), *Decolonizing knowledge: From development to dialogue* (Oxford, 1996), 238.
[83] James C. Scott, *Seeing like a state: How certain schemes to improve the human condition have failed* (London, 1998), 301.
[84] Ibid., 313–19.
[85] Ibid., 311.

of the natural world by Mary Fissell and Roger Cooter. Fissell and Cooter replace the conventional model of knowledge diffusion with an analysis of the diverse sites and forms of natural knowledge: where knowledge was produced and how it was communicated or exercised.[86] The case studies of agricultural knowledge-making provide concrete examples of how the model of knowledge diffusion 'cannot account for the social relations of eighteenth-century agriculture'.[87] Yet it is in their discussion of medical knowledge that they offer the most useful concept for the present study: 'knowledge appropriation', whereby a burgeoning medical profession simultaneously borrowed from and criticised folk knowledge, partly through the production of books.[88]

Book Knowledge

When the diffusion model is applied to books as specific vectors of knowledge transmission, it makes similar errors. The problem again is that it treats books themselves as socially neutral. This is most evident in the inability of historians to explain fully why most farmers were dismissive or hostile to farming books, since their intrinsic value as universal vehicles of knowledge is considered axiomatic. Yet recent histories of print culture have deepened our understanding of how books were made, circulated and used in the early modern period, and challenged our modern assumptions.[89] Print is not neutral, but a specific technology that interacts with knowledge and society in complex ways. There are two key ideas concerning book knowledge in particular that must be recognised.

First, books are adapted to store and communicate certain kinds of knowledge better than others. It is no longer credible to treat books as vehicles for transmitting knowledge *par excellence*.[90] We are increasingly aware of how didactic books actively construct knowledge and perform

---

[86] Fissell and Cooter, 'Natural knowledge', 131. See also Schaffer, 'Enlightenment brought down to earth'. For other critiques of the model of knowledge diffusion, see Stuart MacDonald, 'Agricultural improvement and the neglected labourer', *AgHR*, 31 (1983) 81–90; Yves Segers and Leen Van Molle, 'Introduction: Knowledge networks in rural Europe. Theories, concepts and historiographies', University of Leuven, Belgium (27–29 August 2014).

[87] Fissell and Cooter, 'Natural knowledge', 145.

[88] Ibid., 146.

[89] For introduction and overview: James Raven, *What is the history of the book?* (Cambridge, 2018); Howsam, *Old books and new histories*. Key texts: McKenzie, *Bibliography and the sociology of texts*; Robert Darnton, 'What is the history of books?', *Daedalus*, III (1982).

[90] See Elizabeth Eisenstein, *The printing press as an agent of change* (Cambridge, 1979). See especially response and critique in Adrian Johns, *The nature of the book: Print and knowledge in the making* (Chicago, 1998).

multiple social functions beyond the mere transmission of information or ideas.[91] Once we recognise that written knowledge is simply one of many forms of knowledge, we can be attentive to its relation to practical knowledge and the problem of codification, that is, translating or extracting into written form.[92] Written instructions can never contain all the knowledge required, and even simple recipes assume the reader possesses extra-textual knowledge to interpret and apply them to practice.[93] In a recent theorisation, Matteo Valleriani describes the production of books as one kind of 'externalisation' of practical knowledge, which involves qualitative changes to its structure. Codified knowledge selects, abstracts and alters practical knowledge, substitutes objects for symbols, integrates it with other areas of knowledge, and thereby acquires a conceptual independence from the practice itself.[94] Such discrepancies between practical knowledge and its representation can create tensions between texts and practice. These tensions have been highlighted by studies of 'how-to' books; the manuals and treatises for crafts, trades and household activities, often in the form of recipes.[95] A common conclusion is that manuals were often not written by or for practitioners, as textual instructions had a limited use in master-apprentice forms of training.[96] In short, books are widely recognised as inadequate communicators of complex practical knowledge that do not function as neutral vehicles for transmission, but actively transform knowledge in the process of their production and interpretation. Hence agricultural books must be contextualised within existing systems of practical knowledge and analysed for how they codified

[91] A relevant example is Wendy Wall's argument that the publications of the early seventeenth-century author Gervase Markham served to create a distinctively English national husbandry. Wendy Wall, 'Renaissance national husbandry: Gervase Markham and the publication of England', *Sixteenth Century Journal*, 27 (1996).

[92] See especially literature on 'books of secrets': William Eamon, *Science and the secrets of nature: Books of secrets in medieval and early modern culture* (Princeton, 1994); Elaine Leong and Alisha Rankin (eds), *Secrets and knowledge in medicine and science, 1500–1800* (Farnham, 2011).

[93] Sven Dupré, 'Doing it wrong: The translation of artisanal knowledge and the codification of error', in Matteo Valleriani (ed.), *The structures of practical knowledge* (Switzerland, 2017).

[94] Matteo Valleriani, 'The epistemology of practical knowledge', in Matteo Valleriani (ed.), *The structures of practical knowledge* (Switzerland, 2017). See also Jochen Büttner, 'Shooting with ink', in Matteo Valleriani (ed.), *The structures of practical knowledge* (Switzerland, 2017), 118–19.

[95] Natasha Glaisyer and Sara Pennell (eds), *Didactic literature in England, 1500–1800: Expertise constructed* (Aldershot, 2003); Bushnell, *Green desire*; Ricardo Córdoba (ed.), *Craft treatises and handbooks: The dissemination of technical knowledge in the middle ages* (Turnhout Belgium, 2013); Büttner, 'Shooting with ink'; Viktoria Thaczyk, '"Which cannot be sufficiently described by my pen." The codification of knowledge in theater engineering, 1480–1680', in Matteo Valleriani (ed.), *The structures of practical knowledge* (Switzerland, 2017); Elizabeth Tebeaux, *The emergence of a tradition: Technical writing in the English Renaissance, 1475–1640* (New York, 1997).

[96] Dupré, 'Translation of artisanal knowledge', 170.

knowledge. A study along these lines has already identified oral traces in early agricultural writing from 1200 to 1700, showing how both manuscript and printed works used syntax typical of speech.[97]

Second, as a medium of knowledge, books are not equally valuable for all members of society in all contexts. Literacy is notoriously difficult to define as well as measure, but we know that the structure of literacy was closely aligned with the structure of society. In the seventeenth century, yeomen were far more likely to be literate than husbandmen, while very few women and male labourers were able to sign their name.[98] By around 1750, the majority of the population were most likely able to read the printed word, even if they could not write.[99] In the enlightenment model, illiteracy is treated as a simple barrier to the diffusion of knowledge, which unfortunately placed a proportion of rural society beyond the reach of useful knowledge. But regardless of the ability to read, the more fundamental problem is 'the value of literacy'.[100] Why would sixteenth- or seventeenth-century husbandmen and housewives desire printed information or instruction on husbandry? Knowledge of growing food and keeping animals was acquired, stored and transferred through practice and custom, and the proverbs, gossip, jokes and tales of oral culture were packed with information.[101] Further, literacy was still a major tool and marker of social differentiation in eighteenth-century England; hence illiteracy was not simply a post-publication limitation.[102] For much of the early modern period, books were a relatively exclusive form of knowledge, which could be constitutive of their function. Print was a technology largely dominated by a learned elite at the beginning of our period, and only gradually became central to lower levels of society and extended over all areas of social life.[103] Hence, the fact that agricultural books were mostly read by

---

[97] Elizabeth Tebeaux, 'English agriculture and estate management instructions, 1200–1700: From orality to textuality to modern instructions', *Technical Communication Quarterly*, 19 (2010), 353, 359.

[98] David Cressy, *Literacy and the social order: Reading and writing in Tudor and Stuart England* (2006), 127. Richard Sullivan collated evidence that around 27 per cent of husbandmen were literate in Middlesex in 1683–84; at least 50 per cent of yeomen were literate in rural northern counties by 1650; approx. 80 per cent yeoman and 50 per cent husbandmen were literate between 1750 and 1850. Sullivan, 'Measurement of English farming', 281.

[99] Adam Fox, 'Words, words, words: Education, literacy and print', in Keith Wrightson (ed.), *A social history of England, 1500–1750* (Cambridge, 2017), 138.

[100] Cressy, *Literacy*, 2. See the same point about sixteenth-century French peasant society in Davis, 'Printing and the people', 194.

[101] Cressy, *Literacy*, 13–14; Adam Fox, *Oral and literate culture in England, 1500–1700* (Oxford, 2000), 23–25.

[102] David Allan, *Commonplace books and reading in Georgian England* (Cambridge, 2010), 4.

[103] James Raven, *Publishing business in eighteenth-century England* (Woodbridge, 2014), 258.

the gentry was not a design flaw, but a design feature. Books packaged a particular kind of knowledge for the benefit of particular social groups, and primarily to the advantage of men rather than women due to unequal levels of literacy. Small farmers and farm workers did not form an undifferentiated illiterate mass, but they stood in a different relation to a printed manual than a gentleman landowner. Even as reading became an almost universal skill, writing and publishing remained socially confined, leaving many as passive participants rather than active contributors.[104] Moreover, the codification of customary knowledge into books meant a shift from a communal to an individual mode of knowledge transfer; from author to reader, rather than from elder to younger generations. The question to examine is what effect did the increasing effort to store and transfer knowledge using books have on different sections of the rural community? The diffusion model is incapable of describing the technical and social problems that arose by the systematic compilation of written knowledge about a practical art overwhelmingly performed by people who had minimal use for it.

A few studies of 'how-to' books or craft manuals from the fifteenth century onward provide models of how to analyse book knowledge in relation to social and economic power.[105] In a study of manuscript books on mechanical arts in fifteenth-century southern Germany and northern Italy, Pamela O. Long describes how the patronage of rulers seeking technological mastery encouraged artisans to write manuals on their art.[106] This codification and rationalisation of the mechanical arts facilitated new divisions of labour and a transformation in the social organisation of knowledge, 'from a kind of artisanal know-how transmitted for the most part orally ... to a group of rationalised disciplines informed by principles and explicated in books'. But rather than transform artisans into learned men, it 'prepared certain of the mechanical arts for appropriation by learned culture'.[107] A similar argument has been made about the creation of the *Encyclopédie* in eighteenth-century France, which constituted a large-scale project to observe and record the secrets of crafts and trades. Cynthia J. Koepp claims that the great encyclopaedia amounted to

[104] General point made in Daniel Woolf, *The social circulation of the past: English historical culture 1500–1730* (Oxford, 2003), 297.
[105] For an alternative interpretation: Pamela H. Smith, 'Craft techniques and how-to books', in Mark Clarke et al. (eds), *Transmission of artists' knowledge* (Brussels, 2011), 75–77.
[106] Pamela O. Long, 'Power, patronage, and the authorship of Ars: From mechanical know-how to mechanical knowledge in the last scribal age', *Isis,* 88 (1997), 4.
[107] Ibid., 39–40.

a 'subtle and comprehensive expropriation of that nonliterate knowledge' for the benefit of an enlightened managerial class.[108]

Two histories on the art of navigation provide a strong contemporary case study. Margaret Schott examines the transformation of navigation from traditional craft learned through practice to a theoretical and codified science learned partly through books over the early modern period. Schott weaves together many themes with close parallels in agriculture, including the codification of the sailor's knowledge based on observation, intuition and memory, the shifting balance between practice and theory, and the turn to textual authority signalling a new conception of expertise.[109] This account is complemented by Eric Ash's earlier work, which argues that navigational instructional manuals in late sixteenth-century England were produced in the context of a royal administration engaged in technically complex projects and a humanist culture seeking to extract practical knowledge from unlearned practitioners and systematise it for educated men. Ash argues that humanist-trained authors produced a range of technical treatises to publicly demonstrate their mastery and attract patrons rather than to teach practitioners. Through the writing of manuals, the crafts themselves were fundamentally reconceived. Manuals not only provided instructions but tried to explain why these instructions worked. Such manuals helped create new divisions of labour, whereby the 'expert mediator' in possession of theoretical knowledge was distinguished from the unlearned craftsman.[110]

Hence numerous studies connect the development of written knowledge of traditional arts with the power dynamic in labour relations, emphasising the appropriation of knowledge from practitioners to learned men.[111] The only equivalent example for early modern agricultural books is found within Deborah Valenze's analysis of late eighteenth-century dairying, in which she draws attention to the social impact of printed dairying manuals on the position of dairywomen. In the early eighteenth century, dairying was still an unrecorded customary art, whose knowledge and skills were overwhelmingly possessed by female practitioners. Scientific agriculturists

---

[108] Cynthia J. Koepp, 'The alphabetical order: Work in Diderot's Encyclopédie', in Steven Laurence Kaplan and Cynthia J. Koepp (eds), *Work in France: Representations, meaning, organization, and practice* (London, 1986), 257.

[109] Margaret E. Schotte, *Sailing school: Navigating science and skill, 1550–1800* (Baltimore, 2019).

[110] Eric H. Ash, *Power, knowledge, and expertise in Elizabethan England* (Baltimore, 2004), 8–17.

[111] In a different area of society, Daniel Woolf has similarly described how the supremacy of writing was established in knowledge of the past, in which humanist historiography 'scavenged' and 'appropriated' from custom and memory. Woolf, *The social circulation of the past*, 273.

and men of business, however, sought to 'lay bare the dairy's store of secrets' and to challenge female authority over dairy production. By writing and publishing manuals on dairying, 'male practitioners redefined the art of women and appropriated it as their own'.[112] Male authors acquired much of their knowledge from dairywomen, but used their publications to undermine women's expertise while promoting a vision of commercialised and scientific dairy farming under male supervision.[113] Although Valenze's discussion of agricultural books was only a small part of her argument, her insights can be generalised in two ways: firstly, as women's farm labour in the early modern period extended far beyond dairying, so too did the scope of customary knowledge being appropriated by male writers; secondly, these tensions between custom and science along gender lines can be identified along class lines for agricultural literature as a whole.

There is another area of scholarship, tangential to histories of agriculture and farming books, which is more sensitive to the social and epistemological dynamics in agricultural writing: georgic poetry and literature. However, these have not been fully connected to the socio-economic context outlined above. Studies on the influence of Virgil's *Georgics* in the eighteenth century emphasise how the ancient didactic poem dramatised the relationship between writing and farming ('two antithetically class-specific activities'), and between teacher and pupil, raising fundamental questions about authority.[114] Georgic writing resolves these tensions by equating the labour of writing with the labour of farming.[115] In a nuanced version of this argument in the context of agricultural science in nineteenth-century America, Benjamin Cohen credits the 'georgic ethos' with mediating the shift from a 'tradition-laden, experience-based, locally derived knowledge of the land' to a 'systematic, codified, and universal knowledge'.[116] However, debates about the 'credibility' of agricultural literature (the problem of 'book-farming') are treated as primarily a cultural clash between rural and urban communities, dismissing tensions between economic classes.[117] In an earlier exploration of eighteenth-century georgic

[112] Deborah Valenze, 'The art of women and the business of men: Women's work and the dairy industry c.1740–1840', *Past & Present*, 130 (1991), 153.
[113] Ibid., 155.
[114] Kurt Heinzelman, 'The last georgic: Wealth of Nations and the scene of writing', in Stephen Copley and Kathryn Sutherland (eds), *Adam Smith's wealth of nations: New interdisciplinary essays* (Manchester, 1995), 180.
[115] Ibid., 184.
[116] Benjamin R. Cohen, *Notes from the ground: Science, soil, and society in the American countryside* (London, 2009), 8.
[117] Ibid., 57–58, 76.

prose in Britain, Laura Sayre also highlighted the 'forced translation of farming knowledge from the world of speech and action to the world of writing and research'.[118] While Sayre acknowledges the particular class divisions involved in this process, these are intentionally subsumed under the technical problem of codifying farming knowledge.[119] Yet Sayre does make a passing claim that will be extended in detail in Chapter 3: that agricultural literature represented 'precisely the appropriation of agricultural knowledge by the literate classes from the illiterate or semi-literate classes, a conversion of wisdom and experience from oral to written culture'.[120] This powerful insight was left unexplored and unconnected to the wider upheavals in rural society. We need to go further by examining how agricultural books were linked to issues of economic power.

Knowledge and the Division of Labour

The enlightenment model follows neoclassical economics in analysing how knowledge contributes to labour productivity and economic growth, summed up in the concept of 'human capital' – the knowledge and skills to perform tasks and create economic value (an individualised concept that further erases social relations). Historians have applied this frame to eighteenth-century agricultural literature, arguing that the growth of agricultural books was part of an emerging 'knowledge-based economy'.[121] However, the role of knowledge in the economy can be approached using alternative Weberian and Marxist analytical frameworks. The former directs attention to the distribution of knowledge within the market; the latter directs attention to the distribution of knowledge within the production process.[122] While agricultural historians have noted that competition between producers in the market can give rise to conflict over the possession of knowledge, they have tended to ignore conflict within the production process. For a sociological understanding, we must consider knowledge as a social relation of production, in terms of how knowledge relates to the division rather than the productivity of labour. A key strand

---

[118] Laura B. Sayre, 'Farming by the book: British georgic in prose and practice, 1697–1820', PhD thesis (Princeton University, 2002), 17, see also iii. On this point: Emily Nichole Howard, 'Grounds of knowledge: Unofficial epistemologies of British environmental writing, 1745–1835', PhD thesis (University of Michigan, 2015).

[119] Sayre, 'Farming by the book', 33.

[120] Ibid., 72.

[121] Mokyr, *Enlightened economy*; Jones, *Agricultural enlightenment*. See also Myrdal, 'Agricultural literature in Scandinavia and Anglo-Saxon countries, 1700–1800 as indicator of changed mentality'.

[122] Erik Olin Wright, *Class counts: Student edition* (Cambridge, 2000), 28–29.

of Marxist thought concerns control over the cognitive dimension of labour – the intellectual powers of production – through the extraction of intellectual activity from the labour process.[123] In this sense, the relation between knowledge and production can become a site of conflict.[124]

The role of knowledge in the division of labour has been theorised most influentially by Harry Braverman. His analysis of the theory of scientific management associated with Frederick Taylor ('Taylorism') described how so-called 'ordinary' management traditionally aimed to ensure that workers maximised the use of their knowledge, skills and industry, whereas 'scientific' management aimed to gain direct control over productive knowledge.[125] In Taylor's theory, managers should collect workers' knowledge, reduce it to fixed rules, organise production to separate the conception and execution of tasks, and use the resulting monopoly over knowledge to systematically plan the labour process.[126] Braverman argues that Taylorism was only an advanced and elaborate form of the general tendency to separate mental and manual labour in capitalist production. Similarly, Marglin argues – referring to nineteenth-century England – that full control of management over workers required 'a thoroughgoing reorganisation of the knowledge of production'.[127] Only by transforming worker's experiential knowledge into explicit rules accessible to management alone could there be sufficient managerial control.[128] Agriculture is usually neglected in these accounts, although Braverman hinted that agricultural estates were early sites of large-scale management of labour before industrialisation. Scott also briefly noted the analogue between the factory owner and the 'large capitalist agricultural producer', who faced the problem of transforming the '*mētis* knowledge of farmers into a standardized system' to increase managerial control.[129] However, there have

---

[123] Alfred Sohn-Rethal, *Intellectual and manual labour: A critique of epistemology* (New Jersey, 1978), 122–23, 157–58.

[124] For example, Julia Wrigley, 'The division between mental and manual labor: Artisan education in science in nineteenth-century Britain', *American Journal of Sociology*, 88 (1982).

[125] Frederick Taylor, *The principles of scientific management* (London, 1911). David Spencer, 'Braverman and the contribution of labour process analysis to the critique of capitalist production – twenty-five years on', *Work, Employment & Society*, 14 (2000).

[126] Harry Braverman, *Labor and monopoly capital: The degradation of work in the twentieth century* (London, 1974), 113–19.

[127] Stephen A. Marglin, 'Losing touch: The cultural conditions of worker accommodation and resistance', in Frédérique Apffel-Marglin and Stephen A. Marglin (eds), *Dominating knowledge: Development, culture and resistance* (Oxford, 1990), 246–47.

[128] See also Stephen A. Marglin, 'Knowledge and power', in Frank H. Stephen (ed.), *Firms, organization and labour: Approaches to the economics of work organization* (London, 1984).

[129] Scott, *Seeing like a state*, 338.

been few studies of the relation between knowledge, the division of labour and management in early modern agriculture.[130]

The occupational distribution of knowledge, however, is more complex than a binary opposition between worker and employer, as possession and control of knowledge may be concentrated at strategic locations among supervisors, overseers, managers or experts.[131] The notion of expertise is central. Numerous historical studies have explored the development of expertise in early modern Britain, often highlighting the role of books in constructing a theoretical body of specialist knowledge upon which expertise is based.[132] Although the term 'expert' is frequently used to describe particular agriculturalists in early modern Britain, little attention has been given to identifying the nature of agricultural expertise and how it developed. Expertise is further associated with the notion of the professional, as an occupation defined by the command of specialist knowledge.[133] The question of professionalisation in agricultural history sits within a broader story of specialisation. In particular, the land surveyor and land steward have both been identified as agricultural occupations that were partly professionalised in the early modern period.[134] Paul Brassley argues that farmers themselves have developed some, but not all, professional characteristics since the nineteenth century.[135] The question of how agricultural literature contributed to agricultural expertise and professionalisation is central to understanding how books shaped the social structure of agricultural knowledge (explored in Chapters 5 and 6).

The Power of Book Knowledge

The only previous analysis that explores the relationship between agricultural writing and social power is an essay on a single ancient Latin text from the late Roman Republic: Varro's *De re rustica*, an agricultural treatise composed in his old age around 37 BCE. While the historical contexts

[130] Notable exception is Tom McLean, 'The measurement and management of human performance in seventeenth century English farming: The case of Henry Best', *Accounting Forum*, 33 (2009), 65.
[131] See discussion in Wright, *Class*, 16–20.
[132] In particular, see Rabier (ed.), *Fields of Expertise*; Ash, 'Introduction: Expertise'.
[133] Corfield, *Power and the professions*, 2.
[134] On surveyors, see F. M. L. Thompson, *Chartered surveyors: The growth of a profession* (London, 1968), chs 1, 2; McRae, *God speed the plough*, 169–76; Robson, 'Improvement and epistemologies', 602. On stewards or agents, see G. E. Mingay, 'The eighteenth-century land steward', in E. L. Jones and G. E. Mingay (eds), *Land, labour and population in the industrial revolution: Essays presented to J.D. Chambers* (London, 1967); Sarah Webster, 'Estate improvement and the professionalisation of land agents on the egremont estates in Sussex and Yorkshire, 1770–1835', *Rural History*, 18 (2007).
[135] Paul Brassley, 'The professionalisation of English agriculture?', *Rural History*, 16 (2005).

are very different, the patterns identified are highly instructive. Aude Doody explores the 'authority of writing' in two senses: as a reliable source of knowledge and as the power to make decisions or give orders. Indeed, agricultural texts conferred this double authority onto elite Roman readers 'so that the landowner has both the authority and the expertise to instruct his manager, who in turn instructs the workers on how to farm the land'.[136] Whereas knowledge acquired through labour and experience tends to be passed on between workers, written knowledge was designed to meet the needs of an elite managerial class. In this way, a manual or treatise helps construct and maintain a knowledge hierarchy that corresponds to the social hierarchy: '[a]gricultural literature allows knowledge to flow downwards'.[137] Whereas the enlightenment model treats written knowledge as a liberating and democratising force, Doody highlights that when literacy and economic power are aligned, writing can be a device to control the flow of knowledge. 'Writing on agriculture', Doody concludes, 'was an important means of asserting control over knowledge about the land'.[138] The following chapters argue that this was especially true in early modern Britain.

We now have strong empirical and theoretical grounds for a study of agricultural books that explores their contribution to social changes in early modern Britain. We can infer from the major trends that there was a concentration of managerial control over cultivation in Britain in the seventeenth and eighteenth centuries, requiring a change in the social system of knowledge. We can combine this with a sociological understanding of early modern books as tools for the codification and appropriation of practical knowledge by a learned managerial class in order to increase control over production. Whereas the enlightenment model views book knowledge as a technical power, a power over nature, this sociological model views book knowledge as a social power, a power over people. The standard research question *how did books contribute to the dissemination of knowledge?* is replaced with *how did books contribute to the control of knowledge?* The question *how did books contribute to the productivity of labour?* is replaced with *how did books contribute to the division of labour?*

---

[136] Aude Doody, 'The authority of writing in Varro's De Re Rustica', in Jason König and Greg Woolf (eds), *Authority and expertise in ancient scientific culture* (Cambridge, 2017), 185.
[137] Ibid., 186.
[138] Ibid., 201.

CHAPTER 2

Learning without Books
The Mystery of Husbandry

The memoirs of John Cannon (1684–1743) provide a rare insight into the learning experience of a farmworker around the turn of the eighteenth century. The surviving 700-page manuscript, written around 1742 but compiled from earlier drafts, describes the life of a young farm labourer, an ambitious excise officer and finally an old schoolmaster.[1] Born in Somerset to a family of farmers and butchers, Cannon gained some formal education before being taken out of school aged thirteen to labour on his father's and later his uncle's farm for ten years. Aged twenty-three, he gained a commission in the excise and never returned to farming. While his writings about his early experiences are not the direct utterances of a young ploughboy, the memoir nonetheless reveals the perspective of someone 'bred to husbandry'. Significantly, his descriptions touch directly on the relation between the practical art of husbandry and book learning.

Throughout the section on the years 1697–1707, Cannon presented husbandry and books as belonging to two opposing worlds. He described how, aged thirteen, he was 'taken off from my books to sheepkeeping & other rural employements of husbandry & instead of noble lectures of learning was obliged to endure painful & wearisome excersises of husbandry for my daily task'.[2] This prompted various attempts to escape his training in husbandry to read books. Around age fifteen, 'my father thought fit to put me to the plow which I by practice became master of under my father's directions', along with various other farming tasks. But

---

[1] With thanks to Tim Hitchcock for sharing a selected transcript. Biography and quotations from John Money (ed.), *The chronicles of John Cannon, excise officer and writing master: Pt. 1, 1684–1733 (Somerset, Oxfordshire, Berkshire)* (Oxford, 2009). Original manuscript here: MS DD/SAS C/1193/4, 'Memoirs of the birth, education, life and death of: Mr John Cannon. Sometime Officer of the Excise & Writing Master at Mere Glastenbury & West Lydford in the County of Somerset' (1684–1743).
[2] The disruption of education due to the demands of family farming was common in this period. See Keith Wrightson, *English society, 1580–1680* (London, 1982), 150.

Cannon 'was never without but some book or other in my pocket' to read at every opportunity. He explained how, 'when sent for the cattle to go to plow', he would slip off to 'read under a hedge', and had to make excuses for his long absences, 'all to Indulge my darling the delight I took in my books'.[3] Cannon's sense of becoming a master of the plough under his father's tutelage must have been typical for many young boys throughout arable regions, but he was surely unusual in carrying a book in his pocket. It is significant that husbandry and reading were conflicting – almost exclusive – activities in Cannon's mind.

Cannon declared that by age sixteen he had 'attained under the vigilance of my parents the whole mistery of husbandry & the whole management of the plow & almost all other of my fathers Concern'.[4] He added to this perception of his knowledge in a description of a quarrel with his uncle about how they were going to plough a field. Cannon 'inadvertently asked how [his uncle] knew husbandry, being always bred & used the trade of a baker', and claimed that since he was trained by his father, who was 'counted the best plowman in these parts, it followed I must then know better than [my uncle]'.[5] Hence Cannon contrasted his own direct practical learning under the guidance of an experienced ploughman (his father) with the inferior knowledge of his uncle, primarily a baker. In other words, Cannon believed that only he possessed the mystery ('mistery') of husbandry and mastery of the plough, which did not concern the mere performance of the task, but the knowledge or judgement of the best method.

It does not appear that Cannon ever read any books on husbandry, but he loved reading histories and advice books on sex and midwifery.[6] He also described a local shepherd with a shared enthusiasm for history, poetry and astronomy.[7] It may be that he simply never encountered any books on the topic, but he clearly thought book learning and husbandry belonged to different worlds. In contrast to his farm labours, book learning was crucial to becoming an excise officer, for which he diligently read about accounting and arithmetic. Cannon also mapped the contrast between book learning and husbandry onto himself and his brother; whereas his greatest love was books, his brother 'gave himself wholly to the plow & other such matters'.[8] The conflict between his love of books and position as a farm

---

[3] Money (ed.), *Chronicles*, 29–30.
[4] Ibid., 33.
[5] Ibid., 55–56.
[6] Ibid., 30, 35–36.
[7] Ibid., 42–43.
[8] Ibid., 44.

labourer was clearly a source of anxiety for Cannon, as indicated by the series of quotations he collected on the theme of learning. Curiously, one of these cautioned against thinking that learning only came from books, since 'any artisan whatever, if he know the secret and mistery of his trade may truly be called a learned man'.[9]

The example of John Cannon should serve as a caution against the assumption underlying the enlightenment model that the chief obstacle to the dissemination of agricultural knowledge was the low literacy among common husbandmen, housewives, servants and labourers.[10] The ability to read did not equate to a demand for reading certain kinds of books. The celebrated (and satirised) Wiltshire thresher, Stephen Duck (c.1705–56), read and wrote poetry as a route to escape the barn, not study it.[11] In Cannon's memoir, we find a young man with a strong sense of his mastery of husbandry, but which he viewed as antithetical to his book learning. A literate ploughboy who placed great value on learning from books, but who abandoned his plough at every opportunity to read about the secrets of the female sex, not the secrets of his trade.

Around the time that John Cannon described how he learned the 'whole mistery of husbandry' from his father and through daily practice, a number of books were published claiming to have 'discovered' or to be 'revealing' the 'mystery of husbandry'. The terminology is significant. The term 'mystery' is primarily associated with early modern crafts and artisanal knowledge, which was to some extent socially exclusive. This chapter offers an analysis of the discourse of the 'mystery of husbandry' (and closely associated discourse of 'secrets') as a way to explore analogies between craft and farming knowledge in relation to the fundamental theme of this book: the social system of knowledge. It borrows ideas from modern peasant studies to argue that early modern husbandmen and housewives would have possessed a 'peasant epistemology' analogous to an 'artisanal epistemology'; practical knowledge that is difficult or impossible to translate into text. It suggests that the phrase 'mystery of husbandry' partly captured this notion of expertise, while also signalling underlying tensions with regard to knowledge and authority. When linked to broader socio-economic changes in farming, the emergence of the term 'mystery of husbandry' in the seventeenth century can be seen as a symptom of tectonic shifts in the social system of

---

[9] Quoted from John Howell, *Epistolae ho-elianae* (London, 1650). Cannon, 'Memoirs', 30–32.

[10] For example, Horn, 'Contribution of the propagandist', 323.

[11] E. P. Thompson and Marian Sugden (eds), *The Thresher's Labour by Stephen Duck and The Woman's Labour by Mary Collier* (London, 1989).

agricultural knowledge. In short, the knowledge of husbandry was being commodified in an increasingly competitive commercial environment. By seeking to characterise how the art of husbandry was learned and practiced *without* books, this chapter establishes the key groundwork for later chapters to better understand the social disruption of farming books.

Mysteries, Crafts and Secrets

The English word 'mystery' (alternate spelling 'mistery') had two meanings with distinct etymologies, but which were often associated or conflated. From the Latin *mystērium*, meaning a secret, secret rites or religious truth, derived the theological sense of a 'mystical presence or nature' beyond human comprehension or known only to a select few. From the Latin *misterium,* meaning duty, office or trade, derived the social sense (closer to our modern term 'ministry') of a craft, art or trade, along with its skill or expertise.[12] The mystery of a craft or trade was a kind of property gained through a formal apprenticeship and subsequent membership of a guild, in relation to which it could also be conflated with 'mastery'. It signalled the possession of both knowledge and membership of a community. In the late medieval town, mystery meant ownership of a set of social obligations and political rights, not merely a technical ability.[13] Among late medieval and early modern artisans, 'skill' and 'mystery' were close synonyms.[14] A wage labourer may have the technical ability to perform certain tasks, but not necessarily possession of a skill, in the sense of the full mystery of the trade.[15] Hence mystery carried a dual sense of knowledge and authority.[16] The early modern use of the 'mystery' or 'mysteries' of crafts and trades could combine both meanings to gain its full force; a set of secrets about the natural world known only to those apprenticed in the craft.[17]

---

[12] 'mystery, n. 2', *OED Online*, www.oed.com/view/Entry/124645 (8 February 2018).

[13] Margaret R. Somers, 'The "misteries" of property: Relationality, rural industrialization, and community in Chartist narratives of political rights', in John Brewer and Susan Staves (eds), *Early modern conceptions of property* (London, 1995), 73–74. Pamela Smith, 'Secrets and craft knowledge in early modern Europe', in Elaine Leong and Alisha Rankin (eds), *Secrets and knowledge in medicine and science, 1500–1800* (Farnham, 2011), 50.

[14] 'skilful, adj. and adv.', *OED Online*, www.oed.com/view/Entry/180862 (8 February 2018). Somers, '"Misteries" of property', 67, 74; James R. Farr, *Artisans in Europe, 1300–1914* (Cambridge, 2000), 284; John Rule, 'The property of skill in the period of manufacture', in Patrick Joyce (ed.), *The historical meanings of work* (Cambridge, 1989), 107.

[15] Farr, *Artisans*, 284–86.

[16] On this point, Marglin, 'Knowledge and power', 151.

[17] Karel Davids, 'Craft secrecy in Europe in the early modern period: A comparative view', *Early Science and Medicine,* 10 (2005).

The term 'mystery' in association with arts, crafts or trades was widely present in sixteenth-century literature, became increasingly prevalent in the seventeenth century, before gradually disappearing from common usage and becoming a consciously archaic term in the eighteenth century.[18] It was primarily retained in legal discourse, for example, an apprentice might be defined as someone bound to a tradesman who is obliged 'to teach him his Mystery or Trade'.[19] Samuel Johnson's 1755 dictionary only gave the third sense of 'mystery' as a 'trade' or 'calling', suggesting the spelling should then be 'mistery'.[20] Yet as a sign of its decline in scientific discourse, the definition given in a 1728 dictionary was only the general meaning of 'secret' or 'hidden' with a theological explanation, but no reference at all to crafts or trades.[21]

The mystery of trades was linked to a sixteenth-century genre of 'books of secrets', which claimed to reveal the secrets of nature discovered by crafts and medicine through recipes and how-to instructions.[22] Technical or instructional books published in Europe in the late sixteenth century revealed the mystery of crafts, creating the possibility that intensive reading could be a substitute for a formal apprenticeship.[23] Books of secrets were an 'attempt to put into writing the tacit, experiential knowledge of crafts-people'.[24] These could be secret both in a natural-theological and in a social sense; hidden in the things of nature and hidden from those not trained in the craft. 'Secrets', then, were techniques that had to be learned through practice. More precisely, 'secrets' came to mean specifically 'scattered, unpublished knowledge', rather than simply unwritten, and represented an epistemological shift from manuscript to print. Whereas manuscript miscellanies were viewed as repositories of a collective corpus of practical knowledge, the competitive pressures of the book market drove the claim that printed practical books contained new knowledge.[25]

---

[18] For example, a treatise of mechanical arts listed both spellings of mystery/mistery as another term for 'art', 'trade', 'craft', or 'occupation'. Simon Sturtevant, *Metallica; or The treatise of metallica* (London, 1612), 9, 11, 36, 52, 53.

[19] Dictionary definition: '"Mystery" ... An Art, Trade, or Occupation'. See also 'Apprentice'. Giles Jacob, *A new law-dictionary* (London, 1729).

[20] Samuel Johnson, *A dictionary of the English language*, 2 vols (London, 1755).

[21] Ephraim Chambers, *Cyclopædia*, 2 vols (London, 1728), 611.

[22] Eamon, *Science and the secrets of nature*; Elaine Leong and Alisha Rankin, 'Introduction: Secrets and knowledge', in Elaine Leong and Alisha Rankin (eds), *Secrets and knowledge in medicine and science, 1500–1800* (Farnham, 2011).

[23] Eamon, *Science and the secrets of nature*, 113.

[24] Smith, 'Secrets and craft knowledge', 54.

[25] Melissa Reynolds, '"Here Is a Good Boke to Lerne": Practical books, the coming of the press, and the search for knowledge, ca. 1400–1560', *Journal of British Studies*, 58 (2019), 282.

Hence the concept of mystery was linked to the common belief that it was difficult or impossible to communicate craft knowledge in writing, or that even if it could it was currently hidden and unpublished. Such attitudes were frequently expressed. The sixteenth-century Swiss physician Paracelsus contrasted book learning with learning-by-doing: 'How can a carpenter have any other book than his axe and his wood? How can a bricklayer have any other book than stone and cement?'[26] Joseph Moxon explained that his *Mechanick Exercises* (1677) fell short of a guide to handicrafts 'because Hand-Craft signifies cunning, or Sleight, or Craft of the Hand, which cannot be taught by Words, but is only gained by Practice and Exercise'.[27] In the early seventeenth century, Francis Bacon's proposed project of compiling a 'history of trades' aimed to explore the 'mysteries and seacrets [sic]' of arts and crafts, later pursued by the Royal Society and most comprehensively realised in Diderot's *Encyclopédie* from the 1740s.[28]

Husbandry is rarely included in histories of crafts and artisans that discuss mystery. Similarly, in histories of books of secrets, husbandry is rarely included explicitly, although there are overlaps in both early modern and modern bibliographies, notably works such as Sir Hugh Plat's *The Jewel House of Art and Nature* (1594).[29] However, the overlap between gardening and secret books has been identified.[30] This neglect is perhaps a consequence of the complex and ambiguous relationship between husbandry and crafts in classifications of knowledge. Between classical antiquity and the renaissance, agriculture was sometimes grouped with crafts or mechanical arts and sometimes carefully distinguished.[31] In the influential Aristotelian division of knowledge, agriculture was viewed as a form of *praxis* (action) requiring *phronesis* (judgement in uncertain situations), rather than *techné* (knowledge of making).[32] In Xenophon's *Oeconomica* (fourth century BC),

---

[26] Quoted in Lis and Soly, *Worthy efforts*, 418.

[27] Quoted in Smith, *Body of the artisan*, 230.

[28] Walter E. Houghton, 'The history of trades: Its relation to seventeenth-century thought: As seen in Bacon, Petty, Evelyn, and Boyle', *Journal of the History of Ideas*, 2 (1941); John R. Pannabecker, 'Diderot, the mechanical arts, and the Encyclopédie: In search of the heritage of technology education', *Journal of Technology Education*, 6 (1994).

[29] Only a few brief references in Eamon, *Science and the secrets of nature*. Richard Weston's 1769 catalogue of agricultural books includes many 'books of secrets': Weston, *Tracts*, 16. See also Ayesha Mukherjee, 'The secrets of Sir Hugh Plat', in Elaine Leong and Alisha Rankin (eds), *Secrets and knowledge in medicine and science, 1500–1800* (Farnham, 2011).

[30] Bushnell, *Green desire*, 55; Margaret Willes, *The making of the English gardener: Plants, books and inspiration, 1560–1660* (London, 2011), ch. 9 'Secrets Revealed'.

[31] Whitney, 'Paradise restored'; George Ovitt Jr, 'The status of the mechanical arts in medieval classifications of learning', *Viator*, 14 (1983).

[32] See discussion of distinction in Hellawell, '"The best and most practical philosophers"', 34.

a dialogue on household management, agriculture was associated with cre-ating wealth, maintaining health, and the development of good character for the political or military realm.[33] In the Neo-Platonist tradition of the early medieval period, agriculture was often grouped with medicine and navigation as an intermediate art, distinct from crafts that manufacture artificial products, since by contrast they assisted natural processes and aided the fruition of natural products.[34] Hence the early modern period inherited mixed ideas about the status of agriculture. Pamela O. Long recently articulated this complex relation by distinguishing early modern artisans engaged in 'craft production' from practitioners such as farmers who 'carried out complex practical tasks'.[35] Yet beyond scholarly classifica-tions, the more significant difference between early modern husbandry and crafts lay in the social structures of practice and learning.

Practising Husbandry

Husbandry was not a single or uniform practice. In the sixteenth century, especially, the practice of farming was characterised by variety and shaped by a combination of local factors, including the physical environment, structures of landholding and property rights, the presence of industry and markets, the organisation of fields and established custom.[36] In a strict sense, there was no single agricultural economy, no single occupation of 'husbandman' or 'farmer', and therefore no single body of agricultural knowledge.[37] The 'art of husbandry' was an umbrella term for the produc-tive and maintenance activities of diverse rural households.

Almost all farms were mixed farms, concerned with both growing crops and keeping livestock, but the balance between arable and pastoral varied widely, creating distinct patterns of labour.[38] Further variety came from managing areas of woodland, a garden, a yard with pigs and poultry, keep-ing bees or growing a specialist commercial crop such as hemp or flax. The pattern of activities depended on the balance of producing for household consumption or market exchange. These practices were carried out in a

---

[33] Long, *Openness*, 16, 22.
[34] Whitney, 'Paradise restored', 44–49.
[35] Long, *Artisans/practitioners*, 4.
[36] Descriptions of 'farming countries' in Kerridge, *Agricultural revolution*, 41–180.
[37] Mauro Ambrosoli argues that before the Civil War the agricultural maxims and practices around England 'cannot be considered as an integrated body of knowledge'. Ambrosoli, *Wild and the sown*, 274.
[38] Much of this section is borrowed from Overton, *Agricultural revolution*, ch. 2 'Farming in the Sixteenth Century'.

variety of field systems characterised by a complex combination of topography, property rights and farming regulations. The two main types were 'closed' and 'open' fields. Whereas closed fields were often under the control of a single farmer, open fields with scattered strips of land and common grazing required the coordination and regulation of sowing times, crop rotations and management of livestock. Key farming operations were managed through manorial courts or village meetings, often overseen by elected officials.[39] Such common fields regulated by manorial courts persisted into the eighteenth century.[40] Farming practices were further influenced by the type of tenure: freeholders had a great deal of independence, but customary tenants could be subject to greater manorial control or local custom, and leaseholders might be required to follow a prescription in a lease. From the sixteenth to the eighteenth centuries, leasehold gradually replaced copyhold (customary) as the dominant form. Historians have tried to reduce this complexity by identifying regions of uniform agricultural practice, usually based on areas with a distinctive soil and climate but associated with particular field systems or commercial patterns.[41] However, such generalisations can disguise the variety of farm types within regions.[42]

People worked on farms in diverse ways. Many combined farming with other crafts or even professions; most clergymen were endowed with some land (the glebe) for their living, for example. Land was the source of wealth and status for the elite, and some gentlemen and esquires engaged in farm management. Those directly carrying out farming activities were ranked by status from yeomen to husbandmen to cottagers, servants and labourers. Farm size was the key factor that structured the division of labour, which further depended on the balance of crops and livestock. A small farm would mostly be worked by a husbandman and his family, labour being roughly divided along gender lines, with the housewife responsible for the dairy, garden and farmyard, and the husband responsible for the fields.[43] Hence the small farmer would perform a wide range of tasks throughout the year. On larger farms, yeomen would hire servants and

---

[39] Tom Williamson, 'Joan Thirsk and "The Common Fields"', in Richard Jones and Christopher Dyer (eds), *Farmers, consumers, innovators: The world of Joan Thirsk* (Hatfield, 2016).

[40] Neeson, *Commoners*, 134.

[41] See mapping of farming regions in Joan Thirsk (ed.), *AHEW: 1640–1750 Vol 5 / I. Regional farming systems* (Cambridge, 1985); discussed in Richard Jones and Christopher Dyer (eds), *Farmers, consumers, innovators: The world of Joan Thirsk* (Hatfield, 2016), Part I.

[42] Overton, *Agricultural Revolution*, 50–53.

[43] Only one husbandman in ten employed any servants, Everitt, 'Farm labourers', 400. On gendered division of work, Jane Whittle, 'Housewives and servants in rural England, 1440–1650: Evidence of women's work from probate documents', *Transactions of the Royal Historical Society*, 15 (2005).

day-labourers; hence there was a greater division of labour, especially on arable farms. Activities varied from non-skilled (such as weeding or stone-gathering) to highly skilled (such as ploughing or dairying). The art of ploughing, for example, required careful training, and dedicated plough-men could develop valuable expertise.[44] With the increase in average farm size and growing regional specialisation in an expanding market, there was a tendency for an increasing division of labour over time. However, even in the late eighteenth century, Adam Smith observed that the 'nature of agriculture … does not admit of so many subdivisions of labour' as manu-facturing, since 'the ploughman, the harrower, the sower of the seed, and the reaper of the corn, are often the same'.[45] Reflecting on the same obser-vation a few years later, John Millar enthused about the diverse talents of the farmer in comparison with specialised labourers in manufacture: 'What an extent of knowledge, therefore, must he possess!'[46] In summary, the art of husbandry varied by geography, season, farm and occupation, such that it did not contain a single body of knowledge. As a consequence, farm work was characterised by the need for a considerable range of skill, knowledge, and understanding adapted to highly specific environments.

Learning Husbandry

The knowledge of husbandry was local and customary, in the sense that it was part of the rules and practices regulating all kinds of social activities in the early modern village.[47] Bound up with popular memory, customary practice was inseparable from wider rural culture, including moral and religious concerns.[48] Custom was partly held in oral traditions, with its 'huge wealth of proverbial lore' and maxims containing advice for many occupations, including farming.[49] It has been suggested that an early English book on husbandry by Thomas Tusser was essentially an articula-tion of East Anglian oral knowledge of farming.[50] Traditional proverbs and sayings continued to emerge into print in the eighteenth century, for

---

[44] Everitt, 'Farm labourers', 431–32.
[45] Adam Smith, *An inquiry into the nature and causes of the wealth of nations* (London, 1776), 8.
[46] John Millar, *An historical view of the English government*, 4 vols (London, 1803), iv, 153–54.
[47] Richard W. Hoyle, 'Introduction: Custom, improvement and anti-improvement', in Richard W. Hoyle (ed.), *Custom, improvement and the landscape in early modern Britain* (Farnham, 2011).
[48] Andy Wood, *The memory of the people: Custom and popular senses of the past in early modern England* (Cambridge, 2013).
[49] Fox, *Oral and literate culture*, 23–25.
[50] Ibid., 152–53.

example in the work of William Ellis.[51] Custom was also codified in the by-laws and field orders of common-field regulation, as once or twice a year the regulations would be read publicly and nailed to the church door.[52]

The knowledge and skills of husbandry was passed down through the generations by older, more experienced practitioners, beginning with relatives. Children from the age of seven or eight would begin helping with miscellaneous tasks around the fields and house, such as fetching water, tending poultry, picking fruit, scaring birds and gleaning corn.[53] Like John Cannon, they would gradually be introduced to more physically demanding and skilful tasks. Wage assessments show children could start earning as young as ten (boys) or twelve (girls), with wages rising each year as new skills were learned. Harrowing and carting could be done by thirteen-or fourteen-year-olds, while ploughing was mastered around sixteen or seventeen. Young people working in agriculture had to master a wide range of tasks requiring considerable strength, skill and understanding.[54]

Even among labourers, expertise in a particular craft could be passed on from one generation to the next, as children worked alongside their parents, leading to certain arts acquiring 'their own peculiar customs and mystique'.[55] Labourers would move between regions, hired by farmers seeking a particular set of skills.[56] A new plough type was worth little without a ploughman who knew how to use it. Similarly, the ability of dairymaids from particular regions was highly valued.[57] Such practices in the eighteenth century indicate that farm labourers possessed knowledge that could not be acquired by other means.[58] However, the level of appreciation of labouring knowledge should not be overstated, as assessments of large estates also show a relatively low appreciation of the skills of many servants.[59]

---

[51] The nineteenth-century folklorist James Britten listed over thirty proverbs and folk sayings scattered throughout the eight volumes of William Ellis' *The Modern Husbandman*, printed in 1740s. James Britten, 'Proverbs and folk-lore from William Ellis's "Modern Husbandman" (1750)', *The Folk-Lore Record*, 3 (1880). Ellis introduces specific advice as 'common sayings', which mainly cover knowledge of the natural world but also include guidance on farm management, such as: 'The old maxim, Change of pasture makes the calf fat'. William Ellis, *The modern husbandman*, 8 vols (London, 1750), iii, pt 2, 44.

[52] Neeson, *Commoners*, 111.

[53] Keith Wrightson, *Earthly necessities: Economic lives in early modern Britain, 1470–1750* (London, 2000), 49–50.

[54] Ilana Krausman Ben-Amos, *Adolescence and youth in early modern England* (London, 1994), 73–77.

[55] Everitt, 'Farm labourers', 433.

[56] On skilled labour mobility, Jones, *Agricultural enlightenment*, 111–18.

[57] For example, the 'Berkley Dairy Maid', Valenze, 'Art of women', 147–48.

[58] MacDonald, 'Agricultural improvement', 87.

[59] Steve Hindle, 'Work, reward and labour discipline in late seventeenth-century England', in A. Shepard et al. (eds), *Remaking English society: Social relations and social change in early modern England* (Woodbridge, 2013), 279.

The early modern period has been described as lacking any formal agricultural training.[60] Yet although no formal apprenticeships existed in husbandry, the institution of service constituted a kind of informal and irregular apprenticeship.[61] In common with craft apprentices, servants in husbandry tended to be young, unmarried, hired in return for lodgings and food, and expected to acquire some knowledge and skill.[62] It was a life-cycle employment to prepare for independence in adulthood. Servants advertised their skill at annual hiring fairs by wearing emblems or carrying tools of their craft, such as the shepherd's crook, the carter's whip, or the milkmaid's pail.[63] Contemporaries acknowledged the similarity by describing servants as employed in the 'art' or 'craft' of husbandry.[64] Elizabethan statutes enabled poor children to be indentured as parish or pauper 'apprentices' in husbandry or housewifery, although this partly reflected the range of low-skilled tasks suitable for children.[65] But service in husbandry was distinct from craft apprenticeships in a number of ways: servants were hired on quarterly or annual contracts and might switch masters every one or two years, rather than be bound to a single master for seven; there was no formalised training; the family or household was not subject to equivalent guild regulations; they were hired to contribute to the farm, not in exchange for payment by parents; they were a mix of men and women, whereas apprentices were predominantly male.[66] The parallels are thus only partial, but significant. The absence of formal apprenticeships does not erase the informal and customary forms of teaching and learning. As Arthur Young put it in the late eighteenth century, 'an English husbandry servant is educated very generally to the business from his childhood'.[67] We have plenty of anecdotal evidence that informal

---

[60] Jules N. Pretty, 'Farmers' extension practice and technology adaptation: Agricultural revolution in 17–19th century Britain', *Agriculture and Human Values*, 8 (1991), 137.

[61] Around of 13.4 per cent population were servants between 1574 and 1821 and around 60 per cent of 15–24 year olds. Kussmaul, *Servants*, 4.

[62] Ibid., 73–75.

[63] Michael Roberts, '"Waiting upon chance": English hiring fairs and their meanings from the 14th to the 20th century', *Journal of Historical Sociology*, 1 (1988), 138.

[64] In warrants ordering compulsory service. Whittle, *Agrarian capitalism*, 225–26.

[65] Joan Lane, *Apprenticeship in England, 1600–1914* (London, 1996), 14; Kussmaul, *Servants*, see 'Appendix 6'.

[66] On distinct pattern of employments before and after 1660: Jane Whittle, 'A different pattern of employment: Servants in rural England c.1500–1660', in Jane Whittle (ed.), *Rural servants in Europe 1400–1900* (Woodbridge, 2017).

[67] Arthur Young, 'How far is agriculture capable of being made one of the pursuits, in which men of a certain rank may educate their children, as at present in commerce and manufactures?', *Annals of Agriculture*, 21 (1793), 249.

training and educational networks existed in the late eighteenth century.[68]
It was common for farmers to send sons to regions known for excelling
in certain methods.[69] Some boys were apprenticed to yeomen with substantial premiums for training in farm management.[70] In 1790, William
Marshall noted that large farmers in midland counties placed their sons
'as PUPILS, with superior farmers, at some distance from their father's residence'.[71] Such quasi-apprenticeships have been identified as effective ways
of transferring knowledge between farms.[72]

Before the sixteenth century, agricultural writing was mostly limited
to a few classical manuscripts held in ecclesiastical collections and private
aristocratic libraries, and the scattered pages in vernacular manuscript miscellanies passed down within households as part of a corpus of practical
knowledge on a range of topics such as medicine, cooking, hunting and
hawking.[73] A rare example of written advice being passed from father to
son is striking for its absence of instructions about farming. When, in 1593,
a dying gentleman in Devon wrote a memoir for his young son, he provided extensive details of landholdings and guidance on how to manage
his inheritance, along with a host of moral and practical advice. But aside
from a few descriptions of the 'good tillage' of old family members and the
maxim that the labours of husbandry must be done 'in good season and in
due order', there was not even a brief summary of the principles of farming
or tips on best methods across 140 folios.[74]

However, we do begin to find substantive commonplace books compiled on larger farms or estates from the late sixteenth century, showing
how families compiled their own written knowledge specific to their local
circumstances.[75] A well-known example is the 'Farming Book' of Henry
Best, who owned the manor of Elmswell in the East Riding of Yorkshire
from 1618 to 1645.[76] The notebook was a mixture of highly specific

[68] Sinclair, *Code*, 75–76.

[69] Pretty, 'Farmers' extension practice', 138.

[70] Lane, *Apprenticeship*, 166–67.

[71] William Marshall, *Rural economy of the Midland counties*, 2 vols (London, 1790), i, 117–18. Discussed in Kussmaul, *Servants*, 77.

[72] Jones, *Agricultural enlightenment*, 99.

[73] On Latin and Greek classical manuscripts: Ambrosoli, *Wild and the Sown*, ch.1; Fussell, *Classical tradition*, chs 2, 3. On vernacular manuscript miscellanies: Reynolds, 'Practical Books', 272.

[74] Anita Travers (ed.), *Robert Furse: A Devon family memoir of 1593* (Exeter, 2012), 18.

[75] The notebooks of Sir Hamon Le Strange were organised such that they 'resemble manuals in their own right.' Griffiths, 'Sir Hamon Le Strange', 215. See the late-sixteenth-century manuscript miscellanies of two gentlemen, Thomas Fella and John Kay of Woodsome. McRae, *God speed the plough*, 208–9.

[76] See also a short manuscript describing local methods of farming from mid-seventeenth-century Scotland: Alexander Fenton, 'Skene of Hallyard's Manuscript of Husbandrie', *AgHR*, 11 (1963).

instructions and general statements, which joined local common sayings with passages quoted from Tusser's printed book.[77] Henry Best's notebook illustrates that written instructions could be a part of teaching and learning on some seventeenth-century estates, but he is not representative of most farmers in this period.

Therefore, when the first books on husbandry were being printed in sixteenth-century England, and for a long time after, the knowledge of husbandry was highly diverse and localised. It was acquired primarily through labour, held and exercised by practitioners, passed on within the family and through service, taught by oral instruction and demonstration, and embedded and maintained as customary practice. Overwhelmingly, practitioners in husbandry did not learn the art of husbandry by reading. Acquiring, storing and sharing agricultural knowledge in textual form was a marginal activity.

A Peasant Epistemology?

Husbandry was, therefore, similar to other crafts in being a practical art learned via personal teaching and oral instruction, and acquired and exercised through labour. Studies of craft knowledge, or 'artisanal epistemology', have emphasised the bodily nature of knowing for artisans, transmitted through practice rather than books.[78] The notion of artisanal knowledge attempts to capture the positive aspects of a distinctive way of knowing linked to the production of things, which exceeds ideas of 'tacit knowledge', often defined negatively as that which cannot be written down.[79] But the focus on those who make things tends to exclude the farmer, who instead assists nature's production.[80] Is it possible to identify a 'peasant epistemology', a way of knowing distinctive to practising farmers? There are only occasional hints towards such an idea in current historiography: for example, Benjamin Cohen identified a broad 'praxis-oriented approach to agricultural knowledge' in nineteenth-century America, meaning 'to work the land is to know it'.[81]

---

[77] Woodward (ed.), *Books of Henry Best.*
[78] Smith, *Body of the artisan*, 'Introduction'.
[79] Michael Polanyi, *The tacit dimension* (London, 1983); L. Hakanson, 'Creating knowledge: The power and logic of articulation', *Industrial and Corporate Change*, 16 (2007). Jones noted that tacit knowledge existed outside books: 'Unquestionably a great deal of agricultural knowledge remained tacit, that is to say not inscribed in books or systematized in compendia.' Jones, *Agricultural enlightenment*, 220.
[80] Smith makes a brief reference to how the 'peasant knew and read nature … this peasant engaged in philosophy': Smith, *Body of the artisan*, 155.
[81] Cohen, *Notes from the ground*, 78.

However, in recent decades a variety of disciplines have investigated farmers' local and practical knowledge in contemporary contexts.[82] The writings of the American essayist and farmer Wendell Berry have been especially influential in advocating a comprehensive vision of farming knowledge as highly complex, tacit, learned through labour, held in a community, local, and trans-generational – in contrast to the universalism, reductionism and experimentalism of modern agricultural science.[83] Crucially, Berry argues that farming knowledge is irreducible to written rules. The farmer, he wrote, 'must be master of many possible solutions'.

> The good farmer's mind, as I understand it, is in a certain critical sense beyond the reach of textbooks and expert advice … To the textbook writer or researcher, the farm — the place where knowledge is applied — is necessarily provisional or theoretical; what he proposes must be found to be generally true. For the good farmer, on the other hand, the place where knowledge is applied is minutely particular, not a farm but *this* farm, *my* farm, the only place exactly like itself in all the world.[84]

These themes grew into a distinct disciplinary theme as cultural anthropologists and geographers began to study 'indigenous technical knowledge' (ITK), focused on traditional peasant communities.[85] Recent research into agricultural science, rural sociology and environmental sustainability has developed a new appreciation for the knowledge and expertise of peasants in the modern world. While we should be cautious about projecting continuities back into early modern Britain, these studies help sketch an outline for a distinctive peasant epistemology.[86]

The core of a peasant epistemology can be distilled into three overlapping points. First, farming is a complex and dynamic system, in which the same situation never precisely recurs, making it difficult for practitioners to predict

---

[82] For example, as discussed earlier, concept of mētis to characterise practical farming knowledge that is exercised in unique, complex and non-repeating environments: Scott, *Seeing like a state*, 313–19.

[83] First major work covering many of these themes: Wendell Berry, *The unsettling of America: Culture and agriculture* (3rd edn; Berkeley, 1996). Jeffrey Filipiak, 'The work of local culture: Wendell Berry and communities as the source of farming knowledge', *Agricultural History*, 85 (2011), 181–84.

[84] Quoted in Marglin, 'Farmers, seedsmen, and scientists', 221.

[85] Dennis M. Warren et al. (eds), *The cultural dimension of development: Indigenous knowledge systems* (London, 1995); Paul Richards, *Indigenous agricultural revolution: Ecology and food production in West Africa* (London, 1985).

[86] Summarised recently in Christina Lundström and Jessica Lindblom, 'Considering farmers' situated expertise in using AgriDSS to fostering sustainable farming practices in precision agriculture', *13th International Conference on Precison Agriculture, July 31–August 3, 2016, St. Louis, Missouri, USA* (2016).

and control the environment.[87] Second, farmers, therefore, require adaptable knowledge that can be applied to a series of non-identical situations. This has been called *situated expertise*, based on the need for action in a given situation.[88] Experienced farmers develop situated expertise on their own farm through solving a series of different practical problems and developing tacit knowledge.[89] Third, the learning process in farming is best understood as experiential rather than experimental, since problems are solved by experience from non-identical situations, rather than observations of controlled situations with known variables. Expert farmers, in this view, do not follow strict rules. Rules are only extracted from experiential knowledge to simplify problems for beginners.[90] This notion of farmers' situated expertise has been supported by in-depth empirical studies.[91] Key to these models of farmers' knowledge is the role of uncertainty and the ability to respond to a changing environment in an appropriate way at the appropriate time.[92]

It is, therefore, reasonable to infer that early modern husbandmen and housewives may have possessed a similar kind of situated expertise, or peasant knowledge, analogous to the much-studied artisanal epistemology of craftsmen, which was acquired independently of book-learning and was difficult or impossible to fully capture in writing. Such situated expertise maps convincingly onto the notion of the 'mystery of husbandry'. Indeed, some medieval studies do describe a sophisticated level of judgement that we could call a peasant's situated expertise.[93] Unfortunately, there have been few attempts to apply such ideas to early modern agriculture.[94] While

---

[87] For more on farming as complex system, see S. J. R. Woodward et al., 'Better simulation modelling to support farming systems innovation: Review and synthesis', *New Zealand Journal of Agricultural Research*, 51 (2008).

[88] For a theoretical model of situated expertise, see Hubert L. Dreyfus and Stuart E. Dreyfus, 'Peripheral vision expertise in real world contexts', *Organization Studies*, 26 (2005).

[89] See Volker Hoffmann et al., 'Farmers and researchers: How can collaborative advantages be created in participatory research and technology development?', *Agriculture and Human Values*, 24 (2007).

[90] Lundström and Lindblom, 'Farmers' situated expertise', 3.

[91] Anna Krzywoszynska, 'What farmers know: Experiential knowledge and care in vine growing', *Sociologia Ruralis*, 56 (2016); Fergus Lyon, 'How farmers research and learn: The case of arable farmers of East Anglia, UK', *Agriculture and Human Values*, 13 (1996).

[92] On this point, see Marglin, 'Farmers, seedsmen, and scientists', 238.

[93] A study of smallholding peasants in Cambridgeshire in the late fourteenth century has demonstrated complex decision-making regarding cropping patterns, requiring a subtle understanding of the respective advantages of different crops in a changing environmental and institutional context. Alexandra Sapoznik, 'Resource allocation and peasant decision making: Oakington, Cambridgeshire, 1360–99', *AgHR*, 61 (2013).

[94] The closest is Elly Robson's study of the customary epistemologies of the landscape. Robson, 'Improvement and epistemologies', 2. Separately, David Mitch emphasised the 'distinctive mental agility' of nineteenth-century farm workers, but this concerned a labour force under the direction

the substance of an early modern peasant epistemology is not explored in further detail here, the general notion supports an extended analogy between craft knowledge and farming knowledge, and a serious consideration of the perception of the mysteries and secrets of husbandry.

From the Art of Husbandry to Business of Farming

We can now summarise why husbandry has not been considered a 'mystery' alongside other crafts and trades, and therefore neglected in studies of craft knowledge. Sixteenth-century husbandry was characterised by five features: it was heterogeneous, diffuse, subsistence-oriented, open and irregular. First, husbandry was peculiarly diverse in its operations, both on individual farms and across society as a whole, and therefore did not identify a definitive set of tasks or method of production. In the two main books on husbandry in the sixteenth century, neither Fitzherbert nor Tusser presented their guidance as new, nor as the 'secrets' of a 'mystery' or craft (although these terms were popularised more from 1558, after their initial publication).[95] Second, the art of husbandry was too widely spread among an overwhelmingly rural population. Between two-thirds and three quarters of the population engaged in some kind of farming, with many craftsmen working a scrap of land or grazing a cow on the commons. The art of husbandry was a set of widely shared customs in which large sections of the community participated (particularly at harvest), rather than an exclusive mystery.[96] The struggles of husbandmen and other agricultural workers in the sixteenth century were not around protecting monopolies or restricting access to their trade.[97] Third, the dominance of family-based farming orientated towards household consumption meant that husbandry did not contain commercial secrets to the same degree as other crafts and trades. A rough distinction can be drawn between books of secrets that revealed skills used to make money, and books for family use (including

---

of managers rather than independent peasant producers. David Mitch, 'Learning by doing among Victorian farmworkers: A case study in the biological and cognitive foundations of skill acquisition', *LSE Working Papers in Economic History* (1994), 36.

[95] John Fitzherbert, *Here begynneth a newe tracte or treatyse moost profytable for all husbandmen* (London, 1523); Thomas Tusser, *A hundreth good pointes of husbandrie* (London, 1557). See Reynolds, 'Practical Books', 281.

[96] Recent studies argue that male by-employments were not nearly as ubiquitous as previously claimed, as the evidence of probate inventories systematically overstates their prevalence and scale. Keibek and Shaw-Taylor, 'Early modern rural by-employments'.

[97] See the literature of 'agrarian complaint'. McRae, *God speed the plough*, ch. 1.

husbandry) that shared knowledge and recipes that were at least partially exercised outside a commercial context.[98]

Fourth, contemporaries often remarked – in contrast to crafts hidden in workshops – that the husbandman's art was openly displayed in the fields. This notion has a long history: in the ancient Greek treatise by Xenophon, the character Isomachus 'contrasts the openness of agriculture with the secrecy of crafts', since 'the farmer works openly and is pleased to explain his work'.[99] It combined two senses of openness: the physical environment and the character of the husbandman. In a Latin treatise by the German Conrad Heresbach, translated into English in 1577, it was claimed that whereas the guild crafts kept to themselves the 'chiefe mysteries of their knowledge', the 'husband rejoyceth to have every body made prime to his skill' and gladly shared his knowledge.[100] Similar notions can be found in the eighteenth century. A Scottish agricultural periodical praised the farmer for being free of the 'jealousy' of other professions, 'who generally affect a mystery in their business', and for being 'free, open, and communicative, ready to assist his neighbours, not only with his labour, but with his advice'.[101] Such statements were part of the general moral battle between town and country, yet there was considered something intrinsically different about the open practice of husbandry: '[a]ll rural operations are more or less public', wrote William Marshall in 1804, 'are, as it were, performed on a stage'.[102] A reviewer the same year wrote that 'the out-of-door operations of agriculture can contain no secrets or *mystery*, like those of manufacture'.[103]

Fifth, husbandry had no institutional equivalent of the guild system to both maintain secrecy and regularise training. The tensions that developed over the seventeenth century between the 'private' trade knowledge of guilds and the 'public' knowledge of science, which involved revealing the commercial secrets by which individuals earned a living, cannot easily be observed in husbandry as a whole.[104] Service in husbandry was not formalised education to the same degree as craft apprenticeships. Similarly, while husbandry shared a number of features with medicine – widely spread across society, centred on the family and household, and largely exercised outside of institutional settings – husbandry had no equivalent of

[98] Hunter, 'Books for daily life'.
[99] Long, *Openness*, 23.
[100] Conrad Heresbach and Barnaby Googe, *Foure bookes of husbandry* (London, 1577), 17.
[101] Printed collectively in *The northern farmer: Or select essays on agriculture* (London, 1778), 13.
[102] William Marshall, *On the landed property of England* (London, 1804), 327.
[103] C., 'Hints to agriculturists', *The Farmer's Magazine*, 5:18 (1804), 213.
[104] Hunter, 'Books for daily life', 521.

the apprentice-based training of barber-surgeons and the university-based learning of physicians.[105]

Yet long-term trends shifted the conditions of husbandry closer to other crafts as a commercial trade and distinct occupation. Recent estimates suggest that the large-scale structural shift in labour away from agriculture took place earlier than previously thought, primarily in the seventeenth century. Broadberry *et al.* estimate that the total share of the labour force engaged in agriculture (rather than industry or services) fell from over 60 per cent around 1520 to below 40 per cent by around 1700, then briefly sta-bilised, before falling again from the mid-eighteenth century to around 30 per cent by 1800. The male workforce occupied in agriculture fell dramati-cally from 65 per cent around 1552 to 43 per cent around 1710.[106] Similarly, Wallis *et al.* suggest a decline of the male agricultural workforce from 68 per cent of the total workforce around 1600 to 48 per cent around 1720.[107] At the same time the proportion of women spinning increased from 11.5 per cent in 1590 to 22.6 per cent in 1750.[108] These estimates indicate that the critical shift from a majority to a minority occupation occurred in the seventeenth century, in conjunction with urbanisation and the rise of rural industry and textile communities.[109]

Agricultural work itself was increasingly performed in competitive con-texts. The expansion of local markets encouraged further regional spe-cialisation within a national market.[110] The spread of commercial farming meant that farmers were in greater competition with each other.[111] The growth in farm size and rise in wage labourers meant that people were more likely to be working on a farm under a contractual relationship. Landlords and tenants were increasingly in competition over the balance of farming profits.[112] In all these situations knowledge was being exercised within com-petitive contexts: labourers seeking employment and wages on the basis of their skills; commercial farmers buying and selling goods in the market at

---

[105] Wear, *Knowledge and practice*, 21–25.

[106] Broadberry et al., *British economic growth*, 363.

[107] Wallis et al., 'Structural change'. See also Keibek, 'Male occupational structure'.

[108] Whittle, 'Land and people', 165.

[109] English urban population increased from 5 per cent in 1520 to c.8 per cent in 1600 and c.17 per cent in 1700. E. A. Wrigley, 'Urban growth and agricultural change: England and the continent in the early modern period', *Journal of Interdisciplinary History*, 15 (1985), 688.

[110] On marketisation of agriculture, see Overton, *Agricultural Revolution*, 133–49. On commercialisa-tion generally, see Wrightson, *Earthly Necessities*, ch. 12.

[111] For example, see Patricia Croot, *The world of the small farmer: Tenure, profit and politics in the early modern Somerset levels* (Hatfield, 2017).

[112] Overton, *Agricultural Revolution*, 182.

the best price; tenants and landlords negotiating the most advantageous rent. Hence long-term trends were increasing the value and heightening tensions around the ownership of knowledge of husbandry. As the art of husbandry evolved into the business of farming, it became more like other trades: possessed and exercised by a select group who had an interest in protecting the knowledge upon which their livelihood was based.

Mystery of Husbandry 1600–1800

The earliest identified use of 'mystery of husbandry' in English agricultural literature is particularly notable. In *Maison Rustique* (1600), an English translation from a sixteenth-century French work, it was stated that the landowner must have 'skill in matters of Husbandrie', but that this might be learned through formal education. The hired 'Farmer', in contrast, should have been brought up on a farm since his youth, be 'well experienced in matters and businesses belonging to husbandrie', and have 'attained the mysterie of husbandrie'.[113] The term 'mystery' is used here in a sense consistent with both the sense discussed in relation to crafts and with John Cannon's use cited earlier: that is, a property acquired through labour and experience. The French origin ('le mestier de la rustication') suggests that this was an unusual formulation in English at the time. It appeared again in Gervase Markham's 1613 book of husbandry, in which he claimed to write from experience by stating, 'I am not altogether unséene in these misteries I write of: for it is well knowne I followed the profession of a Husbandman'.[114] Yet across all his works on husbandry the use of the term 'mistery' or 'mystery' was relatively rare.

The identification of husbandry as or with 'mystery' increased from the mid-seventeenth century. A 1647 pamphlet against tithes appealed to the authority of 'Husbandmen that understand the mystery and calling of Husbandry'.[115] Walter Blith's *English Improver Improved* (1653) used 'mystery' throughout, although mostly to refer to specific aspects of husbandry, including the draining of lands, the planting of fruits, the cultivation of particular crops such as saffron and flax, and the 'very mystery of Ploughmanship'.[116] One of the first texts to consistently refer to husbandry as a mystery was *An Essay for Advancement of Husbandry-Learning* (1651)

---

[113] Charles Estienne Jean Liébault, and Richard Surflet, *Maison rustique, or the countrie farme* (London, 1600), 28.
[114] Gervase Markham, *The English husbandman* (London, 1613), ch. 1.
[115] Anon., *The husbandmans plea against tithes* (London, 1647), 28.
[116] Walter Blith, *The English improver improved* (London, 1653), 45, 219, 240, 260.

by Cressy Dymock, which explicitly sought to refashion husbandry along the lines of other trades in proposing a '*private Colledge* or *Society* of good Husbandry'. Dymock declared that students would learn 'the whole and every part of this so *honourable* an *Art*, so *deep* a *Mystery*', and described husbandry as the 'most Auncient, Noble, and honestly gainfull *Art, Trade,* or *Mystery*'.[117] The college would institutionalise the learning of husbandry by offering seven-year apprenticeships for boys aged fifteen or upwards. Pupils would be forbidden 'to discover all or any part of the same Art or Mystery to any person whatsoever' without consent.[118]

The associated rhetoric of secrets was also increasingly applied to husbandry in the context of publicising knowledge. It was mostly used in relation to auxiliary specialisms, such as in Gervase Markham's book on horsemanship, the *Faithfull Farrier* (1629), whose titlepage alone promised to lay open all the 'Secrets of Horsemanship, which the Author never published, but hath kept in his Brest, and hath beene the Glory of his Practise'.[119] In a six-page 1637 pamphlet on improving barren land, John Shaw stated that he knew many husbandmen who understood 'secrets in husbandry' that were not generally known, but he did not want to make public the secrets practised by others.[120] Hence he exhibited some anxiety about publicising little-known points of husbandry. Such anxieties were challenged by Samuel Hartlib and his circle of reformers, whose radical educational proposals and publishing activities were driven by the belief that knowledge was a public good.[121] A pamphlet called *The Reformed Husbandman* (1651) noted that most advanced arts had 'concealed mysteries, which cannot be attained without the consent and information of those that are the Masters of their Trade', yet considered the art of ploughing to be 'evil mannaged' and in need of a 'Remedy', or 'special secret'. The author wrote that he would conceal his full knowledge for the time being, but since God had endowed him with this secret he did not intend to 'hide this Talent in a napkin'.[122] Other works by Hartlib promised to share secrets in the title pages: the *Legacy* (1651) offered the commonwealth 'Secrets in reference to

---

[117] Cressy Dymock, *An essay for the advancement of husbandry-learning: Or propositions for the errecting College of Husbandry* (London, 1651), 4, 9.
[118] Ibid., 10.
[119] Discussed in Allison Kavey, *Books of secrets: Natural philosophy in England, 1550–1600* (Chicago, 2007).
[120] John Shaw, *How to order any land* (London, 1637).
[121] Charles Webster, *The great instauration: Science, medicine and reform, 1626–1660* (London, 1975), 475–76; Eamon, *Science and the secrets of nature*, 326.
[122] Samuel Hartlib and Cressy Dymock, *The reformfd [sic] husband-man* (London, 1651). A reference to the parable of the talents in Matthew 25:26.

Universall HUSBANDRY', and *The Compleat Husband-man* (1659) claimed to lay open 'many rare and most hidden secrets'.

From the 1660s, this trope of revealing or discovering the mystery of husbandry defined the presentation of agricultural literature.[123] The full title of John Worlidge's 1669 treatise was a bold announcement: *Systema Agriculturæ; the Mystery of Husbandry Discovered*. A 1684 manual proclaimed to 'unravel the whole Mystery of Husbandry'.[124] Leonard Meager's *The Mystery of Husbandry* (1697) contained the term in its full title twice. Timothy Nourse's 1700 manual for country gentlemen was reprinted in 1708 with the revised title *The Mistery of Husbandry Discover'd*.[125] However, after this half-century burst, the term 'mystery' is found less often and less prominently in eighteenth-century agricultural literature, while the associated term 'secret' was mostly found in its common everyday usage rather than reflecting its richer artisanal origins.[126] Indeed, the 1716 reprint of Worlidge's treatise removed the reference to the mystery of husbandry (re-titled *A Compleat System of Husbandry and Gardening*).

The notion of revealing or discovering the mystery of the husbandry was nevertheless ambiguous, reflecting the two traditional meanings of mystery. In one sense, 'mystery' could mean that the knowledge held by illiterate practitioners was being made public to educated gentlemen and the wider literate community. From this perspective the relatively brief life of the vocabulary of 'mystery' and 'secrets' appears straightforward: once the mystery and secrets were discovered or revealed, they ceased to be so. A mystery reduces quickly to an art or science. The best secrets of husbandry were revealed in the first flush of publications, but once this literature had a basis, perhaps later authors and booksellers could not so easily claim to be revealing hidden knowledge.

In another sense, however, it meant almost the reverse. This was 'mystery' in the sense of the hidden secrets of nature, rather than secrets of a trade, although the uses overlapped. This ambiguity or duality was present in a number of publications. An anonymous pamphlet of 1612 presented a dialogue between a gentleman student Physiologus and an 'ignorant'

[123] See also publications on other topics, whose titles promised the 'mystery' of astronomy, cookery, or vintners, reflecting general trends in the book trade.

[124] J. S., *Profit and pleasure united, or the husbandman's magazine* (London, 1684), 'Epistle to the Reader'.

[125] Timothy Nourse, *Campania fœlix, or a discourse of the benefits and improvements of husbandry* (London, 1700).

[126] In the eighteenth century the term 'secrets' came to simply mean techniques and lost its associations 'with esoteric wisdom' and 'the artisan's cunning'. Eamon, *Science and the secrets of nature*, 4.

country farmer Geoponus, in which the scholar taught the 'misteries of nature' to the farmer (rather than being revealed by the farmer).[127] Cressy Dymock's 1651 proposal for a college stated that pupils would learn the mystery of husbandry, 'not onely in the more customary and Common way' but through 'rational trials & real Experiments'.[128] Dymock acknowledged the status of husbandry as a mystery, but simultaneously invoked the idea of deeper mysteries yet to be revealed. Walter Blith's use of the 'Mystery of Improvement' hinted that his improved methods uncovered further secrets unknown to customary practice.[129] Worlidge's treatise stated that the husbandman must know 'the secret Mysteries … of the Productions and Increase of Vegetables'.[130] Similarly, in *A New System of Agriculture* (1726) John Laurence referred to 'the whole Mystery of Vegetation and Improvement'.[131] With this second sense, it was possible to reverse the transfer of knowledge: to 'lay open all such important Secrets, as are fit for Countrymen and Peasants to know'.[132] Here Laurence was echoing Pierre le Lorrain, abbé de Vallemont (1649–1721), whose translated treatise made the same plea that 'important Secrets should likewise be imparted to Countrymen and Peasants'.[133] Those in possession of the true mystery of husbandry had been switched.

This shift from the 'mystery of husbandry' to the 'mystery of vegetation' was partly a shift from the view that common husbandmen possessed a hidden knowledge of cultivation to the view that the true secrets of cultivation remained hidden in nature. Hence Laurence's book was presented less as revealing the secrets of practitioners, and more as teaching those practitioners the secrets of nature of which they were ignorant. However, these meanings overlapped and the second sense was not always simply an inversion of the hierarchy of knowledge between farmer and scholar. Thomas Tryon, raised in youth as a shepherd, wrote in 1684 about how shepherds 'Tutor'd their Children in the Mysteries of undisguised Nature'.[134]

---

[127] *A familiar dialogue betwixt one Physiologus a gentleman student of Athens and his country friend Geoponus* (Oxford, 1612), 24.

[128] Dymock, *Essay*, 4.

[129] Blith, *English improver improved*, 'Epistle to the Industrious Reader'.

[130] John Worlidge, *Systema agriculturæ; the mystery of husbandry discovered* (London, 1669), 1.

[131] John Laurence, *A new system of agriculture* (London, 1726), 77.

[132] Laurence was referring to knowledge in the *Philosophical Transactions* of the Royal Society. Ibid., 'Preface'.

[133] Pierre Le Lorrain Vallemont, *Curiosities of nature and art in husbandry and gardening* (London, 1707), 'Preface'.

[134] Thomas Tryon, *The country-man's companion* (London, 1684), 95.

In the eighteenth century, the most common appearance of the term in print was simply listings of Worlidge's seventeenth-century publication in sales catalogues or adverts, or in the continual publication of the 'perpetual almanac' *Erra Pater* or *The Book of Knowledge*, whose subtitle usually promised the reader the 'whole mystery of husbandry'.[135] However, in the latter it was explicitly used as an archaic term.[136] Further scattered references to the mystery of husbandry in the old sense were relatively rare in eighteenth-century agricultural books, but are particularly revealing for that reason. The following examples are all articulations of the attitudes of common husbandmen, suggesting that the term had a longer currency among common husbandmen and labourers (as with John Cannon) and support the hypothesis that it was used in contexts where there was a conflict over knowledge. In *Husbandry Anatomized* (1697), the Scottish author James Donaldson claimed there was no 'great Mistery in what I have here published'.[137] But he confronted the question again when considering that the 'thick scul'd Peasant' might object to his treatise with the response:

> We and our Fathers, have been bred in Husbandrie these many Generations, and if there had been any Mistery in it to find, would not they have found it out before this time? Are you Wiser than all that ever have been bred and exercised in Husbandry hitherto?[138]

In this imagined exchange, the peasant, confident that he is in full possession of the 'mistery' held by generations of men bred to husbandry, confronts the writer who claims some alternative source of knowledge independent from custom. Donaldson's reply was modest: 'What you or your Fathers have been bred to, or what Misterys they might have found, I question not', he wrote, only claiming that what may be new for them was known to be true by the experience of others around the kingdom.[139] The usage of mystery, therefore, appears at a moment of conflict between two ways of learning or knowing. Similarly, in 1727, Richard Bradley, prolific agricultural author and professor of Botany at Cambridge, complained about farmers who rejected all improvements and questioned his advice

---

[135] For example, *The book of knowledge shewing the wisdom of the ancients in four parts* (London, 1720). See Mary E. Fissell, 'Readers, texts, and contexts: Vernacular medical works in early modern England', in Roy Porter (ed.), *The popularization of medicine 1650–1850* (London, 1992).

[136] For discussion of husbandry and astrology in almanacs, see Louise Hill Curth, *English almanacs, astrology and popular medicine, 1550–1700* (Manchester, 2007), 110–11.

[137] James Donaldson, *Husbandry anatomized, or, an enquiry into the present manner of teiling and manuring the ground in Scotland* (Edinburgh, 1697), 'To the Right Honourable'.

[138] Ibid., 122.

[139] Ibid., 123.

due to his lack of practical experience: 'they will ask me whether I can hold a plough, for in that they think the whole mystery of husbandry consists'.[140] This caricature contains the matter in a nutshell: the view of common husbandmen that labouring experience conferred on them the possession of the mystery of husbandry, which could not be attained otherwise.

This view was coming under attack by agricultural improvers and writers. In an anonymous treatise published in 1755, the gentleman author dismissed the 'the weak, old Argument' that 'there are certain Secrets in the Practice of this Art, which the Farmers keep among themselves; and which Gentlemen, or Those they employ, must be ignorant of'. The author declared 'how easy it is for any Man to be instructed in the Farmer's whole Treasury of Knowledge: For all, beyond that little Store, is Terra incognita to the deepest of their Discoveries'.[141] Here the two senses of mystery are contrasted: the secrets learned by the farmer were trivial compared to the secrets waiting to be unlocked by the science of agriculture. The argument of Cuthbert Clarke's 1777 dialogue on the theory and practice of husbandry was subtler. 'That there are mysteries in the art of husbandry', the husbandman Agricola stated, 'no one hath presumed to dispute; but it is, however, the opinion of most husbandmen, that practice alone is sufficient to unfold them'. But the character of Philosophus, articulating Clarke's view, replied that theory was required to investigate the mysteries of husbandry, as practice 'comprehends nothing beyond the act of performing'.[142]

The late eighteenth century nevertheless retained some notion that practitioners of the art could keep knowledge hidden or private. In 1764, Walter Harte described farmers keeping their knowledge to themselves in a national context. In a historical sketch of the seventeenth century, he wrote that Flemish farmers did not publish any books on the subject as 'their intention was to carry on a private lucrative trade without instructing their neighbours', such that Englishmen had to travel to observe their methods themselves. He declared it was the discovery of eight to ten new manures that constituted the 'chief mystery of the Flemish husbandry'.[143] On a smaller scale, in 1779, William Marshall scoffed at the common farmer who, after making discoveries, congratulated himself for 'being

---

[140] Richard Bradley, *A complete body of husbandry: Collected from the practice and experience of the most considerable farmers in Britain* (London, 1727), 95.

[141] A Country Gentleman, *A new system of agriculture* (London, 1755), 90–91.

[142] Cuthbert Clarke, *The true theory and practice of husbandry* (London, 1777), 9–11.

[143] Walter Harte, *Essays on husbandry* (London, 1764), 45.

cunning enough to keep them as family-secrets; and consequently, on being able to monopolize to himself and his heirs, the advantages which may accrue'.[144] The point was discussed in detail in an anti-enclosure pamphlet of 1785, which observed that 'farmers aim at making a mystery of their business in conversation with gentlemen', even with 'their transactions lying open to observation'.[145] The pamphleteer defended the notion that certain kinds of knowledge could be kept hidden among practising farmers. Specifically, the author claimed that there were at least three 'mysteries in practical farming' unknown to gentlemen: the nature of the soil, managing livestock, and managing labourers ('the clowns'). The first two mysteries could be acquired 'only by close attention and long experience', while the third was only ever obtained 'by those who have been brought up from their childhood among the clowns, whom they consider as of their own class'.[146] The pamphlet argued generally that agriculture could not be learned through observation, conversation and reading. In 1783, the physician and political reformer George Edwards also defended restrictions on publicising agricultural knowledge, arguing that 'the mysteries of it should not be revealed' to those who would use it 'to the disadvantage of the farmer or the tenant'.[147]

In the latter half of the century, most scattered uses of 'mystery' in agricultural literature referred to specialist activities involving new crops or methods, rather than the whole art.[148] In a number of remarks by William Marshall (1745–1818) in his *Rural Economy* series, which surveyed agricultural practice across the kingdom, the term 'mystery' was explicitly used in the context of a craft secret known to a select group of practitioners who sought to maintain an exclusive hold over the art in question to secure their social and economic position. Discussing the Midland counties, Marshall noted the following contrast: 'In Norfolk, every plowman and every harrow boy is a turnip hoer: here, hoing is a mystery, practiced only by a few, who have it in their power to make their own terms'.[149] Elsewhere he described how the 'art of pond-making' in Yorkshire was

---

[144] Marshall, *Experiments*, 9.
[145] *A political enquiry*, iv.
[146] Ibid., vii.
[147] George Edwards, *A plan of an undertaking intended for the improvement of husbandry, and for other purposes* (Newcastle, 1783), 6.
[148] In reference to growing turnips in John Mills, *A new system of practical husbandry*, 5 vols (London, 1767), iii, 156. In reference to quick lime in James Anderson, *Essays relating to agriculture and rural affairs* (Edinburgh, 1775), i, 234. In reference to managing bees in the title page of William Thompson, *The new gardener's calendar; or, every man a complete gardener* (London, 1779).
[149] Marshall, *Midland counties*, ii, 8.

'still partially hid under the veil of mystery' and all who practised were 'in reality or pretence, pupils of the first inventors'.[150] He noted that the people of Morton in the West of England 'monopolised, and practised as a mystery, the culture of Potatoes, during a length of time'.[151] However, in each case, it designated a local specialism rather than the general occupation of the husbandman. Together they suggest a changing picture, whereby the whole mystery of husbandry had been, over the course of a couple of centuries, almost entirely 'revealed' and made accessible to learned men, with mere pockets of obscurity remaining where particular labourers or farmers maintained a privileged possession of the knowledge and skills required.

One of these pockets of obscurity was dairying, a customary art still primarily in the hands of women in the early eighteenth century. In Valenze's account of the transformation of the art of dairying into a male-dominated science and business, she describes in detail the precise labours of cheese-making in which 'a seemingly mysterious matriarchal authority prevailed'.[152] Agricultural authors like William Marshall were at the forefront of this transformation. Discussing Gloucestershire, he argued that the knowledge of dairy management was 'confined', because it was practised in physical seclusion and largely performed by women.

> The manufacturing of cheese is not like the cultivation of lands. This is a *public employment*, open to any one who travels across the site of cultivation: that, a *private manufactory* - a craft - a mystery - secluded from the public eye… The dairy room is consecrated to the sex …'[153]

Marshall evoked the ancient idea that tillage was open for all to see, in contrast to cheese making, which was akin to a craft in a workshop and remained a kind of mystery. It was doubly hidden since the practitioners were women, whom Marshall did not consider as belonging to the 'public' realm of gentlemen. Cheese-making was 'a knack involved in mystery', which could not progress so long as it was practised by women, acquired through direct experience and passed down through personal instruction. He called upon 'every man of science, who has opportunity and leisure', to gain access to the dairy room to record, systematise and advance the art.[154] Here the demystification of farming was explicitly gendered.

---

[150] William Marshall, *Rural economy of Yorkshire*, 2 vols (London, 1788), i, 153.
[151] William Marshall, *Rural economy of the West of England*, 2 vols (London, 1796), i, 199.
[152] Valenze, 'Art of women', 157.
[153] William Marshall, *Rural economy of Glocestershire*, 2 vols (London, 1789), ii, 184–85.
[154] Ibid., ii, 185–86.

Two examples from fiction reinforce the overall impression. In Tobias Smollett's *Humphry Clinker* (1771), a gentleman trained in the law named Charles Dennison is determined to retire into the country, but is advised against it by people who assure him 'that farming was a mystery known only to those who had been bred up to it from the cradle', and consequently 'every attempt made by gentlemen miscarried'.[155] But Dennison is not deterred: if a 'peasant without education' could succeed, then surely, he told himself, he could too:

> He had studied the theory of agriculture with a degree of eagerness and delight; and he could not conceive there was any mystery in the practice, but what he should be able to disclose by dint of care and application.[156]

In Richard Graves' *The Spiritual Quixote* (1783), the character of Mr Rivers responds to a proposal to take up a farm with a similar attitude: 'I was very ignorant of the mystery of modern Farming, yet, having been so much conversant in the Classics, I had conceived a romantic notion of Agriculture … I was therefore agreeably struck with the idea of turning Farmer'.[157] In both cases, the 'mystery of farming' was invoked only to be immediately dismissed as redundant. The late eighteenth-century gentleman, armed with deep education in the classics, theoretical knowledge from studying books on agriculture, and confidence in his natural superiority, was not intimidated by the lingering notion that farming was a mystery.

To large tenant farmers with a scientific spirit, such as Marshall, the gradual demystification of the art of husbandry was an unquestioned triumph: 'Until the present Century, FARMING, like RELIGION, was an hereditary mystery, transferred from father to son, and had no other foundation than chance-produced CUSTOM'.[158] Aside from the few exceptions discussed, the disenchantment of husbandry was largely complete by the late eighteenth century. A 1766 agricultural dictionary defined husbandry straightforwardly as 'the business or employment of a farmer, or person who cultivates land'.[159] In the early nineteenth century, Sir John Sinclair opened his treatise with the retrospective observation that the 'art of Agriculture was formerly involved in doubt and mystery', as practitioners 'followed the customs of their fore-fathers' without reflection.[160] In 1865,

---

[155] Tobias Smollett, *The expedition of Humphry Clinker*, 3 vols (London, 1771), iii, 204.
[156] Ibid., 205.
[157] Richard Graves, *The spiritual Quixote*, 3 vols (London, 1783), ii, 86.
[158] William Marshall, *Minutes of agriculture, made on a farm of 300 acres* (London, 1778), 4.
[159] Society of Gentlemen, *The complete farmer: Or, a general dictionary of husbandry* (London, 1766).
[160] Sinclair, *Code*, iii.

John Chalmers Morton could confidently declare that, from the perspective of 'the physiologist, the chemist, the botanist, and entomologist, the "mystery" of agriculture … has disappeared'. The facts of agriculture were merely instances of general laws known to men of science. Further, as a trade, the notion of anything 'mysterious' had been exploded, as no trade needed special protection.[161]

If we return to John Cannon's memoir, we can appreciate that his specific sense of attaining the 'whole mistery of husbandry' from his father and through daily practice, independent from book learning, was perhaps only possible for a period of around two centuries, roughly between the late sixteenth to the late eighteenth century. Before, the knowledge of cultivation was part of the common stock of the rural community; after, it was detailed extensively as a scientific discipline in hundreds of books for specific occupations. In neither case could it be properly termed a 'mystery' in the full sense. However, during this transition the knowledge of husbandry became an increasingly valuable market asset, and consequently, the possession of knowledge became an area of contestation, as landlords sought greater control over their tenants, tenants sought greater control over their workers, and farmers competed with each other.

The gradual application of the term 'mystery' or 'mistery' in seventeenth-century literature was linked to this shift in the conditions in which the art of husbandry was exercised. Mystery implied knowledge possessed by a select group who had acquired it through customary practice. The publication of instructional books on husbandry, which from the early seventeenth century were beginning to claim a knowledge superior to existing customs, both represented and contributed to changing perceptions. As books aimed to make 'public' and open knowledge that was to some extent confined within customary practices, they articulated their purpose in the language of mystery and secrets. Printing, however, did not make private knowledge public, but more accurately made widespread knowledge newly accessible to literate persons, who, not incidentally, were largely those who did not possess the mystery of husbandry. Books were, therefore, a key first step in the commodification of agricultural knowledge, which was also its demystification. Previously, the art of husbandry did not have a fully independent existence outside customary practice, or the minds and bodies of farmworkers who applied it in daily labour, with only marginal exceptions. Once partially stored in books it could not only

---

[161] John Chalmers Morton, 'Agricultural education', *Journal of the Royal Agricultural Society of England*, 1 (1865), 436–37.

be bought and sold in the form of print but could more easily be harnessed and utilised as a separate input in commercial farming.

In agricultural literature 'mystery' had an ambiguous meaning. On the one hand, it evoked the mix of knowledge and skills attained by those bred to husbandry; on the other, it described the secrets of the earth's fertility that remained unknown to rustic clowns. This duality was not contradictory, but marked the conceptual space being traversed. Agricultural writers aimed both to reveal the mystery of husbandry as practised by the best husbandmen and to discover new mysteries that would bring the art of agriculture to perfection. The dwindling use of 'mystery' in the eighteenth century, whether in reference to specialist local methods, or to express the attitudes of common husbandmen, or to identify what gentlemen writers believed they had overcome, testifies to the world being swept away by the culture of improvement. The following chapters develop the argument that agricultural book knowledge was itself a key factor in the long-term demystification of the art of husbandry.

CHAPTER 3

Standing on the Shoulders of Peasants
The Appropriation of the Art of Husbandry

In the satirical poem *Pursuits of Agriculture* (1808), an anonymous author took aim at the philosophical and scientific pretensions of 'agriculturists', based on the activities of the Norfolk Agricultural Society.[1] Most strikingly, in the first canto, the poet turned the narrative of progress by self-described 'improvers' on its head.

> Oh! fair advancement of true science,
> Most worthy of complete reliance;
> What vast improvement must be made
> By this progression retrograde!
> Teachers are taught*, the learned want
> The knowledge of the ignorant![2]

The successive oxymorons – 'progression retrograde', 'teachers are taught', 'knowledge of the ignorant' – inverted the role agriculturists proclaimed for themselves as enlightened men of science, spreading new knowledge to ignorant husbandmen. The poet elaborated in the footnoted commentary:

> *Taught*. The mode of instruction adopted by the *Agriculturists* is *Socratic*; with this difference indeed, that the questioning sage always saw exactly what point he meant to come to; but the *Agricultural querists* are avowedly in the dark …[3]

It insinuated that the knowledge of members of agricultural societies was first extracted from those they claimed to teach, by collecting information from farmers through 'queries'. Further, the author was convinced that gentlemen were often deceived, expressing his surprise that they did not 'see through some of the answers they get to their queries'.[4] The second

---

[1] *Pursuits of agriculture: A satirical poem* (London, 1808), 5.
[2] Ibid., 35–36.
[3] Ibid., 36–37.
[4] Ibid., 40–41.

canto returned to the same theme when describing the way reporters for the Board of Agriculture interacted with working farmers:

> Force him by dint of strong suggestion,
> Pump him and squeeze by artful question,
> To tell, what he and all his neighbours
> Know and perform of rural labours.
> Then, as they quaff their wine or ale,
> Take notes of many a wondrous tale[5]

The reporters had 'plenty of letters from Dukes, Lords, Baronets, M.P.s, D.D.s and simple Squires, to independent yeomen… charging them on their allegiance, to give all possible information'.[6] Summarising the relationship between farmers and agricultural writers, the poet jokingly addressed the 'clown': 'Tell all ye know … Tis your's to give, 'tis their's to mix / And all in meet arrangement fix'.[7]

In the same manner that the poet inverted the contemporary narrative of improvement and agricultural writers, this chapter inverts the established historical narrative about the role of agricultural books in an 'agricultural enlightenment'. The established narrative focuses on the transfer of knowledge from writers to practising farmers, which usually flowed downwards on the social scale. It dwells on a single overarching question: to what extent did printed books contribute to the dissemination of knowledge, the spread of technological innovations, and ultimately increases in agricultural productivity?[8] This narrative obscures the origins of knowledge compiled in books and the profound cultural shift required for genteel authors to position themselves as authorities on farming.

This chapter offers a new narrative about the transfer of agricultural knowledge from practitioners to writers, which usually flowed upwards on the social scale. It takes seriously a general provocation by Peter Burke, who speculated that the 'intellectual revolutions of early modern Europe … were no more than the surfacing into visibility (and more especially into print), of certain kinds of popular or practical knowledge'.[9] Burke acknowledged this would be an exaggeration, but suggested such a counter-narrative might contain some truth. As established in Chapter 1, the main socio-economic trends in early modern agriculture necessitated a

---

[5] Ibid., 130–31.
[6] Ibid., 131.
[7] Ibid., 159.
[8] Most recently, Jones, *Agricultural enlightenment*.
[9] Burke, *Social history of knowledge*, 15.

social redistribution of knowledge as the typical farm changed from a small subsistence farm using family labour to a large commercial farm using hired wage labour. Control over cultivation was gradually concentrated into fewer hands, and decisions about farming were being made by a significantly smaller proportion of the agricultural community. The diffusion model is completely inadequate to describe the multiple and dynamic ways that knowledge circulated within this evolving social order.

A key dynamic is best understood as a process of knowledge *appropriation*. The term 'appropriation' can be used loosely, but Mary Fissell and Roger Cooter provide a useful definition: 'the cultural acquisition of knowledges, or the ways in which they are borrowed from one social setting and reformulated in another'.[10] While they apply it primarily to eighteenth-century medicine, here it applies to agriculture.[11] The description of 'borrowing' and 'reformulating' helps distinguish two processes that formed the appropriation of the art of husbandry in the early modern period: the collection of the existing knowledge of the art, and the transformation of a low practical art into a high literary science. Aspects of these processes have been recognised before without considering their implications for rural social relations. The first process captures how oral or customary knowledge was recorded in written form, making it accessible and useable in new contexts. Whilst the activities of agricultural improvers collecting information about best practices have been identified, little consideration has been given to how this affected relations with the practitioners themselves.[12] The second process captures how the ideal of the husbandman was redefined in terms of elite virtues, by transforming the customary art of husbandry into the noble science of agriculture. Similarly, while it is well established that gentlemen in the early modern period became newly engaged and enthusiastic about the study and practice of agriculture, there has been a repeated failure to consider how their involvement in direct farm management disturbed labour relations, beyond debates about landownership or the depopulating effects of enclosure. Since knowledge of cultivation was overwhelmingly held and exercised by practitioners in husbandry, the construction of a book-based knowledge (even with 'improved' methods) was partly reliant on the practical knowledge of husbandmen and housewives – which at the

---

[10] Fissell and Cooter, 'Natural knowledge', 149.

[11] Fissell and Cooter discuss agriculture in the same chapter, but frame their discussion around knowledge-as-property.

[12] For example, see account of improvers 'compiling, validating and disseminating knowledge', in Popplow, 'Economizing agricultural resources', 264.

same time it sought to supersede. Too often, the instinctive bias of scholars towards texts implies that the transfer of 'a truism for cultivators for thousands of years' into 'learned discourse' automatically constituted a form of progress, as if writing makes knowledge real.[13]

Recent studies have demonstrated the utility of the concept of appropriation for understanding the full range of social effects arising from the development of book knowledge.[14] Since knowledge of most arts, crafts and trades in early modern Europe was held by practitioners and transferred through verbal instruction and practical demonstration, the development of didactic texts served elite interests by preparing mechanical arts 'for appropriation by learned culture'.[15] The only study that has explicitly used the concept of appropriation with respect to eighteenth-century agricultural knowledge is Valenze's analysis of the women's art of dairying.[16] We can now extend Valenze's insight regarding dairy manuals to agriculture literature as a whole.[17]

To practitioners who possessed the mystery of husbandry – many of whom were unable to read – a manual on farming was not obviously necessary or useful. In contrast, educated gentlemen who had not learned the art of husbandry through practice had ample motives for acquiring knowledge of husbandry through reading books. Therefore, broadly speaking, books of husbandry served the interests of landed, learned and leisured society. However, there was no simple appropriation of knowledge from one class to another, but a more complex process whereby the art of husbandry was reformulated for the use of educated men over the course of a couple of centuries, a process assisted by increasing levels of literacy and education.[18] To borrow Daniel Woolf's description of the tussle between printed history and memory, it was a case of 'co-option' rather than 'ruthless oppression'.[19] An analogy with trends in landownership is instructive. The concentration of landownership was not the result of a simple direct transfer of land from one group to another, but rather a differentiation within peasant society, as a minority of

[13] Warde, *Invention of sustainability*, 143.
[14] Ash, *Power, knowledge, and expertise*; Long, 'Power, patronage, and the authorship'; De Munck, 'Corpses, live models, and nature'.
[15] Long, 'Power, patronage, and the authorship', 40.
[16] Valenze, 'Art of women', 153.
[17] The concept of appropriation of agricultural knowledge has been used in modern studies with regard to the relationship between Western corporations and 'indigenous knowledge' in the developing world. Vandana Shiva, *Biopiracy: The plunder of nature and knowledge* (Berkeley, 1998).
[18] Fox, 'Words'.
[19] Woolf, *The social circulation of the past*, 297.

prosperous peasants increased their landholdings and rose to become large yeoman farmers and even gentlemen over generations, while the majority became landless wage labourers.[20] Similarly, we can hypothesise a differentiation within peasant society with respect to the acquisition and form of agricultural knowledge, as a minority participated in literate culture and the development of book knowledge, while the majority continued to practise customary modes of husbandry sustained through oral tradition. In the eighteenth century, this perhaps followed the familiar cleavage within the middling sort between those who emulated the gentry and those who fashioned a distinct middling identity.[21] However, this misleadingly implies the change was passive and organic, without taking account of the motivations and ideologies of writers and readers. Rather than explore a general hypothesis of the social differentiation of knowledge, this chapter examines the extent to which agricultural books functioned as a tool of appropriation for educated gentlemen (analogous to focusing on enclosure when considering the diverse processes that contributed to the polarisation of landownership). It primarily describes an opposition between gentlemen landowners and working husbandmen as representatives of the higher and lower ends of rural society, but it does not presume or aim to validate a binary patrician-plebeian model.[22] Hence, where possible, it also offers some indications of how the expanding middling sort, or rural bourgeoisie – mostly yeomen at the beginning of our period and large tenant farmers towards the end – participated in these developments.

The central argument of the chapter is that there was a partially conscious effort by educated gentlemen to appropriate the art of husbandry from the mid-seventeenth to the end of the eighteenth century. To make this case, it firstly clarifies the role of the gentry with respect to husbandry in the sixteenth and early seventeenth centuries, with a short overview of the economic and cultural context. Next, it shows how the art of husbandry was re-imagined for gentlemen, by elevating it to a science of agriculture and undermining the authority of common husbandmen and housewives. It then identifies the mechanisms of appropriation, before highlighting its gendered dimension. Finally, it draws attention to how common farmworkers resisted the extraction of their knowledge by their social superiors.

---

[20] Whittle, *Agrarian capitalism*, ch. 4.
[21] Henry R. French, 'The search for the "middle sort of people" in England, 1600–1800', *Historical Journal*, 43 (2000), 288.
[22] As articulated in E. P. Thompson, *Customs in common* (New York, 1991).

Origins of Gentry Farming

The art of husbandry was appropriated in a slow and uneven process spanning the entire early modern period, but we can roughly distinguish two phases separated by the mid-seventeenth century. Sections of the gentry became more engaged in agriculture in the sixteenth century through a combination of financial need and intellectual interest, but it is only in the period 1660–1800 that we can discern a self-conscious project of appropriation within the movement for agrarian improvement. In the late fourteenth and early fifteenth centuries, most landlords ceased direct management and leased out their demesnes, effectively handing over control of agricultural production on a quarter of cultivated land in Britain to a new group of farmers, who became increasingly independent and followed their own methods of husbandry.[23] However, in the sixteenth century, in response to falling incomes, landlords began demesne-farming again as part of 'a resurgent landlordism' among gentry and aristocratic families, along with surveying and re-valuing land, and using enclosure to convert arable to pasture and to cultivate wastes.[24] Joan Thirsk argued that many gentlemen were not only responding to economic concerns but also were inspired to turn their attention to farming by the new availability of classical treatises, beginning with the *Scriptores rei rusticae*, printed in Venice in 1472, a compilation of the ancient writings of Cato, Varro, Columella and Palladius.[25] Thirsk noted that after generations of leaving the practicalities of farming to others, gentry families had 'plainly lost touch with day-to-day details'.[26] However, she claimed that Greek and Roman texts provided gentlemen with an 'intellectual reason for turning their attention to farming in a serious and professional manner'.[27]

While Thirsk acknowledged that not all gentlemen became farmers, her argument needs qualification on two points in order to properly understand the developments in the later seventeenth and eighteenth centuries. Firstly, gentlemen who became directly engaged in agricultural

---

[23] Dyer, *Making a living*, 346.
[24] R. W. Hoyle, 'Rural economies under stress: "A world so altered"', in Susan Doran and Norman Jones (eds), *The Elizabethan World* (Abingdon, Oxfordshire, 2011), 445–47. The long history on this subject recently treated in Jane Whittle (ed.), *Landlords and tenants in Britain, 1440–1660: Tawney's agrarian problem revisited* (Woodbridge, 2013).
[25] Thirsk, 'Making a fresh start', 18. Similar argument made earlier with regard to continental Europe in Beutler, 'La littérature agricole en Europe'.
[26] Thirsk, 'Making a fresh start', 16–18.
[27] Ibid., 29. As evidenced in commonplace books, annotated copies of printed books, the catalogues of private libraries, as well as estate correspondence. For contents of private libraries, see Ambrosoli, *Wild and the sown*, 257.

production faced serious social and cultural obstacles, as addressed in studies of sixteenth and seventeenth-century gentility.[28] Although the separation of the gentry from agricultural production was contested and blurred in practice, the cultural orthodoxy maintained that gentility was incompatible with husbandry, as the tilling of fields and tending of beasts was inextricably linked to the base and ignoble peasantry.[29] The boundary between gentry and yeomanry, between the virtues of a gentleman and the business of farming, was certainly becoming more porous, but it had by no means been erased before the seventeenth century.[30] Secondly, it is helpful to distinguish roughly between estate management and the minutiae of farming – or 'farming structure' and 'farming technique'.[31] First and foremost, the sixteenth-century gentleman landowner was encouraged to 'know one's owne', meaning to gain knowledge of the extent, nature and value of his land and resources, not necessarily knowledge of detailed farming operations.[32] The majority of English landlords were rentiers, more interested in extending acreage than intensifying cultivation.[33] We should not collapse all active landlordism into the business of farming. Similarly, as Rob Bryer argues, even though sixteenth-century farmers employed wage labour, they did not all exhibit a 'capitalist mentality' in seeking to change the methods of production in pursuit of a return on capital.[34]

Further, it is also worth noting the tangential nature of much gentry interest in agriculture, especially through horticulture and horsemanship.[35] Husbandry had only just begun its transformation into a genteel

---

[28] A good discussion of gentility in Shapin, *Social history of truth*, 42–62.

[29] J. P. Cooper, 'Ideas of gentility in early modern England', in G. E. Aylmer and J. S. Morrill (eds), *Land, men and beliefs: Studies in early-modern history* (London, 1983), 52–54; Philippa Maddern, 'Gentility', in Raluca Radulescu and Alison Truelove (eds), *Gentry culture in Late Medieval England* (Manchester, 2005); Felicity Heal and Clive Holmes, *The gentry in England and Wales, 1500–1700* (London, 1994).

[30] On both opportunity and difficulties of yeoman families rising to the gentry in fifteenth and sixteenth centuries: Campbell, *English yeomen*, 35–36; Christopher Carpenter, *Locality and polity: A study of Warwickshire landed society, 1401–1499* (Cambridge, 1992), esp. 134–37; Maddern, 'Gentility', 24.

[31] 'Farming structure' is concerned with 'the creation of a favourable environment for efficient farming' through 'enclosure of common fields, consolidation of scattered holdings, reclamation of wastes, revision of tenures, drainage', etc., to maximise rents. G. E. Mingay, *The gentry: The rise and fall of a ruling class* (London, 1976), 97.

[32] McRae, *God speed the plough*, Ch. 6.

[33] French and Hoyle, *Character of English rural society*, 11.

[34] Bryer, 'Genesis of the capitalist farmer', 370–71.

[35] On horticulture, Thirsk, 'World-wide farming web', 19. On horsemanship, see the writing career of Gervase Markham, who wrote on farriery long before husbandry: Thirsk, 'Plough and pen', 301.

art and business. In an essay on agriculture written around 1650, the poet Abraham Cowley suggested agricultural enthusiasm was slow to spread: the 'proprietors of the land are either too proud, or, for want of that kind of education, too ignorant, to improve their estates' – some were too proud 'not only to till the ground, but almost to tread upon it'.[36] Likewise, John Evelyn inserted a new passage into the second edition of his book on forestry in 1670, decrying the fact that yeomen families rising into the gentry sought to escape farming: 'when men have acquired any considerable Fortune by their good Husbandry… they account it a shame to breed up their Children in the same Calling in which they themselves were educated'.[37]

The increased engagement of the English gentry in agriculture, epitomised by men such as Evelyn, did not follow a steady, linear path from the sixteenth to the eighteenth century. According to Walter Harte's assessment, written in 1764, after the Restoration in 1660 the gentry had shown 'a false aversion to what had been the object and care of mean despised persons' which threw 'a damp upon agriculture', whereas after the peace of 1748 'almost all the European nations, by a sort of tacit consent, applied themselves to the study of agriculture'.[38] Another short history, written in 1766, claimed that husbandry 'flourished' briefly in the 1650s, but the industry of the country gentry dissipated after the 1660s and 'husbandry passed almost entirely into the hands of farmers', not to be fully revived until the early eighteenth century by Jethro Tull.[39] Hence a consensus grew that elite enthusiasm for agriculture had flourished briefly in the tumultuous decades of the mid-seventeenth century, receded in the following half-century or more, then returned with new intensity by the mid-eighteenth century.

This chronological pattern in England roughly corresponds to major economic and cultural trends. The mid-late seventeenth century in particular was a period of rapid institutional change provoked by the civil wars, including the demise of anti-enclosure legislation, revision of rents after royalist land sales, and the burst of conversions from copyhold into leasehold.[40] The century after the Restoration was a long agricultural depression, with price stagnation and falling rents. Market pressure

---

[36] Abraham Cowley, 'Of agriculture', *The works of Mr. Abraham Cowley vol. 2* (London, 1707), 706.
[37] John Evelyn, *Sylva, or a discourse of forest-trees* (2nd edn; London, 1670), 'To the reader'.
[38] Harte, *Essays*, 48, 62.
[39] Gentlemen, *Complete farmer*, 'Agriculture'.
[40] Ormrod, 'Agrarian capitalism', 209–13; Hoyle, 'Tenure', 17.

squeezed out small farmers and encouraged engrossment to form larger farms to benefit from economies of scale.[41] However, there is a lack of clarity about the effects on gentry farming.[42] On the one hand, it has been suggested that the gentry abandoned large-scale commercial farming, with an increase in landlord absenteeism (although this did not necessarily equate to neglect).[43] Gentry landowners were perhaps reluctant to engage in commercial farming, partly due to lack of experience.[44] On the other hand, it has been argued that falling prices encouraged landlords to seek innovative methods of husbandry, and that they were often forced to take direct control after tenants abandoned farms.[45] Elizabeth Griffiths offers a more nuanced account, based on Norfolk estates: that landowners energetically intervened in the farming of tenants from 1660s to 1680s, before withdrawing from active management from the 1690s.[46] The balance of evidence suggests that the new farming enthusiasm of some gentry from the late sixteenth century was dampened in the decades around the turn of the eighteenth century.[47] This was certainly so in contrast to the heightened agricultural enthusiasm in the later eighteenth century, with rising prices, increased farm profits and rents, and an acceleration of enclosure through acts of Parliament.[48] From the 1750s, there was a surge in the appetite for the potential gains from farming, and landowner investment shifted from adding acreage to improving land management.[49]

In the cultural sphere, a key intellectual influence from the 1620s was the experimental philosophy of Francis Bacon (d.1626).[50] Whereas classical agricultural literature bestowed honour on careful estate management, a greater stimulus to study and practise agriculture originated in the belief that experimental philosophy could unlock nature's hidden treasures. The spirit of 'improvement' combined Baconian philosophy

[41] French and Hoyle, *Character of English rural society*, 28–31.
[42] Hoyle, 'Introduction: Custom', 25.
[43] Mingay, *Gentry*, 83; James M. Rosenheim, *The emergence of a ruling order: English landed society 1650–1750* (London, 1998), 69–70.
[44] Margaret Davies, 'Country gentry and falling rents in the 1660s and 1670s', *Midland History*, 5 (1977).
[45] Heal and Holmes, *The gentry*, 117; Rosenheim, *Emergence of a ruling order*, 49, 63.
[46] Elizabeth Griffiths, 'Responses to adversity: The changing strategies of two Norfolk landowning families, c.1665–1700', in R. W. Hoyle (ed.), *People, landscape and alternative agriculture: Essays for Joan Thirsk* (Oxford, 2004).
[47] Rosenheim, *Emergence of a ruling order*, 67–68. See Mingay, *Gentry*, 84.
[48] Mingay, *Gentry*, 91–94.
[49] Clay, 'Landlords', 590.
[50] Webster, *Great Instauration*.

with Puritan eschatology in the belief that scientific innovation would create a new paradise on earth, by applying reason to increase the fertility of nature.[51] But the movement for agrarian improvement created a problem whose implications are rarely explored: who should implement such changes? The answer, in short, was learned men. This attitude was made clear in the publications of the circle around the reformer Samuel Hartlib in the 1640s and 1650s, especially the pamphlets of Gabriel Plattes.[52] This new spirit was directly linked to the publications of agricultural books in a review of 1675, whose author noted that it was 'but half an Age, or in fresh memory' since improvements had begun to 'bear credit'. After the civil wars, 'some were by necessity constrain'd to seek out all advantages they could hear of ... And thus, on a sudden, the humor and spirit of a People is alter'd. Books of Husbandry are sold off as fast as the Press can print them'.[53]

If we consider the interest of elites as expressed in national institutions, after the brief surge of activity led by the Royal Society from 1664, there was effectively no institutional support in England for over almost a century, until the formation of the Society for the Encouragement of Arts, Manufactures and Commerce in 1754. Similarly, the numbers of agricultural publications increased around the 1650s and 1660s, stagnated over the next half-century or so, before rising sharply in the 1740s and 1750s.[54] We can also trace the chronological pattern in terms of the shifting meanings of 'improvement'; from increased revenues through estate reforms in the sixteenth century, to extending cultivation in the early seventeenth century, to 'the intensification of farming practice by new techniques, new crops, and rotations' in the later seventeenth and eighteenth centuries.[55] It is in this latter phase of improvement that gentlemen actively aimed to appropriate the art of husbandry.

In the Scottish Lowlands, feudalism was in decline in the late seventeenth century, with a shift in concerns from military power to profitable estates, manifested in two Acts in 1695 facilitating land consolidation.

---

[51] Warde, 'Idea of improvement'; McRae, *God speed the plough*; Anthony Low, *The georgic revolution* (Princeton, 1985); Paul Slack, *The invention of improvement: Information and material progress in seventeenth-century England* (Oxford, 2015).

[52] Webster, *Great Instauration*, 471; Oana Matei, 'Husbanding creation and the technology of amelioration in the works of Gabriel Plattes', *Society and Politics*, 7 (2013), 88; Gabriel Plattes, *A discovery of infinite treasure, hidden since the worlds beginning* (London, 1639).

[53] A review of *Epitome of the art of husbandry* (1675). 'An accompt of some books', *Philosophical Transactions*, 10 (1675), 321.

[54] See Figures 0.1 and 0.2.

[55] Hoyle, 'Introduction: Custom', 2–3.

The 1708 Union with England stimulated greater exchange in ideas and agricultural products, followed shortly by the formation of the Society of Improvers in the Knowledge of Agriculture in Scotland in 1723.[56] The first half of the eighteenth century saw slow changes in tenant structures, but the key turning point was the Jacobite defeat in 1746 and the consequent loss of juridical powers, after which Scottish landowners became zealous improvers. A series of reforms rapidly commercialised Scottish farming, including the introduction of long leases, the transition to rents in cash, the abolition of communal land, and consolidation of farming units.[57] This new relationship to the land and nature was theorised by enlightened thinkers, many of whom were improving landowners themselves.[58] While in England agricultural reforms were driven by large capitalist farmers as much as landlords, the Scottish landowners were more heavily interventionist. But in the second half of the eighteenth century, agricultural reformers and landowners across England and Scotland broadly shared a vision of commercialised farming led by enlightened landlords.

The initial convergence of the cultural and economic incentives for gentlemen landowners to seek knowledge of agriculture was clear in John Worlidge's groundbreaking treatise *Systema Agriculturæ* (1669). Addressing the gentry and yeomanry, he called for landowners to seize the opportunity for a social transformation created by falling rents:

> in this opportune season, when ... so many of your Tenants exercised in onely the *Vulgar Methods of Agriculture*, are forced to withdraw their hands from the *Plough*, and revert to their *Tenements* into your own possessions, that you yourselves may cultivate that which is your own, and you that continue in your *Farms* may by your *Industry* manage them after the best and most advantageous Ways ...[59]

Here the financial motive to take over farm management was infused with the belief that the landowner could improve the 'vulgar' methods of his tenants. Worlidge seemingly perceived changes around him in Hampshire, however, as his revised 1675 address observed that the gentry were 'every day more and more addicted to this Noble, though heretofore neglected Science'.[60]

---

[56] Devine, *Transformation of rural Scotland*, 1–2.
[57] Davidson, 'Scottish path 2', 431.
[58] Schaffer, 'The earth's fertility', 139.
[59] Worlidge, *Systema*, 'Preface'.
[60] John Worlidge, *Systema agriculturæ* (London, 1675), 'Preface'.

Elevating the Art of Husbandry

The social thrust of eighteenth-century agricultural improvement was captured in Robert Dodsley's poem *Public Virtue* (1753). Dodsley – a bookseller whose publications included agricultural works – exhorted 'ye sons
of Wealth':

> Turn to the arts, the useful pleasing arts
> Of Cultivation; and those fields improve
> Your erring fathers have too long despis'd.
> Leave not to ignorance, and low-bred hinds,
> That noblest science, which in ancient time
> The minds of sages and of kings employ'd[61]

The encouragement for gentlemen to turn to the art of cultivation was
based on two distinct, but related, suppositions: that agriculture was a
noble science, and that current practitioners were too ignorant to practise
it properly. The first has received more attention than the second.[62] Yet
they were two aspects of a single vision of transferring control over cultivation from the lower to the upper levels of society. The elevation of the art
of husbandry to a science was simultaneously the elevation of gentlemen
over common husbandmen with respect to farm management. Books of
husbandry did not simply inspire gentlemen to turn their attention to
cultivation, but redefined cultivation as an art requiring education and
learning, by promoting the idea in form and content that husbandry was a
literary and intellectual activity.

The negative associations of agriculture were so deeply embedded that
a sustained intellectual effort was necessary to legitimise the agricultural
interests and activities of gentlemen. The classical writers provided the chief
resource. The poet Abraham Cowley set the tone with an influential essay
written around 1650, which argued that agriculture was an honourable
activity suitable for great men, helping to establish the virtues of husbandry
that would define the literature for the next 150 years.[63] Referencing to the
sacred name of Virgil, Cowley argued that this 'so pleasant, so virtuous, so
profitable, so honourable, so necessary art' was a kind of philosophy and

---

[61] R. Dodsley, *Public virtue: A poem* (London, 1753), 19. Dodsley published Lisle's *Observations in husbandry* (1757) before retiring in 1759. James E. Tierney, 'Dodsley, Robert (1704–1764)', *ODNB* (Oxford, 2004), https://doi.org/10.1093/ref:odnb/7755 (11 January 2018).

[62] Warde correctly points out that the 'reflex condemnation of custom and conservatism' does not provide an accurate picture of general practice, but does not probe the social motives behind this concerted campaign. Warde, *Invention of sustainability*, 57, see also 115 on Bradley.

[63] For example, Cowley is referenced in Switzer (1715), Ellis (1750), Harte (1764), Mills (1764), Peters (1770).

a suitable profession for young gentlemen.[64] Many subsequent manuals and treatises were prefaced with accounts of classical heroes – poets, philosophers, princes – who had studied or practised agriculture. For many writers, it was enough that 'books of Husbandry were composed by men whose exalted station proves the high value then set upon the Art which they taught'.[65] Others claimed that ancient writers 'disdain'd not to take a Part in it themselves'.[66]

Yet the key change from the mid-seventeenth century, inspired by Bacon, was the re-imagining of husbandry as a branch of natural philosophy, not simply an ancient and noble art. In 1651, a Hartlib publication argued that the husbandman must not only know his own grounds but also must know 'even all Subterrany things, and to be a petty Philosopher'.[67] This was a striking claim: it was no longer sufficient for the husbandman to know his own soil through daily experience.[68] In 1669, Worlidge included an extended panegyric to the noble 'science of agriculture', aimed at those 'who judge it below their Honour or Reputation'. In reference to the ancients, he claimed that 'Wise and Learned Men' not only studied agriculture but 'did also exercise themselves in Tilling the Earth'. But Worlidge went a step further and offered his book as a provisional guide, 'until our Philosophers and Heroes of Science and Art, handle the Plough and Spade, and undertake the more plenary discovery and description of these Rustick Operations', which 'require not onely an experienced hand, but a Judicious and Ingenious Pen'.[69]

Over the following decades, Worlidge's book was reprinted multiple times, but no new agricultural authors actively advanced these ideas further until the 1720s, perhaps a reflection of diminished gentry interest.[70]

[64] On the importance of Virgil: Frans De Bruyn, 'From Virgilian georgic to agricultural science: An instance in the transvaluation of literature in eighteenth-century Britain', in Albert J. Rivero (ed.), Augustan subjects: Essays in honor of Martin C. Battestin (67; London, 1997), 55–56.
[65] Mills, New system, i. iv.
[66] Richard Bradley, A survey of the ancient husbandry and gardening (London, 1725), 'Epistle'. Dickson described how the first Roman nobles cultivated land with own hands, whereas later great men maintained close study and attention while others performed operations. Adam Dickson, The husbandry of the ancients (Edinburgh, 1788), 41–43.
[67] Samuel Hartlib, Samuel Hartlib his legacie: Or an enlargement of the discourse of husbandry used in Brabant and Flaunders (London, 1651), 83.
[68] The emphasis on enriching the soil began with Markham. Warde, Invention of sustainability, Ch. 3.
[69] Worlidge, Systema, 'Preface'.
[70] Some books, such as Leonard Meager's The mystery of husbandry (1697), were more concerned with establishing the excellence, necessity and usefulness of the calling of husbandry through biblical references.

Richard Bradley, appointed professor of Botany at Cambridge in 1724, took up Worlidge's mantra. Bradley's vast literary output advocated that husbandry should be founded on philosophy, but its implications could be socially ambiguous. In 1721, Bradley argued that 'Husbandry and Gardening ought to fall under the Care of expert Philosophers and reasonable Men'.[71] Elsewhere in 1726 he stated that the farmer 'ought to be a Philosopher, to Study the Nature of every Soil'.[72] Hence the desire to reform husbandry as a branch of natural philosophy gave rise to a question: should farmers become philosophers, or instead submit to their guidance? This was evident in the publication of the Scottish physician Robert James, whose title *Rational Farmer and Practical Husbandman* (1743) hinted at a division between the learned and unlearned cultivator. James stated that his aim was 'to Explain to the industrious Husbandman' the reasons behind the use of manure and different methods of tillage.[73] Hence the redefinition of husbandry as a science opened the way for the learned man (e.g. a physician) to claim superior knowledge over the practical husbandman. From the 1750s, this was primarily through the introduction of the independent science of chemistry (see Chapter 4).[74]

In the 1770s, most writers agreed that agricultural science required an understanding superior to practical knowledge. As Matthew Peters put it, 'there is something more in husbandry than ploughing, sowing, and harrowing, 'tis an understanding of the science, without which man is but a grub in husbandry'.[75] A 1779 essay by the influential Scottish writer James Anderson on the advancement of agriculture offered an analogy with navigation. Although the young sailor 'wishes only to navigate his ship properly from one port to another', he must first

> study the nature of numbers and proportions, which seems to have no immediate relation to the object he has in view. In like manner the farmer, who wishes to obtain a competent knowledge of his art, must attend to some accessory circumstances that do not seem at first sight of indispensable necessity, but which, if not known, will for ever retard his progress.[76]

---

[71] Richard Bradley, *A general treatise of husbandry and gardening, for the month of April* (London, 1721–1722), 'Preface'.

[72] Richard Bradley, *The country gentleman and farmer's monthly director* (London, 1726), vii–lx.

[73] Robert James, *The rational farmer, and practical husbandman* (London, 1743), 1–2.

[74] Francis Home, *The principles of agriculture and vegetation* (Edinburgh, 1756).

[75] Matthew Peters, *Winter riches* (London, 1771), 166. Also see Alexander Hunter, *Georgical essays*, 4 vols (London, 1770–1772), i. 21.

[76] James Anderson, *An inquiry into the causes that have hitherto retarded the advancement of agriculture in Europe* (Edinburgh, 1779), 28.

In this perspective, the farmer cannot acquire the knowledge he needs through practical experience alone, but must gain theoretical knowledge with no immediate or obvious relation to growing crops or keeping livestock. However, this can resolve itself through a division of labour, in which the gentleman author instructs the husbandman on his business. In this manner, Cuthbert Clarke, a lecturer on natural history, declared the intention of his agricultural book of 1779:

> by resolving the hitherto random Art of Husbandry into a SCIENCE; and, I hope, with propriety and clearness; pointing out to the husbandman, what, at all times, is best to be done in the course of his business.[77]

The intellectual shift that subsumed the practical art of husbandry within the science of agriculture was effectively complete by 1800 (at least within printed literature). A marker of this shift was the subtle change in definition in the dictionary entry for 'agriculture' in *The Complete Farmer*. The original definition in the first four editions from 1766 to 1793 was 'the art of tilling, manuring, and cultivating the earth', which was revised in 1807 as 'the science which explains the art or means of cultivating and improving the earth'.[78] The same shift was noted by the anonymous poet of 1808 quoted earlier:

> *Agriculture*, which has commonly been reputed an *Art*, is now promoted to the dignity of a *Science* … The *professors* and *students* of this *science* are all supposed to be intimately acquainted with the systematic language, not only of their own, but of other connected sciences; especially of Natural History and Natural Philosophy.[79]

The Denigration of Common Husbandmen

The belief that agriculture was a noble science fit for gentlemen was accompanied by the claim that current practitioners were unfit to cultivate the land. Whilst it is well established that agricultural writers argued for 'improved' methods to replace customary husbandry practice, the extent to which this implied that 'improvers' should replace common husbandmen in the management of cultivation has received far less attention. From the mid-seventeenth century, agricultural writers began to casually deride or forcefully attack the capability of uneducated husbandmen. This

---

[77] Clarke, *True theory*, 'Dedication'.
[78] Gentlemen, *Complete farmer*; Society of Gentlemen, *The complete farmer* (5th edn; London, 1807).
[79] *Pursuits of agriculture*, 65.

went beyond the general moral rebukes directed at 'dishonest' husband-men, servants and labourers, or the attacks on the inhabitants of wastes as idle and uncivilised, to the specific accusation that husbandmen were ignorant of how best to grow food and keep livestock. Agricultural writ-ers argued that to establish a rational and experimental husbandry, it was necessary for educated gentlemen to exercise varying levels of oversight over practitioners.[80]

An early extended critique was put forward in 1639 when an obscure projector Gabriel Plattes diagnosed 'the deficiencie of the Husbandmens knowledge' and common practice as the cause of 'barrennesse', 'pover-tie and beggarie'.[81] In another pamphlet, he argued that wealth was lost in England because husbandmen did not possess 'the compleat Art of Agriculture'.[82] Similarly, in 1649, Walter Blith criticised the 'very practitio-ners' of husbandry for their prejudice in 'depraving every new Invention'.[83] In response to new improvements, the common husbandman would reply (according to Blith): 'who taught you more wit than your forefathers, would they have neglected so great advantage if there had been any?' The model of learning by labouring alongside and imitating an older practi-tioner was no longer viable for the improvers.[84] In his 1664 treatise on forestry, John Evelyn wrote of 'ignorant Hinds and Servants, who are… more fit to Learn then to Instruct'.[85]

The authors of agricultural books in the decades around the turn of the eighteenth century were less concerned with advocating social reform, but these early criticisms were revived and elaborated in the 1720s and rose to a crescendo in the 1770s and 1780s. All offered variations on the same theme: common husbandmen blindly followed their fathers, did not understand the reasons behind their methods, did not read to expand their knowledge, and did not know how to proceed on a scientific basis. Many of these criti-cisms were summed up by the charge that husbandmen were illiterate, in the broad meaning that divided classically educated readers of Latin from rustic laymen.[86]

[80] There are strong parallels with contemporary trends regarding 'popular errors', especially in medi-cine, as physician-authors attacked folk medicine and attempted to enforce a hierarchy of knowledge whereby physicians would oversee midwives and surgeons. Fissell and Cooter, 'Natural knowledge', 148–49; Eamon, *Science and the secrets of nature*, 261.
[81] Plattes, *Discovery*, 47.
[82] Gabriel Plattes, *The profitable intelligencer* (London, 1644).
[83] Walter Blith, *The English improver* (London, 1649), 'To the Husbandman, Farmer, or Tenant'.
[84] See further criticisms of English husbandry as 'deficient' in Hartlib, *Legacie*, 6, 89.
[85] John Evelyn, *Sylva, or a discourse of forest-trees* (London, 1664), 'To the Reader'.
[86] Fox, 'Words', 131; Eamon, *Science and the secrets of nature*, 93.

Bradley criticised English husbandmen in 1721 for not being able to 'give any other Reason for what they do, than that their Fathers did the same before them'.[87] The critique of husbandmen was paired with an encouragement for the gentry in John Laurence's 1726 treatise: he moaned that 'the Culture of the Earth is now fallen to the Lot of Men, whom we esteem servile and born to Labour', and wished 'that Men of Thought and Leisure would apply their Study and Care to improve their Estates' and to 'perfect the Knowledge of Agriculture'.[88] In 1732, the Scottish diplomat and army officer Sir John Dalrymple wrote that husbandry had been, until recently, 'intirely managed in *Scotland* by the Vulgar, who, like Moles, blindly run on in the Tract their Fathers had made before them'.[89] Later in 1756, the physician Francis Home introduced his treatise on agricultural chemistry with a summary of its present deficiency:

> This art is, in general, carried on by those whose minds have never been improved by science, taught to make observations, or draw conclusions, in order to attain the truth … [who] can never know more than what they have learned from their fathers … What can be expected from that class?[90]

The lower orders not only lacked knowledge but also were incapable of attaining any. In 1757, Robert Maxwell expressed his frustration that 'few Farmers can be brought by reasoning only, to forsake Customs which are highly unreasonable and destructive'.[91] A book reviewer in the same year observed that husbandry had been 'left wholly to the unlettered farmer, who plods on in the track of his forefathers, without knowledge and reflexion to strike out new improvements'.[92] In 1775, W. Donaldson commented that in ancient Rome agriculture was 'thought too momentous to be referred to the arbitration of common husbandmen', who passively 'acquire accidental knowledge, which they cannot explain, nor do they understand'.[93] Attacking both this labour-based system of learning and specifically the authority of women, Josiah Twamley diagnosed that the problem in the art of dairying was that it was 'taught by Mother to

---

[87] Bradley, *General treatise*, 'Preface'.
[88] Laurence, *New system*.
[89] Sir John Dalrymple, *An essay on the husbandry of Scotland* (Edinburgh, 1732), 5.
[90] Home, *Principles*, 2–3. Point repeated in Matthew Peters, *The rational farmer: Or a treatise on agriculture and tillage* (2nd edn; London, 1771), 6.
[91] Robert Maxwell, *The practical husbandman: Being a collection of miscellaneous papers on husbandry* (Edinburgh, 1757), vii.
[92] 'Art. I. Observations in husbandry', *Critical Review*, 3 (1757), 1.
[93] William Donaldson, *Agriculture considered as a moral and political duty* (London, 1775), 33. Same point in Cuthbert Clarke, *The true theory and practice of husbandry* (London, 1781), 'Preface'.

Daughter' from experience, 'without ever calling in the assistance of either Philosophy' or the knowledge of its application.[94]

These attacks were projected back into history. In 1773, *Scots Farmer* suggested Scottish agriculture had fallen into a 'languishing state' between the Reformation and the Union, when it was left 'in the hands of the meanest country people', without leadership.[95] William Marshall also complained in 1778 of 'the slow progress which Agricultural Knowledge has heretofore made under the patronage of the illiterate', and announced that 'the Pen seems not less necessary to FARMING than to PHYSIC, PHILOSOPHY, or any other abstruse ART or SCIENCE'.[96] An extended critique of 'the prejudices and untractableness of illiterate Farmers and their servants' was put forward by the Rev. William Lamport, a member of the Bath Agricultural Society, in 1780.[97] He argued that '[h]usbandry can rise no higher than the knowledge of those who are engaged in it will permit'.[98] In a brief narrative, he claimed that before the Reformation no improvement in agriculture had been possible, as landowners had left cultivation in the hands of 'meaner vassals', and 'the mind of the peasant was not enlightened by the rays of science'.[99] In the seventeenth century, however, the disadvantages of 'the management of common farmers' had been gradually overcome with the aid of philosophers such as Bacon.[100] Lamport specified 'illiterate peasants' as the main obstacle to progress, as they were incapable of theoretical reflections or 'making any experiments on scientific principles'.[101] Yet books alone were not equipped for this task: '[t]he ideas of illiterate farmers will not be much rectified by many of our publications on husbandry, which some cannot, and the generality are too opinioned to read'.[102] Indeed, Lamport described common farmers as existing within an entirely separate and closed community of knowledge, as they 'communicate their ideas to each other in their own way' and were unable to learn anything from each other but their shared local customs. They 'are a

---

[94] Josiah Twamley, *Dairying exemplified, or the business of cheese-making* (Warwick, 1784), 16.

[95] *Northern farmer*, 3, 8.

[96] Marshall, *Minutes*, 'The Digest', 121. Same critique in Anthony Fothergill, 'On the application of chemistry to agriculture, and rural oeconomy', *Letters and papers on agriculture, planting, &c. selected from the correspondence-book of the Society instituted at Bath*, 3 (1786), 59.

[97] William Lamport, 'A proposal for the further improvement of agriculture', *Letters and papers on agriculture, planting, &c. selected from the correspondence-book of the Society instituted at Bath*, 1 (1780), Appendix, 7.

[98] Ibid., 12–13.

[99] Ibid., 15.

[100] Ibid., 16, 19.

[101] Ibid., 21–22.

[102] Ibid., 26–27.

class of people *sui generis*, and stand at a distance, as it were, from a man of learning'.[103] Common husbandmen must, therefore, be sufficiently educated to be rendered 'teachable' by gentlemen of landed property, and clergymen such as him.[104] Lamport thus exemplified the common belief among agricultural writers that cultivation had to be taken out of the hands of ignorant and illiterate husbandmen, and placed under the care and supervision of men of education, equipped with a body of theoretical literature.

The project of appropriation was distilled in an eccentric book published in 1755 by an anonymous 'Country Gentleman', called *A New System of Agriculture: Or a Plain, Easy, and Demonstrative Method of Speedily Growing Rich*. The first half (roughly 80 pages from 180 total) was essentially an anthology of previous English agricultural literature. It included a total of fifty-two separate quotes, by twenty-one named authors, from books published between 1577 and 1707. In fact, all indications suggest this section was originally compiled before 1720, since there are no quotations from the major agricultural writers in the 1720s, 30s or 40s. The selected quotes themselves were all statements that were designed to convince landed gentlemen that agriculture was noble and profitable, and they should be far more active estate managers. The author outperformed his peers in sheer hyperbole: agriculture was

> not only the most *gainful* Employment, but the most *noble, just*, and *honourable*; --- an Employment, which the wisest Writers of Antiquity, *Priests, Poets, Princes* and *Philosophers*, have celebrated, and preferred before All other; and the greatest Emperors, and mightiest *Heroes* of the Universe, not only delighted in, but practiced with their own Hands.[105]

The excessive praise of agriculture's nobility was mirrored by the hostile condemnation of common cultivators: 'Tis a very great Misfortune to England, that the Cultivation of her Lands is in the meanest of her People; Men, whose Obscurity of Birth, and Narrowness of Education, do not only render them unable to make Improvements but unwilling to hear of them'.[106] Indeed, the author had collated the most extreme expressions of class prejudice against common husbandmen from texts printed over two centuries. This was not a simple farming manual, it was a *manifesto* for the extension of gentry control over cultivation in England.

---

[103] Ibid., 28–29.
[104] Ibid., 49.
[105] Gentleman, *New system*, 5.
[106] Ibid., 2–3. Similar sentiment in Malachy Postlethwayt, *The universal dictionary of trade and commerce, translated from the French* (London, 1757), 963.

The author gave the clearest expression of the dual role of agricultural literature in this project to establish the supremacy of the landowning class. First, in the sheer cultural gravitas of its literary tradition. The compilation of quotes is an explicit strategy of persuasion, the 'Proofs' that agriculture is reputable and profitable: 'I will bring a Croud of witnesses, whose Depositions you shall hear'.[107] A literary tradition extolling the virtues of agriculture was itself a potent method of dignifying farming. Second, by conveniently packaging sufficient knowledge to aid gentlemen in the practice of farm management. Hence the author provided a reading list of twenty-three publications on agriculture for his fellow country gentlemen that would 'give the utmost Knowledge requisite'.[108] This work made it abundantly clear that agricultural books were being deployed in the service of wider social reform.

While *A New System* was an extreme example, the same social project was spelt out by the leading voice of agricultural improvement, Arthur Young: it was the duty of the nobility and gentry to practise agricultural improvements and spread knowledge; to fail would be 'to reduce themselves to the level of those whom they ought to instruct' and 'to submit to that ignorance and backwardness' of previous centuries. 'Common farmers love to grope in the dark: it is the business of superior minds … [to] shine forth to dissipate the night that involves them'.[109]

Mechanisms of Appropriation

While educated gentlemen were critical of the customary knowledge of husbandmen and housewives, they were aware that – as a group – they were themselves mostly ignorant of the art of husbandry, with little practical experience. Gentlemen faced a fundamental problem: the traditional way of learning the art of husbandry was through labour, but gentility was based on the avoidance of manual labour. Hence a suitable way to acquire knowledge was to observe practitioners at a civil distance, collect notes into a systematic order, and perhaps publish for other gentlemen. Indeed, Thirsk described the growth of agriculture literature after 1649 as a period 'when parsons and landed gentry with enquiring minds gathered practical information and wrote it up faithfully and clearly'.[110] She

---

[107] Gentleman, *New system*, 7. See also the concluding statement on p. 79.
[108] Ibid., 80–81.
[109] Young, *Rural oeconomy*, 20–21.
[110] Thirsk, 'Agricultural innovations', 546.

praised a number of authors for diligently collecting knowledge, such as the surveyor of crown lands Walter Blith in the 1640s and 1650s, and the clergyman landowner Edward Lisle in the 1690s, who illustrated 'the painstaking gathering of experience from a multitude of sources'.[111] Similarly, the sixteenth-century French author Charles Estienne, whose works were translated into English, has been praised for his 'ethnographic' methods of interviewing peasants in the field.[112] However, in such accounts, the social significance of these processes is neglected, which constituted an active redistribution of knowledge up the social scale and its reformulation for the benefit of the learned elite.

An intellectual rationale for the codification of all mechanical arts and crafts was put forward in the early seventeenth century in Francis Bacon's scheme for a natural 'history of trades', to establish the experiential knowledge of mechanical arts as the new basis for natural history.[113] The plan was to collect into writing the mysteries and secrets of every art and craft.[114] Experience, Bacon wrote, must be made to 'learn her letters'.[115] Given the social separation between craftsman and philosopher, this was an explicit project to appropriate knowledge. Although the empirical knowledge of artisans and practitioners was vital, the new experimental science was to be led by superior minds. Hence the 'history of trades' programme has been identified as a crucial episode in the long-term 'transfer of manufacturing knowledge from the craftsmen to management' in the development of industrial society.[116] It was advanced by the various encyclopaedic projects of the eighteenth century that aimed 'to translate a more or less illiterate "world of work" into printed words'.[117]

Husbandry was one of many manual arts that had to be written down and illuminated by science, prompting natural philosophers and amateurs to study the arts of practising husbandmen and housewives, servants and labourers.[118] For example, in 1651, a correspondent of Samuel Hartlib

---

[111] Ibid., 573. On Walter Blith, see Thirsk, 'Plough and pen'.

[112] Beutler, 'La littérature agricole en Europe', 1287.

[113] Kathleen H. Ochs, 'The Royal Society of London's history of trades programme: An early episode in applied science', *Notes and Records*, 39 (1985); Houghton, 'History of trades'.

[114] Bacon listed a 'History of Agriculture, Pasturage, Culture of Woods, &c' at no.115 of his catalogue of histories to be completed. James Spedding et al. (eds), *The works of Francis Bacon* (Boston, 1861–1879), viii, 357–62.

[115] Eamon, *Science and the secrets of nature*, 9.

[116] Ochs, 'Royal Society of London's history of trades', 150.

[117] Koepp, 'Alphabetical Order', 233; Richard Yeo, *Encyclopaedic visions: Scientific dictionaries and enlightenment culture* (Cambridge, 2001), 151.

[118] Yeo, *Encyclopaedic visions*, 154.

described how he learned the art of making woad through observing people in the country: 'the time when they sowe it, when first they weed it, and cut it. I saw the manner of their gathering it, grinding, balling, drying it, and after sweating and curing it'.[119] The Royal Society took up the history of trades project in the 1660s, by collecting information on all manner of trades from masonry to glass making.[120] For example, a manuscript report to the Society detailed the precise process of cheese-making based on the observations of experienced dairywomen in Cheshire who had mastered the process through practice.[121] Similarly, a recent study of the 'history of fish' emphasises the reliance on fishermen's first-hand experience to the creation of written natural knowledge.[122] Agriculture as a whole was catered for by the 'Georgicall Committee', founded on 30 March 1664, which resolved to 'compose as perfect a History of Agriculture and Gardening as might be' by collecting all the best books on the subject and creating a survey to gather information from farmers around the country.[123] The survey was ultimately a failure, partly due to the lack of responses. But the objective was clear: the new science of agriculture was to be built upon an initial accumulation of existing knowledge from those experienced in the art of husbandry.

Informally, outside institutions, there is plenty of evidence that written agricultural knowledge was obtained from practitioners by writers with minimal direct experience themselves. Any sharp separation between practitioners and gentlemen breaks down under scrutiny into a more variegated spectrum, but part of the knowledge contained in agricultural books was initially held by practising husbandmen and housewives who never wrote or read anything themselves. Many agricultural writers described their mode of acquiring knowledge through a mix of reading, observation, conversation, and occasional experiment. John Mortimer was a merchant who retired to an estate in 1696 and published *The Whole Art of Husbandry* in 1707. Mortimer stated that the book was largely a collection

[119] Hartlib, *Legacie*, 109.
[120] Houghton, 'History of trades'; Rob Iliffe, 'Capitalizing expertise: Philosophical and artisanal expertise in early modern London', in Christelle Rabier (ed.), *Fields of expertise: A comparative history of expert procedures in Paris and London, 1600 to present* (Newcastle, 2007), 70.
[121] Paolo Savoia, 'Cheesemaking in the scientific revolution: A seventeenth-century Royal Society report on dairy products and the history of European knowledge', *Nuncius*, 34 (2019), 448. Includes a transcription of 'On the making of cheese, etc.' by William Jackson, 449–55.
[122] van Trijp, 'Fresh fish', 21.
[123] Reginald Lennard, 'English agriculture under Charles II: The evidence of the Royal Society's "Enquiries"', *EcHR*, 4 (1932), 23–24; Royal Society, 'Enquiries concerning agriculture', *Philosophical Transactions*, 1 (1665), 91–92.

of existing ancient and modern writings, but added that 'I have also observed the Practice and Experiments of several diligent Husbandmen in most Countries, and have not only improved them, but added many useful Experiments of my own'.[124] Similarly, Giles Jacob, a legal writer, explained that his book *The Country Gentleman's Vade Mecum* (1717) was the result of copious reading and an examination of 'the real Management in the Country, and the Opinions of experienc'd Country Gentlemen, and Observations of the most eminent Husbandmen and Gardiners'.[125] Adam Dickson, a Scottish clergyman and author of an agricultural treatise published in 1762, spent time in his youth with farmers who were 'not unfit to converse with men of letters' and 'from them, as well as from his own observations, acquired the exact knowledge of facts, and of the practice of husbandry'.[126] In 1770, Arthur Young even advised his readers (who he presumed to be inexperienced in husbandry) on how to extract knowledge from more experienced farmers. Not only should the reader 'make enquiries after different methods of farming' through conversation with labourers and farmers,

> [b]ut a greater source than all this is observation: let him look over his hedges, and see what his neighbours do with their land: let him walk about the country for the same purpose, and compare the practice which he *sees* with the opinions which he *hears*.[127]

More systematic efforts developed towards the end of the eighteenth century. The four primary examples were the tours of Arthur Young, the regional reports of William Marshall, the Scottish estate reports of Andrew Wight, and the county reports of the Board of Agriculture. Between 1768 and 1771, Young published three tours of England reporting on farming practice around the kingdom, 'especially the local practice of common farmers'.[128] However, these grew organically, and Young's observations were shaped by his contacts and manner of touring. In 1780, Marshall proposed a more methodical plan for collecting agricultural knowledge to the Society of Arts in London, in which a reporter should reside in an area for twelve months and 'minutely observe and register the living practice which surrounds him'. The crucial underlying assumption of Marshall's plan was

[124] John Mortimer, *The whole art of husbandry* (London, 1707), 'To the Royal Society'.
[125] Giles Jacob, *The country gentleman's vade mecum* (London, 1717), 'Preface'.
[126] Posthumous note by editor in Dickson, *Of the ancients*, ix. Also Adam Dickson, *Treatise of agriculture* (Edinburgh, 1762), iii.
[127] Young, *Rural oeconomy*, 101.
[128] Quoted from Betham-Edwards (ed.), *Autobiography*, 31.

that common farmers 'could not probably communicate their knowledge, with any degree of precision: for their art being the result of habit, it is too familiar to be minutely described'. From the perspective of educated men, the art of husbandry was trapped in mute labouring bodies.[129] Hence a professional observer was needed: 'the art of agriculture must ever remain imperfect while it is suffered to languish in the memory, and die with the practitioner: RECORD, only, can perpetuate the art'.[130] The need for learned society to appropriate the mystery of husbandry was driven partly by a fear that customary knowledge could be lost, and partly by a belief that it could not progress until it had been stored and systematised in texts.

Andrew Wight, a farmer at Ormiston, conducted surveys of Scottish estates between 1773 and 1784 on behalf of the Commissioners for the Annexed Estates and published reports in 1778 and 1784. In the preface, the Commissioners explained the full political vision behind the surveys: their first motive was 'to civilise the people of those estates', and their second motive was 'to lead on gradually the tenants to improve their husbandry': hence a survey of each farm was necessary. The purpose of the book was 'collecting the experience of all into one view'.[131] The merits of systematic surveys into husbandry was gaining advocates around this time. In 1785, the physician Anthony Fothergill called for an 'inquiry' to 'supply many curious and useful facts' only known to practitioners, which could be used to elucidate the underlying principles of which 'even the artists themselves are generally observed to be grossly ignorant'.[132]

When the Board of Agriculture was established in 1793, therefore, it was only extending such exercises when it began the first national survey of British agriculture, eventually producing 193 volumes covering the counties of England, Scotland and Wales.[133] Hence the formation of the Board can be seen as a culmination of the effort to collect a written record of the customary art of husbandry, representing the first centralised body for managing agricultural knowledge in Britain. It was clear to some commentators that the Board was an engine for the appropriation of the art of husbandry. A satirical letter in the Whig-supporting *Morning Chronicle* on 1 August 1794, purportedly from 'A Gentleman Farmer', offered mock-praise to the Board for preserving the social hierarchy and the proper

[129] William Marshall, *Rural economy of Norfolk*, 2 vols (London, 1787), i. vi–ix.
[130] Ibid., i. vii.
[131] Andrew Wight, *Present state of husbandry in Scotland*, 2 vols (Edinburgh, 1778), i. vi, ix.
[132] Fothergill, 'Application of chemistry to agriculture', 64.
[133] There were 90 original surveys printed from 1793 to 1797: Holmes, 'County agricultural surveys: Part 1'.

'claims of Aristocracy' by ensuring that it only communicated its information to gentlemen: 'so that the art of husbandry is not to be preposterously
communicated without distinction to husbandmen'. Pointedly noting the
long tradition of linking dangerous levelling ideas to agrarian reform, the
author urged everyone 'to take care that farming shall now be a liberal profession, and that it shall not be debased by coming into the hands of the
vulgar'.[134] The short article, therefore, mimicked the language of advocates
of the Board, emphasising the apparent paradox of the attempt to take
farming out of the hands of farmers.

The first professor of agriculture, Dr Andrew Coventry (employed at
Edinburgh University from 1790), articulated the ideological underpin-
nings of these activities. He ended his course of lectures, published in
1808, by noting that a 'great deal of information may be likewise gained
by conversing with husbandmen', as although the 'practical husbandmen may not deliver their observations with the method of a professed
writer, yet they possess what the other sometimes wants, the subject'.[135]
His aim for his students was to distil agricultural knowledge for them,
including

> to collect and fix that prime stock of practical knowledge which is current
> among husbandmen — that legendary lore which has descended through
> generations; and thus to unite the facts which are detached, and embody
> as it were under a useful form the experience of mankind in the profession
> of husbandry.[136]

It is remarkable that the first professional agricultural theorist at the
beginning of the nineteenth century understood part of his mission as
fixing and systematising the mystery of husbandry held by common
husbandmen.

Agricultural books had multiple sources of knowledge. It is true that
most authors possessed at least some first-hand knowledge or familiarity
and many others conducted their own experiments. Nonetheless, authors
repeatedly indicated that their knowledge was in part appropriated from
practising husbandmen. Gentlemen used their social power to learn what
husbandmen were doing, before collecting it together and shaping it into
the form of a new science, which was then held up as a justification for
directing the activities of those same husbandmen.

---

[134] 'Board of Agriculture', *Morning Chronicle*, 1 August 1794.
[135] Andrew Coventry, *Discourses explanatory of the object and plan of the course of lectures on agriculture and rural economy* (Edinburgh, 1808), 187.
[136] Ibid., 188.

Masculinisation of Knowledge

The appropriation of knowledge also had a gendered dimension. The elevation of the art of husbandry was also a process of masculinisation, accompanying the increasing exclusion and marginalisation of women in farming. By transforming husbandry into agricultural science and abstracting the customary art from its household context, authors largely erased the role of women within agricultural production.[137] Women composed a significant part of the agricultural workforce as housewives and servants in the sixteenth and seventeenth centuries, performing around a third of all agricultural work.[138]

The two major sixteenth-century English books on husbandry by John Fitzherbert and Thomas Tusser tended to retain the household context, presenting advice for the duties of the husbandman and housewife working in (unequal) partnership, as 'good husbandry / maintaineth good household / with huswifery'.[139] However, the twin arts of husbandry and huswifery became increasingly separated in advice literature, beginning with the publications of Gervase Markham's *The English Husbandman* (1613) and *The English Huswife* (1615). Notably, a late-seventeenth-century plagiarisation of Fitzherbert removed references to the housewife and huswifery.[140] Aspects of earlier huswifery books, such as medicine and cookery, were being published in specialist manuals by the late seventeenth century.[141]

In the eighteenth century, major agricultural writers such as Richard Bradley and William Ellis published separate manuals for the country housewife.[142] However, these books obscured how elements of huswifery were being absorbed under the male discipline of agriculture. While husbandry and huswifery were often distinguished as work outside and inside

---

[137] On the agricultural work performed by women, see Verdon, 'Farmers' wives', 27; Richard W. Hoyle, 'Introduction: Recovering the farmer', in Richard W. Hoyle (ed.), *The farmer in England, 1650–1980* (Farnham, 2013), 16–17; Whittle, 'Housewives and servants'; Briony McDonagh, *Elite women and the agricultural landscape, 1700–1830* (London, 2018).

[138] Whittle and Hailwood, 'Gender division of labour'.

[139] Quote from opening verse in Thomas Tusser, *Five hundreth good pointes of husbandry, united to as many of good huswifery* (London, 1573).

[140] Joseph Blagrave, *The epitome of the art of husbandry* (London, 1669).

[141] For example, Hannah Woolley, *The cook's guide: Or, rare receipts for cookery* (London, 1664); Hannah Woolley, *The compleat servant-maid; or, the young maidens tutor* (London, 1677). This was an unauthorised revision of early work by Woolley, which included six pages of advice for the dairy-maid, pp. 157–163.

[142] Richard Bradley, *The country housewife and lady's director* (3rd edn; London, 1728); William Ellis, *The country housewife's family companion* (London, 1750).

the house, these boundaries were blurred in both prescription and practice, as many activities of the housewife overlapped with the art of husbandry.[143] Indeed, even 'indoor' activities such as cooking required knowledge and skills exercised 'outdoors', for example in the cultivation of herbs.[144] By the eighteenth century, some of these activities were already become separated from the role of women, such as brewing.[145] Similarly, women's gardening work was increasingly relegated as a decorative activity, in contrast to the profit-oriented gardening of men.[146] In systematic agricultural treatises, sections on activities traditionally performed by women – brewing ale or making wine, managing poultry, preserving fruits, managing bees, planting herbs and even dairying – were mostly presented as abstract labours or as a responsibility of the husbandman, rather than under a section for a housewife. For example, Thomas Hale's collated papers published in 1756 treated dairying as one of many duties of the husbandman, only mentioning the housewife incidentally.[147] Hence whereas sixteenth-century books tended to divide advice between husbandry and huswifery, eighteenth-century books increasingly subsumed most of these labours under agriculture.[148] Indeed, in a discussion of the discourse of 'oeconomy', Karen Harvey argues that household management became a hierarchical rather than a spatial division of labour, with women managing day-to-day tasks and men in charge of overall management.[149]

The transfer of knowledge from women practitioners to male authors was often done quietly. For example, Edward Lisle's book includes hints that he learned from talking with and observing neighbouring housewives and dairymaids as well as farmers (e.g. 'a very good dairy-woman in Leicestershire assured me').[150] However, the authority of a man writing about activities known to be widely performed by women usually required some justification. Since a man could not claim to have direct

---

[143] Amanda J. Flather, 'Space, place, and gender: The sexual and spatial division of labor in the early modern household', *History and Theory*, 52 (2013); Pamela Sharpe, *Adapting to capitalism: Working women in the English economy, 1700–1850* (London, 1996), ch. 4.

[144] Karen Harvey, *The little republic: Masculinity and domestic authority in eighteenth-century Britain* (Oxford, 2012), 29.

[145] Whittle, 'Housewives and servants'.

[146] Jennifer Munroe, 'Gender, class, and the art of gardening: Gardening manuals in early modern England', *Prose Studies*, 28 (2006); Rebecca Bushnell, 'The gardener and the book', in Natasha Glaisyer and Sara Pennell (eds), *Didactic literature in England, 1500–1800: Expertise constructed* (Aldershot, 2003), 111, 130.

[147] Thomas Hale, *A compleat body of husbandry* (London, 1756), 551.

[148] On the 'gendered nature of agricultural knowledge', see McDonagh, *Elite women*, 135.

[149] Harvey, *The little republic*, 33.

[150] Edward Lisle, *Observations in husbandry*, 2 vols (London, 1757), i. 354.

experience of the art of huswifery, they were relatively open about taking (at least some of) their knowledge from women. Fitzherbert acknowledged that due to a lack of personal experience he could only offer basic guidance on the work of huswifery, and was not able to provide details on 'howe they shulde do and execute their labour and ocupacyons'.[151] In the short pamphlet *A Dairie Booke for Good Huswiues* (1588), the author Bartholomew Dowe was at pains to emphasise that he did not have direct knowledge of dairying, as he had never made any butter or cheese, but was merely passing on to the housewives of south Hampshire what he had observed as a boy in Suffolk. Within the dialogue, the man assumes his pedagogic role apologetically, explaining to the woman that he did not pretend 'to teache you or others, how ye should make whitmeate, for it were unseemely that a Man that never made anie, (but hath seene and behelde others in dooing thereof) should take upon him to teache women that hath most knowledge and experience in that arte'.[152] The male author presents himself a mere conduit between women. In Markham's book for the housewife, the bookseller felt the need to add an explanatory note at the beginning, pre-empting the sceptical reader who may ask 'what hath this man to doe with Hus-wifery, he is now out of his element', by stressing that the printed book merely arranged 'an approved Manuscript' by a lady of singular rank.[153]

Similar apologies remained in the following century. In 1727, Bradley defended himself for writing on a topic that 'falls within the Ladies Jurisdiction' and explained his aim was to 'assist' rather than 'instruct'. He identified his role as an 'Amanuensis', mostly presenting instructions 'as are practised by some of the most ingenious Ladies, who had Good-nature enough to admit of a Transcription of them for publick Benefit'.[154] Likewise, in 1750, Ellis stressed that he was sharing the best practice of the wives of country gentlemen, yeomen and farmers, among whom he had lived and travelled.[155] The anonymous compilers of the *The Farmer's Wife* (1780) explained that the receipts for making wines were 'communicated by a country lady, who is distinguished for her skill in this kind

[151] Fitzherbert, *Boke of husbandry*, fo. xlviii
[152] A 'dairie booke for all good huswiues' annexed to Torquato Tasso, *The housholders philosophie wherein is perfectly and profitably described, the true oeconomia and forme of housekeeping* (London, 1588), [unnumbered].
[153] When a female authorship was not declared, a dedication to a female aristocrat may have functioned to add credibility. Hunter, 'Books for daily life', 515–19
[154] Bradley, *Country housewife*, viii–ix.
[155] Ellis, *Country housewife's family companion*.

of housewifery'. Later, John Lawrence confessed in his *New Farmer's Calendar* (1800) that his knowledge of dairying was borrowed from his wife.[156]

As already mentioned, the specific processes of appropriation of dairying from women to men have been detailed by Valenze, in which she highlights the role of male cheese factors who were able to exploit their position as a mediator within the trade to 'systematically' obtain information from skilled dairywomen. Factors-turned-authors such as Josiah Twamley were then able to communicate this to the wider world of men.[157] The title page of Twamley's 1784 book on dairying was transparent in declaring that its substance was 'collected from the most experienced Dairy-Women, of several Countries', even while the author attempted to supplant their authority.[158] When knowledge crossed the most visible customary gender lines, therefore, the act of appropriation required some acknowledgement. But on the whole, since significant areas of farm work had only moderate gender orientation, women's role as sources of codified agricultural knowledge were more likely to be erased or obscured.

Yet this dimension of appropriation was complex. Elite women in management roles were also readers of agricultural treatises, and therefore recipients of such knowledge.[159] The household accounts (1610–1654) of Lady Alice Le Strange shows she joined her husband, Sir Hamon, in actively managing their Norfolk estate and home farm, and most likely took advice from the books on husbandry in their library.[160] Mrs Elizabeth Prowse (1764–1810), a widow who managed a 2,200-acre estate in Northamptonshire for more than forty years and was closely involved in implementing improvements on the home farm, bought the latest publications by Nathaniel Kent and Arthur Young.[161] Further, while no women authored agricultural books, the *Annals of Agriculture* did include a handful of articles and letters from female landowners, such as Elizabeth Ilive on potatoes.[162] Hence the intersection of gender and class channelled knowledge in multiple ways.

---

[156] Quoted in Valenze, 'Art of women', 156.
[157] Ibid., 161, 155.
[158] Twamley, *Dairying exemplified*.
[159] See McDonagh, *Elite women*, esp. 47–51.
[160] See also Jane Whittle and Elizabeth Griffiths, *Consumption and gender in the early seventeenth-century household: The world of Alice Le Strange* (Oxford, 2012), 39–42.
[161] Briony McDonagh, '"All towards the improvements of the estate": Mrs Elizabeth Prowse at Wicken (Northamptonshire), 1764–1810', in Richard W. Hoyle (ed.), *Custom, improvement and the landscape in early modern Britain* (Farnham, 2011), 287.
[162] McDonagh, *Elite women*, 145.

Resistance to Appropriation

The actions of genteel authors observing, collecting and systematising the methods of practising husbandmen have been previously narrated as if eighteenth-century society was an idealised scientific community of equals engaged in a shared enterprise of knowledge exchange. But it is a mistake to imagine that knowledge could circulate between different levels of rural society without friction, somehow free from the relations of power that shaped everything else. The social tensions created by these acts of appropriation can be seen in the occasional indication from writers themselves about the resistance they encountered from common husbandmen, servants and labourers.

In 1733, William Ellis warned gentlemen about trying to learn from their neighbours:

> the common Farmer is as subtle a Man in his way as any Mechanick whatsoever, and will be so far from leading any Gentleman into the true method of Farming, that most of them very justly hold it as contrary to their Interest; for, say they, if this is encouraged, how shall we come by Farms to occupy.[163]

Here the conflict over knowledge was given a specific rationale: the competition for tenancies, which were not only given to the highest bidder but also those judged to possess the best knowledge and skills. In 1764, Walter Harte hinted at a similar conflict of interests, noting that 'the husbandman and the bailiff both know full well it is not for their interest that a gentleman should be intelligent in matters of husbandry'.[164]

Arthur Young acknowledged the controversy around gathering information by advising his reader to acquaint himself with farmers who 'will not take a pleasure in misleading him'. The reader must be subtle in his approach: 'Let him invite them to dinner, and now and then give them a bottle of generous wine, and chat freely about country business. He will find it no difficult matter to learn from them the chief of what they know'.[165] Indeed, he described using these techniques himself on his tour of Northern England in 1770:

> some art was requisite to gain intelligence from many farmers, &c. who were startled at the first attack. I found that even a profusion of expence was often necessary to gain the ends I had in view: I was forced to make more

---

[163] William Ellis, *Chiltern and vale farming explained* (London, 1733), Preface.
[164] Harte, *Essays*, 197.
[165] Young, *Rural oeconomy*, 102.

than one honest farmer half drunk, before I could gain sober unprejudiced intelligence … I met with some farmers who gave me accounts too improbable to credit; whether from ignorance, or an intention to deceive, I know not …[166]

Further, Young noted that while gentlemen were often extremely helpful, some common farmers 'were jealous of my designs'.[167] Such passages reveal the suspicion and bitterness created by small acts of appropriation, usually elided by abstract descriptions of *gathering* practical information. These passages are all the more striking as they appear in books that repeatedly proclaimed how superior minds must shine a light on common farmers.

An extraordinarily clear statement explaining resistance to the appropriation of knowledge was given, significantly, in an anti-enclosure pamphlet published in 1785 by an anonymous society of farmers. The author explained that 'it gives the clown pleasure to delude and mislead the gentleman in his notions of farming; and this disposition arises partly from a jealousy lest the gentleman should know as much as himself'.[168] This supports the claim that farmworkers could be equally as guarded as craftsmen in sharing knowledge that could threaten their position. A similar point was made in the commentary on the 1808 poem quoted at the beginning of this chapter, in a reference to common farmers. While some may reveal 'detached parts' of their art, they cannot be 'induced to disclose all'.

> Husbandry is not to them a liberal science, which they are disinterestedly desirous of promoting and diffusing, on philosophical and philanthropic principles. It is their trade, and a gainful one. And is it not the very first lesson taught to every apprenticed boy, that the *secrets* of *trade* are to be kept?[169]

The author suggested that more could be learned 'at half a score *farmers'* ordinaries [inn or tavern], if a landlord could be present at them effectually disguised, than could be drawn out by ten reams of *queries*, and by *agricultural meetings* and *cattle-shews*, held day after day for a year together'.[170] In other words, it would be better for the gentleman to covertly overhear the unguarded chat between farmers than to ask them directly. Hence not only were gentlemen seeking to learn from common farmers but also many of these practitioners in husbandry were cautious or actively resistant to sharing their experience with self-styled men of science.

---

[166] Arthur Young, *A six months tour through the North of England*, 4 vols (London, 1770), i. xiv.
[167] Ibid., vii.
[168] *A political enquiry*, vii.
[169] *Pursuits of agriculture*, 48.
[170] Ibid., 48–49.

It should now be clear that the effort by historians to interpret the role of agricultural books solely using a model of knowledge diffusion is woefully inadequate. Indeed, the presumption that books were primarily vehicles for disseminating knowledge from expert authors to amateur practitioners was in fact the outcome of a sustained propaganda campaign over the seventeenth and eighteenth centuries. By contrast, a model of knowledge appropriation and a renewed attention to the stated intentions of agricultural authors show how books were used to transfer knowledge up the social scale. The art of husbandry was appropriated in two senses: the ideal husbandman was increasingly reimagined as a learned gentleman, and knowledge of the art was codified in books for gentlemen readers. While the growing enthusiasm of the gentry (first English, later Scottish) is a commonplace in agricultural history, the effects on social relations have been systematically neglected, beyond direct conflict over landownership. Yet the spirit of improvement included efforts to transfer control over cultivation up the social spectrum, from the unlearned to the learned. The printed book was a central tool of this process, both in promoting new visions of gentry-led agriculture and in creating a body of written information for use in gentry farm management. This appropriation deserves at least equal scholarly attention to the dissemination of knowledge, although neither model offers a comprehensive account of the myriad flows of knowledge.[171]

The argument here can only sketch the key relations, but the mechanisms of appropriation can be discerned in outline. Gentlemen collected their observations and conversations with practising farmers and farmworkers, both men and women, ordered this material into a suitable method, and sometimes published the result for their peers. These activities ranged from the personal jottings of individual landowners to the systematic surveys of institutions. The need to appropriate the art was driven by a fear that customary knowledge could be lost, a belief that it could not progress until it was stored and systematised, and a conviction that agriculture had to be taken out of the hands of the 'meanest people'. Plenty of signs exist that such efforts were resisted or evaded by farmers and farmworkers who recognised that the authority they possessed in virtue of their experience was being threatened.

---

[171] A broader investigation, beyond dissemination and appropriation, might adopt Pamela Long's idea of early modern 'trading zones' between practitioners and men of learning, and the formation of what Ursula Klein calls 'hybrid experts'. Long, *Artisans/practitioners*, ch. 4; Ursula Klein, 'Hybrid experts', in Matteo Valleriani (ed.), *The structures of practical knowledge* (Switzerland, 2017).

To be clear, 'appropriation' describes the consequences as much as conscious intention. Regardless of the motives of all individual authors, some of whom came from the ranks of the yeomanry or larger tenant farmers, the systematic codification of a practical art in a semi-literate society was necessarily socially disruptive. A book-based system of agricultural knowledge, in which knowledge was stored in writing and acquired through reading, assisted an entirely different social and occupational structure than a labour-based system of knowledge, in which knowledge was stored in customs and passed down generations through speech and demonstration. While these dual systems of knowledge overlapped, they were largely aligned with different class interests.

This transformation in the system of knowledge was a crucial phase in the development of agrarian capitalism, as landowners and capitalist farmers sought to monopolise knowledge of farming in order to increase control over the labour process. Signs of this process can be discerned in the sixteenth and early seventeenth centuries, but the active and self-conscious effort to appropriate aspects of the art of husbandry itself only properly emerged from the mid-seventeenth century as part of the campaign for improvement. The attention of landowners was extended beyond managing rents to managing cultivation itself, from managing resources to managing production (even if only indirectly through the selection and direction of tenants). Agricultural books were a crucial tool for enclosing customary knowledge in a form that assisted the gentry as a whole in bringing the cultivation of land more firmly under their control.

CHAPTER 4

Learning without Labour
Codification and Managerial Knowledge

The relationship between writing and farming was transformed over the early modern period. To be more precise, there was a shift in authority from practice to writing as a source and form of knowledge about farming. The complexities and cultural paradoxes involved are neatly illustrated by a small pamphlet published in 1601 by Edward Maxey.[1] Intervening into a previous exchange, the pamphlet is notable for its struggle to balance the authority between writing and speech, and between writer and farmer.[2] It takes the form of a dialogue between a 'Ploughman' and a 'Schollar', consciously imitating verbal and personal instructions – but, notably, the scholar was being instructed by the ploughman. Maxey, a 'Gent', styled his authorial persona as a 'plaine Ploughman', and thus artificially constructed the speech of a farmworker to mask the form of his advice as the printed words of a gentleman. Throughout, Maxey attempted to navigate the challenge of offering written instructions on a practical art in a society in which the best farming knowledge was believed to be held by practising husbandmen and ideally communicated in face-to-face conversation.

These tensions between writing and farming were not new: agricultural writing goes back at least to Hesiod's *Works and Days* (c.700 BCE). While the invention of printing in the fifteenth century did not introduce a radical break with the manuscript tradition, it did make possible new ways of making, storing and communicating knowledge, and thus gave rise to new tensions. Over time, however, there was an inversion as writing was slowly transformed from a marginal to a dominant form of agricultural knowledge. Writing increasingly penetrated farming practice and more fundamentally the system of knowledge. In the sixteenth century, agricultural writing was

---

[1] Edward Maxey, *A nevv instuction [sic] of plowing and setting of corne, handled in manner of a dialogue betweene a ploughman and a scholler* (London, 1601).
[2] The exchange was between: Sir Hugh Plat, *The newe and admirable arte of setting of corne* (London, 1600); Anon., *God speede the plough* (London, 1601).

explicitly derived from farming practice and recognised as a less authoritative form than speech. By the end of the eighteenth century, writing was not merely a partial record of what was known by experienced farmers, but was becoming central to the production, acquisition, accumulation, transfer and exercise of knowledge. The pen was increasingly asserted over the plough.

In the enlightenment model, studies focus on the extent to which books contained and disseminated 'useful knowledge' – knowledge applicable in practice to increase productivity – with mixed conclusions.[3] But 'useful' for whom? Knowledge has many uses. We need to examine the motives and processes behind the creation of specific forms of written knowledge. Writing about husbandry and practising husbandry were very different things.[4] The logic of practice orders actions in time and space, framed by seasonal rhythms and land boundaries; the logic of the page has no temporal or geographical order, and thus opens up the possibility for new orders.[5] The development of agricultural book knowledge in the early modern period combined at least three distinct processes: translation from oral to written form (recording what had already been articulated); translation directly from practice (articulating previously tacit knowledge); and adaptation of existent writing (formed by the first two).[6] All three can be understood as contributing to a general process of codification, or the articulation of knowledge in a fixed and standardised form.[7] Codification, as theorised by Matteo Valleriani, is necessarily the selection and adaptation of practical knowledge, determined by its social and institutional context. As such, codified knowledge acquires independence from practical knowledge, distinguished by its degree of abstraction and the range of connections to other fields of knowledge. From a socio-economic perspective, codification was stimulated by a shift in value from products themselves to the knowledge required to produce them, and linked to divisions of labour that created experts and managers above practitioners. In analysing the codification of the art of husbandry, therefore, we must be sensitive to

[3] Jones is dismissive of books before the late eighteenth century as constituting a useless 'branch of belles-lettres'. Jones, *Agricultural enlightenment*, 6.
[4] See analogous point in Büttner, 'Shooting with ink'.
[5] As Wendy Wall argues in regard to the 'textual husbandry' of Gervase Markham, both print and husbandry shape each other: the writer brings order to wild information as the husbandman brings order to the field, and 'practices of writing – organising, inventing, classifying, innovating, distributing, and marketing – become interwoven into the subjects of gardening, farming, tending house, dairying'. Wall, 'Renaissance national husbandry', 783.
[6] The shift from orality to textuality in technical instructions in the period 1200 to 1700 is explored in Tebeaux, 'English agriculture and estate management'.
[7] Hakanson, 'Creating knowledge', 51.

both the cognitive and socio-economic dimensions of knowledge.[8] Such points are illustrated in the eighteenth-century's paradigmatic project of codification, Diderot's *Encyclopédie*, which aimed to record and integrate the mechanical arts with the liberal arts and sciences and promote open research to undermine craft guild control, but which struggled to represent craft methods and obscured crucial aspects of technical knowledge.[9]

We already possess excellent general surveys of early modern agricultural literature, including specific genre and sub-genre classifications.[10] Most recently, Heather Holmes adopted a twelve-fold classification for Scottish books 1700–1800.[11] Further, a number of studies have characterised the kind of knowledge contained in early modern agricultural books.[12] However, we lack a systematic analysis of books as a site of knowledge-production, sensitive to both the epistemological and social dimensions. Although two unpublished theses have identified the general problem that, in the words of Emily Nichole Howard, codifying agricultural knowledge required the development of new standards for knowledge-making 'which in themselves have nothing to do with farming, and which must be legible to people other than farmers'.[13] A similar point was made by Laura Sayre, who also noted that farming books were shaped by 'the genteel habit of writing as an instrument of management'.[14] However, neither link these observations to the organisation of labour.

This chapter examines how farming was codified between 1660 and 1800 in ways that transformed the system of knowledge production to correspond

---

[8] Valleriani, 'Epistemology of practical knowledge'.

[9] Pannabecker, 'Diderot, the mechanical arts'.

[10] See bibliographical surveys: Fussell, *Farming books 1523–1730*; Fussell, *Farming books 1731–1793*. Also, Goddard, 'Agricultural literature', 361–62.

[11] Categories: 'specific aspects of agricultural affairs such as crops, implements or livestock'; 'the science of agriculture'; 'agricultural systems'; 'farming tours or surveys'; 'agricultural economics'; 'commentaries on the current state of agriculture and rural affairs'; 'ready-reckoners of prices and weights and measures'; 'extracts from other books'; 'encouragement of agricultural development'; 'catalogues of agricultural products, usually relating to trees and other plants'; 'dictionaries (gardening rather than agriculture)'; 'religious, political or classical frameworks providing advice to farmers'. Holmes, 'Agricultural publishing', 504. See also: Holmes, 'Circulation', 48–51.

[12] A useful map of 'discursive formations' of agricultural treatises is presented in Keith Tribe, *Land, labour and economic discourse* (London, 1978), 54–61. On the shift from a moral to a rationalist framework see McRae, *God speed the plough*. On the classical focus on soil productivity, see Fussell, *Classical tradition*, 182, and S. Todd Lowry, 'The agricultural foundation of the seventeenth-century English oeconomy', *History of Political Economy*, 35 (2003), 83. On the influence of Mediterranean agronomic tradition, see Ambrosoli, *Wild and the sown*, 243–44, 260. Pamela Horn only remarked generally that from 1760 to 1800 books became 'more specialised and more scientific in their approach': Horn, 'Contribution of the propagandist', 319.

[13] Howard, 'Grounds of knowledge', 7, 109.

[14] Sayre, 'Farming by the book', 57.

with new divisions of labour. The analysis is not concerned with genre or style, but with the relation between text and practice, and the organisation of knowledge. Four dominant organising principles are examined: *systematic, theoretical, experimental* and *observational*. These categories derive from contemporary understandings, but they are not strictly contemporary categories. They describe the dominant forms of book knowledge from 1660 to 1800, but do not encompass all agricultural writing. Crucially, each mode had a different solution to the problem of how knowledge is best acquired and communicated. None of these modes were strictly instructional, in the sense of a procedural guide to performing tasks associated with straightforward 'how-to' books. While this mode was present, it was largely secondary to others. Only a few books or pamphlets could be described as simple instructional manuals, and these mostly appeared in single editions and received few comments from other writers.[15] Particular attention is devoted to specific texts that introduced, developed or epitomised an important innovation; that were popular or influential within the literature, according to the number of editions and the opinion of later writers; and that contributed to the construction of a specifically 'agricultural' knowledge.

The key argument is that all four modes of codification subordinated labour and custom in the production of knowledge and acquisition, and therefore undermined the authority of the common husbandman and farmworker, but in distinct ways. The systematic mode prioritised gathering and ordering information from diverse sources into a single coherent system. The theoretical mode prioritised the construction of theoretical principles independent of farming practice, from which good practice was to be derived. The experimental mode prioritised artificial forms of practice coordinated and recorded by writing, formally distinct from daily farming experience. The observational mode prioritised (written) observation over direct experience as a source of knowledge, thereby privileging the manager over the labourer in the acquisition of knowledge.

The first section characterises the classical and medieval literary tradition inherited by the seventeenth century, most of which did not challenge the primacy of labour for acquiring knowledge. It then traces the development of a new relationship between text and practice linked to the construction of 'agriculture' as a literary category and an independent body of theory. The main analysis then consists of the explication of the

---

[15] For example, *A true method of treating light hazely ground: Or, an exact relation of the practice of farmers in Buchan* (Edinburgh, 1735); or the twenty-two-page pamphlet, *Cabbage and clover husbandry* (London, 1775).

four key modes of codification from 1669 to 1792, which shows how specific technical challenges were solved to meet the particular social interests fostered by capitalist agriculture. An underlying trend is that many forces that shaped the organisation of book knowledge did not arise out of the practice of farming, but rather originated in external cultural traditions, and therefore increased the gap between the ways of knowing practitioners and theoretical agriculturalists. The unifying theme of eighteenth-century agricultural literature was the development of a book knowledge that encouraged the learning and teaching of farming without labour. This constituted a form of enclosure, as knowledge was extracted from custom and parcelled up for individual cultivators.

The Invention of Agriculture

The shifting categories applied to cultivation in early modern England – roughly indicated by the changing meaning and frequency of use of 'husbandry', 'agriculture' and 'farming' – has been obscured by bibliographic surveys that apply a single anachronistic definition, such as 'farming text-book' or 'practical treatise on farming'.[16] The term 'agriculture' was not used in sixteenth-century English books on husbandry and was only gradually introduced during the seventeenth century. The construction of 'agriculture' from the 1660s onwards signalled a new phase in the relationship between writing and farming. To appreciate this development, we must first establish the intellectual and literary traditions that seventeenth-century English writers used to construct the category of 'agriculture', and how it differed from 'husbandry'.

Sixteenth-century English writers could draw upon two distinct literary traditions: Anglo-French medieval treatises on estate management, and classical Greek and Roman texts. The influence of the *Scriptores rei rusticae* – the collected ancient works on husbandry, first printed in Venice in 1472 – upon English gentlemen generally has been well documented.[17] The ancient authors provided a moral and aesthetic model, establishing the nobility of agriculture and a template for how to write about cultivation. The central Greek text by Xenophon (c.430–356 BCE), *Oeconomicus*, was a Socratic dialogue on the art of household management, which addressed cultivation as a discipline of *praxis* (action) rather than *techné* (making).[18] However, it

---

[16] For example, Fussell, *Farming books 1523–1730*.
[17] Fussell, *Classical tradition*; Thirsk, 'Making a fresh start'.
[18] Long, *Openness*, 16.

is striking for the insistence that farming was easy to learn and success was due to 'diligence, not knowledge'.[19] Later Roman treatises by Cato (c. C2nd BCE), Varro (116–27 BCE) and Columella (c.4–70 CE) to some degree circle around a loose narrative of acquiring, setting up and managing a farm.[20] Yet each adopted a different style, from Cato's 'imperatives', to Varro's playful dialogues and Columella's 'how-to' approach.[21] Moreover, Virgil's poem *Georgics* was seen by contemporaries, and indeed early modern readers, as an authoritative text on agriculture.[22] Only Varro attempted to formalise agriculture as a system of knowledge, although this was essentially an abstraction from Cato.[23] Pliny the Elder's (23–79 CE) *Naturalis Historia* placed agriculture or 'the natural history of grain' within a massive encyclopaedic framework of natural history. Palladius' (c.350–450 CE) *Opus Agriculturae* adapted Columella into a calendar form and became the 'recognised text of noble agriculture' in medieval England.[24] Such treatises were successively revised, adapted, extracted and translated over the middle ages.[25]

Medieval England produced texts of an even narrower scope; certainly no complete guide to the art of husbandry, nor a complete theory of agriculture. The two major Anglo-French treatises on estate management that survive in abundant copies are the *Seneschaucy* (c.1260–76) and *Husbandry* by Walter of Henley (c.1276–85).[26] These arose from an English legal tradition independent from classical writing and were produced for the administrators of great estates.[27] Their long-term influence is difficult to identify, as no later English agricultural writers from the sixteenth to the eighteenth centuries explicitly based their work upon them. However, the manuscripts were in circulation, and versions of Walter's treatise were printed in 1508 and 1589.[28] Moreover, Fitzherbert's *Boke of Husbandry* (1523) displayed the influence of Walter's text and was perhaps

[19] Warde, *Invention of sustainability*, 34.
[20] Fussell, *Classical tradition*, 12–37.
[21] Aude Doody, 'Virgil the farmer? Critiques of the Georgics in Columella and Pliny', *Classical Philology*, 102 (2007), 183.
[22] M. S. Spurr, 'Agriculture and the georgics', *Greece and Rome*, 33 (1986).
[23] F. R. D. Goodyear, 'Technical writing', in E. J. Kenney and W. V. Clausen (eds), *Cambridge history of classical literature vol. 2* (Cambridge, 1982), 669.
[24] Ambrosoli, *Wild and the sown*, 13, 26.
[25] Fussell, *Classical tradition*, 12.
[26] Oschinsky, *Walter of Henley*.
[27] Although Fussell suggested the authors had read the classical works. Fussell, *Classical tradition*, 74–75. Ambrosoli, *Wild and the sown*, 10.
[28] William Lambarde translated a copy of Walter from French to English and took notes in his commonplace book. Ambrosoli, *Wild and the sown*, 239. See Walter of Henley, *Boke of husbandry* (London, 1508); Walter of Henley, *The booke of thrift* (London, 1589).

the primary vehicle for continuing medieval modes of thought about husbandry.[29] The *Seneschaucy* was arranged according to the duties and qualifications of estate offices (including manorial servants such as ploughman and dairymaid). The text did not seek to instruct any officer below the steward on how to perform his or her duties, but assumed they acquired their knowledge independently.[30] *Walter* (itself a response to the *Seneschaucy*) was presented in the style of a father's sermon to his son, which addressed the main processes or objects on a farm. But *Walter*, according to Oschinsky, 'did not want to teach his students the ploughman's craft'.[31] Hence these medieval texts were not intended to provide complete instructions on how to be a farmer, but rather guidance on the supervision of tasks and keeping of accounts.

The two main books on husbandry published in the sixteenth century had 'no hint of theory'.[32] Both were organised around the duties and labours of the husbandman and to a lesser extent the housewife. Indeed, historians have categorised them in general terms, as handbooks 'dealing with every-day information', 'practical books for the gentleman' (with books on hunting, hawking and military manuals) and 'books for daily life' (the household, husbandry and personal conduct).[33] The first new manual to be printed in English was by a member of a major gentry family: John Fitzherbert's *Boke of Husbandry* in 1523, written broadly for the gentleman or yeoman.[34] The book was organised as a miscellany, a compilation of advice over 150 short thematic sections, which covered technical methods, principles of household management and moral and theological concerns.[35] The second major publication of the sixteenth century also presented itself as a miscellany: Thomas Tusser, a trained court musician, wrote *A hundreth good pointes of husbandrie* (1557), expanded to *Five Hundreth Good Pointes of Husbandry* (1573) with advice on huswifery.[36]

---

[29] George R. Keiser, 'Practical books for the gentleman', in Lotte Hellinga and J. B. Trapp (eds), *Cambridge history of the book in Britain Vol 3: 1400–1557* (Cambridge, 1999), 491; Tebeaux, 'English agriculture and estate management', 359.

[30] Oschinsky, *Walter of Henley*, 281–83.

[31] Ibid., 164.

[32] Warde, *Invention of Sustainability*, 40.

[33] H. S. Bennett, *English books & readers 1457 to 1557: Being a study in the history of the book trade from Caxton to the incorporation of the Stationers' Company* (London, 1952), 109; Keiser, 'Practical books'; Hunter, 'Books for daily life'.

[34] Fitzherbert, *Boke of husbandry*.

[35] Keiser, 'Practical books', 491.

[36] A biographical sketch and bibliographical commentary found in: Thomas Tusser, 'Five Hundred Points of Good Husbandry: Together with a Book of Huswifery', in William Fordyce Mavor (ed.) (Cambridge: Cambridge University Press, 2013).

The advice on the good ordering of the household was in the style of doggerel verse and arranged in a calendar. Although it was reprinted many times and referenced continually for the next few centuries, its organisational form was rarely imitated.[37] Tusser's medley of maxims held little attraction for later agricultural writers seeking to formalise the knowledge of the practical art. As explained by Paul Warde, both these texts appealed to knowledge drawn from daily experience, the notion that 'people who did things for a long time were more likely to know what to do'. Hence Fitzherbert and Tusser, as learned authors, 'did not thus elevate themselves above other farmers'.[38] Further, in key ways, both books helped to reinforce as much as undermine the authority of speech: Tusser's doggerel was designed to be spoken and remembered, while Fitzherbert advised that a gentlemen read aloud relevant chapters to their servants.[39]

The circulation of French and German books produced in the sixteenth and early seventeenth century, and translated into English, was one of the primary routes for the classical agrarian tradition to enter England.[40] For example, the French work *Maison rustique,* translated in 1600, was itself based on the Italian Pier de Crescenzi's (or Crescentius) *Liber cultus ruris,* written around 1305, which was itself largely an adaptation of Palladius, circa fourth or fifth-century BCE.[41] Similarly, *Four Books of Husbandry* (1577), adapted from the German work by Conrad Heresbach, was based on the pattern of Xenophon and Columella.[42] These works were part of the *Hausväterliteratur* or 'house father literature' that promoted ideals of patriarchal order for the male heads of great estates.[43] A survey of English private libraries between 1500 and 1640 shows the widespread ownership of French, German and Italian books, alongside classical authors.[44]

The integration of the continental and classical traditions into a distinctly English framework began with the many publications of Gervase Markham in the early seventeenth century.[45] Markham was from a

---

[37] A total of twenty-three further editions by 1638.
[38] Warde, *Invention of sustainability*, 38–39.
[39] Fitzherbert, *Boke of husbandry*, fo.xlvii.
[40] Fussell, *Classical tradition*, 112.
[41] First published in France in Latin in 1554 by Charles Estienne, then expanded in French by Jean Liebault in 1570. Ambrosoli, *Wild and the sown*, 43; Fussell, *Classical tradition*, 104.
[42] Thirsk, 'Making a fresh start', 25. Warde suggests the translator Barnaby Googe met Heresbach while the latter was on a diplomatic mission in 1570. Warde, *Invention of sustainability*, 36–37.
[43] McRae, *God speed the plough*, 140.
[44] Ambrosoli, *Wild and the sown*, 243–49.
[45] On the career of Markham: Thirsk, 'Plough and pen', 301–6. On an English national framing: Wall, 'Renaissance national husbandry'.

Nottingham gentry family and began as a poet and playwright before a change in fortune led to years as a tenant farmer from which he gleaned new literary inspiration.[46] He penned his own works and put his name to English translations of Heresbach and Estienne. Broadly speaking, his books continued to share Fitzherbert's understanding of husbandry as the set of activities deriving from the husbandman and housewife, although his books have also been credited with a new prioritisation of the soil, rather than household management.[47] In his first work on husbandry in 1613, Markham stated his clear purpose was to 'to set downe the true manner and nature of our right English Husbandry', and described himself as 'onely a publique Notary, who record the most true and infallible experience of the best knowing Husbands in this land'.[48] While he became bolder in his role as a teacher in later publications and more critical of husbandmen, Markham framed his contributions as derived from the best practice of English husbandry.

Hence English and Scottish authors in the late seventeenth and eighteenth centuries had a range of literary models available. Writing about husbandry could be in the form of a philosophical dialogue on the household economy; a handbook for a young landowner; an encyclopaedia on natural history; a monthly calendar of tasks; a specification of estate duties; or a miscellany for rural households. None of these models, however, was based on an understanding of agriculture as a distinct body of theoretical knowledge. Further, they did not challenge the basic assumption that knowledge of cultivation was acquired primarily through labour or practical experience. The pen was guided by the plough.

The key shift in the relation between text and practice can be traced to the emergence of 'agriculture' as an English literary subject. In Thomas Eliot's Latin-English dictionary of 1538, he translated *Agricultura* directly as 'husbandry' – but also defined *Georgica*, *Oeconomica* and *Rusticarius* as all 'pertayninge to husbandry'.[49] So the eventual adoption of 'agriculture' in English for the practice and theory of cultivating the soil and rearing livestock was not inevitable. However, from the latter half of the sixteenth century, the word agriculture began to be used in vernacular printed books, and notably in Francis Bacon's *Advancement of Learning* (1605).[50]

---

[46] Warde, *Invention of sustainability*, 50–52.
[47] Warde, 'Idea of improvement', 136.
[48] Markham, *English husbandman*, 'Epistle' and ch. 1 (unnumbered).
[49] Thomas Elyot, *The dictionary of syr Thomas Eliot knyght* (London, 1538).
[50] Francis Bacon, *The two bookes of Francis Bacon* (London, 1605), 9.

The OED suggests the English term was borrowed from both Latin and French. It was perhaps the influence of the French work by de Serres, *Théâtre d'agriculture* (partly included in the translation of *Maison Rustique* in 1616) that prompted its growing use in seventeenth-century English.[51] It first began to be used in English books on husbandry around the middle of the seventeenth century.[52] The poet Abraham Cowley wrote his Virgil-inspired essay 'Of Agriculture' around 1650.[53] The first use in a printed title was a single page pamphlet by Cressy Dymock, *The New and Better Art of Agriculture* (1668) – the phrasing itself identified a reformed discipline.

The first clear attempt to establish 'agriculture' as an English literary and intellectual category was the publication of John Worlidge's influential treatise *Systema Agriculturæ* (1669), discussed in further detail later. The title retained the Latin, but the English word was used throughout. More significantly, Worlidge sought to define the parameters of agriculture by including 'A Catalogue of such Authors who have written of Agriculture, Or of some Branch thereof, and were consulted with in the Composure of the subsequent Treatise'. The catalogue listed thirty-nine authors alphabetically from the three main traditions – classical, continental and early English print – whose titles described a constellation of topics, including husbandry and huswifery, gardening, natural history, bee-keeping, household management, enclosure and more general miscellanies. None of the book titles listed included the word 'agriculture' (with the exception of the Latin title of Heresbach), indicating that Worlidge was constructing a new literary tradition by assembling a range of books. The flourishing of this new tradition was illustrated a century later, when Richard Weston published his enormous 'catalogue of English authors on agriculture, botany, gardening, &c' with over 800 entries.[54]

Worlidge often used 'agriculture' and 'husbandry' as near-synonyms, but he had a clear preference for the former when defining his subject: agriculture was the 'Science, that principally teacheth us the Nature, and divers Properties and Qualities, as well of the several Soils, Earths, and Places, as of the several Productions or Creatures, whether Vegetable, Animal, or Mineral'.[55] It was the desire to refashion a new scientific category with a classical lineage that motived the substitution of husbandry by

---

[51] Etymons: French *agriculture*; Latin *agricultūra*. See 'agriculture, n.', *OED Online*.
[52] Hartlib, *Legacie*.
[53] Cowley, 'Of agriculture'.
[54] First in 1769, expanded in 1773. Weston, *Tracts*.
[55] Worlidge, *Systema*, 1.

agriculture. The word 'husbandry' was inadequate and came with superfluous moral and social associations, such as frugality, personal discipline, or
simply the general management of daily life.[56] Almost a century later, the
dictionary *The Complete Farmer* (1766) defined *agriculture* as 'the art of tilling, manuring, and cultivating the earth' and *husbandry* as the 'business or
employment of a farmer, or person who cultivates land'. Hence agriculture
was defined as an art or science, while husbandry was defined as a particular social occupation. Husbandry retained its broader association with
the management of domestic affairs.[57] 'Agriculture' was constructed from
'husbandry' by stripping away the moral associations, severing it from its
household context, and integrating it within the broader study of natural
history.[58] Whereas husbandry was unified as the set of activities performed
by the husbandman, agriculture was unified by a set of logical relations
that represented the natural world. Whereas husbandry could only be
learned through labour, agriculture could be learned through books.

The following sections examine the new major modes of organising
written agricultural knowledge that aimed to displace labour as the primary source of knowledge. In a survey of early modern farming calendars,
Fussell observed that the 'procession of the seasons does not change in so
short a time as five hundred years, and consequently the farmer's annual
routine is much the same to-day as it was under the Tudors'.[59] This may
be so; but the organisation of agricultural knowledge was more changeable
than the seasons. Indeed, the long tradition of the agricultural calendar
was relatively rare in the eighteenth century, because most agricultural
writers and readers desired a new relationship between their words and
their farms.[60]

The Systematic Mode

The construction of agriculture was coeval with a new desire to systematise
the art of husbandry; or, more precisely, for a book containing a complete
system. A letter first published by Hartlib in 1651 lamented that 'we have
not a Systema or compleat book of all the parts of Agriculture', dismissing

[56] For example, in the pamphlet: *The art of good husbandry; or the improvement of time: being a sure way to keep money* (1675).
[57] See 'husbandry' in Johnson, *A dictionary of the English language*.
[58] On the separation from household context, see Hunter, 'Books for daily life', 531.
[59] G. E. Fussell, 'Farmers' calendars from Tusser to Arthur Young', *Economic History*, 2 (1933), 520.
[60] The notable exception was the popular work, Arthur Young, *The farmer's kalendar* (London, 1771).

Tusser's verses and existing 'divers small Treatises' as incomplete.[61] A reply letter published in 1659 disagreed, arguing that 'Markham hath comprehended in his works, whatever belongeth to any part of Husbandry and of Housewifery' such that he deserved 'the name of a generall writings'.[62] The choice of 'agriculture' or 'husbandry' in these quotes is revealing of the conceptual shift that occurred around this time: Markham may have produced complete books on husbandry, but they did not constitute a system of agriculture. A few years later, in 1664, John Evelyn expressed his hope for a writer to 'oblige the World with that compleat Systeme of Agriculture'.[63] The same desire would motivate the writing of new systematic agricultural books over the next century. This was part of a culture-wide literary trend, as a host of book titles from the first half of the eighteenth century promised 'compleat systems' on a range of topics such as cookery, geography, military discipline, optics and astronomy.[64]

The systematic mode prioritised the creation of a single, unified body of knowledge to constitute a science of agriculture. It was a response to what writers perceived as the unacceptable fragmentary status of customary knowledge, in at least two ways: the practical knowledge of husbandmen was exercised in a series of discrete, open-ended actions over time, never forming a single whole; and there was no unified set of methods, principles, or terminology across regions with overlapping but distinct customs. While the creation of a system of knowledge was an intrinsically textual project, it did not arise automatically from the printed medium.[65] It was a resolution to a newly perceived problem: earlier miscellanies that divided husbandry into discrete tasks loosely organised by the layout of the farm or estate made it difficult to see the interconnections between different elements.[66]

The systematic mode encompassed a loose grouping of features. First, it aimed for completeness. This may seem trivial, but it was not at all obvious

---

[61] Hartlib, *Legacie*, 105.

[62] Samuel Hartlib, *The compleat husband-man: Or, a discourse of the whole art of husbandry* (London, 1659), 116–17.

[63] Evelyn, *Sylva*, 'To the Reader'.

[64] For example, Charles Carter, *The complete practical cook* (London, 1730); *Atlas geographus: Or, a compleat system of geography*, 5 vols (London, 1711); John Gittins, *A compleat system of military discipline* (London, 1735); Robert Smith, *A compleat system of opticks* (Cambridge, 1738); Charles Leadbetter, *A compleat system of astronomy*, 2 vols (London, 1742).

[65] An extensive and coherent system of knowledge is very difficult to attain or express in oral form. Jack Goody and Ian Watt, 'Consequences of literacy', *Comparative Studies in Society and History*, 5 (1963), 330.

[66] Paul Warde, 'The invention of sustainability', *Modern Intellectual History*, 8 (2011), 155.

that a diverse set of practices, known to vary considerably by soil and climate, could be 'complete' until it had been conceived as an abstract body of knowledge. Second, it aimed for universality: a set of ideas that could apply to all farms and estates. Third, it aimed to be synoptic, to see all things and their relations instantaneously, in order to hold them together in the mind as a totality. As such, it was the perspective of those acting in a managerial or supervisory role, the master or the landlord. Fourth, it aimed to reduce the art of husbandry to an order or a method, a phrase repeated in prefaces throughout the long eighteenth century, along with an associated vocabulary of 'schema', 'analysis', 'epitome' and 'synopsis'. To reduce husbandry to a method was to extract a set of rules from the mystery of husbandry acquired by practitioners, to be transmitted through book learning to those without practical experience.[67]

Worlidge's *Systema Agriculturæ* (1669) marked the beginning of systematic writing, in addition to the beginning of agricultural English literature. It was a popular and influential work – being reprinted nine times and referenced regularly by later writers – setting the standard for the genre for the next century. It has, therefore, been widely regarded by historians as one of the major agricultural books of the seventeenth century.[68] Worlidge was a successful landowner from the market town of Petersfield, Hampshire, belonging to the gentry and urban professional class, who became mayor of his town in 1673, served as deputy steward of Chalton Manor from 1689 and was at one time a steward of Earl of Pembroke's woods. Hence he gained managerial experience in multiple settings.[69] *Systema* was his first publication and the first attempt at a systematic treatment of arable and livestock husbandry, although the content was not especially original, incorporating much from Walter Blith a few decades earlier.[70]

The 282 pages of Worlidge's book exhibited several features that aimed to systematise agricultural knowledge: a synoptic frontispiece, an analysis of the art, a catalogue of literature, a philosophical foundation, a dictionary of terms, a monthly calendar and an alphabetical index. Some of these features can be found in later publications. Over the next century, a significant proportion of agricultural books contained the word 'system',

---

[67] Jones also highlighted the 'quasi-utopian message' in many agricultural books; their faith in 'a supremely rational "system" of agriculture'. Jones, *Agricultural enlightenment*, 6.

[68] See 'Age of Worlidge' in Fussell, *Farming Books 1523–1730*; Thirsk called it one of the 'best examples of influential general handbooks'. Thirsk, 'Agricultural innovations', 569.

[69] Thirsk, 'Plough and pen', 314–15.

[70] Thirsk, 'Agricultural innovations', 561. Blith's book described as the 'first systematic work', Loudon, *Encyclopædia*, 47.

'complete' or an equivalent expression in their titles (see below). Worlidge's frontispiece illustrated the synoptic perspective of the treatise: an image of a large estate from a birds-eye view, displaying a country house surrounded by gardens and walls, with fields beyond, full of trees, grassland, horses, ploughmen, shepherds, even a windmill and church in the distance: the whole of agriculture in a single frame (see Figure 4.1). The image can be read in socio-political terms, but it also defined the intellectual category of agriculture. Similar frontispieces displayed classically ordered great estates over the next half-century (for example, see Figures 4.2 and 4.3).

However, these pictures of grand estates presented an organic whole rather than a conceptual unity. Worlidge attempted the latter by exhibiting the logical relations between parts. In addition to a 'Table of Contents', he provided a more detailed 'Analysis', presenting a detailed structure of the text, and therefore of agricultural knowledge. The title page showed a simpler graphical arrangement to show a set of actions (e.g. sowing) that could be performed upon different land types (e.g. gardens) (see Figure 4.4). Similar graphical arrangements were used in a number of later books according to the 'Ramist method', which created a picture of how parts related to the whole through schematic charts.[71] The most ambitious attempt to represent agriculture as a schematic diagram was in Richard Blome's encyclopaedic *Gentleman's Recreation* (1686), which represented agriculture at two scales, one in relation to all other arts and sciences and one displaying its own elements (see Figure 4.5). For example, 'clover' was placed in the sequence: '*Agriculture or Husbandry > Improvement of Grounds as > Meadows, and Pastures, by > Severall Sorts of French Grasses, as > Clover*'.[72] The crop was not, therefore, positioned according to practical consideration, such as when it is to be sown, but its place in a system of thought. This spatial representation enabled agriculture to be conceived as a single abstract system. Simpler examples are found in books by Timothy Nourse and William Marshall.[73] However, these graphical representations did not become a fixture of every agricultural treatise, and most authors (or printers) were satisfied with detailed tables of contents, which offered a clear structure of topics.

A system of knowledge required a defined vocabulary and set of terminology. Worlidge included a dictionary of 'Rustick Terms', explaining

[71] Walter Ong, *Ramus, method, and the decay of dialogue: From the art of discourse to the art of reason* (Cambridge, MA, 2004), vi–ix; Tebeaux, *Emergence of a tradition*, 53.
[72] Richard Blome, *The gentlemans recreation. In two parts. The first being an encyclopedy of the arts and sciences* (London, 1686), 206.
[73] See 'An Analytical Account of the Argument', in Nourse, *Campania felix*; see 'Systematical Index' in Marshall, *Experiments*.

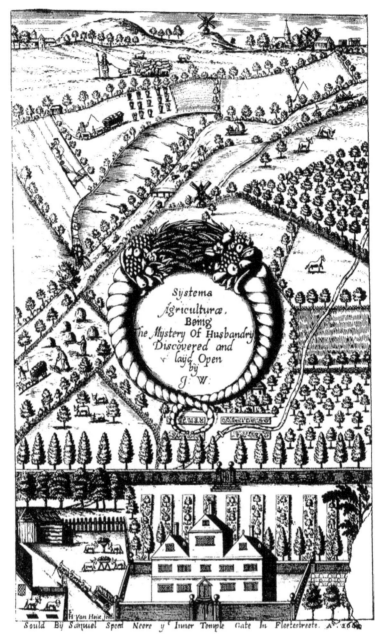

Figure 4.1   Frontispiece to John Worlidge, *Systema Agriculturæ: The Mystery of Husbandry Discovered* (London, Thomas Dring, 1675). Courtesy of The Bodleian Libraries, University of Oxford.

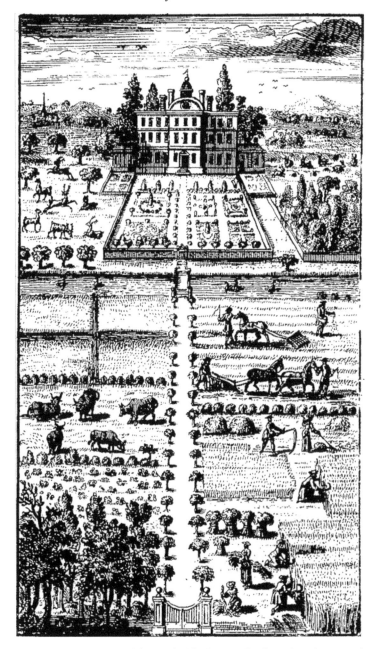

Figure 4.2   Frontispiece to Giles Jacob, *The Country Gentleman's Vade Mecum* (1717).
Courtesy of British Library Board (General Reference Collection DRT Digital Store
968.h.21).

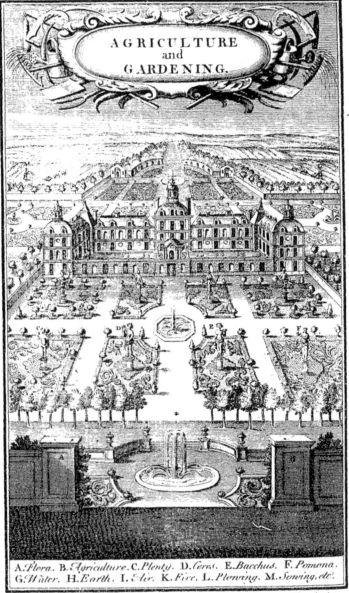

Figure 4.3   Frontispiece from John Mortimer, *The Whole Art of Husbandry* (1721). Courtesy of British Library Board (General Reference Collection DRT Digital Store 1570/2512).

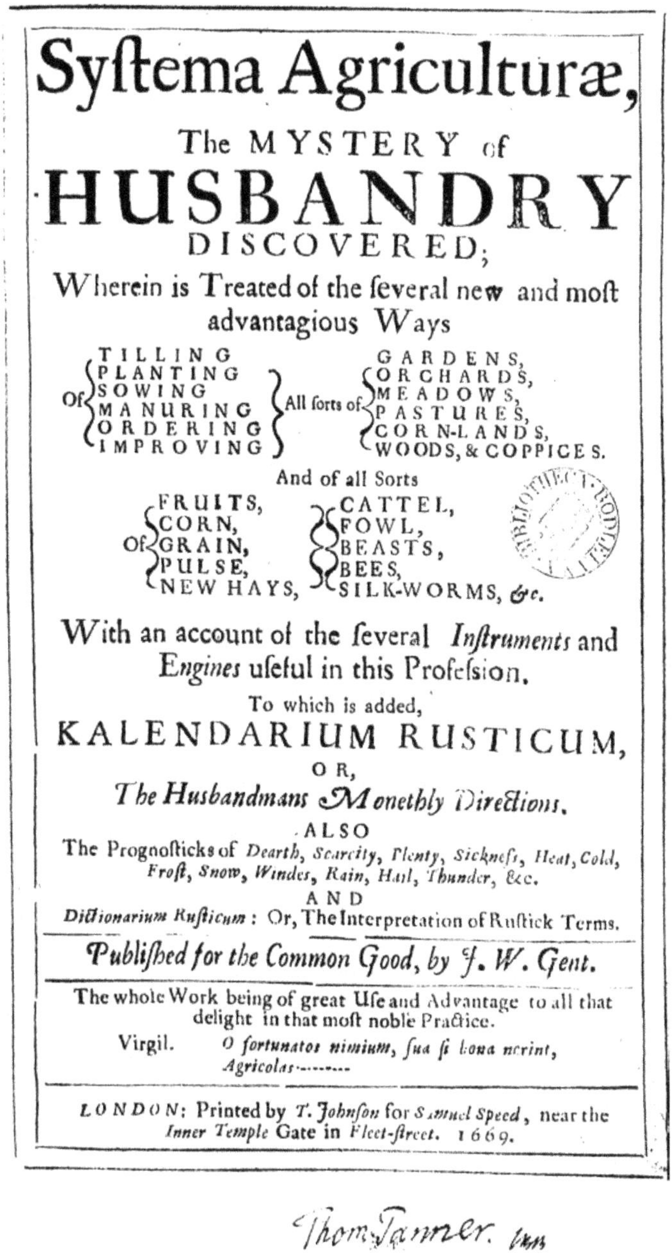

Syſtema Agriculturæ,

The MYSTERY of

·HUSBANDRY

DISCOVERED;

Wherein is Treated of the ſeveral new and moſt advantagious Ways

Of { TILLING / PLANTING / SOWING / MANURING / ORDERING / IMPROVING }   All ſorts of { GARDENS, / ORCHARDS, / MEADOWS, / PASTURES, / CORN-LANDS, / WOODS, & COPPICES.

And of all Sorts

Of { FRUITS, / CORN, / GRAIN, / PULSE, / NEW HAYS, } { CATTEL, / FOWL, / BEASTS, / BEES, / SILK-WORMS, &c.

With an account of the ſeveral *Inſtruments* and *Engines* uſeful in this Profeſsion.

To which is added,

KALENDARIUM RUSTICUM,

OR,

The Husbandmans Monethly Directions.

·ALSO

The Prognoſticks of *Dearth, Scarcity, Plenty, Sickneſs, Heat, Cold, Froſt, Snow, Windes, Rain, Hail, Thunder, &c.*

AND

Dictionarium Ruſticum : Or, The Interpretation of Ruſtick Terms.

Publiſhed for the Common Good, by J. W. Gent.

The whole Work being of great Uſe and Advantage to all that delight in that moſt noble Practice.

Virgil. *O fortunatos nimium, ſua ſi bona nerint, Agricolas*·········

LONDON: Printed by *T. Johnſon* for *Samuel Speed*, near the *Inner Temple* Gate in *Fleet-ſtreet.* 1669.

Thom. Tanner.

Figure 4.4   Title page of John Worlidge's *Systema Agriculturæ* (1669). Courtesy of The Bodleian Libraries, University of Oxford.

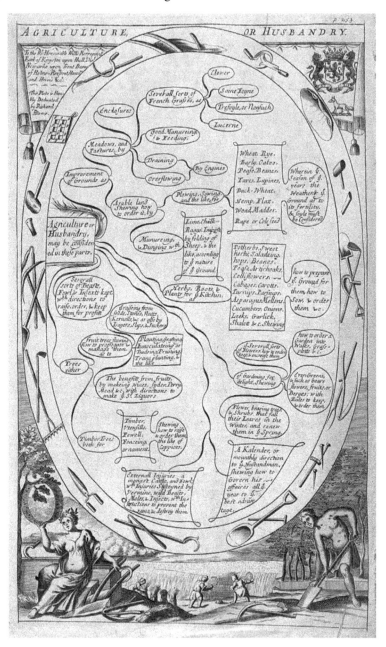

Figure 4.5   A schematic diagram of agriculture in Richard Blome's *The Gentleman's Recreation* (1686), 206. Line engraving. Courtesy of Wellcome Collection. Public Domain Mark.

that 'there is such a Babel of confusion … in their Terms and Names of things' that husbandmen fifty miles apart did not understand each other. Worlidge admitted the peculiarity of defining words for husbandmen, who 'above all others best understand these Terms … so that herein we seem to instruct those that are best able to teach us' – a remark that perhaps revealed more than intended. But he insisted that while individual husbandmen might understand their own terms, English agriculture as a whole lacked a common vocabulary.[74] The editors of *The Compleat Body of Husbandry* (1756) made the same argument, noting the problem of communicating when 'Terms in the Art' and 'Names of Things' were only locally specific or understood by 'the working People'.[75] It was, therefore, the desire to communicate about the topic abstracted from any particular set of local customs that motivated a unified national language of agriculture. This was no doubt encouraged by the greater integration of local and regional markets into a national agricultural economy, which required dealings between hitherto isolated agricultural communities.[76]

The opening chapters set out to establish agriculture on a secure intellectual and social foundation. Chapter 1 covered the philosophy of vegetable production, while Chapter 2 argued for enclosure, which 'capacitates all sorts of Land whatsoever for some of the Improvements mentioned in the subsequent Discourse'.[77] While Worlidge focused on the moral and material benefits, the advantage of enclosure was also epistemological; the enclosing of land into an ordered unit of production paralleled the enclosing of the art of husbandry into an ordered discipline of study. The organisation of knowledge was in general disconnected from any real-world scenario. Worlidge's husbandman was an impossible figure, whose relationship to husbandry was conceptual rather than practical. 'The Judicious and Understanding Husbandman must first consider the Subject whereon to spend his Time, Cost, and Labor …', he wrote, whether 'Meadow, Arable, Pasture, Woodland, Orchard, or Garden', on which may be grown 'Grain, Pulse, Trees, Fruits, or other Vegetables', and stocked with 'Beasts, Fowl, or Animals', etc. This husbandman seemingly possessed an unlimited ability to engage in any aspect of agriculture, regardless of their immediate condition and capacity. Further, the text acknowledged its own limitations as a practical guide, as individual husbandmen had to apply

---

[74] Worlidge, *Systema*, 266.
[75] Hale, *Compleat body of husbandry*, iii.
[76] Overton, *Agricultural revolution*, 136–49.
[77] Worlidge, *Systema*, 10.

their own judgement. For example, Worlidge noted that the season for sowing barley 'differ[s] according to the nature of the Soyl, and situation of the Place', varying from March to May, and therefore 'no certain Rule can be herein prescribed'.[78] In a passage describing the diversity of ploughs, Worlidge's summary ended: 'What else is necessarily requisite in the Plough, you may better finde by your manual and occular experience, than by all the instructions that can here be given'.[79] The systematic mode was thus largely an attempt to collate and order knowledge drawn from experience, but unable to supplant it.

A series of attempts to improve upon Worlidge's system of agriculture were made in the eighteenth century. While many works claimed to be 'complete', only a few genuinely tried to offer a total system. John Mortimer, a London-born merchant who retired to an estate in Essex in 1693, published *The Whole Art of Husbandry* in 1707, which was largely a collection of previous writings on the design of Worlidge's text, but without the philosophical speculations.[80] It was published a further six times throughout the century (the fifth edition grew by 650 pages) and became a key reference point for later writers. The clergyman John Laurence published *A New System of Agriculture* (1726), after previously publishing on gardening, hoping to 'do my Part to extend and enlarge the Knowledge of Agriculture in all its Parts'.[81] Laurence chastised some previous authors who had 'obscured the Subject … especially the Dictionary Writers, by inserting all promiscuously, both good and bad, from other Authors'. In other words, they did not provide an ordered system, but produced indiscriminate compilations. In 1717, Bradley stated he had been 'waiting for a Compleat System of Agriculture, and have read many a fair promising Title, but have found nothing within but a barren bulk of old Repetitions', and eventually published his own attempt, *A Complete Body of Husbandry* (1727).[82] Bradley believed that Mortimer had 'laid the best plan for such a design', but was too dependent on previous authors.[83] In 1733, Stephen Switzer judged that all these efforts had failed. The writings of Walter Blith and Samuel Hartlib had given birth to improvement, but 'from all of them not enough to form a regular System of Agriculture and Planting'.[84]

---

[78] Ibid., 36.
[79] Ibid., 207.
[80] Mortimer, *Whole art of husbandry*, 'Introduction'.
[81] Laurence, *New system*, Preface.
[82] Richard Bradley, *New improvements of planting and gardening* (London, 1717), Preface.
[83] Bradley, *Complete body of husbandry*, ii–ix.
[84] Stephen Switzer, *The practical husbandman and planter*, 2 vols (London, 1733–1734), xlvii.

Switzer identified Mortimer's book as the most accomplished, but observed that the author 'was confined much at Home, so his Composition… falls infinitely short of what it at first seem'd to promise'.[85] The attempts of Laurence and Bradley were dismissed: the former limited by his profession, while the latter was a gentleman 'of too much Pleasure' for the proper undertaking.[86] Beyond these personal critiques, Switzer claimed that a complete system was not 'in the Power of any one Man', since the topic was so extensive.[87] Thus the perceived failure of writing a complete system gave rise to doubts, which later stimulated the development of new forms.

Fresh efforts at systematisation were made in the 1750s and 60s. However, as if to vindicate Switzer, the publication of *The Compleat Body of Husbandry* (1756), an enormous volume totalling 751 pages in folio, was a collective project.[88] The papers of an unknown man called 'Thomas Hale' were sorted by a group of editors, who engaged others, such that 'every *separate Branch* fell under the Care of a *distinct Person*, who was a Master of that *Subject*'.[89] The editors were conscious about the challenge of creating a coherent treatise on such an extensive subject. Explaining the design of the work, they described the journey of the reader from the general to the particular, leading 'the practical husbandman through the several branches of his profession', as if travelling through the conceptual space of a Ramist diagram. As a result, 'the farmer will be fully instructed how he is to conduct himself in the *Field*, the *House*, the *Dairy*, the *Stable*, and in *Haymaking* and *Harvest-work*'.[90] However, a reviewer found the book so voluminous and full of errors that, after an extended dissection spanning ninty-eight pages and seven issues (from May 1757 to May 1758), he grew 'heartily tired of the undertaking' and left it incomplete.[91]

The attempt to encompass a complete system in a single work reached a new scale with the five volumes of John Mills' *A New and Complete System of Practical Husbandry* (1762–65), which when printed together in 1767 totalled an extraordinary 2,393 pages. Mills was fully immersed in

---

[85] Ibid., liii–lv.
[86] Ibid., xiv–xv.
[87] Ibid., xlvii.
[88] Issued in sixty-one numbers from 28 June 1755 to 21 August 1756.
[89] On the puzzle of Thomas Hale's identity, and doubts about his existence, see G. E. Fussell, 'Who was the 'celebrated Thomas Hale'?', *Notes and Queries*, (1947).
[90] Hale, *Compleat body of husbandry*, iii–iv.
[91] Unknown author called 'Okey'. Review began in O., 'A compleat body of husbandry', *Monthly Review*, 16 (1757). On authorship: Benjamin Christie Nangle, *The Monthly Review: First series 1749–1789: Indexes of contributors and articles* (Oxford, 1934), 32.

the book trade and had previously been involved in two other publishing projects: the French edition of Ephraim Chambers' *Cyclopaedia* (c.1743), and the English translation of Duhamel du Monceau's *Practical Treatise of Husbandry* (1759). In his view, 'no one in our language, except Mr Worlidge, has even attempted to comprize the whole of this Art' or 'reduce it into a regular system'.[92] It was primarily a compilation of earlier works, especially Worlidge, Evelyn, Tull and his own translations of Duhamel, which sacrificed any pretence of a clear system for sheer magnitude. The dominant desire was to incorporate everything into a single work, '[t]o give the reader the most extensive view of the subject'. Yet the scale of the work signalled its lack of system, which Mills himself acknowledged in his choice to supply all available ideas rather than specific methods.[93] This approach earned him a rebuke from a reviewer: 'If Mr Mills knows not how to give the necessary directions … why did he undertake to write a work', which 'requires not only the knowledge to be acquired by reading … but also a very considerable share of practical and experimental knowledge'.[94] Another reviewer sarcastically remarked that little practical experience could be expected of 'most *London* writers'.[95] Mills' book was the last in the Worlidge lineage and a *reductio ad absurdum* of the aim to produce a complete system of all agricultural knowledge. The obstacles were considerable: the diversity of farming conditions; the rapidly expanding literature on the subject; and the introduction of experiments generating new information. From 1669 to 1762, from Worlidge to Mills, the complete system of agriculture grew ten-fold from 282 to 2,393 pages. It was unsustainable.

An important cultural driver behind systematic works was the tradition of commonplace books.[96] These were notebooks largely containing quotations from intellectual authorities, collected under different headings, which became central to sixteenth and seventeenth-century humanist learning and practice.[97] Schoolboys were taught to compile extracts on various themes ('commonplaces') to provide a stock of knowledge and aid to memory, which shaped reading and writing habits for generations.[98] By

[92] Mills, *New system*, i. xiv.
[93] Ibid., xiv–xv.
[94] 'Art. II. A new and complete system of practical husbandry', *Critical Review*, 18 (1764), 89.
[95] P., 'A new and complete system of practical husbandry', *Monthly Review*, 32 (1765), 323, 334.
[96] Ann Moss, *Printed commonplace-books and the structuring of Renaissance thought* (Oxford, 1996); Mary Thomas Crane, *Framing authority: Sayings, self, and society in sixteenth-century England* (Princeton, 1993).
[97] A 'locus communis' was 'a general argument capable of being used in different situations'. Yeo, *Encyclopaedic visions*, 104.
[98] Moss, *Printed commonplace-books*, v.

the eighteenth century, the practice was being used to create collections of natural knowledge, indicated by John Locke's new method.[99] Many published treatises clearly began as commonplace books for personal use. For example, Edward Lisle initially collected notes for personal use in the 1690s, which he prepared for publication around 1713, but he died in 1722 leaving disordered notes. The notes were lightly edited and published by his son in 1756–57, largely retaining their original form as short observations and quotes collected under headings, mixing classical maxims with the musings of neighbouring farmers.[100] Hence a reviewer remarked that it had 'more the appearance of a *common-place-book*, than a regular system'.[101] Similarly, a reviewer of John Mills' enormous treatise scoffed that it appeared 'to have been hastily compiled from the half-digested chaos of a common-place book'.[102] From these examples, therefore, it is clear that a humanist cultural practice, external and alien to farming, shaped the way generations of agricultural writers organised their notes and their knowledge.

A further example also illustrates why books of complete systems were effectively abandoned after the 1760s: Arthur Young's life-long project to compile his own agricultural system, 'Elements and Practice of Agriculture', began around 1775 and continued to be edited until 1818, shortly before his death in 1820.[103] The unpublished manuscript describes its origins as a commonplace book:

> [It] was not originally undertaken with the design of publication, but to form a collection of all those passages which I met with in reading books, which treated professedly, or incidentally, of agricultural subjects, — which I arranged alphabetically, for my own private use …

After a few years, Young decided 'that they might be arranged, compared and connected in such a manner as to be equally useful to the public'.[104] This was no doubt a typical beginning for agricultural books in the previous century. Yet it kept expanding beyond Young's control, as he was digesting so many new books that it was impossible to incorporate them for an up-to-date publication. After persisting for decades, Young wrote

---

[99] M. D. Eddy, 'Tools for reordering: Commonplacing and the space of words in Linnaeus's *Philosophia Botanica*', *Intellectual History Review*, 20 (2010), 228.

[100] Lisle, *Observations*, iii–v.

[101] P., 'Observations in husbandry', *Monthly Review*, (1759), 437.

[102] 'Art. II. A new and complete system of practical husbandry', 91.

[103] British Library, Add MS 34821–34854, 'Elements and practice of agriculture', 'Arthur Young' (1818). Prepared for the press in 1818, but not printed. Betham-Edwards (ed.), *Autobiography*, 445–46.

[104] 'Young', 'Elements', 2.

(around 1810) that his papers should not 'be considered in the light of a compleat treatise including the whole range of husbandry, (a work by the way to which no individual is, or can be competent)'.[105] By the time he died, ten folio volumes of manuscript sat in his library at Bradfield Hall.

The ambition for completeness faced the problem of ordering the whole of agricultural knowledge into a single work. The format of a dictionary or encyclopaedia offered a clear solution. Before the seventeenth century, encyclopaedic works were intended to reflect the natural order of the world, but early eighteenth-century dictionaries of arts and sciences broke with the thematic arrangement by subject and adopted the alphabetical ordering from language dictionaries and indexes in technical books.[106] With the apparent expansion of knowledge from the experimental sciences, alphabetical ordering was a convenient way to incorporate new information, as entries could be added without disturbing the overall organisation. Yet this seemingly abandoned any system of logical relations between the parts of natural knowledge.[107] Organising agricultural knowledge alphabetically signalled a further degree of abstraction from practice into a wholly literary form of classification; there is no correspondence between the first-letter ordering of the names of things and the ordering of those things in practice. The arrangement of husbandry into a dictionary of terms was, therefore, a wholesale re-ordering of the art of husbandry, for the purposes of reading and writing.[108]

We have already noted that Worlidge included a short dictionary of rural terms in 1669. A general encyclopaedia of country affairs, handicrafts and trading, *Dictionarium Rusticum & Urbanicum*, was published in 1704.[109] But the first proper agricultural encyclopaedia was not produced until 1766, notably soon after Mill's multi-volume treatise. *The Complete Farmer: Or, a General Dictionary of Husbandry* was a large volume of 751 pages in dense font, edited by members of the Society for the Encouragement of Arts, Manufactures and Commerce, who extracted 'every Thing valuable from the best Writers on this Subject'.[110] Following tradition, they claimed their dictionary was the 'First Attempt to give a COMPLETE SYSTEM of every branch of Husbandry'. It was explicitly a response to the problem

---

[105] Ibid., Preface, 7–8.
[106] Yeo, *Encyclopaedic visions*, 8–9, 18.
[107] Ibid., xv.
[108] Koepp, 'Alphabetical Order', 233.
[109] *Dictionarium rusticum & urbanicum* (London, 1704).
[110] A later imitation was published as *A general dictionary of husbandry, planting, gardening* (Bath, 1779).

that recent 'useful Discoveries and Improvements are scattered through a multitude of volumes, written in different languages, and published in different countries'.[111] With the continuing increase of agricultural books in the latter decades of the eighteenth century, the value of a dictionary or encyclopaedia for literary agriculturists was clear, and many more were produced in the first half of the nineteenth century.[112] As Thomas Potts explained in the preface to his 1807 agricultural dictionary, if every farmer needed an 'Agricultural Library' then an encyclopaedia was 'most likely to answer to every useful purpose intended by such recommendation'.[113] Farming books begat more farming books.

The fact that the systematic (and encyclopaedic) mode was not 'well designed' for direct application to practice has given rise to suggestions that such books were useless.[114] This is to misunderstand their purpose: they were not designed to instruct practitioners, but to systematise the art of husbandry for the benefit of educated men. They were primarily designed for theoretically inclined managers and amateur philosophers who wanted to transform the diverse customs of husbandmen into a complete, universal, synoptic and ordered system of knowledge. The deeper problem from the perspective of authors and readers was that as reference tools they were still derivative of customary labour-based knowledge and did not challenge the authority of unlettered experience.

The Theoretical Mode

The theoretical mode is defined here as agricultural writing organised upon principles or theories about the natural world. It shared many features with the systematic mode – from which it developed – but prioritised foundations over completeness. It accepted the impossibility of offering exhaustive advice on every aspect of husbandry and focused on establishing true principles and a coherent theory. The shift from the systematic to the theoretical mode can be seen as the shift from an approach inspired by natural history, which described and classified the world, to an approach

[111] Gentlemen, *Complete farmer*, Preface.
[112] See G. E. Fussell, 'Nineteenth-century farming encyclopedias: A note', *Agricultural History*, 55 (1981). For example, Loudon, *Encyclopædia*; John Baxter and John Ellman, *The library of agricultural and horticultural knowledge* (Lewes, 1830); Johnson, *The farmer's encyclopædia, and dictionary of rural affairs*; John Chalmers Morton, *A cyclopedia of agriculture, practical and scientific* (Glasgow, 1856).
[113] Thomas Potts, *The British farmer's cyclopædia, or, complete agricultural dictionary* (London, 1807), 'Preface'.
[114] Jones, *Agricultural enlightenment*, 81.

inspired by natural philosophy, which offered causal explanations of the world.[115] As a form of codification, the theoretical mode served to elevate books with respect to labour, and writers with respect to practitioners.

A theoretical or philosophical approach to agriculture, focused on the question of plant nutrition and growth, can be traced to the influence of the French potter Bernard Palissy (c.1510–89) through Sir Hugh Plat.[116] Yet it was the Baconian philosophy of the Hartlib circle in the mid-seventeenth century that firmly established natural history and natural philosophy as foundational for husbandry.[117] In 1644, Gabriel Plattes stressed the importance of causal explanations and declared that all former agricultural writers were 'ignorant in the fundamentall points and causes of Vegetation and Multiplication'.[118] The Royal Society fellow John Evelyn took up the challenge in 1676, with a philosophical discourse on soil and vegetation, reflecting on useful improvements for the husbandman.[119] The theoretical foundations for agriculture would be constructed from the emerging science of chemistry, specifically with regard to plant physiology and nutrition. Robert Boyle was an early advocate for the application of chemistry to husbandry, writing in 1671 that 'Chymical experiments ... may probably afford useful directions to the Husbandman'.[120] A few general studies and books on vegetation were published in the late seventeenth and early eighteenth centuries.[121] In 1727, Bradley published a separate volume of theoretical reflections, but did not organise his agricultural manuals around a particular theory.[122]

Jethro Tull was the first to use a theory of plant nutrition as the basis for a book of husbandry. He was the major innovator in the theoretical mode with *The New Horse-Houghing Husbandry* (1731) and greatly expanded *The Horse-Hoeing Husbandry* (1733).[123] These books inspired later agricultural

---

[115] On modes of knowledge in eighteenth century see John Pickstone, 'Science in nineteenth-century England: Plural configurations and singular politics', in Martin Daunton (ed.), *The organisation of knowledge in Victorian Britain* (Oxford, 2005), 33.

[116] Warde, *Invention of sustainability*, 47; Lis and Soly, *Worthy efforts*, 194.

[117] Webster, *Great instauration*; McRae, *God speed the plough*, 159–60.

[118] Plattes, *Profitable intelligencer*, 88.

[119] John Evelyn, *A philosophical discourse of earth, relating to the culture and improvement of it for vegetation* (London, 1676).

[120] Quoted in John Russell, *A history of agricultural science in Great Britain 1620–1954* (London, 1966), 26.

[121] Archibald Clow and Nan L. Clow, *The chemical revolution: A contribution to social technology* (London, 1952), 461.

[122] Richard Bradley, *Ten practical discourses concerning earth and water, fire and air, as they relate to the growth of plants* (London, 1727), 1.

[123] A supplement full of notes was published in 1736, again with further additions and 'conclusion' in 1740, followed by a second edition with all additions in 1743, and later editions with small revisions in 1751 and 1762.

writers in the eighteenth century. Tull's literary innovations were perhaps more significant than his innovations in methods of husbandry. Rather than attempting to systematise the art of husbandry by ordering all relevant information into a single work, Tull presented a new theory of cultivation. He explicitly – and controversially – distanced himself from classical agricultural writing in both form and content.

Tull (bap.1674, d.1741) was educated as a lawyer and began farming on part of his Oxfordshire estate from 1699, where he created his famous (although not entirely original) seed drill. His farming experience, combined with travels in France and Italy in 1711–14, led him to develop a new method using new instruments.[124] Crucially, Tull's innovations were stimulated by his continual antagonism with his servants and labourers.[125] It was, Tull later explained, because he began farming 'when Plough-Servants first began to exalt their Dominions over their Masters' that prompted him to turn to the cultivation of St Foin in search of greater profits. It was then due to his suspicion that his labourers 'had conspir'd to disappoint me' – from fear that changing methods 'might prove a Diminution of their Power' – which led him to consider giving up entirely 'unless I could contrive an Engine to plant St Foin more faithfully than such Hands would do'.[126] Indeed, he dreamt of 'Automata to do the Business appertaining to Tillage without Hands'.[127] He initially had no desire to publicise his ideas, only doing so aged 57 after encouragement from patrons and correspondents. Tull's theory – an attempt to rationalise his practice – was based on the principle that all plant food comes from the soil through the roots. He explained that his methods were designed to pulverise the earth into smaller elements to assist absorption by the roots, with no need for any manure or fallowing, central to traditional husbandry.[128] This was, as a friend suggested, 'Husbandry Mathematically Explained'.[129] Yet the results of his new approach to husbandry were, as identified by Sayre, to 'reinforce the power of the landlord'.[130]

The 1731 book was a slim 165 pages, later referred to as a 'specimen'. Tull self-consciously wrote a new kind of book and criticised previous authors

---

[124] Ernest Clarke and G. E. Mingay, 'Tull, Jethro (bap.1674, d.1741)', *ODNB* (Oxford, 2004), https://doi.org/10.1093/ref:odnb/27812 (18 October 2016).

[125] Schaffer, 'The earth's fertility', 135; Sayre, 'Farming by the Book', 124.

[126] Jethro Tull, *The new horse-houghing husbandry: Or, an essay on the principles of tillage and vegetation* (London, 1731), xiii.

[127] Jethro Tull, *The horse-hoing husbandry: Or, an essay on the principles of tillage and vegetation* (London, 1733), vi.

[128] Sayre, 'Pre-history of soil science'.

[129] Jethro Tull, *A supplement to the essay on horse-hoing husbandry* (2nd edn; London, 1740), 273.

[130] Sayre, 'Farming by the book', 124.

who 'had formed no manner of Principles'. The text was organised around his principles of vegetation; the first chapter concerning crop rotations began with three theoretical propositions.[131] He explained his intention to publish a larger treatise, with the first nine chapters dedicated to 'prove those Principles in Theory', then six chapters to show 'how these Principles are to be put in Practice'.[132] The 1733 edition eventually contained twenty-five chapters, consisting of three parts, on theory, practice and tools: a new system with principles, methods and instruments, each deduced from the other.[133] Whilst he insisted on the need for experience, he believed that 'when a Thing is first fully proved in Theory, I think one Instance of Fact in Practice may be sufficient for its Confirmation'.[134] He distinguished between offering 'principles' and 'directions': while directions could be given for some crops, the circumstances for wheat were so various that it was impossible to give 'bare Directions in them all … unless the Principles themselves accompany those Directions'.[135] When discussing his four-coultered plough, he claimed that pocket-sized models of instruments and fixed rules would make the new husbandry 'more easy and certain than the *Old*', since 'a Man may practice the old random Husbandry all his Life, without attaining so much Certainty in *Agriculture* as may be learn'd in a few Hours from such a Treatise'.[136] The rules were to be set by the theorist and followed by the practitioner. Tull advised his readers to become 'Master of the Treatise, by making an Index himself to it'. He insisted that his method could not be 'properly performed without a thorough Knowledge of the Principles, which cannot be expected of such illiterate Persons… therefore until the Scheme becomes common, the Management must be under the Direction of the Master himself'.[137] Hence Tull's theory, method and book were explicitly aimed at concentrating power on the farm manager or landowner.[138] The 'new husbandry' was to be learned by a gentleman reading and studying his book and imposing it on his servants.

Tull's theory divided commentators. In 1733, Switzer attacked his critique of Virgil's husbandry (prompting a ferocious defence from Tull) and,

---

[131] Tull described the effort to write a '*general System of Agriculture* without any competent Knowledge of Roots' as being as 'presumptuous, as if he should pretend to be a great *Mathematician* and *Surveyor* without understanding the four first *Rules of Arithmetick*'. Tull, *Supplement*, 225.

[132] Tull, *New horse-hoing*, iv–vii.

[133] Tull, *Horse-hoing*, viii.

[134] Ibid., iii.

[135] Tull, *New horse-hoing*, xviii.

[136] Ibid., 131.

[137] Tull, *Supplement*, 248.

[138] Sayre notes that by 'seeking to establish in a text universal rules', Tull contradicted his own critique of Virgil and other classical authors. Sayre, 'Farming by the book', 161.

in 1757, Francis Home challenged the scientific validity of his claims.[139] However, his methods found supporters in America, Ireland and Scotland, and most significantly in France through Duhamel.[140] A letter to *The Gentleman's Magazine* in 1764 expressed a common view that Tull was the first Englishman 'to reduce agriculture to certain and uniform principles' and had contributed more than anyone to 'establishing a rational and practical method'.[141] The perceived transformation marked by Tull is evident in the dictionary definition of husbandry from 1766, which divided husbandry into 'old' and 'new', or 'that which has been practiced in all countries from the most early times' and 'that introduced by the ingenious Mr Tull'.[142] However, Tull was almost certainly more influential upon the development of agricultural writing and theory than directly upon practice. The power of Tull's husbandry was its simplicity; it was the antithesis of the great systematic tomes published in the previous half-century. In the words of a friend and admirer, Tull 'had comprised the whole art of Husbandry in one single aphorism'.[143] Yet they also admitted that they were more inclined to the practice of the Old Husbandry, and knew two gentlemen 'of small fortunes ... who hurt themselves by the practice' of Tull's new husbandry.[144] Indeed, the full practice of horse-hoeing husbandry was only taken up in a few places with limited success, and practical difficulties with the design of the seed drill meant it was not widely produced until the mid-nineteenth century.[145]

Following Tull, the gradual introduction of chemistry into agricultural writing came from trained physicians, especially in Scotland.[146] Indeed, the application of medical thinking had a lasting impact on agricultural book knowledge.[147] In the early eighteenth century, attention was directed to

[139] On debate between old 'Virgilian' and new 'Tullian' husbandry: Frans De Bruyn, 'Reading Virgil's Georgics as a scientific text: the eighteenth-century debate between Jethro Tull and Stephen Switzer', *ELH*, 71 (2004).

[140] Between 1753 and 1757 Duhamel issued a translation of Tull's work, followed by his own commentary and experiments, then re-introduced Tull's ideas back into English through *Elements de l'agriculture* (1754). Sayre, 'Pre-history of soil science', 854.

[141] Quoted in Fussell, *Farming books 1731–1793*, 5.

[142] Gentlemen, *Complete farmer*.

[143] David Henry, *The complete English farmer; or a practical system of husbandry* (London, 1771), viii–ix.

[144] Ibid., xv.

[145] Clarke and Mingay, 'Tull, Jethro'.

[146] Although a little-known work first written around 1704 and published posthumously in Dublin in 1764 by the Church of England clergyman and antiquary, Henry Rowlands, also aimed to established principles of vegetation using chemistry as a foundation. Henry Rowlands, *Idea agriculturæ: The principles of vegetation asserted and defended* (Dublin, 1764).

[147] For an account of the impact of chemistry on American agriculture in the early nineteenth century, see Cohen, *Notes from the ground*, 34–36.

applying chemistry to agriculture by the Society of Improvers in Scotland, established in 1723, and in the lectures of the physician William Cullen at Glasgow University in the 1740s; but neither produced publications at the time.[148] A book that has received little comment was *The Rational Farmer* (1743), by London physician and medical author Robert James (bap.1703, d.1776). James intended to explain the 'Principles of Vegetation' to husbandmen.[149] However, the book only covered about a third of the plan listed in the introduction and did not go beyond fundamental theory. It was essentially an introduction to chemistry for husbandmen, explaining terms such as 'effervescense', and concluded with the claim that 'the Reader is, by this Time, become almost a Chymist'.[150] It was not until the second half of the eighteenth century that a 'solid knowledge foundation' was laid for a system of agriculture.[151]

The first major work applying chemistry to agriculture was the Scottish physician Francis Home's *The Principles of Agriculture and Vegetation* (1756), written as a dissertation for a gold medal award by the Edinburgh Society.[152] Home's book was socially significant for explicitly dividing the theorist and practitioner, offering 'to fix some general principles on which the artist may depend'.[153] He did not aim to 'teach the practical part of farming', but only 'to sketch out the great outlines of this art'. Home acknowledged that existing customs already contained a degree of regularity, but argued that practising farmers – 'those whose minds have never been improved by science' – could make no further advance. This was because the art of husbandry did not automatically 'lead to an account of itself; or depend on principles which its practice can teach'. Therefore, '[s]omething beyond this art is necessary to the knowledge of the art itself'. This was a transformative idea: the theory of husbandry must originate independently of the practice of husbandry. For Home it had to be deduced from the sciences of mechanics and chemistry, hence the essay aimed 'to try how far chymistry will go in settling the principles of agriculture'.[154] While Home did not wish to teach the practice of farming

---

[148] Charles W. J. Withers, 'William Cullen's agricultural lectures and writings and the development of agricultural science in eighteenth-century Scotland', *AgHR,* 37 (1989).
[149] James, *Rational farmer,* 1–2.
[150] Ibid., 152.
[151] Jones, *Agricultural enlightenment,* 161.
[152] Francis Home (1719–1813) was later president of the Royal College of Physicians of Edinburgh from 1775 to 1777. Iain Milne, 'Home, Francis (1719–1813)', *ODNB* (Oxford, 2004), www.oxforddnb.com/view/article/13640 (16 September 2016).
[153] Home, *Principles,* iv.
[154] Ibid., 2–5.

to farmers, he did wish to establish that they did not – and *could not* by practical experience alone – possess a true knowledge of agriculture. The consequence of this argument was that the practical farmer must either learn chemistry or be dependent on the guidance of an expert chemist.

Similar Scottish works followed that attempted to explain husbandry with chemistry by the clergyman Adam Dickson (1762) and physician George Fordyce (1765).[155] Another Scottish physician, Alexander Hunter, wrote and edited four volumes of *Georgical Essays* (1769–72).[156] As an example of the influence of medical thinking, the first volume on the theory of husbandry included an essay on the 'analogy between plants and animals'. Reflecting on the role of human anatomy in medicine, Hunter reasoned that an anatomical investigation of plants 'is the only rational method of arriving at any certainty concerning the laws of the vegetable oeconomy'.[157] Hunter stated simply that 'to be a good husbandman, it is necessary to be a good chymist'.[158] Another medically trained Scottish gentleman, James Hutton, who studied agriculture and farmed in the mid-eighteenth century, also applied his theoretical training in compiling his unpublished 'Elements of Agriculture' in the 1790s.[159]

Chemistry entered more general agricultural treatises in the 1770s and 1780s. In 1771, Matthew Peters noted that the reader might ask: 'What has chymistry to do with agriculture? He must be told, that on the knowledge of that art, a great part of tillage depends'.[160] In 1787, George Winter organised his theory of husbandry on the basis that the 'principles of Agriculture are deduced from Mechanics, Chemistry, and Natural Philosophy'.[161] However, some writers on agriculture resisted the intrusion of the new science of chemistry. In 1771, a book probably authored by David Henry, a printer who published the *Gentleman's Magazine* and owned a farm in Kent, critiqued the experiments of Francis Home: 'it was before known to the husbandman without the aid of chemistry, that certain mixtures were necessary in the course of regular practice, to quicken and promote vegetation'. Despite the enthusiasm for chemical experiments, 'there has not

[155] Dickson, *Treatise*, iii–iv. George Fordyce, *Elements of agriculture* (Edinburgh, 1765). Fordyce was a pupil of William Cullen. N. G. Coley, 'Fordyce, George (1736–1802)', *ODNB* (Oxford, 2004), www.oxforddnb.com/view/article/9878 (21 September 2016).
[156] Hunter, *Georgical essays*, i. iii.
[157] Ibid., 80.
[158] Ibid., 23.
[159] Jean Jones, 'James Hutton's agricultural research and his life as a farmer', *Annals of Science*, 42 (1985), 585.
[160] Peters, *Winter riches*, xiv.
[161] George Winter, *A new and compendious system of husbandry* (Bristol, 1787), 16.

one species of manure been added to the Farmer's Catalogue, from the days of Hartlib, to the days of Dr. Home'.[162] Henry preferred the simple maxims of Tull to the experiments of Home. Taking a stronger position, *The Scots Farmer* argued in 1773–74 that it was a philosophical mistake 'to mix chemistry and farming together', since the chemist handled 'dead inanimate substances', while the farmer was concerned with 'the nourishment, growth and life of a plant'.[163] In 1779, the *General Dictionary of Husbandry* distinguished the 'simple operations of Nature in Vegetation' from the obscurity of 'Metaphysics or the Arcana of Chemistry'.[164]

Yet this conflict was slowly being resolved through the division of labour and expertise laid out by Francis Home: agricultural theory required chemistry, but not every farmer needed to be a chemist. This was the argument of Lord Kames, a correspondent of the physician William Cullen, in 1776:

> To be an expert farmer, it is not necessary that a gentleman be a profound chymist. There are however certain chymical principles relative to agriculture, that no farmer of education ought to be ignorant of.[165]

The physician Anthony Fothergill echoed this remark, and specifically distinguished between a common husbandman and a 'gentleman who wishes to improve his estate', who 'ought to be well versed, at least, in the principles of philosophical chemistry'. Hence varying degrees of chemical knowledge were mapped onto a stratified class of farmers. Indeed, in an allusion to the old mystery of husbandry, Fothergill argued that private interests had hindered progress 'by casting a veil of secrecy over the different processes, but chemistry assists us in drawing aside the veil'.[166] Chemistry uncovered the mystery of husbandry and placed it into the hands of educated men. Agricultural chemistry gathered momentum as a quasi-independent discipline towards the end of the eighteenth century, simultaneously declaring its practical usefulness while developing a body of knowledge in relative isolation from traditions of husbandry.[167] In a lecture to the Board of Agriculture in the early nineteenth century, Humphry

---

[162] Henry, *Complete English farmer*, vii–viii.
[163] Republished as *Northern farmer*, 193–94.
[164] *General dictionary of husbandry*, iii.
[165] Lord (Henry Home) Kames, *The gentleman farmer: Being an attempt to improve agriculture by subjecting it to the test of rational principles* (Edinburgh, 1776), 292. See William C. Lehmann, *Henry Home, Lord Kames, and the Scottish Enlightenment: A study in national character and in the history of ideas* (The Hague, 1971), 84.
[166] Fothergill, 'Application of chemistry to agriculture', 59–64.
[167] On nineteenth-century agricultural chemistry: Jones, *Agricultural enlightenment*, Ch. 7.

Davy acknowledged 'that a philosophical chemist would most probably make a very unprofitable business of farming'.[168]

In summary, the theoretical mode of writing was crucial to two key trends: the formal separation of the theory from the practice of agriculture, and subsequently the notion that a theory of husbandry must be developed independently from the practice of husbandry. As such it moved away from the systematic mode, which was primarily an effort to collate, order and refine existing customs. The development of books written by and for theorists and the introduction of chemistry further removed much of agricultural literature from the customary knowledge of practising farmers.

The Experimental Mode

A struggle emerged towards the end of the eighteenth century between two visions of agriculture: a deductive, laboratory-driven agriculture based on chemical theory, and an inductive, experiment-driven agriculture based on field trials.[169] This was manifested in books, and some organised their content around experiments rather than theory (although these modes often combined).[170] The distinction between 'experiment' and 'experience' is crucial as this was how book knowledge was often distinguished from the knowledge of practitioners. In the seventeenth century, the Royal Society used 'experience' to mean both a report of a discrete event and what is acquired over time through practice.[171] The former would come to be called 'experiment' and be used in contrast to mere 'experience'. Writing in 1797, James Anderson stated that '[e]xperiment hath been adopted with a view to supply these deficiencies of *experience* in agriculture ... An experiment in agriculture is a particular operation, undertaken with a view to elucidate some fact that is doubtful'.[172] In one sense, experiment was an experience improved by writing; a structured, recorded experience, capable of being integrated into a system of knowledge. A farming book in the experimental

---

[168] Humphry Davy, *Elements of agricultural chemistry: A course of lectures for the Board of Agriculture* (London, 1815), 24. On Davy as 'first true agricultural scientist', see Clow and Clow, *Chemical Revolution*, 500–1.

[169] Jones, *Agricultural enlightenment*, 165.

[170] For a definition and discussion of the history of agricultural 'experiments', Fussell, 'Agricultural Science'.

[171] Peter Dear, 'The meanings of experience', in Katharine Park and Lorraine Daston (eds), *Cambridge history of science: Vol 3: Early modern science* (Cambridge, 2006).

[172] James Anderson, *Recreations in agriculture, natural history, arts, and miscellaneous literature* (London, 1799), vol. 1. 28.

mode was, therefore, explicitly a challenge to the authority of labour-based knowledge derived from accumulated experience.

From the late seventeenth century, 'an all-embracing culture of experimentation suffused English life', stimulating ideas of experimental husbandry in the first half of the eighteenth century, particularly in the publications of Bradley.[173] Tull also distinguished between the 'cumulative experience' acquired by every ploughboy, and the 'singular, contrived events' of experiments designed to test a theory.[174] In the early 1760s, Dickson stated that his treatise was based on a journal of 'the different operations and experiments', while Mills made experiments his 'chief guide'.[175] In 1764, Walter Harte pronounced that 'what we want chiefly in husbandry, is a series of experiments, judiciously made, and faithfully related'.[176] By the 1770s, it became almost mandatory for authors to state that their book was based on both years of experience and their own specific experiments.[177]

Enthusiasm for experimental husbandry was epitomised by Arthur Young in his enormous two-volume publication *A Course of Experimental Agriculture* (1770), which claimed to be 'An exact Register of all the Business Transacted during Five Years On near Three Hundred Acres of various Soils', including 2,000 original experiments.[178] At over 1,800 pages 'this register of Experimental Husbandry' was a self-conscious departure from the systematic mode. He rejected the very idea of a complete system of agriculture contained in one book, 'for the variety of soils, vegetables, and modes of culture, is so great, that a thousand admirable works might be published, and yet the subject incompletely treated'.[179] Young followed the maxim 'keep minutes of everything' and presented the book as 'the real transcript of my practice'. However, Young would later come to regret the excesses of this book as a naive error and tried to destroy all copies.[180]

In his preface, Young reviewed the entire history of agricultural literature and judged it a failure. The classical authors had 'no just idea of experimental agriculture' and therefore 'no notion of registering experiments'. Young critiqued Columella and others, who 'eternally lay down

---

[173] Jones, *Agricultural enlightenment*, 167.
[174] De Bruyn, 'Reading Virgil's Georgics', 670–71.
[175] Dickson, *Treatise*, iii; Mills, *New system*, xv.
[176] Harte, *Essays*, 34.
[177] For example, Kames, *Gentleman farmer*, ix.
[178] Arthur Young, *A course of experimental agriculture*, 2 vols (London, 1770).
[179] Ibid., i. vi–vii.
[180] C. S. Haslam and Arthur Young, *The biography of Arthur Young: From his birth until 1787* (Rugby, 1930), 94.

their instructions, by whole chapters, in the directive stile; teaching their readers how to act, before they convince them by experiments that they understood it themselves'.[181] Young lamented that few modern authors had followed the experimental style advocated by Bacon. Blith's experiments were 'so extravagantly successful' they could not be believed; Worlidge was 'totally devoid of experiment'; Mortimer only collected common ideas of husbandry; Lisle offered observations from experience, but did not communicate the detailed circumstances necessary to inform further experiments; Tull composed 'reflections, instructions, and opinions' about his experiments rather than 'a plain narrative of his experience'; Ellis deserved attention for sharing useful knowledge on common husbandry, but little else; Bradley 'talks of them, but gives none'; and Dickson published a 'volume of reflections without one trial'.[182] It was not sufficient to write generally about experience or experiments; the writer must provide a full register with every detail. Only a handful of writers since the 1750s received his praise: the French author Duhamel, Francis Home, his friend Walter Harte and the Irishman John Wynn Baker.[183]

Young claimed that only a detailed register would allow every man to judge for himself and compare with his own soil, since the variety of farming conditions meant that the generalisations from any individual's experience were unreliable. In agricultural writing, experience must be 'the structure itself, not the foundation'. Hence books must be organised as a detailed record of that experience. 'If one tenth of the books published on this art had consisted only of a *record of cases*, agriculture, by this time, would have received the same perfection as medicine'.[184] Rather than beginning with general reflections on plant nutrition, Young described the particular conditions of the fields he occupied in Suffolk from 1763 to 1768. This experimental husbandry was a form of husbandry built upon writing, as the farmer must record and publish in a standardised format.

Two notable features about authoring a book of experiments are identifiable in an ill-tempered exchange with a reviewer for the *Monthly Review* (possibly the clergyman Thomas Comber).[185] First, it was as much a literary innovation as a farming one. Young's book of experiments contained a long essay of literary criticism dissecting the canon, prompting the reviewer to

[181] Young, *Course of experimental agriculture*, vii–viii.

[182] Ibid., viii–xi.

[183] Ibid., xv–xvii.

[184] Ibid., xv–xvi.

[185] Identity suggested in Nangle, *Monthly Review*, 12. Comber had already published a response to Young's *Farmers letters*.

comment that Young must be 'an *exact* and almost *universal* scholar' as well as a farmer.[186] Young hit back that the reviewer only wanted to treat him in the 'character of a critic' because he 'kn[e]w nothing of husbandry'.[187] To this the reviewer replied that he had wanted to 'consider you as a *farmer*, not as a *fine writer*', but had found Young 'quitting the *experimental path*' and 'deviating into that of the *Belles Lettres*'. In response to Young's temerity, the reviewer offered a mock apology for using the 'language of an university, not of a *farmer*', and sneered at Young's inadequate grasp of Greek and Latin.[188] This exchange illustrates that agricultural writers necessarily entered the realm of letters, with all its distinctive rules and protocols, however loudly they begged to be treated as farmers. Secondly, it also showed that the value of experimental husbandry depended on the character of the experimenter and author. As we know from Steven Shapin's work, truth in the new experimental sciences was founded upon the credibility of the gentleman.[189] 'Before we can reasonably depend on an *experimenter*', wrote the reviewer, 'we must know the *man*, as well as his *name*'.[190] Indeed, it was the doubt cast upon Young's character that offended him. Hence the experimental mode raised new questions as to the character and credibility of the author and experimenter, upon whose personal honour and reputation the value of the book rested. As Warde correctly infers, experimental knowledge was based on trust in the 'virtuous improver'.[191]

A similar justification and plan was given by William Marshall in *Experiments and Observations* (1779), a shorter work that combined experimental records with reflections. An exasperated Marshall asked why, at a time when advances were made in arts such as astronomy, botany and navigation, agricultural had never been 'professedly considered as a branch of EXPERIMENTAL PHILOSOPHY?' Indeed, he found it difficult to extract from the whole of agricultural literature 'one authentic sheet of COMPARATIVE EXPERIMENTS'. Not even the great Virgil had made or recommended scientific experiments. Cautiously, Marshall offered his book as 'an OVERTURE TO EXPERIMENTING, rather than as a COURSE OF EXPERIMENTS'. But the experimental principle was fundamental.[192] The illiterate

---

[186] C., 'Art. X. A course of experimental agriculture, &c. continued', *Monthly Review*, 44 (1771), 230.
[187] Arthur Young, *The farmer's tour through the East of England*, 4 vols (London, 1771), iv. 'Addenda', 512.
[188] C., 'To Arthur Young, Esquire', *Monthly Review*, 46 (1772), 169–70. This referred to fact that Young had not attended university and was apprenticed with a wine merchant.
[189] Shapin, *Social history of truth*.
[190] 'Art. Xii. A course of experimental agriculture', *Monthly Review*, 44 (1771), 164.
[191] Warde, *Invention of sustainability*, 119.
[192] Marshall, *Experiments*, 'Introduction to experiments'.

farmer trusted his memory, but the scientific farmer 'not only observes and records the useful information which occurs to him in the course of his practice, by INCIDENT; but discovers by EXPERIMENT'. Marshall explained that registers of experiments must be 'digested' and then '*systematized*', otherwise they would be 'an almost useless chaos of valuable information'.[193] Hence the experimental mode used the written word to create and symbolise a similar cleavage as the theoretical mode, in this case between the experienced practitioner and the experimentalist.

The experimental mode that materialised during the eighteenth century was, therefore, both a reaction against and a realisation of the systematic and theoretical modes of agricultural writing, by building a new foundation for the collective project of constructing a system of agriculture. Books in this style did not provide direct instructions, nor was it possible for the majority of farmers to replicate them. Indeed, Joseph Wimpey was critical of the efforts to derive general rules from 'particular experiments made on a small scale'.[194] Further, it relied on trust in the written word and the author's credibility. Even the agricultural writer David Henry argued that a single farmer 'growing rich by the sole practice of the New Husbandry, would to me be a more convincing proof of its superiority over the Old, than a thousand calculations of profit and loss upon paper'.[195] For many, direct observation or the verbal assurance of a neighbour still had more credibility than a book.

The Observational Mode

The increasing space given to reporting on agricultural experiments was part of a general shift away from prescription towards description. The observational mode generalised this approach, organising knowledge on the basis of methodical observations. Rather than a record of particular experiments, the observational mode offered a record of general best practice. Previous authors had based their guidance on the observations they made of their servants, labourers and neighbouring farmers, but they aimed to 'reduce to method' their various sources of knowledge. In contrast, writing in the observational mode made a virtue of its origins.[196] In

[193] Ibid., 2.
[194] Joseph Wimpey, *Rural improvements* (London, 1775).
[195] Henry, *Complete English farmer*, xiv.
[196] Emily Nichole Howard argues that major late eighteenth-century agricultural writers rooted their claims to knowledge in their personal story, such that agricultural prose became 'an alternate form of life-writing'. Howard, 'Grounds of knowledge', 111.

the seventeenth and eighteenth centuries, observation and contemplation came to be seen as 'productive', as serious forms of intellectual labour.[197] Daniel Defoe's tour of England in 1724 exemplified the labour of 'the professional observer'.[198] This productive observation was used by authors such as Marshall to solve key technical and social problems of agricultural books. Prioritising observation over experience as a source of knowledge achieved two things: it privileged the manager over the labourer in the acquisition of knowledge, and it privileged a particular form of writing ('minutes') in the communication of knowledge.

Observational writing had been present in seventeenth- and early-eighteenth-century agricultural books, but Young made observational writing central when he invented the farming tour as a genre of agricultural writing, with *A Six Weeks Tour through the Southern Counties* (1768). Touring gentlemen had taken notes on agricultural practices for decades, but Young was the first to publish his notes as a journal-like set of letters on the farming practices around the country.[199] He published three tours of England over a short period: southern (1768), northern (1770, 4 vols) and eastern (1771, 4 vols).[200] The innovation arose almost accidentally, after Young went searching for a farm in 1767, during which he took notes 'chiefly as an amusement on the road'.[201] Young explained his aim was 'to gain as complete a knowledge as possible of the present state of agriculture' in the areas he passed through, including crop rotations, farm size, prices of labour, accounts of stock and the use of horses and oxen.[202] However, it was not treated as a farming tour by all readers, as shown by a review solely interested in Young's account of the art and architecture of great country houses.[203] In the prefaces, he summarised his role as a professional observer: 'the principal part is executed during the journey, recording intelligence on the spot, and at the moment; or minuting at night the transactions of the day'.[204] On multiple occasions, he defended his qualifications for undertaking such surveys and stressed the need for 'practical knowledge of agriculture'.[205]

---

[197] Joanna Picciotto, *Labors of innocence in early modern England* (Cambridge, MA, 2010), 2.
[198] Ibid., 543. Daniel Defoe, *A tour thro' the whole island of Great Britain* (London, 1724).
[199] See unpublished farming journals of George Culley. Anne Orde (ed.), *Matthew and George Culley: Travel journals and letters, 1765–1798* (Oxford, 2002), 16–17.
[200] Arthur Young, *A six weeks tour, through the southern counties of England and Wales* (London, 1768); Young, *Six months tour*; Young, *Farmer's tour*.
[201] Young, *Six months tour*, iii. See also Haslam and Young, *Biography of Arthur Young*, 38.
[202] Young, *Six weeks tour*, 1.
[203] 'A six weeks tour', *Monthly Review*, 38 (1768).
[204] Young, *Farmer's tour*, xix.
[205] Young, *Six months tour*, xiv.

However, if Young was the innovator of the observational genre, Marshall was the theorist. The implication of Young's work, highlighted by Sayre, was that 'only written agricultural experience really counted as experience'.[206] It was Marshall who articulated a justification for this idea most thoughtfully and forcefully. Marshall's distinctive surveying method has been discussed at length, but his striking theory of knowledge and learning has been overlooked.[207] To understand the form of Marshall's reports we need to consider his first publication, *Minutes of Agriculture* (1778).[208] Common to both this first book about his farming and his later *Rural Economy* series was the prioritisation of observational writing and an understanding of knowledge and communication that remained remarkably stable over his publishing career.

Marshall took over the management of a 300-acre farm near Croydon in 1774 and compiled detailed notes over the next few years that led to the publication of his *Minutes*, which combined a detailed diary-like report of daily activities (the 'Minutes') with an attempt to unite these into a theoretical system (the 'Digest'). Marshall explained that, after dismissing the 'imbecility of Books' already written, and attempting to learn from his own experience through rigorous note-taking, he decided to publish his minutes to provide a 'REAL LIKENESS OF FARMING', inviting the reader to 'peruse as he would PRIVATE MANUSCRIPTS in the closet of his Friend'. These were not instructions for readers to follow, and he cautioned the inexperienced farmer against hurrying to the 'field of practice' before considering their particular situation, soil and servants. His aim was 'not to enforce PRECEPTS, but to convey HINTS'.[209] A favourable review appears to have appreciated this point, suggesting that the book would 'serve to teach an inexperienced person how to think, and thus become his own instructor'.[210] In the 'Digest', Marshall argued that agricultural knowledge could only be built upon 'ANALYSIS, EXPERIMENT, and OBSERVATION', through the 'SELF-ATTENDANCE and CLOSE ATTENTION' of the farmer.[211] He divided the source of all agricultural knowledge into 'SELF-EXPERIENCE and the EXPERIENCE OF OTHERS'.[212] Marshall's book received praise the following year from the farmer and essayist James Anderson, who commented that

---

[206] Sayre, 'Farming by the book', 68.
[207] G. E. Mingay and Arthur Young, *Arthur Young and his times* (London, 1975), 16.
[208] Marshall, *Minutes*.
[209] Ibid., 'The approach'.
[210] 'Art. VII. Minutes of agriculture', *Monthly Review*, 60 (1779), 20–22.
[211] Marshall, *Minutes*, 'Digest', 11.
[212] Ibid., 'Digest', 120

the *Minutes* were the 'most complete set of observations relative to this subject that I have seen'.[213]

In 1780, Marshall submitted a 'Plan for Promoting Agriculture' to the Society of Arts (with Young on the board) appealing for funds to conduct a survey of English agriculture. His appeal was denied, but his subsequent role as a land agent gave him the opportunity to partially carry out his plan. Marshall rejected the 'transient view' gained by travelling through a region at one time of year (Young's approach) and affirmed the necessity of year-round residence.[214] The plan was to extend the approach on his own farm – described as 'a plan for acquiring agricultural knowledge, systematically, from self-practice' – to the whole kingdom. He emphasised his qualifications for such a task, which must be performed 'by one who is accustomed to agricultural observation'.[215] Marshall explained that the function of the professional observer was to communicate the knowledge of farmers who were unable to articulate it themselves: '[t]heir farms are the only records in which it is registered'.[216] Hence Sayre described Marshall's ideal of an agricultural writer as a kind of 'ethnographer' whose goal is to 'get the husbandman to speak'.[217]

The method was as follows: pick a branch of agriculture to be studied, select a district that excels in that branch, spend twelve months living 'in the house of the best-informed farmer', and then, 'with daily attention, minutely observe and register the living practice which surrounds [the observer]: not the practice of theoretical, but of professional farmers', recording both established practice and particular improvements.[218] In this plan, Marshall subtly shifted the emphasis (as outlined in the *Minutes*) on the acquisition of knowledge from experience to observation: the 'experience of Agriculture is acquired through adequate observation, either on self-practice, or on the practice of others'. Even personal experience became a special kind of observation. Elsewhere he explained that his method shared the basic mode of acquiring knowledge with the way 'the most illiterate Farmer becomes knowing in his profession', but made an advance through recording and systematising.[219]

[213] Anderson, *An inquiry*, 26.
[214] The 'Plan' was reprinted in Marshall, *Norfolk*, i. iii.
[215] Ibid., vii–viii.
[216] Ibid., vi–vii.
[217] Sayre, 'Farming by the book', 71–72.
[218] Marshall, *Norfolk*, ix.
[219] Marshall, *Experiments*, 'Observations', 8.

The privileging of observation shaped his *Rural Economy* series, composed of six volumes on different regions of England from 1787 to 1798.[220] For example, the Norfolk volumes were divided into a systematised register and particular minutes.[221] 'I am still more and more convinced that PRACTICAL KNOWLEDGE is never conveyed more forcibly than in MINUTES', he explained.[222] A reviewer agreed, finding the 'detached observations' to be 'singularly entertaining and instructive'.[223] Marshall elaborated the point through an analogy with law and medicine, drawing precise relationships between the form of knowledge and the particular profession. The 'minutes' were to agriculture as 'cases' were to physic and 'reports' were to law, that is, 'PRACTICE IN ITS BEST FORM'.[224]

> For an agricultor cannot register an incident, — a surgeon, a case, — nor a lawyer, the proceedings and decision of a court, with any degree of accuracy and perspicuousness, until he has ascertained, and set before him, the facts and attendant circumstances respecting it; — and has revolved in his mind the cause, the operation, and the effect.[225]

By recording minutiæ, the practitioner was encouraged to reflect in new ways. Further, a faithful register enabled the reader to know as much as the author: 'the student gains full possession of the practice of a practitioner … a barrister is enabled to step into court, and a physician into a sick room, without the assistance of self-practice'.[226] Hence the form of minutes (or cases, or reports) had two advantages: it was the best way both to acquire and to disseminate practical knowledge.

Marshall's theory of agricultural minutes advocated for a new system of agricultural knowledge in which writing was fundamental to its production, development and communication. The most extraordinary claim was that the form of minutes allowed the reader to learn as if they were practising farming themselves. Full knowledge was transferred from teacher to student without loss. This conception was only possible by establishing observation as the primary mode of acquiring knowledge rather than experience, since observations could more faithfully be recorded in written form. This had broader social implications. By privileging observation over

---

[220] Norfolk (1787, 1795), Yorkshire (1788, 1796), Gloucestershire (1789, 1796), midland counties (1790, 1793, 1796), west of England (1796, 1797) and southern counties (1798).
[221] Marshall, *Norfolk*, ii. iii.
[222] Ibid., v.
[223] 'Rural economy of Norfolk', *Critical Review*, 65 (1788), 280.
[224] Marshall, *Norfolk*, ii. vi.
[225] Ibid., ii. vi.
[226] Ibid., vii.

direct experience in the acquisition of knowledge, Marshall offered a solu-tion to a key problem for gentlemen farmers. The true expert now became the manager who observed, recorded, reflected and systematised all the labours on the farm. The mere personal experience of an individual worker, unreflective and unarticulated, was insufficient. In other words, agricultural learning was seen in entirely intellectual terms, extracted from the perfor-mance of manual labour. Marshall, therefore, presented the most serious and sophisticated attempt to reconcile the contradictions of agricultural book knowledge that had plagued agricultural writing for over a century.

Two institutions adopted similar approaches to Young and produced official surveys. The first were the estate reports by Andrew Wight, a Scottish tenant farmer, responding to an invitation by the Commissioners for the Annexed Estates to assess estates between 1773 and 1784, result-ing in two publications in 1778 and 1784. The second was the country reports of the Board of Agriculture, established in 1793. The first ninety country reports across England, Scotland and Wales mark the end of our period.[227] Although both Young and Marshall were highly critical of the surveyors and surveying method, the transformation of how agricultural knowledge was organised was institutionalised on the broad model they had established.

The observational mode has been praised for allowing a comparative analysis of farming methods and the promotion of best practices.[228] To this, we could add that it helped bridge the gap between the local and the national. In Young's words, 'writers confined to their closets, or, at most, to a single farm, could not describe what it was impossible for them to know'.[229] However, many contemporaries were sceptical about their achievement. A reviewer in 1794 explained that he was 'somewhat distrust-ful of travelling, or rather galloping authors in husbandry' (referring to Young and others), since they were 'exceedingly liable to be imposed on in those accounts which they pick up in their excursions … and are necessar-ily ignorant of a thousand local circumstances, known only to the practical husbandman, who resides for years on the scene, and amidst the subject of his inquiry'.[230] This identifies a neglected dimension of the fashion for touring. As theorised by Marshall, the observational mode shifted the sense of how knowledge was acquired, from the experience of local practitioners

---

[227] Holmes, 'County agricultural surveys: Part 1'.
[228] Goddard, 'Agricultural literature', 363.
[229] Betham-Edwards (ed.), *Autobiography*, 55.
[230] 'Art.VIII. An agricultural dictionary', *English Review*, 24 (1794), 115.

to the notebook of the travelling observer, surveyor or reporter.[231] A 1770 review of Young's northern tour suggested that from the comparative view of different methods 'the common farmer will be instructed, without the trouble of experiment or calculation, in what method to proceed upon every kind of soil'.[232] The implication was that the common farmer did not know the soil he already worked in.

As the systematic mode tended towards the encyclopaedia, the experimental and observational modes tended towards the periodical. The single treatise was unsuited to communicating an ongoing series of discrete records or reports among readers. In general, it has been recognised that the rise of periodical publications from the seventeenth century created a new relation between print and knowledge, which was maintained through a community of participant readers in a culture of polite correspondence.[233] A few efforts were made to create agricultural-related periodicals from the late seventeenth century, but the format would not properly emerge until the 1760s.[234] It was driven in particular by the desire for what Francis Home called 'a book of experiments' or a periodical to communicate experimental husbandry.[235] Or, as the first serious agricultural periodical *Museum Rusticum* (1763–66) put it, the need for publications that were 'miscellaneous, not systematical'.[236] Both Lord Kames and Young (in 1770) argued that the chief obstacle to registering and publishing experiments was 'the want of a periodical recepticle of such intelligence'.[237] The *Scots Farmer*, a short-lived periodical with monthly issues from October 1772 to November 1774, articulated the need to put knowledge into 'the hands of our Farmers periodically, in a pamphlet form', as the general habits of reading extended 'little beyond a news-papers [sic], a magazine, or a pamphlet'.[238] Anderson developed the intellectual case in 1779, arguing that a method was required for 'collecting together and comparing

---

[231] The observational mode continued into the nineteenth century, both in the radicalised form of the reformer William Cobbett's *Rural rides* (1830) and the conservative form of the Scottish politician James Caird's *English agriculture in 1850–1851* (1852).

[232] 'Art. I. A six months tour through the north of England', *Monthly Review*, 42 (1770), 83.

[233] Adrian Johns, 'Print and public science', in Roy Porter (ed.), *Cambridge history of science: Vol 4: Eighteenth-century science* (Cambridge, 2003), 552.

[234] For a full list of agricultural periodicals, see Buttress, *Agricultural periodicals*. Earliest periodical: John Houghton, *A collection for improvement of husbandry and trade* (London, 1681).

[235] Home, *Principles*, 202–7.

[236] *Museum rusticum et commerciale*, 6 vols (3rd edn; London, 1764–66), i. 'Preface'. A total of thirty-four issues.

[237] Young, *Rural oeconomy*, 193.

[238] Reissued collectively as *Northern farmer*, 9–12.

the experiments of many farmers in different parts of the country'. He ambitiously claimed that a 'periodical performance' would create a 'grand republic of farmers', in which all could freely communicate without regard to social rank. Anderson's utopian plan was to bring farmers into the literary world by inducing them to 'become members of a Georgical Society' where they could be both writers and readers. Indeed, Anderson recognised that 'those farmers who are best qualified to instruct others have often the greatest aversion at becoming authors themselves', since to 'write a book requires an exertion quite foreign to their ordinary course of business'.[239] Anderson later made some effort to put his ideas into practice with a weekly Edinburgh paper called *The Bee* (1790–94) and a monthly journal called *Recreations in Agriculture, Natural History, Arts and Miscellaneous Subjects* (1797–1802).

The first sustained specialist venture, however, was Young's *Annals of Agriculture* (1784–1808). In the first issue, he defined its chief purpose as a vehicle to publish his own experiments and as many communications as he received.[240] The low sales were a constant disappointment, but it built prestige and a network of communications among keen agriculturalists, and may have reached up to 3,000 readers.[241] The *Annals* was a new way to present Young's own agricultural writings but also became a regular forum for contributors who would not otherwise have published. The foundation of Young's plan, and the distinctiveness compared to the previous *Museum Rusticum*, was to only publish contributions by named individuals, according to the accepted standard that experimental knowledge of the natural world must be based on personal authority.[242] Many articles were based on observational tours and Sarah Wilmot estimated that at least 20 per cent of articles from 1784 to 1809 were related to experiments.[243]

In the nineteenth century, the agricultural periodical and newspaper would eventually become the dominant form of agricultural writing.[244] In the enlightenment model, the periodical plays a key role as an efficient disseminator of knowledge. Yet underneath its innovation in publishing format lay the more fundamental innovation in the experimental and observational modes of codified knowledge. The periodical represented

[239] Anderson, *An inquiry*, 30–36.
[240] Arthur Young, *Annals of agriculture vol. 1* (London, 1784), 8.
[241] Horn, 'Contribution of the propagandist', 320; Goddard, 'Agricultural periodicals', 120.
[242] Dear, 'Experience', 129.
[243] Wilmot, *Business of improvement*, 12.
[244] Goddard, 'Agricultural periodicals', 120.

a new phase in the long-term shift in the relationship between writing and farming over the early modern period; an attempt to replace, or at least formalise, the oral circulation of information and extend the primacy of written knowledge. Unrecorded experience was being systematically undermined as an authoritative source of knowledge. The pen was the new chief instrument of agriculture.[245]

Managerial Knowledge

We can summarise the trend in the codification of agricultural knowledge over the early modern period as follows. Early printed books in the sixteenth and early seventeenth centuries collated local husbandry knowledge in loosely organised miscellanies organised around daily and seasonal practice, which was slowly integrated within the classical literary tradition. Writers from the mid-seventeenth century attempted to construct a unified body of agricultural knowledge and produce universal guides. But books of the systematic mode became increasingly voluminous and distant from practice, prompting further innovations from the mid-eighteenth century in the theoretical, experimental and observational modes, which aimed to construct new relations between writing and farming, between theory and practice. All of which aimed to subordinate labour as the primary source of knowledge, whether under principles derived from natural sciences, discrete experiments performed outside the regular operations of farming, or the written reflections of a professional reporter. Books were designed in ways that asserted the authority of written knowledge over practical knowledge.

This is not a story of technological determinism, in which the printing press caused agricultural knowledge to take a particular form. Yet the affordances of printing clearly shaped agriculture in various ways. The construction of 'agriculture' itself was achieved by uniting a set of conceptual relations in books to replace the set of practices grouped under 'husbandry'. Books enabled the ordering of information into complex systems of conceptual or lexicographical relations, entirely alien to the customary art. The capacity of books to store considerable quantities of knowledge, ready to be accessed at leisure, encouraged the publication of tools of reference. The fixed quality of a text encouraged the establishment of fixed principles. The

---

[245] See similar point by Cohen about American agriculture around 1800, Cohen, *Notes from the ground*, 8.

potential universal scope encouraged the proposal of universal rules that were as mobile as the book itself, which created many problems for writers and readers, many of whom were well aware that what was good for one farm was useless for another. The reaction against universality stimulated later modes of writing focused on communicating individual experiments and reporting on local practices. The difficulties of translating practical experience into words led in two directions: either a retreat into abstract theories or innovations such as observational minutes.

In all these ways, agricultural knowledge was shaped by the possibilities and limitations of print. But it was shaped more heavily by the attitudes of educated and wealthy men; a blend of a managerial desire to organise large-scale commercial farm production and an intellectual desire to systematise and integrate agriculture with other sciences. From the mid-seventeenth century, the gentleman landowner (or steward) desired a synoptic knowledge for managing a large estate with a variety of land types rather than detailed instructions on a set of tasks. Thus, agricultural writing became increasingly distant from local practice. The expansion of large-scale farms run by educated tenant farmers in the eighteenth century stimulated new modes of organising knowledge. Writers such as Young and Marshall attempted to balance theory and experience by producing a kind of knowledge that was suitable for the bookish farmer hiring and managing large tracts of land. This new ideal farmer did not learn primarily from custom or theory, but by minuting observations and recording experiments.

As farming books were constructed from the intellectual resources of the gentry and professionals they became deeply infused with the culture of an educated elite. The desire for completeness and theoretical foundations was stimulated by Francis Bacon's reform of natural philosophy. The process of collecting knowledge and writing a book was shaped by the ways of reading, learning and writing using commonplace books. The organisation of books often followed the waves of wider literary trends, such as the dictionary and encyclopaedia used for arts and sciences. Theories of agriculture were organised along models of other experimental sciences, and largely developed by physicians who introduced the science of chemistry. Hence the way agricultural writers thought and wrote about husbandry diverged from the practising husbandman who learned how to work his farm through parental guidance, daily labour and neighbourly conversation.

It is true that agricultural books in the seventeenth and eighteenth centuries were not books written by practitioners for practitioners in the narrow sense, but this does not mean that they were *useless* – for they still served particular social and economic needs. Indeed, they provided managerial knowledge for gentlemen, professionals and large tenants, who were becoming increasingly dominant. Book knowledge was for managers of labour, not labourers. The codification of agricultural knowledge was, therefore, a key element in the wider development of agrarian capitalism by subordinating workers' knowledge, in a similar manner that typified the later development of the factory system.

CHAPTER 5

Dividing Head and Hand
Gentleman Farmers, Agriculturists and Expertise

In 1825, John Loudon's enormous encyclopaedia of over 1,000 pages provided elaborate classifications of the division of labour in agriculture, far more extensive than any previous author.[1] These classifications highlight how far mental and manual labour had been separated in agriculture over the previous two centuries. This division between head and hand operated at two different but overlapping scales: a social division, between those who produced knowledge about agriculture and those who applied it in practice; and a task division, between those who exercised knowledge on a specific farm or estate and those who executed their decisions.[2] The former is the general division between the roles of the scientist and the farmer; the latter is the division between the manager and the labourer. Loudon encompassed both by constructing taxonomies of agricultural occupations (across the economy as a whole) and agricultural tasks (across a typical farm or estate). Loudon (1783–1843) was the son of a Scottish farmer who published many works on horticulture. His background, education, intellectual interests and experiences were typical of earlier authors, and his opportunity to observe and participate in agriculture in multiple ways – as an apprentice to a nurseryman, an attendee of university lectures, a landscape designer, an author, a tenant farmer and a continental traveller – gave him a comprehensive view of the whole.[3] Loudon combined this breadth of knowledge with a 'galaxy of helpers' (in Fussell's judgement) to compile his encyclopaedia.[4]

In a section titled 'Of the Operations of Agriculture', an abstract term for agricultural labour, Loudon divided all labour under three broad headings: 'Manual Labours and Operations', 'Operations requiring the

---

[1] Loudon, *Encyclopædia*.
[2] On Scottish enlightenment and social division of labour: Yeo, *Encyclopaedic visions*, 246.
[3] Brent Elliott, 'Loudon, John Claudius (1783–1843)', *ODNB* (Oxford, 2004), www.oxforddnb.com/view/article/17031 (14 April 2017).
[4] Fussell, 'Farming Encyclopedias', 17.

Aid of Labouring Cattle' and 'Scientific Operations, and Operations of Order and general Management', in a series of 266 numbered articles.[5] The first and second categories covered manual labour and the third covered intellectual labour, although they were enumerated in a sliding scale from the simplest to the most complex operations, such that labours in the middle sections explicitly combine manual and mental elements (for example, weeding required 'a certain degree of botanical skill').[6] In total, Loudon listed sixty-eight distinct manual labours, as presented in Table 5.1, including five 'Mechanical Labours', sixteen 'Agricultural labors of the Simplest Kind', twenty-two 'Agricultural Operations with Plants', thirteen 'Mixed Operations', ten 'Operations requiring Cattle' and two 'Labours with the Crop'. The sections on intellectual labour were less neatly distinguished and quantifiable. The scientific operations covered the exercise of particular kinds of knowledge, chiefly 'measuring surfaces, measuring solids, taking the levels of surfaces, dividing lands; and valuing lands, timber, leases, and farming stock'.[7] The managerial operations covered organising the workforce, accounting and commercial dealings.

The significance of Loudon's taxonomy of farm labour is that it was *itself* clearly designed as a reference tool for the scientific and managerial operations that it delineates. Who required definitions and rankings of sixty-eight distinct manual labours? Not the farm labourers performing them, certainly. Loudon himself acknowledged that manual labours were not best learned by reading: 'no description, however minute, will teach a man to dig, plough, or mow, equal to a few hours' trial in the field'.[8] He maintained that a knowledge of the underlying principles would be useful, but to whom? How exactly would a working farmer benefit from an analytical breakdown of their complex daily labours into the abstract actions of 'wheeling', 'shovelling', 'cutting', 'weighing', 'herding' and so on? The beneficiary was clearly 'the superintendent or master', who performed managerial operations. Superintendents required a panoptic conception of all labour performed under their supervision. The painstaking descriptions of manual labour would be useful for the purpose of '[e]stimating the quantity of work which servants and cattle ought to perform in a given time' and 'estimating the value of work done… founded upon the price

---

[5] Loudon, *Encyclopædia*, Part II, Book V, 449–93 (articles 2875 to 3141).
[6] Ibid., 453.
[7] Ibid., 477.
[8] Ibid., 450.

Table 5.1 *A classification of manual labours in agriculture, tabulated from John Claudius Loudon,* An Encyclopædia of Agriculture *(1825).*

1. 'Mechanical operations'	2. 'Agricultural labors of the Simplest Kind'	3. 'Agricultural Operations with Plants'	4. 'Mixed Operations'	5. 'Operations requiring Cattle'	6. 'Labours with the Crop'
Lifting	Breaking stones	Weeding	Ropemaking	Herding	Stacking
Carrying	Picking	Thinning	Thatching	Cleaning cattle	Housing
Drawing	Digging	Planting	Turning straw or hay	Feeding cattle	
Pushing, or thrusting	Shovelling	Planting, as applied to seeds and tubers	Drawing or sorting straw	Harnessing	
Wheeling	Marking with a line	Transplanting (planting, as applied to plants already originated)	Flail-threshing	Yoking	
	Trenching	Preparation of the plant	Hedging and ditching	Ploughing	
	Ridging	Insertion of the removed plant	Weighing	Harrowing	
	Forking	Watering	Measuring	Horse-hoeing	
	Dragging	Sowing	Stack-building	Drilling	
	Hand-hoeing	Broadcast-sowing	Sheep-shearing	Driving carts	
	Hand-raking	Sawing	Paring and burning turf	and waggons	
	Scraping	Cutting	Burning clay		
	Sweeping	Clipping	Forming compost soils or		
	Screening, or sifting	Splitting	manures		
	Gathering	Pruning			
	Cleaning roots	Mowing			
		[inc. multiple forms of mowing]			
		Reaping			
		Bagging			
		Sheaving and shocking (*binding, stooking*)			
		Gaiting			
		Pulling			
		Digging up, or forking up			

Note. From Book V, Ch I. 'Manual labours and operations' and Ch. II 'Operations requiring the aid of labouring cattle', no. 2875 to 3051, pp. 449–77.

of labor and the time of performance'.[9] The intricate ordering of manual labour assisted the organisation of the workforce into an efficient system:

> The grand point to be aimed at by the steward of an extensive estate, and the occupier of a large farm, is to hit on the proper number of sub-managers; and to assign each his distinct province... the next thing is to keep the whole machine in regular action, to keep every man, from the lowest operator to the highest, strictly to his duty.[10]

The function of a manager in capitalist farming was to analyse the production process and reorganise the separate parts into a profitable system.[11] The minute classification of manual operations was only meaningful once the farm had been reimagined as a machine composed of smaller machines (human and animal). To view this machine as supervised by a pyramid of managers required the prior conceptual separation between mental and manual labour.

In a later section entitled 'Of the different Descriptions of Men engaged in the Practice or Pursuit of Agriculture', Loudon brought the proliferation of occupations into a single and systematic view, distinguishing four general types of 'agriculturalists': 'operators or serving agriculturalists; dealers or commercial agriculturalists; counsellors, professors or artists; and patrons'.[12] Each class was sub-divided in a series of fifty-five articles, some of which indicated further subdivisions. In total, Loudon listed seventy-one distinct kinds of agriculturalists, as shown in Table 5.2.[13] This was the first systematic typology on such a scale, reflecting trends in agricultural specialisation and Loudon's particular vantage point as an agricultural reader and author.

Earlier writers did not apply the same classificatory precision to labour that they applied to soils, crops, manures, animals and instruments. In most English books, there was only a basic sorting of persons engaged in agriculture, which could be roles and responsibilities within a single estate, household, or farm, or rankings within rural society as a whole.[14] The cultivator in texts was usually the husbandman, sometimes joined by a housewife and some servants.[15] A few manuals distinguished a greater variety of

---

[9] Ibid., 482–83.
[10] Ibid., 491.
[11] On this general point: Marglin, 'Knowledge and power', 148.
[12] Loudon, *Encyclopædia*, 1076.
[13] Some types clearly overlapped. Art. 6928 identified 'professional operators' generally, whereas art. 6929 identified 'hedgers', a specific type of professional operator.
[14] For example, the thirteenth-century treatise on estate administration, the *Seneschaucy*, was divided into sections on twelve estate offices. Oschinsky, *Walter of Henley*, 75.
[15] For example, Markham, *English husbandman*.

Table 5.2 *A classification of agriculturalists, tabulated from John Claudius Loudon, An Encyclopædia of Agriculture (1825).*

1. 'Operators or Serving Agriculturalists'	2. 'Commercial Agriculturalists'	3. 'Agricultural Counsellors, Artists or Professors'	4. 'Patrons of Agriculture'
Farm Labourers	Jobbing farmer	Land-measurer	Consumers
(inc. men, women, children)	Itinerant agriculturalists	Agricultural salesman	Amateur agriculturalists
Local residents	Cottage farmers	Appraiser	Connoisseurs
Periodical visitants	Poultry farmers	Land-surveyor	Employers of agriculturalists
Itinerant workmen	Garden farmers	Timber surveyor and valuer	Amateur farmers
Apprentices	Seed farmers	Land-valuer	Noblemen and proprietor farmers
Children of operators	Orchard farmers	Land-agent	Noblemen and gentlemen improvers
Sons of richer persons	Hop farmers	Agricultural engineers	
Journeymen (or professional operators, e.g. ploughmen, cattle herds, shepherds)	Milk or cow farmers	*Drainer*	
	Dairy farmers	*Irrigator*	
	Graziers	*Road engineer*	
	Stock farmers	*Mineral surveyor*	
	Store farmers	*Coal viewer*	
	Hay farmers	*Rural architect*	
Hedgers	Corn-farmers	*Hydrographical and canal engineers*	
Woodman	Wood-farmers	Veterinary surgeon (or agricultural doctor)	
Head Ploughman	Quarry-farmers	*Farrier*	
Farm Bailiff	Mine-farmers	*Cowleech*	
Bailiff and gardener	Salmon or river-farmers	*Gelder*	
Forester or head woodman	Commercial or professional farmers	Agricultural draftsman or artist	
Land steward	*Small farmers (under 100 acres)*	*Designer or painter*	
Under stewards	*Middling farmers (100–300)*	*Land-surveyor*	
Demesne stewards	*Large farmers (300–500)*	*Architect*	
Court farmer	*Extensive farmers (over 500)*	*Inventors (or agricultural machinist)*	
	Gentlemen farmers	Agricultural author	
	Yeomen farmers	Professor of agricultural science	
	Farming landlords		

Note. Loudon presented these types linearly, divided into four sections in numbered articles: Sect 1: 6926–6938, Sect 2: 6939–6961, Sect 3: 6962–6973, Sect 4: 6974–6980, pp. 1076–80. These run from top to bottom, left to right. Additional types mentioned within articles have been added as sub-types in italics.

servants in the context of advice on hiring.[16] Others divided farmers according to their social rank: for example in 1795 James Donaldson divided the farmers of Britain into six classes, based on landownership: the king, the great proprietors and country gentlemen, yeoman and farmers, possessors of small farms, cottagers and the 'unproductive class of husbandmen'.[17] Yet such traditional classifications no longer corresponded to the highly commercialised rural economy, with distinct areas of specialist production and new occupations generated by the market and improvements of estates. Loudon's typology was eccentric but not fanciful. His classification was similar in scope to that used in the 1851 Census[18] as well as schemes used by recent historians.[19]

The key innovation of Loudon's typology was to classify agriculturists in relation to the market, rather than the estate or social order – to distinguish between those hired for labour, those producing for the market, those hired for specialist skill or expertise and those consuming or investing in agricultural products. The scheme was hierarchical on two levels: a loose hierarchy between the four general classes (left to right in the table), but also a clear ranking within each class from the 'lowest' to 'highest' grade. It was a kind of Agricultural Chain of Being; a pyramid with scores of nameless ditchers and reapers at the bottom and the celebrated Duke of Bridgewater at the top.

A notable feature giving texture to this hierarchy was the requisite knowledge and typical level of education (explored further in Chapter 6). The crucial points to note here are the specialist roles at the upper end of the scale for those who have an entirely or predominantly theoretical engagement with agriculture, including the 'professor of agriculture'

---

[16] In 1750 William Ellis listed a ploughman, tasker-servant (thresher), shepherd-servant, odd manservant, and horse-keeper servant, with a promise to write about maid-servants in another book. Ellis, *Modern husbandman*, iv. 140–50.

[17] James Donaldson, *Modern agriculture; or, the present state of husbandry in Great Britain*, 4 vols (Edinburgh, 1795), i. 382.

[18] See Table 54 'Classified arrangement of the occupations of the people in 1851' in *Parliamentary Papers 1852–3*, LXXXVIII, 'Population Tables, vol. I. part II. Ages and occupations'. See a summary in E. A. Wrigley, 'Men on the land and men in the countryside: Employment in agriculture in early-nineteenth-century England', in Lloyd Bonfield et al. (eds), *The world we have gained: Histories of population and social structure: Essays presented to Peter Laslett on his seventieth birthday* (Oxford, 1986), 305.

[19] Using occupational data from 1379 to 1911, the Cambridge Group for the History of Population & Social Structure identified a total of 122 distinct agricultural occupations (76 arable and animal husbandry, 21 gardening, 12 estate work, 13 forestry), grouped into 34 occupational categories (19 arable and animal husbandry, 6 gardening, 4 estate work, 5 forestry). See project 'The occupational structure of Britain 1379–1911': www.campop.geog.cam.ac.uk/research/occupations/datasets/coding/ (accessed 27 February 2018).

('capable of instructing the public') and 'connoisseurs' ('critical or skil-ful lovers of agriculture').[20] Loudon reserved special praise for the unique species of theoretical agriculturist to which he himself belonged: the *agri-cultural author*. 'The agricultural author may be considered as the most universal kind of agricultural counsellor, since his province includes every branch of the art, and comprehends times and practices past, present, and to come'. The agricultural author, therefore, found a niche within Loudon's taxonomy, abstracted from any practical role as farmer or land-owner. The author possessed a powerful, universal knowledge, applicable to any context, and at his best 'communicates original information'. Such authors were encouraged by patrons, while amateur agriculturalists and connoisseurs both promoted agriculture through the 'purchase of books'.[21] Hence within Loudon's occupational typology, we find clear divisions between mental and manual labour beyond the individual farm or estate, through the identification of writers of books and producers of knowledge as a distinct class of agriculturalists. In short, it constitutes a schematic diagram of the social threads between agricultural books, knowledge and labour in the early nineteenth century.

The contribution of agricultural books to these new divisions of labour is the topic of the current and following chapters. This chapter explores how authors separated intellectual and manual labour conceptually, metonymi-cally figured as the division between head and hand, or pen and plough. This was a key consequence, and part of the process, of the appropriation and codification of the art of husbandry, as examined in the previous two chapters. How this fundamental division was manifested is explored by considering the two broad senses outlined above: as both a task division within a farming unit and a social division between theory and practice. The task division was first loosely expressed in the figure of the 'gentleman farmer', whose emergence in eighteenth-century rural society constitutes the initial formalisation of the head/hand separation within the organisa-tion of agricultural production. Gentleman farmers were partly made pos-sible by the widespread availability of printed farming books. The social division of mental and manual labour encouraged the construction of a new kind of expertise, signalled by the term 'agriculturist'. The agricultur-ist possessed book-based theoretical expertise, by virtue of their individual training or ability, in contrast to the labour-based situated expertise of common farmers and farmworkers, by virtue of their membership of a

---

[20] Loudon, *Encyclopædia*, 1079–80.
[21] Ibid., 1080.

local community. The agriculturist could deploy their expertise in a range of roles as counsellors, connoisseurs and public stewards, as it transcended any particular farm or estate.

Both the gentleman farmer and the agriculturist demonstrate the social impact of the accumulation of agricultural book knowledge. Once head and hand were separated, the pen could begin to dominate the plough. Books helped drive the development of a new knowledge-system, named here as *agriculturism*, in which cultivation was directed by a social stratum of men with theoretical, book-based expertise; by agriculturists rather than farmers. If the term 'improvement' identifies the technological impact of book knowledge in terms of the dissemination of useful knowledge, 'agriculturism' identifies the social impact of book knowledge in terms of new divisions of knowledge and labour.

Labour of the Brain

The art of husbandry was not appropriated wholesale by learned culture, but rather extracted in part. Eighteenth-century agricultural writers increasingly invoked a conceptual separation between head and hand, which manifested itself economically and socially as the institutional differentiation between those who *know* and those who *do*. This was a division of labour that, as far as possible, separated intellectual tasks from physical tasks and privileged mind over body. Agricultural books extracted and packaged the cognitive aspects of farming, severing the knowledge of farming from daily labour and custom. This tendency in agriculture was part of a much wider and longer historical development linked to the rise of the new sciences and the capitalist mode of production.[22] In his influential analysis of the capitalist labour process, sociologist Harry Braverman argued that the 'separation of hand and brain', or the separation between conception and execution, was both a general tendency in capitalist development and the 'most decisive single step in the division of labor'.[23] The appropriation of the intellectual forces of production created a division between productive bodies and managerial minds.[24] Whilst

[22] Sohn-Rethal, *Intellectual and manual*, 117–18, 122–23. Wrigley, 'Division between mental and manual labor', 32.

[23] Braverman, *Labor and monopoly capital*, 126. See also Bruno Tinel, 'Why and how do capitalists divide labour? From Marglin and back again through Babbage and Marx', *Review of Political Economy*, 25 (2013); Emmanuel Renault, 'Work and domination in Marx', *Critical Horizons*, 15 (2014).

[24] François Guéry and Didier Deleule, *The productive body*, trans. Philip Barnard and Stephen Shapiro (Alresford, Hants, 2014).

the Marxist historical tradition links this separation to large-scale manufacturing and machine technology, we can see this process occurring in
eighteenth-century agriculture, assisted by printed books.[25]

We will first consider the task division of labour, which followed from
redefining the true role of the husbandman or farmer as primarily consisting of mental tasks. The growing emphasis that agricultural writers
placed on intellectual labour was signalled by the praise of the 'ingenious' husbandmen – rather than good, honest, industrious, or thrifty –
in the late sixteenth and early seventeenth centuries.[26] An early example
teasing out this distinction is found in the 1635 edition of Markham's
The English Husbandman, in which he explained that the labour of the
husbandman was the labour of the eyes, hands, feet and mind: the eyes
'in visiting and beholding his affairs, in apprehending the good and evil
actions of his Servants'; the hands 'in distribution of things necessarie,
wanting, or behoovefull'; the feet 'walking about his Pastures, Meadowes,
Woods, Commons, and Tillage'; and the mind, 'in fore-casting afairs to
come' and 'mannaging affairs present'.[27] The hands and feet perform
the minimal physical labours required for supervision. However, this
did not yet equate to the master concentrating all productive knowledge
within himself, which was only gradually conceived over the eighteenth
century.

The discourse of improvement that flourished from the mid-seventeenth
century not only advocated a new scientific attitude to agriculture based
on reason but began to theorise a division of intellectual and manual
labour. In 1726, Richard Bradley stated simply: 'I consider a Farmer as a
Person whose Business depends more upon the Labour of the Brain, than
of the Hands'.[28] In the same year, John Laurence argued that the husbandman did not gain chiefly 'from the Labour of His Hand', but instead, 'his
Eye to watch, and his Understanding and Judgement to direct, are the
chief Hinges upon which the Success of his whole Business depends'.[29]
The head and hands, of course, had long been identified with different

---

[25] Sohn-Rethal, *Intellectual and manual*, 121. Carlo Vercellone, 'From formal subsumption to general
intellect: Elements for a Marxist reading of the thesis of cognitive capitalism', *Historical Materialism,*
15 (2007), 15–16.

[26] McRae, *God speed the plough*, 161; Warde, *Invention of sustainability*, 106. Joanna Picciotto argues
that 'ingenuity provided the foundation for the concept of intellectual labor': Picciotto, *Labors of
innocence*, 67.

[27] Gervase Markham, *The English husbandman* (London, 1635), 5–6.

[28] Bradley, *Country gentleman*, vii–viii.

[29] Laurence, *New system*, 54–55.

members of the social body. When discussing servants, most authors echoed Timothy Nourse's remark that 'they are the Instruments, or rather the Hands, by which the good Husbandman does subsist and live'. Here the 'Husbandman' was identified with a large farmer or landowner.[30] This contrast between the role of the husbandman and his servants was expressed most succinctly in William Marshall's opening 'diary' entry published in his *Minutes of Agriculture* (1778), in which he explained his decision to discharge his bailiff: 'He has good hands, but a bad head … [he is] a good implement of husbandry … but a bad Husbandman'.[31]

These ideas were connected to a vision of how agricultural production should be organised: namely, large farms with sufficient hired labour to allow the farmer to focus on management, with time for reflection, judgement and reasoning. This ideal was stated most clearly in Thomas Robertson's 1796 report on farm size and organisation, which argued that the best farmers were enterprising tenants leasing land that kept them fully employed. In the criteria for the ideal cultivator, Robertson specified – extraordinarily – 'the SECOND characteristic of a farmer, that He does not perform manual labour'.

> Farming is a liberal art, and consists in appointing and in superintending labour; and in fact, it is less laborious to do a thing, than to tell others what to do, how to do, and to see it done. Were the farmer to hold his own plough, and perform the other menial exercises, he could not have time to make observations, to think, to read, to go to markets, to meet with his neighbours, to ride through the Parish and County, and neighbouring Counties, to see better practices, and get information from all quarters.[32]

The farmer's time should be freed up and dedicated fully to managerial activities, including making observations, thinking, reading and organising complex farming operations with a pen. Marshall mused on how far this ideal could be carried out in 1777:

> Is it impossible to manage a Farm with the pen? Proper orders, properly executed, must produce proper management. — If the orders are injudicious, it is my own fault. — But if the execution be bad, the blame falls immediately on the Ordereé, not on the Labourers — and, of course, it may be readily rectified by a dash of the pen.[33]

---

[30] Nourse, *Campania felix*, 201.
[31] Entry date 18 July 1777 in Marshall, *Minutes*, [unnumbered pages].
[32] Thomas Robertson, *General report upon the size of farms, and upon the persons who cultivate farms* (Edinburgh, 1796), 54.
[33] Marshall, *Minutes*, 29 July 1777.

A profound transformation had taken place over the previous two and a half centuries. In the sixteenth century, the husbandman was fundamentally defined as one who labours, epitomised by Tusser's rhyme: 'The husband is he, that to labour doth fall, the labour of him, I do husbandry call'.[34] Robertson, echoing many writers at the end of the eighteenth century, advocated a reformed husbandman: one who only performed mental labour. Writing around 1776, Adam Dickson described a similar development in the ancient Roman republic: 'When the great men of Rome became so much civilised, as not to perform the manual operations of agriculture, they were still educated in the knowledge of it, studied its improvement, and directed all its operations with exactness and oeconomy'.[35] The growth of agricultural literature was fuelling this transformation in Britain. For example, according to a survey of Fife at the turn of the nineteenth century, farmers had ceased to perform any manual labour in order to focus on superintending their labourers.[36]

However, agricultural writers generally qualified this basic division of labour. Even Robertson qualified his principle, adding that he did not mean 'a farmer should be ignorant of what labour is; he should know how to hold a plough and drive a waggon, build a haystack, and every other operation'.[37] Some experience or familiarity with manual operations was recommended. Dickson advised that a farmer should by no means 'serve in the place of a man at the plough or in the barn', but neither should he allow work to go undone if his servants were unavailable.[38] Depending on the size of the farm and number of employees, such questions could apply equally to an upper servant trusted with the master's authority. In a 1792 manual on agricultural education, William Skirving articulated a clear hierarchy of labours, in which 'planning and directing are always superior and more important services than mere manual labour'. Yet he advocated that both the farmer and upper servant sometimes 'ought to labour with their hands' for health and other benefits, but only when absolutely necessary, not as routine. On a large farm, 'higher concerns must occupy', and a 'cumbered mind, and a fatigued body, are too much for any man to

---

[34] Tusser, *Five hundreth good pointes*, 'The description of husbandry. Chap. 7'.
[35] Dickson, *Of the ancients*, 94.
[36] Quoted from the *Farmers Magazine* (vol. 1, 1802) in Hobsbawm, 'Scottish reformers of the eighteenth century and capitalist agriculture', 17.
[37] Robertson, *General report*, 54.
[38] Dickson, *Treatise*, 44.

persevere under'.[39] Proper management required a comprehensive understanding of the labours involved, but freedom from their daily burden.

Other writers flirted with an alternative ideal in which head and hand
remained united. In the early eighteenth century, Edward Lisle offered
a romanticised vision to his readers: 'if they would plough one day, that
is, busy themselves as husbandmen usually do, and study the other, they
could improve the state of learning far beyond what they now do or can'.[40]
Similarly, when Marshall first turned to farming, he initially dreamed of
spending the day toiling in the fields and the evening in scientific research.[41]
There were undoubtedly some authors who combined a degree of manual
labour with extensive reading and study. One of these was perhaps the
Scottish geologist, James Hutton, whose letters in the 1750s indicate that
he was (rather unhappily) labouring on his own farm: 'I find myself already
more than half transformed into a brute'.[42] Similar claims have been made
of Henry Home, Lord Kames, the jurist, agricultural author and pivotal
figure of the Scottish Enlightenment, who described his daily routine in
1765 as spending the morning 'entirely upon my studies' and the remaining daylight 'attending to farm-operations'.[43] Yet so much is hidden in the
word *attending*. The biographer William Lehman described Kames as a
'dirt-farmer', but this seems to be a euphemism for 'personally supervising
the work of labourers in his own fields'.[44] Kames no doubt got his boots
dirty, but we get closer to capturing his activities in Lehman's quip that
he combined 'relaxation with productive intellectual labor on his farm'.[45]
As Laura Sayre has commented regarding the character of Mr Rivers in
The Spiritual Quixote, this was less 'an ideal balance between intellectual
and physical labor', but 'more precisely, between pure and applied mental
labor'.[46] Even Arthur Young hinted it was impossible to unite the theory
and practice of agriculture in a single individual. The theory of husbandry
demanded 'a very enlarged, as well as deeply instructed mind', which was
incompatible with sufficient practical training.[47] There is little evidence
that the eighteenth century produced a new breed of philosopher-farmers

---

[39] William Skirving, *The husbandman's assistant; containing the employments and instructions to which a judicious and practical farmer would urge the attention of a son* (Edinburgh, 1792), 412–14.
[40] Lisle, *Observations*, xiii.
[41] Marshall, *Experiments*, 4.
[42] Jones, 'James Hutton'.
[43] Quoted in Lehmann, *Henry Home*, 94.
[44] Ibid., 84–85.
[45] Ibid., 94.
[46] Sayre, 'Farming by the book', 346.
[47] Young, 'How far is agriculture', 250–52.

who balanced intensive theoretical study with considerable physical toil; instead, the dominant social and cultural forces served to assign these to distinct social roles, and thereby forged the new breed of gentleman farmers.

The Gentleman Farmer

The formation of the gentleman farmer was an outcome of two convergent processes; the appropriation of the role of cultivator by the educated and landowning class, and the successful social ascent of tenant farmers able to detach themselves from day-to-day farming. Historians have mostly attended to the question of how the gentleman farmer was defined in terms of wealth, education or landholdings, or to contemporary attitudes from those above and below.[48] Less attention has been given to the relative knowledge or expertise they supposedly possessed, which distinguished them from the common farmer, and especially the role of book-learning in cleaving these social categories.

The term 'gentleman farmer' has been applied loosely to the fifteenth, sixteenth and seventeenth centuries, but as a contemporary description, it only came to prominence in the mid-eighteenth century.[49] While a case can be made for applying the label to earlier individuals, doing so understates the controversies surrounding this hybrid category.[50] If the social and cultural roots lay in the ideological influence of classical manuals and the economic incentives for active estate management of the sixteenth century, the figure of the gentleman farmer did not fully mature until the eighteenth, when such men became sufficiently prevalent and accepted to acquire an easy moniker. The gentleman farmer was a species that evolved slowly within the genus of country gentlemen – those who did not reside idly on their land but engaged in the practicalities of farming, while maintaining their gentility through a blend of wealth, education and manners.

---

[48] For example, in Paul Langford, *A polite and commercial people: England, 1727–1783* (Oxford, 1989), 66.

[49] Only in quotation marks in Dyer, *Making a living*, 347; applied to sixteenth and seventeenth centuries in Thirsk, 'Making a fresh start' and Thirsk, 'Plough and pen'; Leslie and Raylor suggest the 'new breed of gentleman farmer' flourished in the seventeenth century, in Michael Leslie and Timothy Raylor, 'Introduction', in Michael Leslie and Timothy Raylor (eds), *Culture and cultivation in early modern England: Writing and the land* (Leicester, 1992), 7.

[50] A rare early use (1616) of 'gentleman farmer' in print was a caution for gentlemen retiring to the country, playing on its oxymoronic character: 'the cattell will famish or diminish, the plough will go untoward … and the best by-word shall be for you: a poore Gentleman Farmer': Thomas Gainsford, *The secretaries studie containing new familiar epistles* (London, 1616), 28.

He could emerge from both ends of the social scale: as a prosperous yeoman imitating the lifestyle of superiors or a gentleman who from necessity or for amusement took full command of a farm.[51] This was part of a wider social phenomenon and expansion of gentility that also produced the 'gentleman tradesman'.[52]

The question of terminology is complex. In certain contexts, 'husbandman' could in principle refer to a gentleman, but was usually only identified with cultivators of low rank and wealth.[53] In the sixteenth and seventeenth centuries, 'yeoman' referred to freeholders or wealthier farmers, distinguished by the size and value of their farms.[54] From the late seventeenth century, 'yeoman' diminished and was mostly replaced by the alternative of 'farmer', a narrower occupational title without the associations of rank.[55] The term 'gentleman farmer' (often a hyphenated compound in early use) specified the highest ranks of farmers. Even in the late seventeenth and early eighteenth centuries, a clear distinction was usually maintained between the role and status of the husbandman/yeoman/farmer and the gentleman. For a gentleman, husbandry was initially a recreation, not a vocation.[56] Timothy Nourse, a retired clergyman, observed in 1700 that whereas 'the Yeoman goes himself and works with his Servants', which allows him to supervise the servant's labour properly, the gentleman 'cannot labour with his own Hands, nor may he go to Market to sell his own Corn'.[57]

Yet from the beginning of the eighteenth century, commentators were clearly groping for new ways to describe a changing social world. In her travel journal (1697–1702), Celia Fiennes described the prosperous men of Kent as 'a sort of yeomanry Gentry'.[58] In Thomas Baker's 1703 play *Tunbridge-Walks*, a yeoman of Kent was described, humorously, as 'half farmer and half Gentleman, his Horses go to Plow all the Week, and are put into the Coach o'Sunday'.[59] 'Gentleman farmer' began to be used in agricultural literature, such as the 1726 retitled edition of

[51] Langford, *Polite and commercial people*, 66.
[52] Alexandra Shepard, *Accounting for oneself: Worth, status, and the social order in early modern England* (Oxford, 2015), 271.
[53] Campbell, *English yeomen*, 28–29.
[54] Shepard, *Accounting*, 244–45.
[55] Hoyle, 'Introduction: Recovering the farmer', 6. The term 'farmer' appears as self-description by court witnesses from 1685, in relation to 'employment' or 'business'. Shepard, *Accounting*, 267.
[56] Jacob, *Country gentleman's*, 'Preface'.
[57] Nourse, *Campania felix*, 202.
[58] Celia Fiennes, *Through England on a side saddle in the time of William and Mary* (London, 1888), 112.
[59] Thomas Baker, *Tunbridge-Walks: Or, the yeoman of Kent* (London, 1703), 3.

the royalist Sir Richard Weston's 1650 pamphlet, and the hyphenated self-description by Jethro Tull in his 1731 preface.[60] But it was only in the 1740s that the term gained widespread use. The first reference to a 'gentleman farmer' in the Old Bailey records occurred in 1744.[61] Literary characters described as 'gentleman farmers' appeared in novels by Samuel Richardson (*Clarissa*, 1748) and Henry Fielding (*Tom Jones*, 1749).[62] A broadside ballad, dated between 1736 and 1763, addressed the 'Gentleman Farmer' in the first line, alerting the gentleman to the challenges of farming and suggesting he should stick to genteel recreations: 'There's hunting and hawking is gentleman's game, / While we poor Farmers must toil on the plain'.[63]

Contemporaries clearly felt there was a shift in the middle decades of the eighteenth century. It was the opinion of Edward Lisle, a clergyman landowner writing around 1713, that it was 'one of the chief misfortunes of this age' that 'gentlemen of the greatest abilities in parts and learning' did not tend 'to live upon and direct the management of their estates'.[64] Since those country gentry who did engage in farming often did so through ill-fortune rather than design, 'it is no wonder the comedians exhibit them on our stage in so despicable and ridiculous a figure'.[65] Yet in 1770, Arthur Young summarised the change he and many contemporaries believed had taken place:

> There is scarce a nobleman without his farm; most of the country gentlemen are farmers; and that in a much greater extent of the word, than when all the country business was left to the management of the stewards … and the merits of tenants; for now the master oversees all the operations of his farm, dictates the management …[66]

The close management of farms by gentlemen was far from universally accepted, however. For example, in 1756, even the agricultural improver

---

[60] *The gentleman farmer: Or, certain observations made by an English gentleman, upon the husbandry of Flanders* (London, 1726); Tull, *New Horse-hoing*, 'Preface'.

[61] Old Bailey Proceedings Online (www.oldbaileyonline.org, version 7.2, 26 July 2017), Ordinary of Newgate's Account, October 1744 (OA17441005).

[62] Henry Fielding, *Tom Jones* (London, 1749), III. viii. xi. 23; Samuel Richardson, *Clarissa*, 7 vols (London, 1748), vii. 141. See Taylor Corse, 'Husbandry in Humphry Clinker, Tobias Smollett's georgic novel', *SEL Studies in English Literature 1500–1900*, 57 (2017); Robert James Merrett, 'The gentleman farmer in Emma: Agrarian writing and Jane Austen's cultural idealism', *University of Toronto Quarterly*, 77 (2008).

[63] 'The farmer', Roud Number: V20791 (London, 1736–1763). Available online: http://ballads.bodleian.ox.ac.uk.

[64] Lisle, *Observations*, ix.

[65] Ibid., xi.

[66] Young, *Rural oeconomy*, 91.

Sir Archibald Grant urged the Scottish gentry to maintain a supervisory and supportive role at a distance:

> Our *Scots* Gentry have of late commenced Farmers, this is certainly going out of their Sphere; their proper Business is to give due Encouragement to the Husbandman, and they will be more useful and ornamental to their Country, by applying themselves to Philosophy and the Sciences, to the Law and the Army, than by following the Plough ...[67]

In a little-known pamphlet from 1783, the physician and political schemer George Edwards went so far as to claim that not only were gentlemen 'not qualified' to improve agriculture due to the complexities of practical farming but that 'gentlemen have no right to be farmers'. It was a 'breach of their moral duty' to enter the business of farming if it disadvantaged farmers.[68] At the same time, farmers were still often treated with contempt, stuck on the margins of gentility.[69]

The gentleman farmer was the ideal reader of most agricultural books. Henry Home, Lord Kames, entitled his 1776 treatise *The Gentleman Farmer*, written expressly for Scottish 'gentlemen of landed estates'.[70] The preface explained the patriotic social role that landowners should play in leading lesser farmers, since they understood the theory of agriculture. Kames encouraged the landholder 'to rouse emulation among his tenants, by kind treatment, by instruction, by example, and by premiums'. He should 'study the rules contained in this little work', then 'convene his tenants once a-year to a hearty meal, and engage them to follow these rules'.[71] Hence such books written by and for gentlemen were to equip them to direct the methods of tenant farmers. Indeed, many agricultural writers described themselves or could be characterised as belonging to the ranks of gentlemen farmers. The anonymous author of *The Farmer's Compleat Guide* (1760) argued that neither 'scholars' nor 'farmers' were the most suitable writers on agriculture, but instead the 'proper person is a gentleman who has a large farm in his own hands'.[72]

As an ideal type, the gentleman farmer was defined in opposition to the common farmer, in part through his superior knowledge. In 1770, Young explained the 'difference between gentlemen and common farmers' – focusing

---

[67] Sir Archibald Grant, *Political observations occasioned by the State of Agriculture in the North of Scotland* (Aberdeen, 1756), 33.

[68] Edwards, *Plan of an undertaking*, 6.

[69] Stafford, 'Representations of the social order', 86–87.

[70] Kames, *Gentleman farmer*, xiii.

[71] Ibid., xi.

[72] Anon., *The farmer's compleat guide* (London, 1760), 2.

only on those gentlemen who farmed for profit rather than pleasure.[73] The advantage of the common farmer was his frugality, as he was able to work alongside labourers for close supervision and labour diligently himself. The gentleman, by contrast, was reliant on the honesty of his servants and could not enforce the same efficiency.[74] However, the gentleman had his own advantages: 'superiority in general knowledge, in reading, and observation' was as valuable as 'the superior industry, common knowledge, and attention of the farmers'.[75] As an example of the benefits of reading agricultural books, he imagined a gentleman living in a country where 'turnips are commonly cultivated, but none hoed', but who discovers 'in turning over his books, that hoeing is a common practice in many counties, and prodigiously advantageous', and therefore adopts the profitable practice himself.[76] Hence general knowledge and book learning enabled the gentleman to surpass the performance of the common farmer. To maintain his genteel status, the gentleman farmer should 'never fight the farmer with his own weapons', but instead use his own, that is, book knowledge.[77] In such a manner, books helped distinguish gentlemen from common farmers in terms of their approach to farm management.

Indeed, the gentleman farmer was so inextricably tied to the growth of agricultural literature that an over-reliance on books was an acknowledged problem, even by authors themselves.[78] An irate book reviewer in 1755 wrote of the damage experienced by 'gentlemen who have managed their estates upon the credit of a writer's *name*, and the promises of his *title-page*'.[79] In 1771, David Henry claimed that it was a universal observation 'that whenever a gentleman enters upon farming with a resolution to model his practice by the instructions he may have received from books' he would lose money.[80] In 1780, John Trusler observed that speculative treatises on farming had 'brought on a considerable loss' for country gentlemen, by inducing them to follow wild experiments rather than 'that plain method which every farmer follows'. Rather than books, they should have

---

[73] The threshold between the two was defined in terms of wealth and the size of the farm. Young, *Farmer's guide*, 247.

[74] Ibid., 268.

[75] Ibid., 271–72. On the superior education of gentlemen farmers, see Dickson, *Of the ancients*, 85.

[76] Young, *Farmer's guide*, 273–74.

[77] Ibid., 276–77. Similar point made in John Lawrence, *The new farmer's calendar* (London, 1800), 130–31.

[78] See Chapter 6 on the 'book-farming' controversy.

[79] 'Art. VIII. A new system of agriculture', *Monthly Review*, 12 (1755), 57. See also 'Art. 18. Agricultura: Or the good husbandman', *Monthly Review*, 56 (1777), 67.

[80] Henry, *Complete English farmer*, iv.

depended on 'an honest country servant, bred to the plough'. Ironically, Trusler was trying to assure his readers that they would be rewarded with profit if they followed the plain methods in *his* book.[81]

An essay by Young raised the question of whether 'there should be such a being at all as a gentleman farmer' and confronted the uncomfortable fact that 'many gentlemen, in all parts of the kingdom, have applied to agriculture, and, generally speaking, with uniform loss, when their whole fortunes have been engaged with ruin'.[82] The problem was that gentleman farmers were, initially at least, 'generally completely ignorant of the art', since knowledge of agriculture could not be 'gained from the mere circumstance of *living* in the country', or by 'following a partridge or a fox, or from admitting a farmer to his table on a Sunday'.[83]

> But books are at hand, and it may be thought that agriculture is to be learned from them. This is to learn an art by studying the theory of it. Was ever an art learned so? If instead of wishing to turn farmer, your inclination lead you to physick, to manufacture, to commerce, would you venture to engage in the practice of any of them, from having studied their principles in books? No man could be such an idiot.[84]

Similarly, Dickson observed that the British gentry might 'indeed acquire knowledge of the theory of it from reading and reflection', which might be enough for the general management of estates, but because of 'their established manner of life, they cannot attain much knowledge of the practice of agriculture'.[85] Hence even among leading authors there was a recognition of the limited capacity for books alone to turn gentlemen into successful farmers.

It was acknowledged that a strict division between intellectual and manual labour risked severing theory from practice. In the second half of the eighteenth century, agricultural writers were equally likely to criticise the study-bound scholar as the earth-bound rustic. A dictionary of husbandry from 1779 stressed the 'essential difference between the learning of a practical observant Farmer and the pedantic performances of a closeted Bookworm'.[86] In general, scholars in early modern England were often the subject of ridicule for their overdependence upon book-learning, and the

---

[81] John Trusler, *Practical husbandry, or the art of farming* (London, 1780), 2–3.
[82] Young, 'How far is agriculture', 233–34.
[83] Ibid., 235.
[84] Ibid., 235–36. Same point made here: Young, *Rural oeconomy*, 95–96.
[85] Dickson, *Of the ancients*, 94.
[86] *General dictionary of husbandry*, i. iii.

identity of a 'gentlemen-scholar' was problematic for the new scientific practitioners.[87] The gentleman farmer faced a struggle to balance the virtues of the scholar and the husbandman: to be learned about farming, but not solely reliant on books; to be experienced in farming, but not to lower himself to the level of the ploughman.

Hence the most promising opportunity for genteel husbandry was in the form of experiments.[88] Young, describing 'experimental husbandry', stated that the farmer's role was 'to invent, – to sketch the grand design of each operation, and to leave the execution to his deputy; now and then viewing the field as his walks or rides render it agreeable'.[89] The division of labour was clear: in experimental trials 'many points should be laid down as rules of conduct to the director of them, who cannot be supposed to have adequate ideas of the nature of trials founded on the principles of vegetation, and carried on with a philosophical precision'.[90] The master farmer was the philosopher; the servant was the (invisible) technician.[91] Experimental husbandry practiced by the scientific-minded farmer offered a way to neatly divide intellectual and manual labour, while ensuring that the theoretical expertise of the gentleman farmer remained rooted in a form of practice (as discussed in Chapter 4).

The Agriculturist

If the gentleman farmer was ideally a manager who made all the decisions and left all the manual labour to his subordinates, then 'agriculturist' came to mean the kind of expert who provided the average farmer with the theoretical knowledge he required. However, these terms overlap, as a theoretical or scientific agriculturist could also be a gentleman farmer. Nonetheless, the figure of the 'agriculturist' provides a way to explore the growing social division of labour, and a more general hierarchy of knowledge, beyond the organisation of a particular farm or estate. This division represents a further extraction of intellectual labour from the daily practice of farming. It was based on the emerging idea that advances in the theory of agriculture were not the responsibility of the professional farmer, or at least not in the capacity of the common practitioner.

---

[87] Steven Shapin, 'A scholar and a gentleman': The problematic identity of the scientific practitioner in early modern England', *History of Science,* 29 (1991), 291.
[88] On experimental husbandry, see Jones, *Agricultural enlightenment*, 162–67.
[89] Young, *Farmer's guide*, 476.
[90] Ibid., 477.
[91] Steven Shapin, 'The invisible technician', *American Scientist*, 77 (1989).

In the encouraging words of Walter Harte, in 1764, 'the natural philosopher, the mechanist, and the man of fortune ... must all join with the
laborious husbandman, in order to advance the art of agriculture'.[92] In
more robust language, William Marshall suggested in 1790 that agricultural knowledge be concentrated among elite farmers: with regard to 'the
LOWER CLASSES OF HUSBANDMEN, who form the main body of occupiers,
their business is to *follow*' the 'superior class of professional occupiers'.[93]
Later, the agricultural chemist Humphry Davy argued that the 'common
labourer can never be enlightened by the general doctrines of philosophy',
and it was 'from the higher classes of the community, from the proprietors
of land' that 'the principles of improvement must flow to the labouring
classes of the community'. Davy explained with two analogies: the 'mari-
ner can trust to his compass' though he does not understand magnetism;
and the 'dyer will use his bleaching liquor', even if he does not know
the name of the substance that gives it potency.[94] The common farmer or
agricultural labourer should likewise trust the tools and techniques created
and identified by his or her intellectual superiors. Just as the individual
farm manager possessed knowledge to instruct his servants, so the class of
the enlightened agriculturists possessed or produced knowledge to teach or
instruct their social inferiors. It was the same hierarchy of knowledge, the
same division of mental and manual labour, manifested on different scales.

To explore this division of knowledge and labour further we need to
consider the changing nature of agricultural expertise. The term 'expertise' and the noun 'expert' were not used in English until the middle
of the nineteenth century. The adjective was used from the fourteenth
century, such that one could be expert in a particular domain, meaning
experienced or skilful, but there was no explicit concept of expertise.[95]
However, recent studies have used expertise as an analytical category to
explain the long-term development of the modern notion.[96] Eric Ash
proposed five-fold criteria for early modern expertise, distilled from
multiple studies: (1) the possession and control of a body of specialist
knowledge; (2) based in part upon the experience of both learning and

[92] Harte, *Essays*, 159.
[93] Marshall, *Midland counties*, i. 119.
[94] Davy, *Elements*, 25.
[95] Peter Dear, 'Mysteries of state, mysteries of nature: authority, knowledge and expertise in the seventeenth century', in Sheila Jasanoff (ed.), *States of knowledge: The co-production of science and social
order* (London, 2004). Although the associated term 'expertness' meant 'skilfulness' in the seventeenth century: Hellawell, 'The best and most practical philosophers', 32.
[96] Rabier (ed.), *Fields of expertise*.

exercising that knowledge; (3) the abstraction of theory from practice; (4) the claim of being distinct from common practitioners or methods; (5) requiring a degree of public acknowledgement or legitimation.[97] Each is best understood as a locus for negotiation and contestation through which expertise developed. We can supplement point (1) with a distinction borrowed from the sociology of science between *contributory* and *interactional* expertise; the former is 'what you need to do an activity with competence', while the latter is 'the ability to master the language of a specialist domain in the absence of practical competence'.[98] Interactional expertise is greater than the recitation of rules, but less than full practical immersion.[99] We can move beyond the question of how much practical knowledge agricultural authors and readers possessed by considering how books fostered interactional expertise, distinct from the situated expertise of experienced workers (as described in Chapter 2). At the lowest level, this was simply the ability to talk in an intelligible way, allowing gentlemen with no practical experience to have meaningful conversations about farming. At the highest level, it enabled readers to be more active managers of farms and estates, which included a kind of meta-expertise in being able to judge the ability of hired workers.[100]

This idea of interactional expertise is similar to the argument made by Ash about the role of navigational manuals in creating early modern 'expert mediators', from which an analogy can be made with agriculture. In the early sixteenth century to be 'expert' in an art was to have personal, hands-on experience. However, the culture and practice of humanist-inspired patronage encouraged new forms of expertise beyond the experiential knowledge of a practitioner, based on a superior knowledge about how and why things worked. Since Elizabethan patrons preferred not to engage with vulgar and unlearned practitioners, expert mediators acted as a social bridge.[101] They produced technical treatises to demonstrate the mastery of an art and attract patrons.[102] In the case of navigation, printed manuals based on mathematical theories helped transform the art of piloting a ship over the sixteenth century, 'from the local and circumstantial to

---

[97] Ash, 'Introduction: Expertise', 5–9.
[98] Harry Collins and Robert Evans, *Rethinking expertise* (Chicago, 2007), 14.
[99] Ibid., 31–32.
[100] In a modern context: Michael S. Carolan, 'Sustainable agriculture, science and the co-production of "expert" knowledge: The value of interactional expertise', *Local Environment*, 11 (2006).
[101] Ash, *Power, knowledge, and expertise*, 9–11. For a slightly different characterization of a similar process in eighteenth-century Europe: Klein, 'Hybrid experts'.
[102] Ash, *Power, knowledge, and expertise*, 15.

the mathematical and universal'.[103] Applying this analysis to eighteenth-century farming, we can see how printed manuals boosted with chemical theory helped transform the localised art of husbandry into the universal science of agriculture. The next chapter will examine the estate steward as an example of expert mediators who offered their universal agricultural knowledge to landowners.

The notion of the expert has occasionally been used to describe developments in early modern agriculture. Typically, agricultural authors are assumed to have been the 'leading experts' of the time.[104] The only study of eighteenth-century agricultural expertise is a brief discussion by Fissell and Cooter, in which publication is presented as only one tactic used by agriculturists to position themselves as 'experts' to select audiences. For example, the gardener and author Stephen Switzer 'worked within a time-honoured system of aristocratic patronage'.[105] Many further examples could be added of authors using their publications to appeal to patrons.[106] The focus here is to identify the general characteristics of book-based agricultural expertise. In relation to Ash's criteria, Chapters 3 and 4 have already detailed how agricultural books abstracted theory from practice and served to create a body of specialist knowledge (points 3 and 1). The following section examines how authors used books to construct a notion of agricultural expertise distinct from that of common husbandmen (point 4) and gain public legitimation (point 5).

In early modern Britain, the term 'expert' meant to be experienced or skilful.[107] The term 'expert husbandman' is found in some printed texts before the eighteenth century, meaning good, capable or skilled, to describe both servants and farmers. Husbandry manuals advised choosing 'a very expert husbandman' for a bailiff (1577); referred to 'expert and skilfull servants' in husbandry, while also stressing that the 'owner of the Farme, be most expert' (1616); and generally used it as a term of praise, such as 'ingenious and expert Husbandman' (1669), or 'most Expert of

---

[103] Ibid., 131–36. For a detailed study of navigational manuals, offering a slightly different account, see Schotte, *Sailing school: Navigating science and skill, 1550–1800*.

[104] Kerridge, *Agricultural revolution*, 102.

[105] Fissell and Cooter, 'Natural knowledge', 142–45. On appeals of authors to patronage, see Dorothy Kathleen McLaren, 'By the book? Farming manuals, animal breeding and "agricultural revolution"' (University of British Columbia MA thesis, 1991), iii.

[106] For example, in 1783 Marshall was offered the role of estate steward by Samuel Pipe-Wolferstan in Staffordshire after the latter had read his earlier books about managing a farm in Surrey, composed when he was a tenant farmer. Horn, *William Marshall*, 20.

[107] Only as an adjective, see 'expert, adj.1', *OED Online*, www.oed.com/view/Entry/66552 (8 February 2018).

the Ancient Husbandmen' (1697).[108] In the first half of the eighteenth century, it was occasionally applied generally to husbandmen or farmers.[109] But in 1722, Bradley argued that husbandry should fall under the care of 'expert Philosophers and reasonable Men', suggesting that husbandry required expertise in philosophy.[110] Yet, from the 1750s, the adjective mostly described practitioners or skilled workers. It was not used to describe those in possession of theoretical or specialist knowledge. Rather than the generic expert husbandman, we find a cast of expert ploughmen,[111] hoers,[112] threshers,[113] women finger-weeders,[114] oxen-driving labourers[115] or simply operators.[116] The meaning had clearly narrowed to the ability to perform a skilled task successfully. Hence Marshall contrasted the learning styles of the 'Philosopher' and the 'Mechanic expert', the latter by habit.[117] Although the use of 'expert' is not a simple tracker for the concept of expertise, the shift is suggestive of a long-term trend: as the ingenious and expert husbandman of the seventeenth century was split into the distinct figures of the ingenious gentleman farmer and the expert labourer by the late eighteenth century. In other words, we can detect the same separation of intellectual and physical ability.

The development of a new theoretical agricultural expertise is best illustrated by the discourse around 'agriculturist'. Chapter 4 described how the English category of 'agriculture' – as a literary topic and a science – was constructed in the late seventeenth century. A hundred years later, it was personified as the 'agriculturist' (or 'agriculturalist').[118] Agriculturist could be used as an umbrella term for anyone engaged in agriculture, including farmers and farmworkers, but was especially used for theorists, as they lacked a term of their own. Since the labels 'husbandman' and 'farmer'

---

[108] Heresbach and Googe, *Foure bookes of husbandry*, 13; Gervase Markham, *Maison rustique, or the countrey farme* (London, 1616), 15, 19; Worlidge, *Systema*, 36; Leonard Meager, *The mystery of husbandry: Or, arable, pasture, and wood-land improved* (London, 1697), 7.

[109] For examples, see Bradley, *Complete body of husbandry*, 249; Tull, *New horse-hoing*, 98; Ellis, *Modern husbandman*, 7 (April).

[110] Bradley, *General treatise*, 2.

[111] Hale, *Compleat body of husbandry*, 338; Dickson, *Treatise*, 234.

[112] John Wynn Baker, *Experiments in agriculture* (Dublin, 1772), 79.

[113] Thomas Bowden, *The farmer's director; or, a compendium of English husbandry* (London, 1776), 156.

[114] Kames, *Gentleman farmer*, 104.

[115] Young, *Six weeks tour*, 64.

[116] Anderson, *Essays relating to agriculture*, 79.

[117] Marshall, *Experiments*, 2.

[118] Both spellings emerged in the 1770s and 1780s, although the short form dominated for most of the nineteenth and twentieth centuries. See 'agriculturist, n.', *OED Online*, www.oed.com/view/Entry/4184 (8 February 2018); 'agriculturalist, n.', *OED Online*, www.oed.com/view/Entry/4179 (8 February 2018).

were already widely used to describe those occupied in farming, 'agricul-turist' was sometimes used to group practising farmers and theorists in a single category – strikingly demonstrated in Loudon's taxonomy of the 'different orders of agriculturalists'.[119] In this sense it could serve to blur the boundary between practitioner and theorist. But it usually referred to someone who was both less and more than a mere farmer. The earli-est use identified was by Marshall (a prolific inventor of words, hardly any of which were taken up), whose 1778 sub-title offered 'Hints to the Inexperienced Agriculturist'.[120] As the son of a yeoman, Marshall claimed he could 'trace his blood through the veins of AGRICULTURALISTS' back four centuries.[121] In the same work, Marshall indicated the label's utility to describe those who primarily studied agriculture, when he explained that (referring to himself) 'although he is not at present a Farmer, he has not lost sight of SCIENTIFIC AGRICULTURE'.[122] However, the term was increas-ingly used to accentuate the distinction between theory and practice. In a lecture written in 1813 for the Board of Agriculture, the chemist Humphry Davy presented his teaching to two distinct audiences: 'both the theoreti-cal agriculturalist, and to the practical farmer'.[123] In 1865, John Chalmers Morton suggested a scientific education would lift a man 'from the rank of a mere journeyman cultivator to that of a Master Agriculturist'.[124] Hence it came to be associated with a theoretical engagement and a rank superior to the ordinary farmer.

George Winter, a member of the Society of Arts in London and of the Bath Agricultural Society, who described himself as a 'Practical Agriculturist' on his treatise titlepage, provided an early portrait in 1787:

> The Agriculturist, whilst riding or walking round his farm, fully enjoys the sweet refreshing breeze, so necessary to the preservation of his health; and while he attends to his business, may entertain himself with rural sports. Every field and experiment present new objects to his view; pleasing researches into the Works of Providence …[125]

The agriculturist was associated with farming for amusement and intel-lectual curiosity. A reviewer stressed this meaning of the new term, by

---

[119] Loudon, *Encyclopædia*, 1076.
[120] Marshall, *Minutes*. The OED lists two further uses of both spellings in the 1780s.
[121] Marshall, *Experiments*, 1.
[122] Ibid., 5.
[123] Davy, *Elements*, 4.
[124] Morton, 'Agricultural education', 443.
[125] Winter, *New and compendious*, 7–8.

describing Winter as 'a gentleman of fortune and a self-instructed AGRI-CULTURIST, who, being under no necessity to labour for a family, has applied himself to agriculture'.[126] Agriculturist was a new nickname to overcome the awkward hybrid of 'gentleman farmer', dissolving the inner tension by collapsing the two terms into a derivative of the honourable science of agriculture, safely distinguished from both the unlearned farmer and the quixotic gentleman. But crucially it also became the favoured term to describe agricultural theorists, whose expertise arose as much from their learning in philosophy and chemistry as their experience on a farm.

The construction of expertise can be understood as a matter of persuading various audiences of one's authority in a chosen domain. The jurisdictional claims of new experts are liable to provoke challenges, dismissals or outright derision. This was certainly the case for agriculturists, who were ruthlessly satirised from around the turn of the nineteenth century. An article in 1810 caricaturing the excesses of improvement and the absurd rationalisations of farming was notably titled 'The Agriculturist'.[127] In a later and more sober assessment, George Robertson captured the critical sentiment with his remark about certain gentlemen improvers: 'he may be a very good agriculturalist but is commonly a very bad husbandman'.[128]

Pursuits of Agriculture was a more elaborate satire in the form of a long three-canto poem, first printed anonymously in 1808 by John Joseph Stockdale.[129] The commentary in footnotes was so extensive that the book was essentially a series of essays prompted by a few lines of verse. The poem used the example of the Norfolk Agricultural Society to take aim at all 'philosophic and scientific agriculturists', or what the poet labelled 'agriculturism'.[130] This echoed the contemporaneous sneer at 'philosophism' (meaning superficial, affected philosophical knowledge). Agriculturism was 'a constant feverish impatience, never satisfied, for something new … that spirit of universal change and perversion, under the guise of improvement'.[131] As an example of the humorous and irreverent tone, the naturalist Sir Joseph Banks, President of the Royal Society from 1778 to 1820, was described as the 'Chief Hierophant' and 'Magnus Apollo of Agriculturism'.[132]

---

[126] '131. A new and compendious system of husbandry', *Gentleman's Magazine*, 58:1 (1788), 622.
[127] Sylvanus, 'The agriculturist', *The Satirist*, 7 (1810).
[128] Quoted in Smout, 'Scottish improvers', 142.
[129] Modelled on Thomas James Mathias' popular satiric poem, *The Pursuits of literature*.
[130] *Pursuits of agriculture*, 5, 8.
[131] Ibid., 137.
[132] 'Hierophant' (Greek): a person who brings religious congregants into the presence of the holy and interprets sacred mysteries; 'Magnus Apollo': great oracle. Ibid., 27.

The poem was scathing of the scientific pomposity, fanciful theories and ludicrous methods of agriculturists. It mocked how they posed as teachers while actually collecting knowledge asking farmers questions and conducting surveys.[133] The act of discovering and publicising improvements for rewards was parodied in this example on livestock breeding:

> The process is simply this — procure *one* 'huge litter' by *any* means, no matter how much out of the course generally practical — write an account of it — say nothing of the extravagant absurdity of your process ... take your *forced* produce as an *average* ... the business is done — the *improvement* is made — you get your prize.[134]

The ambitions of authors received the same treatment in a verse on the County Reports of the Board of Agriculture (still being published at this time):

> May't live much longer than my rhymes,
> That ever, in far distant times,
> Boors, yet unborn, may thumb and pore on
> Thy *agriculturistic koran*.[135]

Here the poet was inspired by a genuine remark they had read, expressing the hope that the reports would become a kind of Bible for politicians and philosophers. Of the recent popularity of the *Geoponica*, a collection of ancient agricultural writings, they joked that even if the books are not read, 'still it is fit that every Agriculturist, of name and figure, should have his Study decorated with such ornamental articles of furniture'.[136] The commentary also launched a series of barbs at their superficiality, observing how agriculturists left their actual business to servants and were highly reluctant 'to have their whole system investigated, and their farms surveyed by strangers'.[137] The poet insisted strongly that they were not criticising actual farmers. Between farmers and agriculturists, 'I make the same distinction as between sane and profitable practice, and wild wasteful whim'.[138] Indeed, the poet claimed that 'farmers and agriculturists ... do not understand one another'.[139] A few passages in the poem are given to

[133] Ibid., 36–37.
[134] Ibid., 15–16.
[135] Ibid., 167.
[136] Ibid., 186.
[137] Ibid., 55, 132.
[138] Ibid., 45.
[139] Ibid., 49.

describing the response of common farmers to the 'hums of agriculturists' (meaning humbug, a hoax).[140]

The agriculturist in the *Pursuits of Agriculture* was a caricature, but there was some truth in the accusations that agriculturists were dependent on the knowledge of working farmers and that their true skill was literary. It was a parody of what here has been more positively characterised as interactional expertise, gained partly through interaction with communities who possess contributory expertise, that is, by conversations with practical farmers.[141] Similarly, the literary affectations of agriculturists can be understood more sympathetically as the expertise of connoisseurship. In this sense, the agriculturist stands in a similar relation to the farmer as the art critic to the artist.[142] The expertise of the agriculturist, as a critic and connoisseur, lay in the analysis, interpretation and evaluation of the art of husbandry. Many gentlemen enthusiasts may have lacked the full practical immersion of a working farmer, but they were not completely ignorant.

In Loudon's typology, the 'counsellor' can be identified as the interactional expert, of which the author was the most universal kind. Under the patrons, the agricultural 'connoisseurs' are described as 'critical or skilful lovers of agriculture' who promoted the art by purchasing books, attending exhibitions, and encouraging counsellors, occasionally writing themselves (naming Sir John Sinclair as an example).[143] We can group counsellors and connoisseurs as members of the broader constellation of agricultural intelligentsia, the class of educated people engaged in intellectual labour – or alternatively as the 'congnoscenti', the 'literati', or, in the phrase of the precocious improver Gabriel Plattes in 1639, the 'Knowledge-mongers'.[144]

There is no better illustration of this kind of expertise than the figure who came to define the age of improvement in the late eighteenth century for both contemporaries and historians: Arthur Young (1741–1820). Young

---

[140] Ibid., 47.

[141] Collins and Evans, *Rethinking expertise*, 35.

[142] See 'technical connoisseurship' in ibid., 15. On the relation between 'connoisseurship' and 'expertise', see Charlotte Guichard, 'Connoisseurship and artistic expertise: London and Paris, 1600–1800', in Christelle Rabier (ed.), *Fields of expertise: A comparative history of expert procedures in Paris and London, 1600 to present* (Newcastle, 2007).

[143] Loudon, *Encyclopædia*, 1080. Rosalind Mitchison, *Agricultural Sir John: The life of Sir John Sinclair of Ulbster 1754–1835* (London, 1962).

[144] Fussell: the contents of farming books were 'known to the ignorant and illiterate farmer, but new and stimulating to the increasing number of cognoscenti'. Fussell, *Classical tradition*, 110. Davidson describes the impact of Scottish Enlightenment on agrarian improvement as an alliance between two leading elements: 'the literati and the great proprietors'. Neil Davidson, 'The Scottish path to capitalist agriculture 3: The enlightenment as the theory and practice of improvement', *Journal of Agrarian Change*, 5 (2005), 40. Plattes, *Discovery*, 67.

has been described as a populariser, a publicist and propagandist.[145] Yet the image of Young as simply an amplifier of ideas or practices fails to capture his role in constructing a new kind of expertise. Fissell and Cooter have highlighted how his writing career secured political patronage.[146] We can further examine how Young's interactional expertise (as critic, counsellor and connoisseur) was rooted in an extensive body of agricultural literature, as an ideal type of the agriculturist.

Young did not merely write about his own and others' farming, but in effect farmed in order to write. He was always a literary man to his core.[147] Before reluctantly turning to farming in 1762 aged twenty-two, he had already published a pamphlet aged seventeen on the war in America, and briefly established then abandoned a monthly magazine, *Universal Museum*, after seeking advice from Samuel Johnson.[148] Suddenly faced with the management of a farm, he immediately gathered all the writings on husbandry he could find, later commenting that 'my love of reading proved my chief resource'.[149] Within one year he was writing letters on the subject to the *Museum Rusticum* and in correspondence with the author of *Essays of Husbandry*, Walter Harte. In a letter sent in 1764, Young praised Harte's book for making him 'quite a dilettante', but not yet 'a virtuoso' in the art of agriculture.[150] During his first years farming he wrote and published three romantic novels before any works on agriculture.[151] By the end of the decade he was publishing books on agriculture in a range of genres: epistolary, tour diaries, calendar tips, experimental records. He was, as he put it, working 'with incredible avidity in the agricultural and literary department', and writing at a furious pace: 'I remember once to have written a quire of foolscap in one day!'.[152] Young recognised his expertise was of an interactional nature, that of a discerning critic rather than simply a practitioner. The real fruit of his labours managing a farm at Bradfield, in Suffolk, between 1762 and 1767, was 'to enable me to view

---

[145] John Gazley, *The life of Arthur Young, 1741–1820* (Philadelphia, 1973), vii; Mingay and Young, *Arthur Young*, 16; Horn, 'Contribution of the propagandist'.

[146] Fissell and Cooter, 'Natural knowledge', 142–43.

[147] Similarly, William Marshall admitted, referring to himself: 'To be an *Author*, indeed, had been long his ambition; but to be an *Agricultural Author* was … an idea which never occurred to him, until he had been near three years a Farmer'. Marshall, *Experiments*, 4.

[148] G. E. Mingay, 'Young, Arthur (1741–1820)', *ODNB* (Oxford, 2004), www.oxforddnb.com/view/article/30256 (2 June 2016).

[149] Betham-Edwards (ed.), *Autobiography*, 29.

[150] Ibid., 34.

[151] Perry, *Novel Relations*, ch. 7.

[152] Betham-Edwards (ed.), *Autobiography*, 45. A 'quire' is four sheets of paper or parchment folded to form eight leaves. A 'foolscap' is folded writing-paper.

the farms of other men with an eye of more discrimination than I could possibly have done without that practice'.[153] It was such expertise that formed the basis for his proudest achievement and lasting legacy: the farming tours around English counties from 1767 to 1771. Young developed the skills of an agricultural connoisseur through the combination of personal experience, touring, correspondence, reading and publication: 'my design is to be of some service to British agriculture, an object I cannot possibly succeed in, except by publishing'.[154] Further, while on his tours he offered his services as a travelling consultant, to 'impart the little knowledge' he possessed.[155]

Young has often been criticised for being unsuccessful at farming. George Washington's secretary, Tobias Lear, reported back to the President in 1794 that 'many who know him well consider him rather as a theorist on the subject of farming … and his own farm is said to be one of the most slovenly in the part of the Country where he lives'.[156] The farmer and sheep-breeder George Culley was particularly disappointed on his visit to Young's farm: 'people that devote their time to writing cannot act or execute. His sheep are scabbed, his cattle ill chose and worse managed, in short he exhibits a sad picture of mismanagement'.[157] But such criticisms mischaracterise the nature of Young's enterprise. In his farming, the production of food was secondary to the production of knowledge. Young's success or failure did not ultimately depend on (or succeed by) producing enough from his farm for consumption and profitable sales. His land was a subject and resource for writing, a foundation for authorship. Young's farms were full of experiments and novelties, difficult for most farmers to replicate.[158] They were part laboratory, part college and part exhibition, as well as 'a reception centre and recruitment station'.[159] He sent sample crops and seeds, he lent and sold ploughs and other implements, he offered advice to visitors, and accepted pupils under his tutelage. All of which made Young an agriculturist, running a sort of consultancy business, rather than a farmer. Mingay judged that although Young was not

---

[153]   Ibid., 30.
[154]   Young, *Farmer's tour*, i. xx.
[155]   Young, *Six months tour*, i. v.
[156]   'From Tobias Lear, London, January 26th[–30] 1794', *The papers of George Washington: Digital edition* (Charlottesville, 2008), http://rotunda.upress.virginia.edu/founders/GEWN-05-15-02-0095 (24 May 2019).
[157]   Orde (ed.), *Matthew and George Culley*, 20.
[158]   Mingay and Young, *Arthur Young*, 11.
[159]   On Young as a 'node' in the European network of knowledge exchange, see Jones, *Agricultural enlightenment*, 113.

an efficient farm manager, he was 'an accurate observer and shrewd asses-
sor of other farmers' practices'.[160] As a connoisseur of husbandry, Young
combined his knowledge of agricultural practices with his knowledge of its
history, philosophy, aesthetics, economics and politics, which he primarily
learned and propagated through books.

Revealingly, Young's life as an agriculturist took him further and further away from farming. Describing the shift in his quality of life after
becoming Secretary to the Board of Agriculture, in 1793, and therefore
based in London, Young wrote:

> What a change in the destination of a man's life! Instead of becoming the
> solitary lord of four thousand acres, in the keen atmosphere of lofty rocks,
> and mountain torrents … behold me at a desk in the smoke, the fog, the
> din of Whitehall.[161]

Reflecting on the early years of the Board, Young described how little
he was engaged with agricultural matters due to his 'incessant' round of
dinners and evening parties.[162] This is characteristic of the nature of interactional expertise: to act as a medium of communication between practitioners and amateurs. It was this particular kind of expertise that was
fostered by agricultural reading and writing, distinct from the contributory expertise of practising farmers.

A similar example of such an expert mediator that provides a revealing
contrast is Charles Varlo, a contemporary of Young. What distinguished
Young was his success in bridging the literary and farming worlds as, in
Sayre's words, 'the most successful *polite* agricultural writer', a gentleman
writer who excelled at winning the admiration and patronage of enlightened landowners.[163] Varlo, however, was from a yeoman family and therefore a step or two below Young in the social ranks. But he was able to
combine his farming experience and writing skills to advance his social
position and join the 'new rural professional class'. Hence Varlo offers a
case study of how book-learning could open up avenues for social advancement for farmworkers from a middling background. Varlo occupied a genuine 'intermediate status', which 'allowed him to work both sides of the
equation—master and servant, tutor and taught'.[164] Indeed, in other areas
of the economy, those in possession of craft knowledge could benefit more

---

[160] Mingay and Young, *Arthur Young*, 11.
[161] Betham-Edwards (ed.), *Autobiography*, 222.
[162] Ibid., 246.
[163] Sayre, 'Farming by the book', 419.
[164] Ibid., 391–93.

from publicising their expertise to acquire patronage than they could from directly exercising their skills.[165]

In an autobiographical essay published in 1768, Varlo tells the reader he was the 'son of a plain English farmer', who was boarded at school at age six for one year, gained some further tutoring at home alongside 'all sorts of drudgery', before further brief stays in school between ages ten and fourteen.[166] Being able to read, write and cast accounts, another farmer made him his clerk to keep the accounts.[167] Later, back on his father's farm, he wrote that he 'applied myself close to learning every thing the country could afford', such that he 'could read and converse upon almost any subject, because I had read much'.[168] Around 1748, he moved to Ireland, where he says he met a worthy bishop and was introduced 'under the name of an ingenious young English farmer'. Since the bishop 'liked my discourse, advice, and methods so well', he was employed to consult on methods of cultivation on his estate. If we are to believe the story, then this is perhaps the key detail. It was Varlo's ability, after years of book-learning, to articulate his practical knowledge and experience in a manner that was persuasive to a bishop that secured him a good position. He was soon employed by the government to advise gentlemen on the growing of flax. He claimed that he continually surprised the bishop by being so 'conversant in history' and all matter of subjects.[169] Varlo not only used his book-learning to rise in social status and achieve greater economic security but later became an agricultural author himself, publishing multiple treatises.[170] Further, his ability to communicate his expertise was at the foundation of his activities in the 1760s and 1770s, as he journeyed across counties to demonstrate his machines, instruct farmers and sell his books.[171] Varlo's story shows how the experience as a servant in husbandry could be combined with book-learning to cultivate a form of expertise that was attractive to his superiors, both as employers and as readers of his own books. The insertion of the long biography in his treatise was precisely because Varlo was seeking to lay claim to a unique expertise – as both a genuinely practical and learned husbandman.

[165] Ash, *Power, knowledge, and expertise*, 15; Iliffe, 'Capitalizing expertise', 60.
[166] Charles Varlo, *The modern farmers guide*, 2 vols (1; Glasgow, 1768), vii. Reprinted and discussed in Clarke and Varlo, *Unfortunate husbandman*. See also Fussell, 'A Real Farmer'.
[167] Varlo, *Modern farmers guide*, xvi.
[168] Ibid., xxxix.
[169] Ibid., xlvi–xlvii.
[170] Charles Varlo, *A new system of husbandry*, 3 vols (York, 1770).
[171] Clarke and Varlo, *Unfortunate husbandman*, 17, 22.

It was the type of expertise exemplified by Young, as a counsellor and connoisseur, which found an institutional foothold with the formation of the Board of Agriculture in 1793, a hybrid between a department of state and a voluntary association.[172] However, ideas for a national body to supervise the husbandry of the kingdom, and the associated idea of employing public officials to oversee husbandmen, was at least 150 years old.[173] An early incarnation appeared in the utopian tract by Gabriel Plattes about the fictional Kingdom of Macaria, which included a 'Councell of Husbandry' to reward and punish.[174] In the 1650s, the educational reformer Samuel Hartlib proposed appointing 'two or more fit Persons of approved skill and integrity' as 'Publique Stewards or Surveyors', one for husbandry and one for forestry.[175] In 1669, John Worlidge wished that England would follow the inspiration of Numa Pumpilius, the legendary second King of Rome, who decreed that supervisors should reward or rebuke the work of husbandmen.[176] These ideas found widespread support in the eighteenth century. Writers on political economy such as Nehemiah Grew (in 1706–7) and Malachy Postlethwayt (in 1757) advocated state-appointed 'surveyors of husbandry' to ensure best practice.[177] In 1784, William Lamport supported the appointment of '[s]urveyors or inspectors of proposed improvements', to ensure that farmers did not exhaust their soil.[178] In 1792, William Skirving advocated the practice of the ancient Romans in appointing *censores agrarii*, to report what is 'praise-worthy' and 'expose ... bad habits'.[179] This arose from what Richard Hoyle has called the 'double thinking' within the culture of improvement; 'that everyman should be entitled to use his lands as he wished, but only if it were improved' – otherwise he should be forced to do so.[180]

[172] Frank A. J. L. James, "Agricultural Chymistry is at present in it's infancy": The Board of Agriculture, The Royal Institution and Humphry Davy', *Ambix*, 62 (2015), 364–65.

[173] On legislation to control practices of husbandry under the Commonwealth. Webster, *Great Instauration*, 476–77.

[174] Gabriel Plattes, *A description of the famous Kingdome of Macaria* (London, 1641), 3.

[175] Hartlib, *Legacie*, 'To the reader'.

[176] Worlidge, *Systema*, 'Preface'.

[177] Edgar Augustus J. Johnson, 'The place of learning, science, vocational training, and "art" in pre-Smithian economic thought', *Journal of Economic History*, 24 (1964), 137.

[178] William Lamport, *Cursory remarks on the importance of agriculture, in its connection with manufactures and commerce* (London, 1784), 70.

[179] Skirving, *Husbandman's assistant*, 66–67.

[180] Hoyle, 'Introduction: Custom', 23.

The appointment of county surveyors or reporters by the Board (which initially published ninety short country reports in 1793–97) highlights the contested nature of agricultural expertise. Who was qualified? Sir John Sinclair was criticised by contemporaries (and historians) for selecting the first reporters based on his personal and political connections rather than their farming experience.[181] Young was himself 'infinitely disgusted' with the appointment of the first surveyors, 'who scarcely knew the right end of a plough'.[182] Marshall, angered by being overlooked for a position on the Board, was especially critical, and laid out the qualifications necessary for 'Surveying' and 'Reporting' on rural practices.[183] First, the reporter must possess practical knowledge of all aspects of rural economy: not only agriculture but planting, woodlands and the management of estates. Second, he should be knowledgeable of various sciences, including natural history, mechanics and higher mathematics, 'to teach him to think with precision'. Third, such knowledge must be combined with the ability to write with clarity. Fourth, he should ideally spend two years studying a region, whilst employed in a suitable position to be able to survey the area, converse with practising farmers and record everything.[184] Hence, for Marshall, to be an expert agricultural reporter was to possess general scientific knowledge, local experience and effective communication skills. Book learning was, therefore, a core component of the expert agriculturist. A mere farmer was ill-qualified to be a surveyor and reporter of farming.

Agriculturism

The emergence in the eighteenth century of an agricultural expertise distinct from the knowledge and skills acquired by labouring husbandmen continued to be a subject of debate and a force that shaped modern agriculture in the nineteenth and twentieth centuries.[185] The American horticulturalist, Liberty Hyde Bailey, who believed that every farmer should be

---

[181] See full bibliography of first surveys in Holmes, 'County agricultural surveys: Part 1'. Mitchison, *Agricultural Sir John*, 149–53.

[182] Betham-Edwards (ed.), *Autobiography*, 242.

[183] See account in William Marshall, *The review and abstract of the county reports to the Board of Agriculture*, 5 vols (York, 1818), i. xxiii.

[184] Ibid., xxx–xxxii.

[185] See Joseph Morgan Hodge, *Triumph of the expert: Agrarian doctrines of development and the legacies of British colonialism* (Athens, 2007).

independent, wrote in the early twentieth century of the intrusion of 'plant doctors, plant breeders, soil experts, health experts, pruning and spraying experts, forest experts, recreation experts, market experts'.[186] Technological developments such as hybrid seeds served to commodify knowledge and render the farmer increasingly dependent on the products of scientists.[187] The introduction of an industrial logic into agriculture encouraged the view that 'farming had become too complex for farmers' and required 'farm management experts'.[188] Such trends prompted a fiery backlash in the writings of Wendell Berry in the late twentieth century, who insisted that the 'expert knowledge of agriculture developed in the universities, like other such knowledges, is typical of the alien order imposed on a conquered land'.[189] Berry was emphatic: 'a farm expert is by definition not a farmer'.[190]

The precondition of all such forms of expertise and commodification was the development of agricultural book knowledge and the increasing divisions between intellectual and manual labour in the seventeenth and eighteenth centuries. As the art of husbandry was codified, the expansion of book knowledge helped form the gentleman farmer, who was characterised positively as possessing superior knowledge to the common farmer, but negatively as lacking practical experience and overly reliant on books. The head and hand, once united in the person of the husbandman or yeoman, were increasingly divided. The ideal gentleman farmer reflected and planned, designed and recorded, measured and calculated; above all, he read and wrote books. Printed books served to sharpen and deepen the internal divisions of labour on the farm, between managers and labourers, between pen and plough.

The cumulative effect of print shaped a new social system of agricultural knowledge, which we can call *agriculturism*. It was the social system and underlying ideology in which cultivation was directed by agriculturists, a class of men with theoretical, book-based expertise. Agriculturism was based on the widespread use of treatises and manuals that created new ways of acquiring, storing, transferring, exercising and legitimating

---

[186] Quoted in Marglin, 'Farmers, seedsmen, and scientists', 193. See Scott J. Peters, '"Every farmer should be awakened": Liberty Hyde Bailey's vision of agricultural extension work', *Agricultural History*, 80 (2006).

[187] Kathy J. Cooke, 'Expertise, book farming, and government agriculture: The origins of agricultural seed certification in the United States', *Agricultural History*, 76 (2002), 25.

[188] Deborah Kay Fitzgerald, *Every farm a factory: The industrial ideal in American agriculture* (New Haven, 2003), 118.

[189] Berry, *Unsettling of America*, 186.

[190] Ibid., 88.

knowledge tangential to the practice of farming. As such, it produced new kinds of agricultural experts beyond the farmer embedded within local custom. However, the efforts to establish a theoretical expertise were not entirely successful and some of their claims were met with hostility or derision (further explored in Chapter 7). The new ideal of expertise had to compete with and overturn an ingrained appreciation for the grounded experience of ordinary husbandmen. Book-based expertise did not eclipse the authority of experienced practising farmers, but established a new hierarchy of knowledge, in which the practical know-how of working farmers was subordinated to the theoretical understanding of learned agriculturists.

CHAPTER 6

Monopolising Knowledge
Professionalisation, Education and Stewards

Agricultural books in eighteenth-century Britain helped construct a new kind of theoretical, book-based expertise to compete with traditional labour-based expertise. However, this emerging form of expertise had to establish itself on a more permanent basis within the dominant social organisation of knowledge. Gentleman farmers were amateurs who would only read as much or as little as needed to pursue a mix of profit and pleasure. Without further social reform, the rest of the rural community would largely continue teaching and learning without the aid of books. But many authors had greater ambitions for their publications and actively sought to institutionalise book-based expertise by encouraging the professionalisation of agriculture. In particular, they advocated for programmes of formal education in order to produce a class of agricultural professionals defined by their command of specialist knowledge or expertise.[1] The effort by educated men to monopolise agricultural knowledge is the subject of this chapter.

Since professionalisation was a further formalisation of the division of intellectual and manual labour, Loudon's 1825 encyclopaedia is again a helpful reference point.[2] For Loudon's hierarchy of occupations corresponded to a rough hierarchy of knowledge and education (see Table 5.2).[3] The lowest-serving agriculturalists – the farm labourers – were partly defined by having received no 'professional instruction' except what they had 'derived casually' or through observation. The farm bailiff, however, should be 'a person of tolerable education', as well as experienced in every area of farming.[4] Education was less an outward distinction among commercial agriculturalists, except as it helped distinguish the 'gentleman

---

[1] Corfield, *Power and the professions*, 2.
[2] Loudon, *Encyclopædia*.
[3] Ibid., 1076.
[4] Ibid., 1077.

farmer' from the yeoman. However, the third class, of counsellors and artists, was fundamentally defined and differentiated by education and training. The land-measurer was often 'the village schoolmaster'; the land-valuer required 'a general knowledge of agriculture in the most extensive sense of the word'; the land-agent must 'possess the knowledge of the valuer in an eminent degree'; and the professor of agriculture was not only 'a self-constituted instructor … but constituted by competent judges as capable of instructing the public'.[5] The label 'professional' appeared loosely in two ways: to distinguish the skill of 'professional operators' (akin to journeymen) from labourers; and to designate the full-time occupation of 'commercial or professional farmers' or those gentlemen who were 'professional farmers on a large scale'. From a modern perspective, we could also characterise Loudon's third class as 'professionals' (although he did not define them as such) as it included surveyors, engineers, architects and the university professor.

In a later chapter, Loudon discussed agricultural training, dividing it into two; for 'practical men' and for 'professional education'. This was not an absolute division between a wholly practical training for labourers and a wholly theoretical education for managers, but rather a staggered progression that in principle permitted a degree of mobility. Indeed, in a comment that reveals the predominant attitudes among his peers, Loudon gently admonished men of property who wished to 'keep down the lower orders' through a denial of education, and warned that this 'monopoly of power and knowledge, however, cannot be maintained for ever'.[6] Nonetheless, Loudon's own proposals envisioned at the very least a high concentration and level of control of knowledge among managerial occupations and propertied men. He had himself been an early beneficiary of formalised education by attending classes on agriculture at the University of Edinburgh, under Andrew Coventry, the first Professor of Agriculture.[7] It is perhaps not surprising, therefore, that in 1809 Loudon had established a 'kind of agricultural college for the instruction of young men in rural pursuits' at Tew Park, a large estate he was managing in Oxfordshire.[8] The purpose of the college was apparent from the title of the pamphlet putting forth his proposal: *The Utility of Agricultural Knowledge to the Sons*

[5] Ibid., 1079–80.
[6] Ibid., 1183–84.
[7] See 'An account of the life and writings of John Claudius Loudon' in John Loudon, *Self-instruction for young gardeners, foresters, bailiffs, land-stewards, and farmers: With a memoir of the author* (Cambridge, 2013), xi.
[8] Ibid., xix.

of the Landed Proprietors of England, and to Young Men Intended for Estate-Agent (1809). It appears no copy of this pamphlet has survived, but his wife Jane later explained that the college was divided into two tiers; Loudon instructed 'sons of landed proprietors', while those intended as subordinate managers as 'land-stewards and farm-bailiffs' were 'instructed by his bailiff'.[9] Its pretentions were mockingly described as an effort to educate young gentlemen 'in the liberal sciences of driving *tandem* and *four-in-hand*!'.[10] The college itself only operated for a few years.

Hence we find the effort to institutionalise book-learning in agriculture in both Loudon's encyclopaedia and personal life. This chapter continues the assessment of the social impact of the accumulation of agricultural book knowledge by examining the increasing determination of authors to monopolise knowledge. First, it considers the role of books in the professionalisation of agriculture, especially through contemporary analogies with medicine. Second, it examines how books were envisioned as part of a new system of learning by analysing proposals for educational reform. Third, it examines the development of the estate or land steward as an example of an agricultural profession that came to be defined by possession of a universal book-based knowledge, through an analysis of manuals for land stewards.

A Learned Profession

In the early modern period, 'profession' could simply mean occupation or vocation, but had an older meaning of a public profession of faith or allegiance. The meaning was gradually refined to mean a skilled service, distinct from crafts and trades. The primary professions were divinity, physick and law, but a more expansive eighteenth-century definition could include all skilled tertiary-sector occupations organised around a corpus of specialist knowledge.[11] Professions were further distinguished from other occupations by an ethos of public service (code of ethics), formalised training and qualification, high social status and prestige and a claimed monopoly on their service.[12] The growth in the number and size of the professions was part of the broader trend of an increasing tertiary sector in the English

---

[9] Ibid., xix. The same two-class education plan was outlined in: 'Review: The utility of agricultural knowledge to the sons of landed proprietors of England', *The Satirist*, 5 (1809), 169.
[10] *Pursuits of agriculture*, 239–43.
[11] Corfield, *Power and the professions*, 18–25.
[12] Ibid., 26. See also definition in Rosemary O'Day, *The professions in early modern England, 1450–1800: Servants of the commonweal* (Harlow, 2000), 9.

economy from the sixteenth to the nineteenth centuries.[13] Since scholars
have identified a set of common organisational features of modern professions, they have suggested a common pattern of professionalisation, a
linear evolution through a set of standard stages – such as excluding the
unqualified (or anyone who would lower public prestige), building a code
of conduct, establishing tests and exams, extending control over educational institutions and statutory registration.[14]

The notion of professionalisation in histories of agriculture sits within
a broader story of economic specialisation through commercialisation.
Land stewards and agents formed a particular kind of specialisation in
eighteenth-century rural society, linked to the rationalisation of estate
administration.[15] Mingay argued that by 'the later eighteenth century land
stewardship was in the course of becoming a recognised profession with
its own distinct body of knowledge and skills', partly indicated by the
publication of manuals for land stewards.[16] This was driven by the increasingly complex market economy, the adoption of new management techniques on landed estates and the rage for improvements. Stewards were
part of a 'growing band of professionals in the countryside', along with
land surveyors and enclosure commissioners.[17] The expert or professional
land surveyor had arisen earlier, driven by reforms of estate management
in the sixteenth century.[18] The case of farmers themselves is more complex.
Paul Brassley argues that, although farmers developed some professional
characteristics over the nineteenth and twentieth centuries, agriculture
never fully professionalised.[19] Using the criteria of Harold Perkin, Brassley
argues that while modern farmers possess uncommon skills or esoteric
knowledge, they largely fail on other criteria: restricted entry, standardised
training, selection by merit, exclusion of those unqualified, status and
authority and independence from the market.[20] This was partly because
agricultural science became institutionally independent from the business

[13] Overview in Barrington Kaye, *The development of the architectural profession in England: A sociological study* (London, 1960), 12–13.
[14] Ibid., 22.
[15] Porter, 'Development of rural society', 844; Beckett, 'Landownership', 590; Clay, 'Landlords', 180;
Turner et al., *Agricultural rent*, 15.
[16] Mingay, 'Land steward', 8.
[17] Porter, 'Development of rural society', 844–48.
[18] Thompson, *Chartered surveyors*; chs 1, 2. McRae, *God speed the plough*, 169–76; Robson,
'Improvement and epistemologies'.
[19] Peter Jones observed that the 'mid-Victorians never considered seriously the idea that agriculture
should be converted into a profession'. Jones, *Agricultural enlightenment*, 182.
[20] Brassley, 'Professionalisation', 247.

of farming, rather than forming the basis for farming as a profession.[21] By 1914, many new farming inputs and techniques were being developed outside the farming community, in research institutions and universities.[22]

The overall picture is of a partial professionalisation of agriculture or a combined professionalisation and annexation of certain elements. However, this apparent failure to professionalise was not for the lack of trying. Such efforts to professionalise are best explored using the jurisdictional model of Andrew Abbott rather than the trait-based approach of Perkins, which lacks flexibility and historical nuance. The jurisdictional model treats the professions as an interdependent system, competing with each other for jurisdiction over certain forms of work, through the control of knowledge and its application ('jurisdiction' meaning various kinds of formal and informal authority, not the narrow legal sense).[23] This perspective is helpful in understanding how professions develop through struggle and negotiation in a competitive environment. To constitute itself as a profession, members or advocates must seek legitimation from society to recognise its system of knowledge and grant it both cultural and social authority.

It is thus possible to study professionalisation by examining competing jurisdictional claims rather than identifying a fixed set of organisational traits (associations, qualifications, code of ethics).[24] Hence we can explore how agricultural authors and books contributed to the professionalisation of agriculture by considering the jurisdictional dispute between educated men and unlearned husbandmen. Indeed, instructional manuals are typically used to make public claims for the application of a particular system of knowledge to an area of social life.[25]

The term 'profession' itself, as with 'expert', does not afford a straightforward way to analyse the professionalisation of agriculture, as it did not bear its current meaning. 'Profession' was used widely in the early modern period to mean almost any occupation to earn a living, and applied fairly consistently to husbandry in this sense.[26] For example, in 1613, when Gervase Markham wished to establish his credibility as an author, he

---

[21] Ibid., 242.
[22] Paul Brassley, 'Agricultural science and education', in E. J. T. Collins (ed.), *AHEW: 1850–1914 Vol 7* (Cambridge, 2000), 597–98.
[23] Peter Jones does not refer to Abbott's model, but describes 'a jurisdictional dispute between the two professional groups – agronomists and chemists' for control of the direction of agricultural science in nineteenth-century Europe. Jones, *Agricultural enlightenment*, 181–87.
[24] Andrew Abbott, *The system of professions: An essay on the division of expert labor* (London, 1988), 19–20.
[25] Ibid., 9, 60.
[26] 'profession, n.', *OED Online*, www.oed.com/view/Entry/152052 (8 February 2018).

claimed to have 'followed the profession of a Husbandman'.[27] Yet from the 1770s onwards many writers used 'profession' to contrast working farmers with theorists. Arthur Young distinguished between gentlemen who had a scholarly interest in farming and gentlemen for 'whom it is a real profession, business, and dependence'.[28] William Marshall drew the explicit distinction: 'not the practice of theoretical, but of professional farmers'.[29] In the 1790s, Andrew Coventry explained his aim in a course of lectures on agriculture to teach 'both the principles of agriculture ... as a science, and its rules as a practical profession'.[30] However, Coventry also represented a new sense of 'profession', as he was the first 'Professor of Agriculture' anywhere in Europe, residing at the University of Edinburgh. Until Coventry, the notion of the profession of husbandry had no specific association with a body of specialist knowledge, only with a practical occupation. Hence the changing use of the term profession is suggestive of the same split between practice and theory as the changing use of expert. As 'expert' was increasingly used to mean the skill of practitioners, 'profession' was increasingly used to mean working, practical farmers, for whom farming was a business. Therefore, it had almost the opposite meaning to the analytical concept under investigation, which is the reform of agricultural occupations on the basis of a command of a body of specialist knowledge.

Hence the idea of an agricultural profession is best introduced in the way in which contemporaries imagined it, which was often through an analogy with medicine. Indeed, there are a number of striking parallels in the development of medicine and agriculture with respect to the relationship between books, knowledge and power. In the early modern period the knowledge and practice of both were largely informal, widely spread throughout society and centred on the family.[31] Further, it has been argued that the development of medical science was marked by the same process of appropriation of popular knowledge as discussed in relation to husbandry.[32] For example, the oral and customary knowledge of herb women was recast in the pages of books into a learned botanical

---

[27] Markham, *English husbandman*, ch. 1.
[28] Young, *Farmer's guide*, 249.
[29] Marshall, *Norfolk*, i. ix.
[30] Coventry, *Lectures on agriculture*, 3–4.
[31] Wear, *Knowledge and practice*, 21–28. The intimate parallels between early modern agriculture and medicine is perhaps best illustrated in almanacs, as rules for husbandry and rules for physic were offered alongside each other and understood within the same astrological system. Curth, *English almanacs*.
[32] See argument in Fissell and Cooter, 'Natural knowledge', 146–52.

framework for the physician and apothecary.[33] We can draw further parallels in terms of professionalisation. David Wear has explored the complex negotiation in the jurisdiction over knowledge and practice between the physician, the surgeon and the apothecary, such as between 'the book-based knowledge of the learned physicians' and 'the practical training and modicum of book learning in medicine of the apothecary-physicians'.[34] The central issue of many early modern medical controversies was the extent to which medicine was an art learned by practice, or a science learned by theoretical study, and the institutional arrangement of various levels of expertise.

These controversies were mirrored in agriculture. The medical comparison was made explicitly by agricultural writers towards the end of the eighteenth century, partly due to the influence of physicians who published agricultural books. These analogies offer an insight into how agricultural writers viewed the occupation of the farmer and their desire to elevate farming to a learned profession. It was claimed that both occupations depended on a body of scientific knowledge and required academic training. Hence it was argued that agriculture required re-organisation along the lines of medicine, with equivalent divisions between practitioners of differing expertise.

In 1777, Cuthbert Clarke offered an extended comparison of the 'expediency of the theories of medicine and husbandry' through a dialogue. The character Philosophus argued that while medicine was ancient, it had only recently been improved by science. In medicine's infancy, the sick were placed at road crossings to be inspected by travellers, whose diverse experiences made them best able to identify sickness. In the same manner, 'collections of facts relative to the effects of certain manures and modes of culture, upon soils of such and such complexions' were being made on agricultural tours, but were not yet united by theory.[35] Clarke went on to compare the 'mere druggist set up for physician', with the 'mere practitioner in husbandry who presume to manage as well … as a person that has a competent knowledge of both Theory and Practice'.[36] Clarke argued that farmers required formal education in the same manner 'that physic can

---

[33] Wear, *Knowledge and practice*, 63–65.

[34] Ibid., 435. See also account of conflict between the 'rational physician' and 'empiricks' on the basis of their understanding of the fundamental causes of disease. Steven Shapin, 'Trusting George Cheyne: Scientific expertise, common sense, and moral authority in early eighteenth-century dietetic medicine', *Bulletin of the History of Medicine*, 77 (2003), 271.

[35] Clarke, *True theory*, 4–9.

[36] Ibid., iv.

only be warrantably practiced by men who have studied anatomy, and the nature of medicine'.[37]

Medicine set the cultural standard for many agricultural writers. In 1779, Young declared that agriculture required more attention than almost any other art, 'ranking in this respect, perhaps, with that of medicine itself'.[38] He believed that if the spirit of improvement continued, then 'we shall soon see husbandry in perfection … and built upon as just and philosophic principles, as the art of medicine'.[39] George Winter remarked that '[p]hysicians are well acquainted with the disorders incident to the human body; it is *their* profession, their study … Why should it not be similar with Farmers?'.[40] In 1780, William Lamport declared that, with respect to education, 'it is with Agriculture as with Physic'. Hence farmers should learn the science behind their art, 'unless quacks may be allowed to perform perfectly well in Agriculture'.[41] However, the comparison with medicine could be used against agricultural writers themselves. Both agriculture and medicine were considered arts and sciences, for which a combination of practice and theory was necessary. In an anti-enclosure pamphlet responding to Lamport, the author claimed that agricultural writers were like physicians who derived from the '*materia medica*' (the body of collected knowledge about healing) 'a specific remedy against every disorder to which mankind are liable, without distinction of age, sex, constitution', as they attempted 'to fix upon one specific plan of husbandry, suitable to every soil in Great Britain'.[42]

Lamport's use of 'quack' – someone who dishonestly claims to have medical knowledge or skill – highlights the struggle over expertise. Polemics against quackery, usually hurled at unqualified medical operators, were, in Roy Porter's words, 'blows in tactical professional infighting'.[43] Accusations arose from the need to build a consensus about what constituted true knowledge in a particular domain and who was entitled to exercise it. Hence its use in an agricultural context is revealing. William Ellis included an anonymous letter in his 1736 publication that observed the poor reputation of recent books on husbandry, viewed by many as 'Quack Advertisements'.[44] Agricultural authors mocked their rivals for

[37] Ibid., 4–5.
[38] Young, 'How far is agriculture', 234 (originally written in 1779).
[39] Young, *Rural oeconomy*, 92.
[40] *The farmer convinced; or, the reviewers of the Monthly Review anatomized* (London, 1788), 34.
[41] Lamport, 'Proposal', 30.
[42] *A political enquiry*, 34.
[43] Roy Porter, *Health for sale: Quackery in England, 1660–1850* (Manchester, 1989), 222.
[44] William Ellis, *New experiments in husbandry, for the month of April* (London, 1736), 36.

including ambitious recipes 'for increasing fertility, like quack medicines', or attacked 'the quackery of deceitful imposters'.[45] Similarly, Thomas Stone compared trusting the opinion of mere farmers about the consequence of enclosure to trusting 'an ignorant empiric' to perform surgery.[46] Joseph Wimpey likened the difference between a good and bad understanding of husbandry to 'the real difference between a Physician and an Empiric'.[47]

In 1787, William Marshall crystallised the rationale for the professionalisation of agriculture in an extended analogy with learned professions. He drew an equivalence between the surgeon or physician, the lawyer or barrister, and the 'agricultor' (borrowed from Latin, synonymous with 'agriculturist'). He explained the difference between the agricultor and the farmer:

> The attorney, the apothecary, and the common farmer, are enabled to carry on their respective professions, or callings, without those scientific helps. The former depend upon the practice of their masters, and their own practice, during their clerkship, or apprenticeship; as the farmer does upon that of his father, and the country he happens to be bred in. But why do we, in difficulties, fly from the apothecary to the physician, and from the attorney to the counsellor? Because they have studied their professions scientifically, have obtained a general knowledge, and taken comprehensive views, of their respective subjects ...[48]

This is the crucial point: the desired agricultural professional was not intended to replace the common farmer, but to establish a more prestigious occupation above him. Most significantly, this professional 'agricultor' was to be formed through the study of science, grounded in a body of literature. Indeed, many years later, in 1865, John Chalmers Morton used a comparison of the ratio of book sales per farmer with the ratio of medical textbooks per doctor to measure the professional standing of farming, linking the professionalisation of farmers with both the medical profession and book-learning.[49] Similar analogies relating to occupational hierarchies were made by others, although with different terminologies. For example, Andrew Coventry stated that a 'mere ploughman can no more be reckoned a husbandman ... than a druggist's porter a physician'.[50] Here the

---

[45] See Anon., *Essay on the theory of agriculture* (London, 1760), 4; Wimpey, *Rural*, 25.

[46] Thomas Stone, *A review of the corrected agricultural survey of Lincolnshire, by Arthur Young, Esq* (London, 1800), 411.

[47] Wimpey, *Rural*, 211.

[48] Marshall, *Norfolk*, ii. vii–viii.

[49] Goddard, 'Not a reading class'. See Morton, 'Agricultural education', 456.

[50] Coventry, *Lectures on agriculture*, 6.

husbandman was refashioned as the master of both theory and practice, whereas the ploughman was an unlearned assistant.

Educational Schemes

The best way to control knowledge and its application to an area of work is through education. Hence regularised education or training is a recognised feature of all professions. Tracking ideas of agricultural education is, therefore, a way of tracking ideas relating to professionalisation and the monopolisation of knowledge. Formal agricultural education was not established until the founding of the Agricultural College near Cirencester in 1845 (officially granted the title Royal Agricultural College in 1880). Yet various proposals had been circulating since at least the mid-seventeenth century.[51] While there were a few attempts to put them into practice, most of these visions were never realised. As a consequence, there has been no dedicated study of early modern agricultural education. Here we will be restricted to unpacking the intention of authors and the role of book-learning in educational proposals. Plans for formalised agricultural education were in part an attempt to institutionalise theoretical expertise derived from agricultural books and establish new pedagogical relationships between educated gentlemen and various subordinate farmworkers. Over time a vision was formed of a highly stratified education system for the primary purpose of preparing the sons of wealthy farmers and gentlemen to join the managerial class of capitalist agriculture. These proposals were put forward in a period of expanding educational provision, a general shift from classical to technical or science-based curricula and an opening of opportunities for the middling sort.[52]

The 1640s and 1650s produced a burst of ideas for educational reforms led by Samuel Hartlib, John Dury and William Petty, which focused on technical or vocational training for the lower orders, including husbandry.[53] The most developed proposal for a dedicated 'College of Husbandry' was put forward by Cressy Dymock in 1651, envisioned as a combined educational institution and scientific society, with training modelled on a seven-year craft apprenticeship for instruction in both practice and theory.[54] It

---

[51] Informally, prosperous farmers sent placed their sons as pupils 'with superior farmers'. Marshall, *Midland counties*, i. 117–18.

[52] Fox, 'Words', 131–35.

[53] Webster, *Great Instauration*, 210–18, 475–76. See also W. H. G. Armytage, 'Education for social change in England 1600–1660', *The Vocational Aspect of Education*, 4 (1952).

[54] Dymock, *Essay*.

aimed to educate the sons of 'Persons of quality' to be leaders of agricultural improvement.[55] Written around the same time, the poet Abraham Cowley's ideas for agricultural education became an inspiration for many eighteenth-century proposals.[56] Cowley argued that the art of agriculture had no proper men to be its professors and it was an 'evil custom' that 'no men put their children to be bred up apprentices in agriculture'. Hence Cowley advocated that 'two or three thousand youths' should be apprenticed at a time, and a college should be founded in each university, along with medicine and law.[57]

This brief enthusiasm for agricultural education faded over the next half century, but re-emerged again in the early eighteenth century. In 1721, Richard Bradley, later appointed the professor of Botany at Cambridge, briefly outlined a course of education for 'those who design to profess or follow Agriculture or the Hortulan Arts', which included instruction in Latin, writing, mathematics, designing and botany, as well as collecting fruit, making observations about plants, talking at every opportunity to 'Ingenious Men' and then travelling around Europe to learn different practices.[58] A short pamphlet in 1723 included a different proposal by the retired Irish country Whig politician, Robert, first Viscount Molesworth (1656–1725), responding to the dearth in corn in Ireland. A central recommendation of his programme of improvement was the instruction of 'ignorant' Irish farmers, through the establishment of a 'School for Husbandry' in every county, in which 'an expert Master of the English methods' would teach with the aid of 'Tusser's old Book of Husbandry'; to be read, copied and learned by heart.[59] Whereas seventy years earlier Dymock had planned a single institution for the advanced theoretical and practical education of young gentlemen, Molesworth advocated schools for common youths for basic education in good husbandry as an explicitly colonial project.

Walter Harte quoted Molesworth's sketch approvingly in 1764, although he judged Tusser's book to be 'obsolete'.[60] Harte adopted a more sympathetic, if paternalistic, attitude towards common farmers, assuming that the 'poor uninstructed farmer' could not make improvements.[61] His

[55] Ibid., 9.
[56] Cowley, 'Of agriculture'. For example, Cowley is quoted at length in Gentleman, *New System*, 13–18.
[57] Andrew Wallace, 'Virgil and Bacon in the schoolroom', *ELH*, 73 (2006), 175.
[58] Bradley, *General treatise*, 167.
[59] Robert Molesworth, *Some considerations for the promoting of agriculture and employing the poor* (Dublin, 1723), 31; Tusser, *Five Hundreth good Pointes*.
[60] Harte, *Essays*, 156.
[61] Ibid., 160.

modest ambition, borrowed from an older German idea, was for a little book of 'plain solid incontestable foundations of husbandry' with wood-cut images for poor children to read in country schools to instil good hab-its.[62] For children of wealthy families, he mentioned Cowley's proposal, but believed agricultural societies in every district would be better than an elite college of students reading classical treatises. Around this period, the need to educate farmers was also advocated by writers on political econ-omy, such as Nehemiah Grew (in 1706–07), Malachy Postlethwayt (in 1757) and Sir James Stuart (in 1767).[63] In 1757, Robert Maxwell, previously secretary to the Society of Improvers in Scotland, urged that husbandry be taught 'in a College-way, as other Sciences are', advocating a professorship in agriculture.[64]

From the 1760s to 1790s, a series of increasingly detailed plans for agri-cultural education were put forward. A self-described 'Old Essex Farmer', with a gentleman's upbringing, shared his own preparation and his ideas for the 'Education of a Youth intended for a Farmer' in a letter published in 1765. His own education, presumably in the early eighteenth century, was based on observations, reading, conversational lessons from his father and tours of England and Europe, with no mention of any practical work. He acknowledged that touring was too expensive for most farmers, but nonetheless recommended the same formal study for all, including 'as much natural philosophy as might serve to give him some idea of the nature of vegetation'. A young farmer need not learn Latin, Greek or French, but should read 'the best of our English writers who have treated of husbandry'.[65] In the same year, in Dublin, John Wynn Baker published the first educational plan orientated towards the development of a special-ist class of professionals in agricultural service across Ireland, rather than a general school for all rural children or an elite college for gentlemen.[66] In 1777, Cuthbert Clarke, a lecturer on natural philosophy, presented a 'plan of education for youth intended for the profession of husbandry'.[67] After arguing for the necessity of theory in husbandry, against the opinion of most husbandmen, he outlined a three-stage programme: develop personal attributes (up to age 5 or 6); teach reading, writing and basic accounting

[62] Ibid., 155.
[63] Described in Johnson, 'Place of learning'.
[64] Quoted in Jones, *Agricultural enlightenment*, 176.
[65] 'A letter from the Old Essex Farmer, in which he gives his opinion relative to the education of a youth intended for a farmer', *Museum Rusticum*, 5 (1765), 87–88.
[66] John Wynn Baker, *Plan for instructing youths in the knowledge of husbandry* (London, 1765).
[67] Clarke, *True theory*, 18.

(age 6 to 9–10); provide a practical apprenticeship in husbandry (age 10 to 16–17).[68] Rather than list any books on husbandry to be read during the apprenticeship, the rest of Clarke's book was designed to provide the theory. For example, he stated that the pupil should have proper instructions for operations such as ploughing, and then proceeded to explain the theory of ploughing.[69]

The difference between educational proposals for the lower and upper ranks of the agricultural community, and the specific educational needs of English agriculture, was evident in William Perryman's *An Essay on the Education of Youth Intended for the Profession of Agriculture* (1777), translated from an earlier 1764 tract, *Essay on the Education of Peasants*, by a Swiss clergyman. The original essay, which filled the first 100 pages of the 108-page book, was generic guidance on raising young people to be useful members of a peasant society. Only a few pages outlined the maxims for training in the practical part of husbandry.[70] Perryman added a crucial supplement for the English farmer, explaining that the original essay was 'chiefly intended for the labouring husbandman', whereas he intended to offer a course of learning for the sons of prosperous tenant farmers.[71] Perryman's own plan for a 'Rural Academy' was designed to add the theoretical education missing in the Swiss proposal, including formal education in surveying, geometry, measuring timber, mechanics, the principles behind instruments and a theory of vegetation. Such training would equip pupils to become estate stewards, replacing the lawyers who were typically employed at the time.[72] Hence Perryman's small book contained two educational plans: one for poor, labouring husbandmen, modelled on idealised peasant child-rearing practices and one for wealthy farmers and estate managers, adapted to the social structure of English agriculture.

In 1778, Arthur Young wrote an essay addressing the question of whether agriculture could be a proper pursuit for the sons of gentlemen, in which he outlined the ideal education. Young's plan was distinctive in two ways: there was a subtle role for book-learning, and it was specifically designed to produce farm managers. Young observed that while 'uneducated' common farmers acquired basic know-how by growing up on a farm and effectively serving 'two or three apprenticeships', gentlemen had no such experience

---

[68] Ibid., 17–39.
[69] Ibid., 42.
[70] William Perryman, *An essay on the education of youth intended for the profession of agriculture* (London, 1777), 82–83.
[71] Ibid., 101.
[72] Ibid., 102–7.

and so were 'generally completely ignorant of the art'. But Young cautioned against the recent habit of gentlemen trying to learn solely from books.[73] In his plan, a young man should be taken from school at sixteen or seventeen, with knowledge of arithmetic, chemistry and mechanics.[74] After this Young envisioned a kind of ten-year apprenticeship, from fifteen to twenty-five, based on annual agreements to lodge with a 'considerable farmer' to receive instruction. Young stressed that pupils should learn the practical operations with their own hands, for the purpose of effective management: 'if he never takes a tool in his hand he will never understand it to that degree which is necessary for instructing ignorant workmen, nor for making contracts with skilful ones'. As part of his management training, the pupil should observe every stage of production, by rising with the servants, following their round of work and recording all details. After completing a practical apprenticeship, Young declared, 'I shall be in no fear of his reading books of husbandry', since he would then be able to 'oppose the theory he finds in books to the practice he has under his eye' and judge the merit of what he read.[75] Young's plan was aimed at educating the farmer as a professional or a businessman, not a pure theorist.[76]

A tradition of educational thought was being assembled, reflected in William Lamport's proposal in 1780 for 'the profession of Agriculture'. It was motivated by the need to make agricultural books more effective, since 'illiterate farmers' could not or would not read. Education was necessary 'to extend and call forth the powers of the mind, and to render it ductile and teachable!'. Lamport advocated education at two levels: 'let Agriculture be studied by gentlemen of landed property, on philosophic principles' and 'let it be taught to their tenants'. Hence he recommended a mix of previous proposals, whereby agricultural societies would use a few fields to instruct pupils, 'either according to the idea of Lord Molesworth, which points to the education of poor men's children; or, according to the ideas of Cowley and Sir William Petty, which respect the education of gentlemen's sons as well as others'. The sons of poor farmers would be educated to be knowledgeable and skilful bailiffs or improving tenants, able to teach inferior servants – because gentlemen, he noted, 'have more important objects in view than to cultivate the neglected understanding of

---

[73] Young, 'How far is agriculture', 234–36.
[74] Ibid., 237–38.
[75] Ibid., 243–47.
[76] Although Young welcomed the University of Edinburgh's proposal in 1789 to endow a professor of agriculture, asking: 'Why not a Professor of Agriculture in every University?': Arthur Young, *Annals of agriculture vol. 11* (London, 1789), 367–68.

every rustic labourer'. It was not specified whether gentlemen's sons were to be instructed at the same schools, or a separate academy along the lines of Cowley, but Lamport stressed that their education would allow the gentleman to 'direct his servants, rather than be imposed upon by them, which must ever be the case when the master is unacquainted with the business he superintends'.[77] While it was valuable to have a 'well-educated bailiff', the gentlemen should not be wholly reliant on him. Hence agricultural education should maintain a clear social hierarchy of knowledge.

A rather different motivation lay behind the Scottish farmer and political reformer William Skirving's 1792 book titled *The Husbandman's Assistant*, which could be described as the first agricultural textbook. It presented both a theory of education and instructions to be used by a tutor in a hypothetical agricultural apprenticeship. Skirving was baffled that there were no regular apprenticeships in husbandry: why was it that 'this universally approved manner of acquiring the practical knowledge of common occupations has been neglected by the farmer?'[78] Most innovatively, Skirving explained his desire to provide instructions for farm labourers, 'the persons to whom chiefly the operations of agriculture must be committed'. He argued that because 'operators' acquired knowledge through practice, they remained 'ignorant of the *rationale*, or the principles of the very works which they can execute perfectly'. While Skirving admitted that 'book-learned farmers have seldom succeeded in the schemes of culture which they have pursued', he argued this was not an excuse for practical farmers to neglect theory entirely. Labouring people learned religious matters well enough in youth and so could be taught science by reading short instructions in leisure hours.[79] Elsewhere he appealed to the value of books, chastising the over-indulged farmers' sons who preferred to 'hang about a smithy for half a day, than read a book of instruction for one hour'.[80]

William Marshall developed the last significant educational proposal of the eighteenth century over a series of books, culminating with his thirty-seven-page pamphlet, *Proposals for a Rural Institute* (1799). The target demographic oscillated between iterations. In 1778, Marshall boasted his agricultural college would accept 'ALL DEGREES OF MEN, from the PEASANT to the PRINCE'; in 1790, he presented a more considered plan to the sons

---

[77] Lamport, 'Proposal', 27–46.
[78] Skirving, *Husbandman's assistant*, x.
[79] Ibid., v–xvii.
[80] Ibid., 62.

of the 'superior class of yeomen', complete with a fee-scale for a range of packages; and by 1799 it was broadened again to 'Agriculturalists, and to husbandmen of every description'.[81] The second version specified a 'LIBRARY, for the reception of books on RURAL SUBJECTS', illustrating the importance of book learning.[82] In 1799, Marshall argued for the necessity of a theoretical education through an analogy with medicine (adding to that discussed above):

> It is true, an illiterate rustic, who never entered a college of agriculture can *farm* … Just so a village doctor, — though he never walked the hospitals, nor attended the theatres, elaboratories, and lecture rooms of science, — can practice physic, — and with a certain degree of success. But why, in difficult cases, call in the physician? Because he has taken a more comprehensive view of the subject, and is better acquainted with the principles of the art itself.[83]

Extending the comparison with the learned professions, Marshall compared the limited education of the 'mere country-bred attorney' and the 'field preacher' with the university-educated professors of law and divinity. Further, whereas the fisherman could merely 'grope along the shore he was bred upon', the 'scientific navigator can cross the wildest ocean', because he had studied the principles of sailing.[84] Marshall's ambition was to create a class of professional agriculturists, distinguished from mere farm-bred husbandmen. However, his appeals for patronage or government support were ignored. He tried to implement his plan by adding a schoolroom onto his Yorkshire house around 1816 but died in 1818 before his college could open.[85]

The concern with education demonstrates that agricultural authors were not simply interested in new crops, tools or methods, but in fundamentally reforming the social relations of production. In addition to these specific proposals, the creation of a body of technical literature was itself an educational initiative, partly to enable the higher levels of the rural community to better manage the land and labour under their control. The dream of a professionalised agriculture founded on formal education was one of the motivating factors behind the creation of

---

[81] Marshall, *Minutes*, 'Digest', 115; Marshall, *Midland counties*, i. 129; William Marshall, *Proposals for a rural institute, or college of agriculture* (London, 1799), 10.
[82] Marshall, *Midland counties*, i. 127.
[83] Marshall, *Proposals*, 12.
[84] Ibid., 13.
[85] Horn, *William Marshall*, 39.

agricultural literature for almost two centuries before it was institutionalised. The mode of learning that had dominated for centuries, of sons and daughters learning by experience on their own farm or a neighbouring one, was being challenged. All authors agreed that practice remained necessary, but that it must be governed by theory: as Adam Dickson put it, 'a little learning is absolutely necessary', and 'a greater degree of knowledge is necessary in the farmer than he can be supposed to acquire who has been bred up to possess only a [small] farm'.[86] However, the proposals exhibited changed over time. The first burst of proposals in the mid-seventeenth century advocated educating the sons of gentlemen with classical texts. From the 1720s, this was joined by a concern with educating poorer farmers. The range of proposals shows writers wrestling with the two core questions: the social question of who was to be educated, and the epistemological question of the balance between theory and practice. Both were resolved by differentiating the level and type of education for different social groups or occupations.[87]

The movement for agricultural education made slow progress in the nineteenth century, and the majority of farmers and farmworkers continued to learn informally 'on the job'.[88] By the twentieth century, however, a three-tier system had emerged: higher education for gentlemen farmers, stewards and some large tenants; intermediate education for bailiffs and small tenants; and lower education for farm labourers.[89] The difficulties of the Agricultural College (founded 1845) in attempting to unite theory and practice are well documented.[90] Despite some of the early rhetoric, the college was an elite institution. It did not attract the sons of farmers: the first sixty students in 1850 were sons of solicitors, clergymen, officers, or landed proprietors.[91] Even towards the end of the twentieth century, only a minority of working farmers had a formal agricultural education: a 1974–75 survey of East Anglia showed that 77.2 per cent of farmers 'had no formal agricultural qualifications at all'.[92]

---

[86] Dickson, *Treatise*, 9–11.
[87] Similarly in educational experiments on the continent: Jones, *Agricultural enlightenment*, 177–78.
[88] Stewart Richards, 'Masters of Arts and Bachelors of Barley': The struggle for agricultural education in mid-nineteenth-century Britain', *History of Education*, 12 (1983), 165. Brassley, 'Agricultural science', 622.
[89] Richards, 'Masters of Arts and Bachelors of Barley', 162. See Brassley, 'Agricultural science', 649.
[90] Roger Sayce, *The history of the Royal Agricultural College, Cirencester* (Gloucestershire, 1992), 27; Brassley, 'Agricultural science', 624; Richards, 'Masters of Arts and Bachelors of Barley', 171.
[91] Brassley, 'Agricultural science', 626.
[92] Paul Brassley, 'Agricultural education, training and advice in the UK, 1850–2000', in Nadine Viver (ed.), *The state and rural societies: Policy and education in Europe 1750–2000* (Turnhout, 2008), 269.

Estate Stewards

The estate steward was envisaged as a key beneficiary of many agricultural educational proposals. It is also the occupation most closely identified with professionalisation, far more so than the farmer.[93] The agglomeration and increasing size of estates in the eighteenth century, combined with high rates of landlord absenteeism and a zest for improvement, led to the rise in England of the full-time estate or land steward and eventually the independent land agency.[94] Only the largest estates needed or could employ full-time stewards to act on behalf of the landowner. They were typically responsible for managing the home farm, garden and parks, handling leases and rents, keeping accounts, and supervising lower servants.[95] Seventeenth-century stewards were often tenants on the estate, but by the eighteenth century they tended to be lawyers.[96] However, approaches to estate management were shifting from maintaining or increasing revenues through more efficient administration, to raising rents through improved agricultural productivity. Improving landlords required stewards able to oversee the farming of tenants and large-scale infrastructure projects, in addition to managing legal and financial relationships.[97] This created a demand for greater agricultural expertise.[98] Commentators criticised lawyers who were ignorant of husbandry and called for specialist stewards with agricultural knowledge, claiming jurisdiction over an area that offered opportunities to rise from middling origins to the minor gentry.[99] Sarah Webster, however, argues that the ideal of the professional land steward found in manuals was only partially realised in the eighteenth century and more accurately applies to independent land

---

[93] For example, Mingay, 'Land steward', 8.

[94] Bailiffs and stewards originated in great medieval estates, but their development over the early modern period has not been traced in detail. See E. Hughes, 'The eighteenth century estate agent', in Henry Alfred Cronne et al. (eds), *Essays in British and Irish History: In honour of James Eadie Todd* (London, 1949), 186.

[95] Beckett, 'Landownership', 592.

[96] See example of Verney estate John Broad, *Transforming English rural society: The Verneys and the Claydons, 1600–1820* (Cambridge, 2004), 113–17.

[97] See example of agents in Wordie, *Estate management*, 16–64. Clay, 'Landlords', 215–16. On lack of technical agricultural knowledge needed for seventeenth-century steward: D. R. Hainsworth, *Stewards, lords and people: The estate steward and his world in later Stuart England* (Cambridge, 1992), 8–9.

[98] Mingay, 'Land steward', 8; John Beckett, 'Estate management in eighteenth-century England: The Lowther-Spedding relationship in Cumberland', in John Chartres and David Hey (eds), *English rural society 1500–1800: Essays in honour of Joan Thirsk* (Cambridge, 1990), 57.

[99] Mingay, 'Land steward', 12.

agencies in the nineteenth century.[100] Therefore, the effort of some writers to establish the need for a steward with agricultural expertise was not wholly successful. The following will explore the role of books and book knowledge in these efforts to professionalise the occupation of steward.

Between 1712 and 1804, seven manuals were published on the duty of the land steward, by George Clerke (1712), Giles Jacob (1713), Edward Laurence (1727), John Mordant (1761), Charles Ley (1786), John Lawrence (1801) and William Marshall (1804). Both Clerke and Jacob described a steward with limited financial and legal responsibilities, with no hint that knowledge of husbandry was required.[101] Laurence's *Duty of a Steward* (1727) was the first manual to argue that stewards should possess agricultural expertise and established the template that others would follow. Laurence was employed as a land surveyor from 1706 on estates across a variety of counties, gradually diversifying his activities from surveying and mapping estates, to valuing land, letting farms and offering advice on husbandry.[102] We know little about the background of John Mordant, but Charles Ley was also a land-surveyor, John Lawrence was initially a writer on horses and animal welfare and William Marshall was variously employed as a steward and was already a prolific agricultural writer by the time he published on the topic.

The first point to note is the obvious one: the very existence of such manuals encourages the notion that stewards can learn their role from a book. Secondly, they contributed to the construction of a book-based expertise by stressing the necessity for theoretical knowledge, by distinguishing the steward's knowledge from that of the country attorney and common farmer, and seeking to gain public legitimacy. Thirdly, they were designed to establish the professional status of the land steward, by founding it upon specialist knowledge, setting ethical rules of conduct and specifying qualifications. Fourthly, Edward Laurence, Charles Ley and John Lawrence also used their books to publicise their expertise, including short, single-page adverts at the front of their books.

All five books argued that stewards should understand agriculture (hence should not merely be lawyers), that their knowledge should cover a wide range of sciences, and that the instruction of tenants on

---

[100] Webster, 'Estate improvement', 61.

[101] George Clerke, *The landed-man's assistant: Or, steward's vade mecum* (London, 1712); Giles Jacob, *The compleat court-keeper: Or, land-steward's assistant* (London, 1713).

[102] Sarah Bendall, 'Laurence, Edward (bap.1674, d.1739)', *ODNB* (Oxford, 2004), www.oxforddnb.com/view/article/16125 (15 March 2017).

their methods was an essential duty. They shared a common diagnosis that uninformed stewards and ignorant tenants were managing estates poorly. The existing practice of 'Country Attorneys' employed by multiple landowners, who allowed tenants to cultivate their farms as they wished, was damaging to the value of estate lands. Laurence's experience led him to believe that the remedy was to reform the role of the steward, who must be 'well vers'd in Country Business'.[103] Mordant's *The Complete Steward* (1761), a re-packing and expansion of Laurence's book, quoted his critique of the hiring of country attorneys.[104] Ley's guide in 1786 rearticulated the assault on the 'impropriety of employing country attornies in the office of stewards'.[105] These moves to establish and protect an area for professional expertise were also apparent in Mordant's criticism 'of advancing menial servants to the office of a steward, that are not duly qualified'.[106]

All authors argued that a considerable range of theoretical knowledge was required. Laurence stated that a steward should be a good accountant and have 'a tolerable degree of Skill in Mathematicks, Surveying, Mechanicks, and Architecture'.[107] Mordant repeated a similar list of qualifications, including knowledge in '*agriculture*, in *trade*, *arithmetic*, the *mathematics*, *mechanics*, &c'.[108] Ley echoed these suggestions and stressed the need for educating young people in both theory and practice to be qualified for the office of steward, since a 'well educated steward or bailiff' was preferable to 'the illiterate'.[109] Almost identical qualifications were listed by William Marshall in 1804.[110] But John Lawrence presented a more complex picture of the role of steward and estate management in *The Modern Land Steward* (1801), distinguishing various levels of knowledge depending on the size and structure of the estate.[111] He identified three types of steward: the lowest 'house-steward', who only required basic knowledge of accounts, the market and the hiring of tradesmen; the middling 'Acting Land-Steward'; and the highest 'Chief Agent' or

---

[103] Edward Laurence, *The duty of a steward to his lord* (London, 1727), 5, 11.
[104] John Mordant, *The complete steward: Or, the duty of a steward to his lord*, 2 vols (London, 1761), i. 213.
[105] Charles Ley, *The nobleman, gentleman, land steward, and surveyor's compleat guide* (London, 1786), 5.
[106] Mordant, *Complete steward*, 208.
[107] Laurence, *Duty*, 50.
[108] Mordant, *Complete steward*, 'Preface'.
[109] Ley, *Nobleman*, 19–21.
[110] Marshall, *Landed property*, 338–39.
[111] John Lawrence, *The modern land steward* (London, 1801), vi.

superintendent, whose role was to coordinate the other stewards. The highest steward required wide-ranging knowledge for infrastructure projects, with 'a thorough insight into the nature of every improvement' and an understanding of political economy. In sum, his 'intelligence ought to be universal'. The acting land steward required 'a practical skill in all the material branches of agriculture', as well as knowledge in accounting, architecture, mathematics, mechanics and measurement.[112] Hence only stewards dealing directly with tenants or managing a home farm required excellent practical knowledge of farming. It was in all cases a role for men of education, however – Lawrence stressed that the labouring classes should not rise higher than a bailiff.[113]

All authors insisted that a sufficient knowledge of agriculture was needed for the supervision of tenants. Laurence stipulated that a steward must be able 'to direct and advise such Tenants as do not understand the best and latest Improvements in Husbandry'.[114] Mordant even argued it was not necessarily a problem if small, illiterate tenant farmers were ignorant of improved methods (compared with a man of substance), since 'it is the duty of the Steward … to instruct them'.[115] This point highlights the complex adjustments in the structure of knowledge on estates and the purpose of hiring a steward as a resident expert. Mordant also stressed the need for the steward to be able to manage and instruct other workmen on the estate. For example, common artificers must be helped, since while they 'may do the mechanick part very well', they lacked 'a proper education in theory'.[116] Ley repeated Laurence's points but also highlighted how the steward must, at the very least, appear to be knowledgeable – in other words, possess a minimal interactional expertise. The problem with country attorneys who knew nothing of husbandry was that they were ineffective at directing farmers, who recognised immediately that they were 'better acquainted with the art of politeness and dress, than with the principles of agriculture'.[117] In Marshall's terms, without agricultural knowledge the steward could not 'properly appreciate the management of occupiers; much less assist them, in correcting their errors, – and improving their practice'.[118] Hence the book-learned steward was to instruct the unlearned farmer in

---

[112] Ibid., 43–46.
[113] Ibid., 48–49.
[114] Laurence, *Duty*, 22.
[115] Mordant, *Complete steward*, 360.
[116] Ibid., 208.
[117] Ley, *Nobleman*, 12.
[118] Marshall, *Landed property*, 338.

the best methods of husbandry (or at least ensure that their practice was not to the disadvantage of the landlord).[119]

John Lawrence was the most emphatic about the centrality of book learning for the steward, which perhaps reflects the growing importance of agricultural literature by the nineteenth century. For Lawrence, through reading books 'we gain perhaps in one year, that knowledge, which might have taken the laborious practice of many to acquire'. Here was the function of books in a nutshell: they offered a shortcut to acquiring knowledge otherwise only obtained through years of labour. 'The library of the lord ought to be a resource to the steward, for the most approved and useful books in every department of agricultural and economical science'. Lawrence even recommended a course of study, including learning the true understanding of tillage and drilling from Jethro Tull and Philip Miller, useful practical hints on culture and livestock from William Ellis, ample details of existing practice from William Marshall's tours, and the principles of modern economy from Arthur Young.[120] Indeed, the breadth of knowledge expected of the steward was scarcely attainable without the availability of books.

It was no coincidence that the eighteenth century saw the simultaneous professionalisation of the estate steward and the flourishing of agricultural literature. They were mutually reinforcing processes, as the ideal steward developed into a specialist occupation grounded in book knowledge. The steward needed his library as much as the husbandman needed his seeds or manure. It is also clear that books were used more precisely to delineate the professional status of the steward, distinct from inferior servants, the farmer or the landlord. They allowed for a sharper division of intellectual labour within estates, concentrating expertise in a single or handful of individuals. The scope of responsibility for the office of the steward was stretched by the availability of treatises and manuals on a diverse range of topics, since without such accessible knowledge, the steward would have been far more reliant on subordinate officers and workers and in a weaker position in attempts to instruct tenants. In summary, the role of agricultural books in professionalisation can be interpreted in two ways. The demand-side explanation is that the growing number of educated men in agricultural service roles, who required extensive theoretical knowledge, stimulated the book trade. The supply-side explanation is that the growing

---

[119] For example, the estate manager for the Marques of Stafford, James Loch, advised the tenants on how to plough and what to read. Jones, *Agricultural enlightenment*, 80.
[120] Lawrence, *Land steward*, 55–56.

number of books on agriculture, which made it possible for men of education to develop extensive theoretical knowledge, stimulated the agricultural service industry.

The vision of professionalised agriculture that emerged in the eighteenth century was only partially achieved, as agricultural knowledge splintered into diverse areas of expertise over the next two centuries. Expertise was channelled into the quasi-professional service occupations of the land steward and surveyor, while also helping to develop an independent body of soil chemists. The effort failed partly because it was subsumed under the greater force of commercialisation. While not wholly opposed, they tugged in different directions. The need to establish public prestige, qualifications, statutory associations and a code of conduct was subdued by market forces. In the commercialised agricultural world of the eighteenth century, the manager-worker relation was far more prevalent than the expert-client relation characteristic of the professions. Agriculture became more of a business than a learned profession; agricultural knowledge became more of a commodity than a protected specialism. The dominant social figure became the capitalist farmer, eventually the agribusinessman, more so than the professional agriculturist.

However, the drive to institutionalise expertise and professionalise agriculture shaped the way industrial agricultural systems grew in the nineteenth and twentieth centuries. In 1995, the fierce critic of modern agribusiness, Wendell Berry, enumerated fifteen assumptions underlying modern industrial agriculture, the first seven of which outlined the dominant system of knowledge.[121]

1. If the world and all its creatures are machines, then the world and all its creatures are entirely comprehensible, manipulable and controllable by humans.
2. The humans who have this power are experts.
3. Experts are made by education.
4. Education only happens in schools.
5. Experts are smarter than other people.
6. Thinking is best done by experts in offices and laboratories.
7. People who do work cannot be trusted to think about it.

The belief that there exists a universal knowledge to be applied to all farms; that such knowledge should be acquired through formal education;

---

[121] Berry, *Unsettling of America*, 'Afterword', 230–31.

that such education produces experts who should exercise control over farming – this was the framework that was first developed by eighteenth-century agricultural authors. This is the system of knowledge of 'agriculturism'. At its core is number 7 in this list: the separation between those who think and those who do. Authors saw book learning as one of the key pillars of an agricultural profession and believed that enlightened men with theoretical expertise should exercise control over cultivation rather than common husbandmen, housewives, servants and labourers. Being bred to husbandry on a farm was no longer sufficient to be a good farmer.

CHAPTER 7

The Master Should Know More
Book-Farming, Power and Resistance

'Malè agitur cum Domino, quem villicus Docet.'
— Cato, *De Agricultura* (Second century BCE)

'Things go ill with the master when his bailiff has to teach him', wrote the ancient Roman senator Cato in the earliest surviving Latin agricultural text dating from the second century BCE. This maxim was quoted by Columella two centuries later in the most comprehensive and celebrated of the classical agricultural treatises, linking it to similar advice in the older Greek dialogue by Xenophon.[1] It became a favourite of early modern writers. In 1616, Markham's English translation of *Maison Rustique* quoted Cato's warning of the consequences when the 'Lord & owner knoweth not to teach & command that which is to be done: but must depend & relie wholly upon his Farmer'.[2] In 1664, John Evelyn of the Royal Society recited the 'Observation of old Cato's' when counselling his fellow gentlemen not to 'commit themselves to the *Dictates* of their ignorant *Hinds* and *Servants*, who are (generally speaking) more fit to Learn then to Instruct'. Evelyn clarified the managerial relationship: 'We are to exact Labour, not Conduct and Reason, from the greatest part of them'.[3] In the following century, Cato's maxim adorned the title page of a bullish manifesto for the gentry control of agriculture, the anonymous *A New System of Agriculture* (published in 1755 but clearly composed in the early 1700s).[4] The same year, Cato was again summoned by Edward Wade to advocate

---

[1] Quote from Columella, *On agriculture*, trans. Harrison Boyd Ash (Loeb Classical Library; Cambridge, MA, 1941), iii. 50–51. Cato and Varro, *On agriculture*, trans. W. D. Hooper and Harrison Boyd Ash (Loeb Classical Library; Cambridge, MA, 1934).
[2] Markham, *Maison rustique*, 19.
[3] Evelyn, *Sylva*, 'To the reader'.
[4] Gentleman, *New system*. Evelyn's gloss was also quoted (32–36), which was likely where the author picked up the original.

for the gentry and aristocracy to take direct control over the cultivation of their estates rather than leave them in the hands of 'ignorant servants'. The anxiety was that, since landowners did not educate their children in agriculture, their descendants were 'so totally void of this useful knowledge as to be easily liable to be imposed upon'.[5] In Walter Harte's 1764 reformulation of Xenophon's version of the maxim, the best husbandman should be 'the school-master of his own bailiff', since a 'gentleman must lose by husbandry, except he understands it'.[6] The first English translation of Columella, which included the lessons from Cato and Xenophon in Book XI, had been published in 1745.[7] The name Columella itself conjured up a vision of a wise philosophical husbandman whom the major writers of their day wished to emulate. Indeed, in correspondence in 1767, Harte referred to Arthur Young affectionately as 'my Columella' in one letter and himself signed another as 'Your most Obliged, & ever affectionate servant Columella'.[8]

In an analysis of another classical treatise by Varro, written between Cato and Columella, Aude Doody connects Cato's dictum directly to the social role of agricultural literature: the point was 'to pass on knowledge, from elite Roman to elite Roman, so that the landowner has both the authority and the expertise to instruct his manager, who in turn instructs the workers on how to farm the land'. Written agricultural instructions 'allows knowledge to flow downwards, from the master to the vilicus, and finally to the workers'.[9] However, Varro's text also displays a pessimism about the 'ability of written texts to hold and transmit information on agriculture'.[10] The dialogue is notable for the way it plays with the tensions between writing and practice, between knowledge acquired by reading and knowledge acquired through experience.[11] These two facets run through the entire western tradition of agricultural writing: the value of writing in

---

[5] Edward Wade, *A proposal for improving and adorning the island of Great Britain* (London, 1755), 8–10.
[6] Harte, *Essays*, 196–201.
[7] Columella, *L. Junius Moderatus Columella of husbandry. In twelve books: and his book concerning trees. Translated into English, with several illustrations from Pliny, Cato, Varro, Palladius, and other antient and modern authors* (London, 1745). Cato and Xenophon quoted on p. 450.
[8] British Library, Add MS 35126, 'From Harte, June 28, 1767', Original letters addressed to Arthur Young, F.R.S., Secretary to the Board of Agriculture [d 1820], with a few holograph draft replies; 1743–1820), f.23–24; British Library, Add MS 35126, 'From Harte, Sept 29, 1767', Original letters addressed to Arthur Young, F.R.S., Secretary to the Board of Agriculture [d 1820], with a few holograph draft replies; 1743–1820), f.29.
[9] Doody, 'Authority of writing', 185–86.
[10] Ibid., 191.
[11] Ibid., 194, 197.

offering knowledge and mastery to an educated landowning class, and the 'weakness of writing as a substitute for lived experience'.[12]

This fundamental tension is apparent in how 'Columella' could be a shorthand for both the achievements and inadequacies of farming books in eighteenth-century Britain; its nobility and absurdity. The conspicuous social and cultural gap between scholarship and farming in eighteenth-century Britain was ripe for comedy. In Richard Graves' novel *Columella* (1779), the eponymous character 'was always talking of Virgil's Georgics, Cowley, and Columella' and therefore 'partly on account of the subject of that author's book on Agriculture, acquired the nick-name of Columella'.[13] In the scene introducing this character, visitors found 'their philosophical friend running across the lawn, with faggot-stick in one hand, and a book in the other', displayed in the frontispiece (see Figure 7.1).[14] The juxtaposition of farming and books, the world of rustic toil and the world of genteel scholarship, was an easy source of humour. Yet it also expressed a concern about the follies of excessive reading and an overly romanticised engagement in farming.[15] The fictional Columella did not learn the ancient Columella's maxims about managerial control, for after taking a farm into his own hands he 'trusted too much to servants to make it advantageous'. Worse, perhaps, was the worry that reading farming books was more pleasurable than profitable: 'He now read over Virgil's Georgics with a practical view, and studied the modern writers on agriculture; but either by his mistaking the precepts, or his hind not executing them properly, his fields hardly paid the expence of cultivation'.[16] This was a familiar tale for the gentleman book-farmer.

The precarious power of book knowledge is the theme of this chapter. The growing presence of agricultural books, and increasingly significant role of book-learning in farm management, culminated in the 'book-farming' controversy in the eighteenth century. It was the most visible symptom of the changing social system of knowledge described in previous chapters. The use of the compound term 'book-farming' (and 'book-farmer') – usually in a pejorative sense – was sufficiently widespread to gain entry into the *Oxford English Dictionary*, meaning 'the practice of farming with knowledge acquired chiefly from books, rather than through

[12] Ibid., 201.
[13] Richard Graves, *Columella; or, the distressed anchoret* (London, 1779), 7.
[14] Ibid., 45–46.
[15] Sayre, 'Farming by the book', 355.
[16] Graves, *Columella*, 186–87.

Figure 7.1   Frontispiece to Richard Graves, *Columella: Or, the Distressed Anchoret* (London, 1779). Courtesy of HathiTrust: https://catalog.hathitrust.org/ Record/000779453.

practical experience'. The first entry from 1794 described how the practical farmer 'sneers at what he contemptuously calls book-farming'.[17] Many historians have noted these criticisms of agricultural literature but overlooked the significance of the scepticism and hostility to book-farming.[18] For example, Peter Jones observed – but did not probe why – farmers were 'rather resistant to book knowledge'.[19]

To fully understand the book-farming controversy, it is helpful to distinguish between weak and strong criticisms. The weak criticism of book-farming condemned an overly theoretical approach to farming or the overly speculative ideas in books. Agricultural writers themselves used it in this sense to distinguish their own work from the fanciful theories of previous or rival authors. It was, therefore, an internal and constructive critique, which is the sense usually identified by historians.[20] However, in its strongest form, to criticise book-farming was to disparage all book-based farming and express a fundamental suspicion of the value of learning about farming from books. This sense was mostly attributed to the attitude of common farmers, but remains unexamined. Instead, many historians have tacitly accepted the judgment of eighteenth-century gentlemen that common farmers were narrow-minded or plain illiterate, repeating contemporary frustrations about the general prejudice against 'book-learning'.[21] In the enlightenment model of knowledge diffusion, resistance to book-farming is viewed as an unfortunate obstacle to progress. For example, Pamela Horn attributed criticisms to the poor quality of content and low levels of literacy in rural society, that is, factors negatively affecting the dissemination of useful knowledge.[22] As an aside, Horn quoted Arthur Young's sarcastic

---

[17] See note on 'book-farmer' in 'book, n.', *OED Online*, www.oed.com/view/Entry/21412 (8 Feb. 2018). Further examples include: (1) 'It is not merely book husbandry, but actually common in some parts of this kingdom'. Young, *Farmer's kalendar*, 37; (2) '… this is not merely book-farming, but is worthy the attention of real practical farmers', Thomas Wright, *The art of floating land* (London, 1799), 18. See also equivalent compounds, such as 'book-astronomer'.

[18] Many studies reference without examining the term. For example, G. E. Fussell, 'Cuthbert Clark, an eighteenth-century book-farmer', *Journal of the Ministry of Agriculture*, 37 (1930). In early twentieth-century American context, see Cooke, 'Expertise'.

[19] Jones, *Agricultural enlightenment*, 62, 84.

[20] An early example to show longevity of this point: 'Their promises were often exaggerated beyond the bounds of belief; mixed with some useful suggestions were others which were either ridiculous or of doubtful value. Men actually and practically engaged in cultivating the soil were, therefore, justified in some distrust of book-farmers'. Rowland Edmund Prothero, *English farming, past and present* (London, 1912), 111.

[21] Goddard, 'Agricultural literature', 366.

[22] Horn, 'Contribution of the propagandist', 320–24.

comment that many farmers only followed the methods of 'their grand-
mothers, and are much too wise to follow book husbandry'.[23] Yet this
remark, which hinted at a deeper antagonism between writers and farmers over the acquisition of knowledge and the nature of agricultural
expertise, was left unexplored.

The best study to date is an examination by Benjamin Cohen of the
book-farming debates in nineteenth-century America, which advances
on British studies by foregrounding the problem of 'credibility'.[24] Cohen
traces the shift from the 'tradition-laden, experience-based, locally derived
knowledge of the land' to 'systematic, codified, and universal knowledge'.[25]
However, while Cohen is sensitive to the social dimension of this conflict,
he argues that book-farming was not a controversy between different economic classes ('not between an upper-class planter and a lower-class tenant, or an educated country squire and a day laborer') but rather a cultural
clash between rural and urban communities, between 'the farming class
and the philosopher class', or 'the active versus the contemplative'.[26] This
may be a fair account of nineteenth-century America, but it is inadequate
for eighteenth-century Britain. The weakness of Cohen's interpretation is
that it fails to fully connect different kinds of knowledge to questions of
economic power.

This chapter examines the spectrum of criticisms of agricultural books
and book-farming in eighteenth-century Britain, combining reported reactions and self-criticisms by authors with contemporary reviews. The first
part reassesses the weak critique of book-farming. The reflexive criticisms
of agricultural writers are usually viewed through the lens of what came
after, as the early teething problems of a rational, experimental science. We
need to reverse this perspective and view them through the lens of what
came before, as the difficulties arising from the process of appropriation
and codification by which agricultural books were constructed. Given that
many books were the product of gentlemen with limited experience writing down what they learned from observation, conversation and reading,
and given the inherent difficulties of codifying a complex practical art and
reducing living custom to a fixed method, it is not surprising that early
manuals failed to provide complete instructions to amateur farmers in
diverse conditions. The exasperations of readers from the mid-eighteenth

---

[23] Ibid., 320.
[24] Cohen, *Notes from the ground*, Ch. 2. Quote from p. 76.
[25] Ibid., 8.
[26] Ibid., 57–58, 78.

century indicate the challenges the gentry faced in attempting to use book knowledge to exert greater managerial control over their farms. We will trace how these frustrations spiralled into a sense of mild crisis by the 1770s, prompting attempts by some authors to reform the genre in order to rescue book-farming.

The second part explores the strong critique. It offers an explanation for why book-farming generated a mixture of indifference, scepticism and hostility from working farmers, by attending to relations of power. It argues that hostility towards book-farming should be contextualised within a wider conflict of interest regarding the social system of agricultural knowledge, rather than simply in terms of illiteracy or the poor quality of manuals. The first direct use of the term in print, referring to the attitudes of common farmers, was in 1767, but the underlying attitudes were prevalent from decades earlier.[27] At stake were fundamental questions about how knowledge of cultivation was acquired, stored and transferred. The opposition of common farmers and servants to book-farming was a species of 'everyday resistance': the daily efforts by subordinate groups to minimise appropriation and exploitation by those who dominate them.[28] Opposition to book-farming constituted resistance to the subordination of the customary knowledge of husbandmen to the book-based expertise of agriculturists, and the use of books as tools of management in the running of estates and large farms. The depth of this class antagonism is drawn out through a close analysis of an anti-enclosure pamphlet from 1785, which articulated concerns about the social disruption generated by agricultural literature. Such evidence, albeit limited, directly connects opposition to the enclosure of knowledge with opposition to the enclosure of the commons. A full appreciation of the book-farming controversy in late eighteenth-century Britain must, therefore, take into account not only the debates between authors about the correct balance of theory and practice but also the struggle between a labour-based and a book-based system of knowledge and the balance of power within agricultural labour relations.

---

[27] Arthur Young, *The farmer's letters to the people of England* (London, 1767), 146. For a very early example, the French author Olivier de Serres commented in 1600: 'There are some who mock all the books of Agriculture, and send us back to the peasants without letters, which they claim to be the only competent judges of this subject, as based on Experience …' ['Il y en a qui se mocquent de tous les livres d'Agriculture, et nous renvoyent aux paysans sans lettres, lesquels ils disent être les seuls juges compétents de cette matière, comme fondée sur l'Expérience …']. Beutler, 'La littérature agricole en Europe', 1293.
[28] James C. Scott, *Weapons of the weak: Everyday forms of peasant resistance* (London, 1985).

Rescuing Book-Farming

The range of attitudes towards agricultural literature reflected a general eighteenth-century ambivalence about the book trade; books were both praised as vehicles of enlightenment and derided as vulgar commodities symbolic of cultural decay.[29] Before surveying the internal critiques, it must be understood that these criticisms were expressed within an overall triumphant narrative about the huge contribution agricultural literature had made to agricultural progress. Between the late seventeenth and late eighteenth centuries, agricultural books were full of self-praise for their heroic role as agents of improvement. John Houghton thought his readers in 1681 would agree that 'the art of agriculture hath not been a little improved by the use of books'.[30] During the middle decades of the eighteenth century, authors such as John Mills and Walter Harte framed narratives of progress around the achievements of earlier authors.[31] In 1778, William Marshall put the story in pseudo-mythic terms: before 1700 farming was trapped in custom, but 'REASON found her plodding through a narrow, blind-lane … He led her from the mire … and introduced her to BOOKS'.[32] Many greeted the stream of publications as a welcome sign that enlightened men were finally engaged in the forgotten classical art. However, despite the general tone of self-congratulation, frustrations were building up. By the early nineteenth century, the high quantity and low quality of agricultural books had become a familiar joke, epitomised by the poetical fiction of the '*Georgoboscophlyariographometer*', a 'mathematical instrument, which on being applied to the titlepage of any treatise, either on tillage or cattle, will immediately shew, by the motion of a certain volatile spirit in a glass tube hermetically sealed, the precise quantity of nonsense it contains'.[33]

The tension that runs through the whole of eighteenth-century agricultural literature was expressed succinctly by Jethro Tull in 1731: 'WRITING and PLOUGHING are two different Talents; and he that writes well, must have spent in his Study that Time, which is necessary to be spent in the Fields, by him who will be Master of the Art of Cultivating them'.[34] This

---

[29] Barbara M. Benedict, 'Writing on writing: Representations of the book in eighteenth-century literature', in Laura L. Runge and Pat Rogers (eds), *Producing the eighteenth-century book: Writers and publishers in England, 1650–1800* (Newark, 2009).

[30] Houghton, *Collection*, 5.

[31] Harte, *Essays*, 42–60; Mills, *New system*, i. vi–ix.

[32] Marshall, *Minutes*, 'The Digest', 4.

[33] *Pursuits of agriculture*, 106. The Greek name was itself a parody of agricultural scientific discourse: *Georgos* (farmer), *boscos* (bucolic, shepherd), *phylaria* (nonsense).

[34] Tull, *New horse-hoing*, 'Preface'.

opening remark went beyond the usual pre-emptive apology about authorial style to highlight the incongruity between texts and fields. Tull castigated previous ornamental books, retelling an anecdote about a 'Great Man', who, 'having perused all their Books of Husbandry', ordered them to be thrown in the fire so others would not waste time reading them, since they had 'treated of an Art, wherein they had formed no manner of Principles'.[35] Although Tull claimed to have read no husbandry books before writing his own, he later ascribed their superficiality to the lack of farming experience of most authors: 'Mr. Lawrence was a Divine, Mr. Bradley an Academick, Dr. Woodward a Physician, Mr Houghton an Apothecary'.[36] Similarly, he sarcastically suggested that a book title by a London-based critic should have been titled *The Cockney Husbandman, Who Never Practised Agriculture Out of the Sound of Bow-Bell'.*[37] However, whereas Tull criticised previous works as mere summaries of a customary art without clear theoretical foundations, many later admonishments targeted excessive theory.

A general dissatisfaction is discernible in the 1730s. For example, the prolific author William Ellis included a flattering letter from an anonymous (perhaps fictitious) gentleman in his preface, which suggested that Ellis' books might not have been received well because the 'World has been so pester'd of late Years with Books upon those Subjects, which have proved no better than arrant Impositions', written 'by Speculation and unexperienced People, that it is no Wonder People now grow more wary in laying out their Money in Books of this Kind'.[38] Ironically, despite his own criticisms of 'meer Scholars', and disparaging a 'downright Theory Author', Ellis' work epitomised the commercialised process that generated abundant volumes filled with speculations.[39] After an early publishing success, Ellis was committed to producing a monthly quota of around 40,000 words, which he filled with repetition, local gossip and anecdotes.[40] In 1748, the Swedish botanist and traveller Peter Kalm recorded a conversation with Ellis' neighbour, who insisted that Ellis made 'more profit out of sitting and scribbling books' than from farming. 'Mr Ellis mostly sits at home in his room and writes books', said the neighbour, 'and sometimes

---

[35] Ibid., 'Preface'. Mentioned again in Tull, *Supplement*, 246. Arthur Young later repeated this story: Betham-Edwards (ed.), *Autobiography*, 55.
[36] Tull, *Supplement*, 257.
[37] Ibid., 248.
[38] Ellis, *New experiments*, 'Preface'.
[39] Ibid., 'Preface'; Ellis, *Chiltern and vale*, 'Preface'.
[40] *Ellis's Husbandry, abridged and methodized* (London, 1772), v–lx.

goes a whole week without going out into his ploughed fields and meadows to look after the work, but trusts mostly to his servant'.[41]

In the 1750s, criticisms arose from the irritation of gentlemen who
wanted farming knowledge from books but found their instructions to be
useless or even harmful. It was previously noted in Chapter 3 that many
gentlemen farmers were known to have lost fortunes through following
the advice in books. In 1757, a reviewer remarked that many readers who
'have tried to realize such visionary schemes' found through experience that
'many a castle has been built in the air'.[42] Another listed seven *great defects*
of agricultural books, which amounted to an *imposition upon the public*:

> In the first place, they generally *copy* from each other. Secondly, In *dif-
> ferent* works, they even *steal* from themselves. Thirdly, They write much
> from *hypothesis*. Fourthly, They are *partial* in the calculation of *profit* and
> *loss*. Fifthly, They often *contradict themselves*, and that even in *one* and the
> *same* work. Sixthly, They seldom tell us for *what* part of *England* their cal-
> culations are made … And lastly, They are very shy of owing where their
> *theory* falls short in *experiment* …[43]

This sums up the main criticisms of agricultural books: plagiarised, speculative, dishonest, inconsistent, vague and untested. Yet, despite the consequent disappointment and failings of readers, 'few books have so quick and
large a sale as those wrote upon this subject'. After detailing the limitations
of respected authors – Bradley, Mortimer, Ellis – the reviewer offered an
explanation for the common defects: agriculture was not simply a '*delight-
ful study*', but 'a *bewitching* one to men whose genius turns that way', who,
therefore, penned equally bewitching and fantastical books. However, the
reviewer saved his sharpest scorn for the mere '*compilers*', of whom he simply warned country gentlemen that they existed – 'and that they *print*'.[44]

The apparent chasm between dreams and reality was cruelly satirised by
one reviewer in 1757 who picked out the career of Gabriel Plattes (fl.1639–44),
a promoter of wondrous schemes for growing corn who 'died in the street,
for want of that bread'.

> So long, therefore, as Writers upon Husbandry are starving, like many of
> the ancient Alchymists, amidst their golden dreams, what encouragement
> can thence be drawn for Farmers to practice schemes that have proved so
> destructive to the Projectors of them?[45]

[41] Quoted in Vicars Bell, *To meet Mr Ellis: Little Gaddesden in the eighteenth century* (London, 1956), 149.
[42] O., 'Compleat body of husbandry', 386.
[43] 'Art. VIII. A new system', 57.
[44] Ibid., 58.
[45] O., 'Compleat body of husbandry', 387–88.

In general, the internal criticisms within late eighteenth-century agricultural literature can be divided into four main kinds: that published books were too long, expensive and complicated to be suitable guides for practice; that books merely plagiarised previous authors and copied errors in order to fill large volumes; that there were simply too many books on the topic creating a mass of confusing information; and that books were too theoretical and full of harmful speculation because the authors lacked practical experience.[46] The first two were present from the first half of the century, while the latter two came to dominate concerns from the 1770s.[47] While authors were no doubt keen to disparage their competitors, the critique of farming books was a genuine reaction to, and reflection upon, their perceived weaknesses and failings. Here we will focus on the perceived problems of overproduction and overtheorising.

The actual term 'book-farming' (occasionally 'book husbandry') emerged as part of the growing anxiety within agricultural books published in the 1760s and 1770s. This was a period of heightened enthusiasm for agriculture among the gentry, professionals and respectable tradesmen. Arthur Young claimed in 1770 that there had been 'more experiments, more discoveries' in agriculture in the previous ten years than in the preceding hundred ones, driven by a 'noble spirit'.[48] Yet the new energies directed towards farming also generated friction and debate. Looking back in 1779, William Marshall was as precise as he was dramatic in his characterisation of the early 1770s, when 'the FALSE SPIRIT OF FARMING then shone out with meridian splendour, and all ranks and descriptions of people had fled to the country' – by 1776, however, 'the rage for Farming which had glowed, or rather burnt out so seriously of late, had now begun to abate'.[49] Others did not see the rage abating so quickly. Writing in 1780, the Rev. John Trusler still sensed the 'general rage for Farming throughout

---

[46] There was a general suspicion of 'book knowledge' prevalent throughout the crafts and mechanical arts in the eighteenth century. For example, on the sea-captain: 'he relies far more upon these, than Book-Knowledge and Accompts', Edward Ward, *The wooden world dissected* (London, 1707), 7.

[47] Example of the first criticism: Lord Belhaven found fault with the 'many large and learned Treatises of Husbandry' for being too general and elaborate for an ordinary reader. Lord (John Hamilton) Belhaven, *The country-mans rudiments: or, an advice to the farmers in East-Lothian how to labour and improve their ground* (Edinburgh, 1713), 3–4. Example of the second criticism: Richard Bradley chastised previous writers for either 'Collecting from Antiquity and foreign Soils' or 'copying from our old English Systems', mostly plagiarising each other with minimal additions of their own. Bradley, *New improvements*, 'Preface'.

[48] Young, *Rural oeconomy*, 92.

[49] Marshall, *Experiments*, 2–3.

the kingdom, among men of landed property, and among others who take it up under a principle of amusement, or gain'.[50]

These were the decades when the number of agricultural titles surged in both England and Scotland, even relative to the general increase in publications.[51] This pattern is notable from contemporary observations and also aligns with a general increase in the writing of technical books.[52] In 1743, Robert Maxwell commented that 'there are few Scots Books wrote upon husbandry'.[53] Yet barely more than three decades later, in 1776, the Scottish jurist Lord Kames opened his treatise with the wry exclamation '[b]ehold another volume on husbandry!'.[54] Reviewers in 1757 and 1765 observed the recent fashion for reading and writing books on agriculture.[55] In 1762, John Wynn Baker commented that 'an infinite number of books have been published upon the subject' and guessed he owned 'upwards of a hundred volumes'.[56] In 1771, David Henry lamented that agricultural books were 'too numerous to be purchased, and too voluminous to be read by those who are obliged, for a livelihood, to employ their time in the practice of husbandry'.[57] The journal *The Scots Farmer* commented in 1773 that 'the books on Agriculture, published in England, would form a little library', although there were still few books by Scottish writers.[58] New authors were forced to acknowledge the perceived problem – for example, Cuthbert Clarke began his 1777 treatise by addressing the concern 'that books on husbandry are already more plentiful than useful'.[59] The sheer quantity of available books by this time is indicated by the vast catalogue of over 800 books on agriculture, botany and gardening, compiled by Richard Weston in 1769 and 1773.[60] The catalogue was designed to help gentlemen enthusiasts with their collections of books on the subject.[61]

A greater problem than the overwhelming mass of advice was the speculation of authors who lacked sufficient experience. A reviewer of

---

[50] Trusler, *Practical husbandry*, 1.
[51] See Figures 0.2 and 0.3.
[52] Mokyr, *Enlightened economy*, 46.
[53] Holmes, 'Agricultural publishing', 504–5.
[54] Kames, *Gentleman farmer*, vii.
[55] O., 'Compleat body of husbandry', 386; P., 'A new and complete system', 334.
[56] John Wynn Baker, *Some hints for the better improvement of husbandry* (Dublin, 1762), 13.
[57] Henry, *Complete English farmer*, iii.
[58] Reprinted in *Northern farmer*, 1.
[59] Clarke, *True theory*, iv.
[60] Weston, *Tracts*.
[61] For context on the perception of too many printed books: Ann Blair, *Too much to know: Managing scholarly information before the modern age* (New Haven, 2010); James Raven, 'Debating bibliomania and the collection of books in the eighteenth century', *Library & Information History*, 29 (2013).

the enormous treatise attributed to Thomas Hale in 1757 commented that a general fault of agricultural writers was 'to build too much upon theory'.[62] The multi-issue review concluded its critique with a succinct couplet: '*Practice* alone must form the Writer's head, / And ev'ry Author to the *Farm* be bred'.[63] The English translation of the French treatise by Duhamel du Monceau, published in 1764, derided 'Theorists who, without having any real knowledge in Husbandry, from their desks pretend to trace systems and lay down rules to Husbandmen'.[64] Lord Kames complained of agricultural writers who 'deliver their precepts from a study lined with books, without even pretending to experience'.[65] The *General Dictionary of Husbandry* (1779) decried 'the pedantic performances of a closeted Bookworm'.[66] The narrative of enlightened progress by William Marshall quoted earlier, was complicated by a tangent, in which books on agriculture led to '*Men of Taste!*' mounting agriculture 'on the Throne of ABSURDITY'. The noble science of agriculture had become 'a chit-chat Companion to the FINE ARTS and BELLES LETTRES!', 'the *hobby-horse of Projectors*, and *the catch-penny of Booksellers*'.[67] In 1794, Thomas Wedge remarked that it was 'an easy thing for a man to sit in his closet, and without any reference either to seasons, markets, or the objects of general practice, in particular districts, to frame such a course of crops as he may think applicable on all soils, in all situations'.[68] The critique against speculative or theoretical authors was, therefore, closely associated with the critique that agricultural books had fallen prey to the hack-writing industry; a 'bookseller contrives a new title, collects books upon the subject, delivers them to his author to pick and cull'.[69] In a letter to Young in 1765, Walter Harte mocked the periodical *Museum Rusticum* as the work of 'one man in a garret, who does not know a blade of wheat from a blade of barley'.[70] Smollet's 1771 novel described a hack writer who 'had just finished a treatise on practical agriculture, though, in fact, he had never seen corn growing in his life'.[71]

---

[62] O., 'Compleat body of husbandry', 386.
[63] O & P., 'Conclusion of the compleat body of husbandry', *Monthly Review*, 18 (1758), 558.
[64] M. Duhamel and Philip Miller, *The elements of agriculture*, 2 vols (London, 1764), i. xv.
[65] Kames, *Gentleman farmer*, vii.
[66] *General dictionary of husbandry*, i. iii.
[67] Marshall, *Minutes*, 'Digest', 3–4.
[68] Quoted in Horn, 'Contribution of the propagandist', 323.
[69] Kames, *Gentleman farmer*, vii.
[70] Betham-Edwards (ed.), *Autobiography*, 39.
[71] Smollett, *Humphry Clinker*, ii. 22.

The combined set of problems was identified in the introduction to the first volume of *The Scots Farmer*, a short-lived journal (1773–74).

> In England, many books have been published of late, with the professed purpose of instructing the Farmer in the universal science of Agriculture: Their titles promise a great deal; but these systems, these complete bodies of Agriculture, have been justly censured as very unfit instructors for the actual Farmer: They may do very well for the amusement of a gentleman in his country retirement; and may incite him to experiments … But, as they are mostly compiled by men possessed with the rage of book-making; who thought it their duty to amass every thing that has been wrote or said on their subject indiscriminately; instead of instructing, they could not fail to lead the ignorant Farmer into a maze of error and confusion.[72]

This is an appropriate summary of the bulk of agricultural literature produced between the 1660s and 1750s: the use of books to construct complete systems of knowledge, primarily for educated gentlemen, but which had questionable value as guides for practice.

The criticisms of theorists and bookworms were accompanied by a general concern among authors about acquiring their knowledge from other books. As noted earlier, these had ancient origins. Richard Bradley's 1725 survey of ancient agricultural literature included a caution from the Roman writer Columella (4-c.70 CE), that 'the Writings of such Authors will rather give us the Rudiments of the Art, than make us compleat Artists … So that our Rules do not pretend to make perfect Husbandmen, but to assist them; nor can any one pretend to be Master in this Art by Reading only'.[73] Perhaps inspired by the old Roman, in 1757 Thomas Lisle stated:

> Nor is the knowledge of husbandry to be acquired by reading without practice. Books may give valuable hints to those who have judgement to make use of them, but, to learn the first rudiments of this art, it is necessary to serve an apprenticeship to it as to other trades.[74]

Such qualifications limited but preserved the value of books as a way of learning about farming. Until the 1760s, most writers explicitly appealed to the authority of earlier books as a source for their own publications. For example, this was still the case for Adam Dickson in 1762, who assured his readers that he had first 'read almost all the books which this age has produced on that subject'.[75]

---

[72] Reprinted in 1778: *Northern farmer*, 9.
[73] Bradley, *Survey*, 4.
[74] In editor's preface to father's treatise: Lisle, *Observations*, ii. vi–vii.
[75] Dickson, *Treatise*, iii.

Yet there appears to have been a shift in opinion around this time about whether previous books were a legitimate source of knowledge. In 1765, Charles Varlo claimed that he had 'borrowed nothing from books' when writing his new treatise.[76] In 1775, Nathaniel Kent also insisted that '[n]othing is borrowed from books' in his manual.[77] Kent was one of the many who performed the linguistic trick of substituting a physical book for a metaphorical one: 'if we consult only the book of Nature … we shall derive infinite advantage from her instructions in all country-business'.[78] The same sentiments were put forward by Kames in 1776 when sharing a moment of philosophical doubt.

> In studying the principles laid down by writers, I found myself in a sort of labyrinth, carried to and fro without any certain direction. After a long course of reading, where there was nothing but darkness and discrepence, I laid aside my books, took heart, and like Des Cartes commenced inquires with doubting every thing. I resorted to the book of nature: I studied it with attention.[79]

Kames questioned the source of earlier writings, but did not reject books as a form of agricultural knowledge. Further, he did not retreat to the notion that only those bred to husbandry could possess the full mystery of the art. Rather than descend to the plough, Kames took up his pen; he planned experiments and contemplated the labours of others. Marshall described a similar experience in the mid-1770s when he took over a farm: 'fearing that from Education and Books he had received false ideas of Agriculture', he had 'resolved to throw aside Books'.[80] Later, Marshall claimed that since 1774 (when he began farming) to the time of writing in 1789, he had 'read nothing on the subject of rural affairs'.[81] He refrained from reading 'lest I might catch ideas, imperceptibly', preferring to gain knowledge from nature, established practices, the individual experience of superior men and his own experience.[82] In short, agricultural authors in the 1770s distanced themselves from their own genre, by trying to liberate their intellectual work from old epistemologies and contemporary associations with hack writing.

---

[76] Charles Varlo, *A treatise on agriculture, intitled the Yorkshire farmer* (Dublin, 1765), iii.
[77] Nathaniel Kent, *Hints to gentlemen of landed property* (London, 1775), iii.
[78] Ibid., 1–2.
[79] Kames, *Gentleman farmer*, xii.
[80] Marshall, *Minutes*, 2.
[81] With the exception of some weeks or months in 1780 'in the reading room of the British Museum, looking over and forming a catalogue of books, formerly written on the subject'. Marshall, *Glocestershire*, i. xxvi.
[82] Ibid., i. xxv–xxvi.

In the late eighteenth century, the rage for farming and the rage for book-making combined to form the rage for book-farming. But the efforts to codify the art of husbandry and transform it into a science of agriculture for gentleman landowners had produced an eccentric genre. As Laura Sayre noted, there was a growing recognition 'that agricultural literature could breed its own forms of quixotism'.[83] It was partly successful in inspiring a new breed of gentlemen farmers, but inadequate as a resource for both gentlemen and for common farmers. A reviewer of Young's *Farmer's Kalendar* captured the problem: 'one of those many instruments which are needless to an *old* and *judicious* husbandman, and dangerous to the *young* and *injudicious*'.[84] Similarly, a reviewer concluded that the *Gentleman Farmer's Pocket Companion* (1790) was of no use to anyone: the directions were 'of little service to the ignorant practitioner, on account of their brevity – but as they are often erroneous, they would mislead those who consult them. The skilful farmer could avoid the errors: – but he has no need of the directions'.[85]

Farming books had to be rescued from the perils of book-farming. As Joseph Wimpey put it in 1775, 'I am very far from intending to decry all books on the subject … the men I complain of, and would discountenance, are your mere book builders'.[86] Major agricultural authors between the 1770s and 1790s attacked the errors of their predecessors and tried to reform agricultural literature on the basis of experiment and observation, as discussed in Chapter 4. These reforms could be linked to a broadening of the socio-economic origins of authors and readers. Whereas many of the treatises published around the beginning of the eighteenth century were compilations by and for country gentlemen in retirement, many of the new manuals in this period were the productions of commercial farmers or stewards for the increasing number of wealthy and educated tenants of large farms. The printer David Henry, who acquired a farm in Kent in the early 1760s, agonised over the central problem in 1771:

> But, surely, something may be done to rescue Book-Husbandry from that contempt into which it has fallen. Unfortunately for farmers, the greatest number of those who have pretended to teach the art, have either been scholars only, or unlearned farmers, either mere theorists or mere practicers …

[83] Sayre, 'Farming by the book', 313.
[84] 'Art. VI. The farmer's kalendar', *Monthly Review*, 45 (1771), 445.
[85] 'Art 29. The gentleman farmer's pocket companion', *Monthly Review*, 3 (1790), 338.
[86] Wimpey, *Rural*, 27.

The former were 'too prone to advance novelties' based on abstractions; the latter were 'too ignorant to reason from effects to causes'.[87] Henry described the dialectic of agricultural literature: from the unlearned, oral and customary world of husbandry emerged its opposite – the scholarly texts of theoretical agriculture – which had to be synthesised by scientific-minded, professional farmers who could balance theory and practice.[88] Farming books needed a firm empirical basis, but in a way that preserved the authority of authors and readers over the unlearned practitioner.

The re-making of the genre was led by the dominant writers of the late eighteenth century, Arthur Young and William Marshall, and to a lesser extent James Anderson. All three had experience of managing large farms and were able to bridge the farming and literary worlds better than most of their predecessors. They combined a deep commitment to the potential of agricultural writing with an equally deep frustration in its mixed achievements. In 1767, only a few years after he took up farming, Young echoed others in denouncing 'those books which are published under the title of *General Treatises – Systems – Dictionaries*, &c. &c. &c. comprehending more soils, articles of culture, &c. than any one man can experimentally have knowledge of '.[89] The compilers of such 'pernicious books' had caused a great deal of damage as they deterred farmers from experiments and tarnished all new ideas. Since readers of such books failed with considerable losses, 'a disgust is taken at the very idea of experiments or *book husbandry*', and 'a whole neighbourhood of farmers clap their hands with pleasure at the gentleman's disappointment, determining never to be misled by books into any *new tricks*'.[90] It was partly the attempt to rescue agricultural literature from social ridicule and a didactic dead-end that Young produced a series of innovations in the form of agricultural book knowledge: a tour, a register of experiments, a calendar, a management manual and finally a periodical.

James Anderson, the Scottish agriculturist and political economist, was more sceptical about overcoming the weaknesses of book-farming through, for example, a register of experiments, as all written knowledge faced the problems of communicating across diverse vocabularies and diverse

---

[87] Henry, *Complete English farmer*, iv–v.
[88] A similar opinion was expressed by George Winter in 1788: 'the oldest Farmers are not always possessed of the greatest knowledge of Husbandry, nor are the most learned in literature at all times the most competent judges of Agriculture – Improvements in Husbandry, are acquired only by experiments and the strictest observations ...' *The Farmer convinced*, 16.
[89] Young, *Farmer's letters*, 144.
[90] Ibid., 146.

environments. Therefore, 'even the best practical treatises are merely local', and the reader could not know in advance if the advice would be applicable on their own farm.[91] Like Young, Anderson believed the periodical was the best way to mitigate the defects of agricultural writing and bridge the opposition between practical farmers and agricultural theorists. His journal *Recreations* (1792–1802) was an attempt 'to establish a channel of information that may be as little liable to objection by these two different descriptions of men'.[92]

The aim to steer a middle way between customary husbandry and speculative book-farming was elaborated most forcefully by William Marshall. Chapter 4 explained his theory of how knowledge is best produced and communicated, upon which basis he offered a theoretical schema that divided farmers into three classes: 'Aboriginal', 'Scientific' and 'Aerial'. 'The first farm from CUSTOM; — the second, from EXPERIMENT and OBSERVATION; the last, from BOOKS and BAILIES'.[93] The Aerialist was 'speculative', 'credulous' and 'habitually bookish' – the quintessential book-farmer. He had 'read the TOURS' (a swipe at Young), and 'sallies forth Knight-errant of Agriculture'. When he failed, he 'changes his BOOKS — changes his BAILEY, and changes his PLAN of management – but all in vain'. Marshall imagined the Aerialist, after complete failure, observing a common farmer 'in a spacious field of flowing corn' and finding 'himself deservedly laughed at by the very persons he affected to contemn'. Marshall criticised both custom and abstract theory, and sought to resolve their errors through the figure of the 'Sciencist' [sic], who proceeded from experiment and observation. The scientific farmer approached agriculture professionally as his study and his business.[94] At the end of this book Marshall directly confronted the apparent contradictions or hypocrisies of his own authorship (original italics):

> It is true, he is *writing a Book*; in which it is also true, he has more than once *laughed at Books*; and he is now absolutely recommending *written Agriculture*. He *writes* a Book *to put the unexperienced on their guard in reading* Books. He *contemns Books*, because there are too many *Books on Agriculture* which are *contemptible*. And when he recommends WRITTEN AGRICULTURE, he means such only as results immediately from DELIBERATE ANALYSIS, ACCURATE EXPERIMENTS, and WELL-DIGESTED OBSERVATIONS.[95]

---

[91] Anderson, *An inquiry*, 6–8.
[92] Anderson, *Recreations*, i. 22–23.
[93] Marshall, *Minutes*, 'Digest', 7.
[94] Ibid., 'Digest', 11–12.
[95] Ibid., 'Digest', 122.

It was a rare moment in which the precarious high-wire act performed by many late-eighteenth-century writers was laid bare. If agricultural literature was to thrive then it had to trim its excesses and pretensions and construct a new basis for its authority upon experiment and observation.

All the above criticisms of agricultural books and book-farming, however forceful, were ultimately constructive and reformist, stimulating debates about the source of knowledge and innovations in form. Sayre shrewdly suggests that the 'superficial ridicule' of commentators about gentry farming were designed to guard against more serious objections, since a foolish and romantic enthusiasm for improvement appeared more 'disinterested' than 'avaricious strategies for increasing estate income'.[96] But this only constituted part of the controversy of book-farming. The authors themselves indicated that the criticisms from practical farmers went much further than complaints about the number of books or their speculative style.

Book Knowledge Is Power

To understand the depth of the controversy surrounding book-farming, we must recognise the general relation between knowledge and power in the sphere of production. That is, we need to consider whether criticisms about agricultural books could be about their social impact (especially on labour relations) as much as their technical qualities. Broadly speaking, knowledge can be viewed as a key factor of agricultural production alongside land and labour.[97] Those who possess productive knowledge possess a degree of power in the production process.[98] To exert control over agricultural production, therefore, it is advantageous to control productive knowledge, or the intellectual powers of production.[99] If the worker possesses more knowledge than the manager who directs them, this creates a problem of asymmetric knowledge.[100]

The popularity of Cato's maxim, as explained at the beginning of this chapter, shows how early modern agricultural literature displayed a deep

---

[96] Sayre, 'Farming by the book', 315.
[97] For discussion on knowledge as a force of production and the notion of 'cognitive capitalism', see Yann Moulier-Boutang, *Cognitive capitalism* (Cambridge, 2011).
[98] On the need to control knowledge: Marglin, 'Losing touch'; Scott, *Seeing like a state*, 334–38.
[99] On how conflict over the intellectual powers of production shaped capitalist divisions of labour, see Vercellone, 'From formal subsumption'.
[100] See the related 'principal-agent' problem, where the worker (agent) is more knowledgeable about their labour than the manager (principal). For example, Alanson Minkler, 'Knowledge and internal organization', *Journal of Economic Behaviour and Organisation,* 21 (1993).

concern with controlling productive knowledge and frequently discussed the problem of asymmetric knowledge between master and servant, and to a lesser extent between landlord and tenant. Hence the English edition of the French treatise *Maison Rustique* (1616) stated that the landowner must possess a minimum amount of knowledge to command his subordinates, to avoid dependence upon them. The lord who read books and enriched 'his memorie with these knowledges, shall live a Free man, and no Bondslave, a Master, and no Prentice, to his Farmer or Baylie'.[101]

The risks to masters who were overly dependent on their servants were regularly raised throughout the eighteenth century. As explained in Chapter 4, Jethro Tull developed his new methods and theories through antagonism with his workers, and his anger at what he felt was the 'exorbitant Power of Husbandry Servants and Labourers over their Masters' is a persistent theme in his writing.[102] In Tull's view, no farmer could profit when the servants were in control of the methods, and many gentlemen suffered because servants refused to implement their master's will. He warned in 1733 that if correspondents sent servants to him to be instructed in his new horse-hoeing methods, they would then be reliant on their servants' knowledge, resulting in the disagreeable situation of 'the Plowman's correcting his Titular Master'.[103] In the same year, William Ellis described the unhappy condition of men who inherited an estate in their youth and were 'obliged to be guided by their head Servant or Ploughman'.[104] Herein lay the potential usefulness of practical guidebooks: 'the World may easily see how vastly useful experimental Rules and Cautions are to the Youth, Heir, Gentleman, unexperienc'd Farmer, and even to the Foreigner'.[105] A 1762 Irish tract on the improvement of husbandry by John Wynn Baker worried about the ignorance of gentlemen and regretted 'the influence that some old farmers, of *supposed experience*, have had upon gentlemen; so as totally to subvert their intentions, even to a counteracting of their schemes'.[106]

The underlying concern was explained with characteristic clarity by Young in 1770, as part of his advice on employing a bailiff (the head servant to whom the management of a farm was often delegated): 'in every

---

[101] Markham, *Maison rustique*, 19–20. Similar point made in Heresbach and Googe, *Foure bookes of husbandry*, 15–16.
[102] Tull, *Supplement*, 238. In the same work, see passages 225–26 and 250.
[103] Tull, *Horse-hoing*, vi.
[104] Ellis, *Chiltern and vale*, 'Preface'.
[105] Ibid., 'Preface'.
[106] Baker, *Some hints*, 10–12.

species of business, the master should know more, or, at least, as much as the man, that no errors may pass in the conduct of the latter, without being seen and understood by the former'. Young acknowledged that 'a young practitioner in farming must necessarily be so much at a loss about a great variety of matters … of which he is ignorant, that if he does not keep a bailey, his whole business will infallibly suffer'. The gentleman farmer must, therefore, first learn from his bailiff before he can exert full control: 'by the help of a bailey, well skilled in common husbandry, he will, in a few years, acquire an equal knowledge; and consequently, have it fully in his power to oversee and controul the bailey himself, and never lay himself open, through his ignorance, to be imposed upon'.[107] In another book published the same year, Young argued that his manual could, therefore, be an alternative, and more reliable, source of knowledge. As 'many gentlemen who make farming a business or a pleasure are at first *totally* ignorant of most things concerning it', and therefore under 'the necessity of being guided by their servants', then 'a work of this sort will to them prove a better guide than a foolish, prejudiced, or perhaps knavish assistants [sic]'.[108] No doubt Young's advice was born from his own experience, after he found himself in 1763, aged twenty-two, running a farm without any knowledge. Similarly, in 1804, Marshall argued that the manager of a farm ought to be the 'master of every implement, tool, and operation', otherwise he would be unable 'to correct a bad workman' or 'to know when to be satisfied with a good one'.[109] The agricultural chemist Humphry Davy later made the point from the reverse perspective, arguing that the 'attention of the labourer will be more minute, and he will exert himself more for improvement when he is certain he cannot deceive his employer, and has a conviction of the extant of his knowledge'. Ignorance in a landowner 'often leads either to inattention or injudicious practices in the tenant or the bailiff'.[110]

As Davy's remark indicated, agricultural writers were also concerned with the relative knowledge of landlord and tenant, as well as the key management relation of master-bailiff. For the most part, eighteenth-century landlords (or their stewards) were keen to lease a farm not only to tenants with sufficient capital to invest, or willing to pay the highest rent but also to those judged to possess the necessary knowledge and skills to be

---

[107] Young, *Rural oeconomy*, 98–100.
[108] Young, *Farmer's guide*, i–ii.
[109] Marshall, *Landed property*, 423.
[110] Davy, *Elements*, 25–26.

profitable and to improve the value of the land (or at least not diminish it).[111] But while there was a preference for knowledgeable tenants, there was also a desire to extend control over their methods. This was manifest in the increasing use of covenants in leases, which were detailed prescriptions specifying a range of matters from crop rotations to the use of certain manures.[112] The author and Church of Scotland minister Thomas Robertson discussed the struggle for power between the landlord and tenant in his 1796 report on the size of farms for the Board of Agriculture. Robertson was a firm advocate of a landlord-tenant system with a strict division of responsibilities, and chastised landowners who were 'a kind of farmer in disguise' and who 'over-rule all the operations of husbandry' in their manner of leasing.[113] By prescribing general systems of management in their leases, they were asserting that 'the owner knows the best principles of farming', instead of the tenant, and assumed for themselves 'the gift of prophecy too, with respect to the weather'.[114] Robertson painted a striking picture in his summary of the system prevailing in large areas of the kingdom:

> The tenants are machines, without will or movement of their own. The landlords are the farmers; for, either by their refusal of leases, or by their restrictions and directories, they, in effect, conduct, or over-rule the whole business, themselves … Thus have we, the great part of the landlords of England, sitting behind the curtain, in the character of farmers-in-mask; guiding by strings a number of puppets, under the name of tenants, upon the stage …[115]

Robertson's argument was slightly against the grain of the majority of literature from the period, which usually encouraged an active landlordism based on a solid foundation of agricultural knowledge. But he was drawing attention to an important area of conflict within the structure of estates: who claimed knowledge of cultivation, and who had responsibility for exercising it?

The struggle over knowledge can be viewed, albeit indirectly, from the opposite perspective of servants to masters, or small tenants to landowners.

---

[111] For example, on the late seventeenth-century Verney estate, 'obtaining the highest rent was balanced against the known skills of candidates'. Broad, *Transforming English rural society*, 141. Sir Joseph Banks even went so far as to argue 'that "unlearned" tenants should be prevented from competing for farms and paying rents they could not afford'. Mingay, *Gentry*, 85.

[112] Turner et al., *Agricultural rent*, 14–15; Clay, 'Landlords', 613–14. Examples of covenants in Ley, *Nobleman*, 368.

[113] Robertson, *General report*, 76.

[114] Ibid., 88.

[115] Ibid., 96.

In a book on ancient husbandry, Adam Dickson made the basic point that farmers in his time learned their art independently: there was a period when Roman farmers had 'received all their knowledge from the proprietors', whereas British farmers had 'as yet received but little instruction from the proprietor; all the knowledge which he possesses, he has acquired from his own observations, and the practices of his predecessors'.[116] In general, the pride of common husbandmen and servants in their customary knowledge and confidence in their superior expertise acquired through labour is well attested. Richard Bradley complained in 1727 at the mocking response he would receive from common farmers when he offered advice: 'they will ask me whether I can hold a plough, for in that they think the whole mystery of husbandry consists'.[117] Tull joked that bailiffs respond to gentlemen switching from customary to new methods of husbandry like a priest responding to a Catholic converting to Protestantism.[118] In an unpublished georgic poem eulogising Tull's new husbandry, written around 1738–44, Edward King commented that 'mere farmers have a strong persuasion that gentlemen cannot understand the nature of Vegetation so well as mere farmers'.[119] Harte cautioned his readers that the common husbandman might think 'that it is impossible for a gentleman to understand such matters' and 'laugh at you in private'.[120] The apparent failure of The Society of Improvers in the Knowledge of Agriculture in Scotland to influence farming practice was attributed to a prejudice among common farmers: 'How should gentlemen', they would ask, 'not bred to the plough, know any thing of Farming?'.[121] In 1790, Marshall stated that the 'great bulk of occupiers consider every man who has not been bred up in the habits of husbandry, or enured to them by long practice, as a visionary; and are more inclined to sneer at his plans, than adopt them'.[122] In 1792, William Skirving noted that servants were so convinced of their customary methods of sowing 'that there have been instances of sowers giving up their places rather than sow to a master's pleasure'.[123]

Such scoffing at gentlemen could be extended to all male agriculturalists concerning areas of traditional female authority, especially

[116] Dickson, *Of the ancients*, 95.
[117] Bradley, *Complete body of husbandry*, 95.
[118] Tull, *Supplement*, 256.
[119] Add MS 56378, 'Agriculture; or drill-husbandry', 'Edward King', Western Manuscripts (1738–1744), f. 77.
[120] Harte, *Essays*, 196.
[121] *Northern farmer*, 5.
[122] Marshall, *Midland counties*, i. 120.
[123] Skirving, *Husbandman's assistant*, 338.

dairying. In 1784, Josiah Twamley shared 'how unthankful an office it is, to attempt to instruct or inform Dairywomen, how to improve their method, or point out rules, which are different from their own, or what hath always been practiced by their Mothers'. His efforts to advise women would be met with bafflement, for 'how should a Man know of any thing of Cheese making?'[124] Knowledge was rooted in gendered roles and experience.

We can consider these grumbles and chuckles at the presumption of expertise by gentlemen and the unwillingness to implement their ideas as a species of 'everyday resistance', or 'weapon of the weak', as first theorised by James Scott.[125] Evading, mocking or frustrating the chosen methods of a gentleman farmer functioned in a similar way to foot-dragging, dissimulation or small-scale sabotage. For example, Tull complained about servants who feigned ignorance at following his new methods, since 'they can do it well when they please', and concluded a story of servants frustrating a nobleman with the judgement that it was 'their Will not their Skill that was wanting'.[126]

It is clear that the balance of knowledge between master and servant, or landlord and tenant, was contested. Therefore, we must understand the impact and response to agricultural books within a context of conflicting interests, rather than assuming that everyone involved in agriculture should have responded to book knowledge equally. Agricultural books reduced the dependence (and feeling of dependence) of gentlemen upon their servants and other social inferiors who usually possessed greater practical experience. It was an alternative and unfamiliar source of knowledge that competed with the advice of servants or customs of tenants, and therefore challenged the knowledge of those bred to husbandry. As Arthur Young put it, when a gentleman turned to farming he was faced with an 'immense mass of advice'; 'every common labourer can point out many things that should be done; the bailey many more; and books, ten thousand times as many'.[127] This managerial function of books was stated clearly by the Rev John Trusler – an incessant compiler of manuals on myriad topics – who explained that his *Practical Husbandry* (1780) was not written for

---

[124] Twamley, *Dairying exemplified*, 10–11. See discussion in Valenze, 'Art of women', 162–63.
[125] Scott, *Weapons of the weak: Everyday forms of peasant resistance*; James C. Scott, *Domination and the arts of resistance: Hidden transcripts* (London, 1990).
[126] Tull, *Supplement*, 225, 250.
[127] Young, *Rural oeconomy*, 96.

instructing men early bred to husbandry; but to give Gentleman, who may think proper to use a certain quantity of land, either for amusement or convenience, such an insight into the nature of farming, as will enable them to check the negligence, correct the ignorance, or detect the imposition, of servants.[128]

We can see, therefore, the importance of books as a tool of the gentleman farmer, who needed to know as much or more than his subordinates, yet could not lower himself to engage in manual labour to learn through practical experience. It is one of the ironies of agricultural books that while they proclaimed the superior intellectual capacity of genteel readers, their pages were full of anxiety about the deeper knowledge of their hired hands. In an American book published in 1824, the authors stated that '*[b]ook-knowledge then is power*, and other things being equal, the farmer who obtains information from books, or other printed works … has the advantage over his unlettered neighbour, who despises book-farming'.[129] Books were, indeed, a new source of power, but in a broader sense than these authors intended. While agricultural books have usually been characterised as disseminating the expertise of gentlemen to less educated practitioners, they should also be seen from the inverse perspective, as serving the needs of ignorant gentlemen who otherwise struggled to exert full command over their servants or tenants.

Social Evils of Book-Farming

In 1799, James Anderson reflected on the 'general prejudice [that] hath long prevailed among practical farmers against books on agriculture'. He gave an unusually balanced assessment of the underlying conflict:

> this indiscriminate prejudice hath produced a disagreeable estrangement between practical farmers and amateurs of agriculture … In the eyes of the amateur the mere practical farmer is accounted a narrow-minded, obstinate, perverse animal, who is determined … to plod on to all eternity in the path his forefather had trodden; and the farmer, in his turn, laughs at the amateur as a visionary, who, mistaking dreams for realities, is in hopes of obtaining immense treasures by those very steps that the cautious farmer knows will often end in his own ruin.[130]

[128] Trusler, *Practical husbandry*, 3.
[129] William Drown and Solomon Drown, *Compendium of agriculture; or, the farmer's guide* (Providence, R.I., 1824), 21–22. Original italics.
[130] Anderson, *Recreations*, 20–21. Same observation made in 1757, 'that the real practical Farmers, and the visionary speculative Authors, have usually entertained a pretty remarkable prejudice against each other'. O., 'Compleat body of husbandry', 387.

By 'amateur', Anderson meant theorists and writers, as opposed to farmers by vocation. Here Anderson gestured towards the fundamental opposition between two ways of knowing that gave rise to the hostility to
book-farming. The problem is that we have plenty of direct evidence of
the perspective of amateur agriculturists and only occasional and indirect
evidence of the perspective of practical farmers from anecdotal encoun-
ters. Yet they give a flavour of the general response. The first Scottish
author on the subject, James Donaldson, anticipated a peasant's cyni-
cism in response to his treatise of 1697: *'From whence came you Sir? That
offers to teach us how to labour our Ground … Are you Wiser than all
that ever have been bred and exercised in Husbandry hitherto?'*[131] Similarly,
in his 1714 book on gardening, the clergyman John Laurence gave an
example of the 'Rebukes' he received from gardeners, 'who hate to be
inform'd by a Scholar':

> What, say they, does this Man come and pretend to teach us, to make our
> Masters think we do not understand our Business? How should he know
> what Stocks are best for Trees, or how to prune them? It is fitter for him to
> be at his Studies, 'a making Sermons'.[132]

On 1 March 1736, a London newspaper carried a curious letter from a
Kentish farmer, which ridiculed a book written by a parson regarding
the disadvantages of farmers selling grain for distilling. Notably, the correspondent claimed the book contained things 'which every Plough-Boy
knows to be false', and pointedly asked if 'this learned Gentleman will
allow a Farmer to be any Judge in his own Affairs, that he was bred and
born in'.[133] Decades later, Charles Varlo imagined how 'bigoted old fashioned farmers' who 'scorn to be book farmers' would react to his book
A New System of Husbandry (1770): 'shall a gentleman because he can
write, pretend to instruct me what to do with my land, does he know
better than myself, who has been brought up to farming business all
my life time, and perhaps on the same land too, a pretty joke indeed'.[134]
These reported views of practical farmers clearly expressed criticisms of
book-farming in social terms, challenging the fact that authors not bred
to husbandry were positioning themselves as teachers of experienced
husbandmen.

---

[131] Donaldson, *Husbandry*, 122.
[132] John Laurence, *The clergy-man's recreation: Shewing the pleasure and profit of the art of gardening*
(London, 1714), 'Preface'.
[133] 'News', *London Daily Post and General Advertiser*, 1 March 1736.
[134] Varlo, *New system*, i. 75.

Authors often indicated that the quality of farming books was irrel-
evant, as common farmers were only willing to learn through practice, and
were uninterested or unaccustomed to learning from books: 'characters
wrote with *pen* and *ink* are not what they can understand … The characters intelligible to them must be wrote with *the plough and the spade*'.[135]
Varlo travelled around selling his books and implements and demonstrat-
ing his methods as he was 'convinced that many farmers to whom I have
explained these interesting methods of husbandry, will practice from what
I have shewed; who, probably would have overlooked them, had they only
read the books'.[136] James Anderson, writing of farmers in 1779: 'Few of
them read much: and they so seldom meet with instruction in books of
agriculture, that these are perhaps less read by practical farmers than books
of any other kind whatever', as they 'despise those who write on the subject of their own profession as idle visionaries'.[137] It was in such a context
that Cuthbert Clarke looked nostalgically to Roman antiquity, when he
believed 'authors had such influence on practical husbandmen, that their
directions were considered as rules for practice', whereas in his time 'nothing can more offend the common husbandman' than deriving knowledge
'from any other resources than practice'.[138] A contributor to the journal
Annals of Agriculture remarked in 1799: 'I think I hear the old obstinate
farmer exclaim against any innovations; his method bags up enough every
year; and while others starve by book-farming, he is getting rich by old
custom'.[139] Another journal disparagingly characterised the small farmer
as one whose 'broad countenance never assumes so triumphant a grin,
as when he can find auditors to relish his stupid observations on book-
farmers'.[140] Significantly, common farmers were portrayed as 'against taking any hint, right or wrong, from books'.[141]

These reported criticisms overlap with those already discussed, but
there are indications of wider discontent towards agricultural writers and
the impact of their publications. In 1794, Charles Varlo described how
some farmers blamed him for contributing to the high price of provi-
sions. They insinuated 'that it is such as I, who made books that opened

[135] Sir Archibald Grant, *A dissertation on the chief obstacles to the improvement of land* (Aberdeen, 1760), 91–92.
[136] Clarke and Varlo, *Unfortunate husbandman*, 21.
[137] Anderson, *An inquiry*, 34–35.
[138] Clarke, *True theory*, 'Preface'.
[139] *Annals of agriculture*, 32 (1799), 112.
[140] *The commercial and agricultural magazine*, 3:12 (1800), 48.
[141] Lawrence, *The new farmer's calendar*, 'Preface'.

their landlords' eyes, made them farmers, know the value of crops, and made them raise their rents'; and he assumed that 'other authors, who have wrote upon husbandry, have met with like replies'.[142] Such anecdotes suggest that negative attitudes towards farming books may have reflected a belief that they were disrupting rural relations by changing the behaviour of gentlemen landowners and others.

We can explore this sense of wider conflict by examining the sophisticated social critique of book-farming advanced in an anti-enclosure pamphlet from 1785. In Chapter 3, it was shown that agricultural writers developed criticisms of the customary knowledge and skills of common husbandmen as justification for appropriating the art of husbandry. This general criticism could support more specific arguments for enclosure, particularly during the peak of Parliamentary Acts of Enclosure in the late eighteenth century. Although rarely an outright justification for enclosures, the underlying belief that commoners were incapable of carrying out what agricultural writers saw as necessary improvements, partly through a lack of education, was embedded within the worldview of enclosure advocates.[143] The pro-enclosure arguments published in 1787 by the land steward Thomas Stone, for example, presumed a particular hierarchy of knowledge.[144] The aim of enclosure was not only to advance individual property rights, or consolidate the holdings of particular landowners but also to ensure that cultivation was under the supervision of learned men. The process of enclosure itself often involved enclosure commissioners, appointed by Parliament, directing decisions about farming while they superimposed a new pattern of landownership, briefly occupying the earlier role of manorial courts.[145]

A particular debate in the 1780s around the consequences of enclosure highlights this struggle over knowledge. The central exchange involved a 1784 pro-enclosure pamphlet by William Lamport, a member of the Bath Agricultural Society, and a reply by an anonymous 'Society of Farmers' the following year, both of which prompted further reviews and pamphlets. The debate centred on the specifics of enclosure, but the opponents

---

[142] Charles Varlo, *Nature display'd, a new work, being a miscellany* (London, 1794), 42–43.

[143] Studies on enclosures usually focus on the moral debates around property, poverty and depopulation. For example, J. M. Neeson, 'The opponents of enclosure in eighteenth-century Northamptonshire', *Past & Present* (1984).

[144] The open field farmer was described as 'so bigoted to the ancient mode of field farming' that he was unable or unwilling to take advantage of enclosed land if it meant deviating 'from the beaten track of his ancestors for the means of subsistence'. Thomas Stone, *Suggestions for rendering the inclosure of common fields and waste lands a source of population and riches* (London, 1787), 25.

[145] J. V. Beckett et al., 'Farming through enclosure', *Rural History*, 9 (1998), 146–47.

articulated fundamentally contrasting views about agricultural knowledge
and books. Lamport's 1784 pamphlet only made occasional reference to the
knowledge or skill of common cultivators, but he had previously explained
his views on these matters in 'A proposal for the further improvement of
agriculture' (1780), which addressed 'the prejudices and untractableness of
the illiterate Farmers and their servants'.[146] In this essay, Lamport criticised the unenlightened management of common farmers and their lack
of reading about husbandry and improvement.[147]

In 1785, *A Political Enquiry into the Consequences of Enclosing Waste Lands*,
advertised as the 'sentiments of a society of farmers in —— shire', was published in reaction to a favourable review of Lamport's pamphlet.[148] This anti-
enclosure pamphlet had multiple authors: an editor who inserted a preface,
and a 'Farmer' who wrote the bulk of the pamphlet, but who was referred
to as the 'amanuensis', since by the use of 'the pronoun I, is in general,
meant, *we the Society*'.[149] We gain a hint of who might have constituted this
society as the pamphlet includes a representation against enclosure signed by
'the Freeholders, Copyholders, Leaseholders, and other Inhabitants of the
Parish'.[150] The main topic of the pamphlet was the high price of butcher's
meat examined through a commentary on Lamport's pamphlet, but both
editor and farmer presented a fierce critique of agricultural books in the
preface and introductory essay. The fact that this extensive attack on book-
farming was linked to arguments against enclosure illustrates how agricultural literature was positioned within the attacks on customary farming
(both land rights and knowledge) and its impact on social relations.

The editor began by stating 'that writers *not brought up in the arts of
Agriculture from their childhood*, can never acquire such an established intimate knowledge … to enable them to state the general system in its true
light'. The ideas in agricultural treatises might be amusing or lead to profitable experiments for men of fortune, but they were no guides for ordinary
farming families. He lamented that lawyers, physicians and clergymen
wrote agricultural books, rather than people 'who have been regularly
brought up from their youth in the employment'. Moreover, he claimed
that practising farmers deliberately hid their knowledge from gentlemen,

---

[146] Lamport, *Cursory remarks*.
[147] Lamport, 'Proposal'.
[148] 'Art. 24. Cursory remarks on the importance of agriculture', *English Review*, 4 (1784), 76.
[149] *A political enquiry*, viii, xi.
[150] The 'Farmer' described himself as having a grammar education, and the experience of travel over
England and the Continent, but had begun farming in his youth and now held his own farm of
near two hundred acres (without the help of a bailiff). Ibid., 16.

'partly from a jealousy lest the gentleman should know as much as himself; and partly from the haughty contemptuous manner in which he is frequently treated'.[151] Explaining the origin of the pamphlet, the editor described how among the society of farmers 'many of the positions laid down in modern treatises … were standing matter for jokes'. Indeed, at first Lamport's pamphlet 'had afforded a subject for merriment', but the political context had provoked a serious response in print.[152] The pamphlet presented itself 'as *information to the legislature*, not as *instructions to farmers how to manage their lands*, which hath been the professed plan of most writers on farming'.[153] This is significant as it shows the authors were sceptical about the very idea of instructional farming books.

The section titled 'A Farmer's Thoughts' was dedicated to an epistemological and social critique of the 'evils' of agricultural books. Agriculture, the writer argued, was a mechanical art that depended on practice, such that 'when the speculative philosopher attempts to give the mechanic or the farmer practical instructions, he is perpetually lost in the mazes of error'. Further, books mistakenly made the leap from local knowledge to universal principles.[154] However, the author did pick out four authors, two ancient and two modern – Virgil, Columella, Duhamel and Tull – who had provided real 'systems of farming' from experience. In contrast, he painted an unflattering picture of 'modern compilers on husbandry', who

> learn a few principles from preceding writers, or gather crude hints in London coffee-houses … run from county to county to glean up partial, or perhaps romantic details of particular modes of husbandry, with which some practical farmers may have been pleased to amuse them …[155]

Consequently, 'literary men' were 'often deceived by specious writers', which gave rise to disagreements 'between the man of science and the farmer', who 'accuse each other of ignorance and obstinacy'. Modern treatises were mere 'farming romances', at best encouraging good general principles, but certainly no guide for practice.[156]

The farmer's main concerns were the social 'evils' arising from the printing of agricultural books, of which he listed five. First, the failures of tradesmen deluded by reading books, which were parodied as 'knights-errant in farming':

[151] Ibid., iii–vii.
[152] In response to a recommendation that the Crown's forest lands be sold and enclosed.
[153] *A political enquiry*, x–xiii.
[154] Ibid., 13.
[155] Ibid., 3.
[156] Ibid., 2–4.

I could give names of honest industrious London tradesmen, who have quitted business with fortunes sufficient to retire upon during the rest of their lives, merely for the sake of turning farmers, upon the plan of Mr A or Mr B and have died insolvent with broken hearts, or are now languishing in prisons.[157]

Secondly, that landowners raised rents in full knowledge that neighbouring farmers would see the land as overvalued, but that 'it will catch the eye of a *cockney*, who inflated with an idea of his superior knowledge, compared with that of a common farmer, will think an advance of a few shillings per acre of no great importance'. This drove up the rent for other farmers. But there were 'other evils arising from the publication of these books' which were more complex. The third complaint was that since farmers 'succeed so ill in their undertakings when governed by books', an observing farmer then 'rejects every idea of modern improvement', even those that might be useful. The writer believed that books were inadvertently hindering progress. Fourth, when the 'new-fashioned farmers' came from London they introduced 'expensive luxuries' and ruined the simplicity of rural life. Yet, fifthly, an evil of 'greater magnitude' was 'their tendency to mislead the legislature' as 'many acts of parliament have been passed of late years, upon the false principles which those books have inculcated'.[158]

In summary, the pamphlet articulated a critique of agricultural books that went beyond a stubborn lack of interest. The writer(s) argued that agricultural books misrepresented the art of husbandry and disrupted social relations (i.e. the problems arising from the codification and the appropriation of husbandry). Why did the pamphleteers spend time attacking agricultural books, authors and readers in the opening of an anti-enclosure pamphlet? Because they not only wanted to challenge the substantive arguments regarding the effects of enclosure but to undermine the authority upon which those arguments were based. It was a critique of men such as Lamport who claimed an authority on agricultural matters on the basis of superior education. The pamphlet clearly had some influence. The specific argument about agricultural writers found agreement in the *English Review*.[159] John Howlett published a counter-argument in 1787 because the farmers' pamphlet 'had had considerable influence in different parts of the kingdom'.[160] Similarly, Thomas Stone chose to criticise the farmer's pamphlet because he knew 'how likely gentlemen are to be misled

[157] Ibid., 5.
[158] Ibid., 6–8.
[159] 'Art. VI. A political inquiry', *English Review*, 6 (1785).
[160] John Howlett, *Enclosures, a cause of improved agriculture* (London, 1787), ii.

by professors of practical husbandry, when they are not well acquainted with it themselves'.[161] Hence the pamphlet exchange was a symptom of an underlying battle over expertise, which spilled over into print. Two visions opposed each other about how the cultivation of England should be managed: either by farmers who gained knowledge and skills through inherited customs and practical experience or by enlightened gentlemen in possession of fundamental scientific principles who could direct the labour of others. Books were a central tool in this struggle. The self-directed criticisms of book-farming were only the moderate end of the full spectrum of anti-book-farming sentiment.

A Mixed Legacy

By the nineteenth century, agricultural books had acquired an ambiguous status. Printed books had made significant advances into the organisation of agriculture, and were bought and read by landowners, stewards, some educated farmers, along with members of the non-agricultural professions. But their penetration into rural life was controversial and had become a source of conflict between learned agriculturists and common farmers. A review of a new husbandry book in 1800 insisted that 'the information to be derived from books is not to be despised', since 'a well-written practical agricultural work' was ideally 'a record or memorial of the processes of others'. On this basis, despite the varied quality, the reviewer concluded 'that the country may congratulate itself on the publication of so many agricultural books as have lately appeared'.[162] Yet in the same year, even the President of the Board of Agriculture admitted that 'a plain man can maintain his family on the husbandry of his ancestors; but rare is the example of a book-farmer making his rent'.[163]

The scorn towards book-farming among many in the farming community continued throughout the nineteenth century and was only gradually overcome. Peter Jones argues that in the 1790s a new effort was made to produce 'books for use' rather than unaffordable 'massy volumes', but there is little evidence of a dramatic transformation.[164] In any case, Jones acknowledged that farmers around the turn of the century did not necessarily need

---

[161] Stone, *Suggestions*, 50.
[162] 'Art. V. The new farmer's calendar', *Monthly Review*, 33 (1800), 140.
[163] John Somerville, *The system followed during the two last years by the Board of Agriculture* (London, 1800), 16.
[164] Jones, *Agricultural enlightenment*, 64.

anything beyond 'orally transmitted information'.[165] Heather Holmes argues
on the evidence of subscription lists that Scottish readership was already
widening in the 1780s and 1790s to include tenant farmers – indeed, by
1816, Sir John Sinclair was commending Scottish farmers for 'their habit
of reading'.[166] A study of a subscription library at Selkirk from 1799 to 1814
also shows the expanding circulation of agricultural literature in Scotland.[167]
Nicholas Goddard suggested that by 1850 all English farmers accepted written information, but elsewhere showed that the 'antipathy' towards agricultural books was only gradually eroded by the end of the nineteenth century.[168]
Even in a 1908 bibliography of agricultural writers, Donald McDonald was
cautious in his assessment: 'a prejudice has hitherto existed among farmers
against the agricultural knowledge contained in books, but there are signs
that these stagnant cultivators are gradually disappearing'.[169]

The Gentleman's Magazine published a 'Review of the Eighteenth
Century' in 1800, which devoted a couple of paragraphs to agriculture.
'Agriculture and Botany', it declared, 'were an hundred years ago left to
the laborious husbandman and the practical gardener'. At that time, discoveries were accidental, 'knowledge was partial, and ignorance almost
universal'. But, it triumphantly announced, 'now it is different'.

> The scientific theorist and the practical labourer have shaken hands, and
> united into one common stock the result of their labours; and, however
> men may differ in opinions, or in rank, there exists an universal harmony
> as to their connexions and conduct as men, in search of useful truths ....[170]

This was a fantasy that only the most optimistic agricultural writer could
have affirmed. There was instead significant discord between men of different ranks in rural society, and especially between the self-identifying
theorist and practitioner.

The controversies around book-farming in the late eighteenth century
have previously been viewed from the perspective of agricultural improvers seeking to disseminate knowledge, and therefore analysis has focused on
understanding why books may have been poor vectors for dissemination.
This interpretation fails to contextualise criticisms of book-farming in two

[165] Ibid., 59.
[166] Holmes, 'Circulation', 77; Holmes, 'Agricultural publishing', 509. See also Smout, 'Scottish improvers'.
[167] Towsey, 'Store their minds'.
[168] Goddard, 'Agricultural literature', 370. Goddard, 'Not a reading class'.
[169] McDonald, *Agricultural writers*, 3.
[170] 'Review of the Eighteenth Century', *Gentleman's Magazine* (1800), 173–74, with note published originally 'From the ORACLE of Jan 1'.

ways: it adopts an anachronistic perspective from the vantage of nineteenth-century agricultural science, and it takes no account of the relation between knowledge and power. The weak book-farming critique should be interpreted in the context of the longer history of agricultural literature, constructed through the codification and appropriation of the art of husbandry. One of the motivations driving the production of agricultural books was to transfer greater control over cultivation to men of learning. But the codification of a practical art posed significant challenges and produced texts that were difficult to apply to a wide range of practical contexts. Hence the reported struggles of gentlemen using farming manuals provoked internal debate among agricultural authors about how to reform the genre to make books more effective tools of management. Some agricultural writers responded by trying to forge a new middle way between the customs of illiterate peasants and theories of speculative scholars. By the 1790s, agricultural writing was being reshaped to assist the experimental or business-oriented farm manager who emerged as a major force in British farming.

The strong book-farming critique should be interpreted in the context of the antagonistic social relations within agricultural production, and the problem of asymmetric knowledge between master and worker, or landlord and tenant. Indeed, if we bring together the various statements of agricultural writers – the necessity that the master knows as much as his servants, the typical ignorance of gentlemen farmers not bred to husbandry, and the value of books in providing an independent source of knowledge for gentlemen – then it is clear that a core motivation for publishing and buying agricultural books was to equip gentlemen with the means to establish full command over their farms and estates. If we further consider the reported scepticism of common farmers to the very possibility that gentlemen could possess a superior knowledge of husbandry, and the argument about the disruption to social relations advanced in the anti-enclosure pamphlet, then we can begin to comprehend the apparent hostility to book-farming. Agricultural books could be used to undermine the customary knowledge gained through labour, undermining both a way of living and the status of common husbandmen and agricultural workers within the farm, estate, or wider commercial market. In this light, the resistance to book-farming takes on a new significance as a symptom of a deeper tension between old labour-based and new book-based systems of knowledge, which mapped onto class struggles over control of the intellectual powers of production during the rise of agrarian capitalism. The enclosure of knowledge was resisted openly and persistently; sneering at book-farmers was akin to hedge-breaking.

Conclusion
New Histories of Knowledge

A strange forgetting has taken place over the last two centuries. Agricultural writers from the late seventeenth century proudly declared the impact of the printed word in advancing the ancient art of husbandry in England and Scotland. But they always believed this was part of the social reform of agriculture, not merely a technological project: applying reason to increase nature's fertility required educated men to replace or supervise common cultivators. Books, pamphlets and periodicals were the chief tools of such men and therefore the most visible expression of agricultural progress or 'improvement'. This set the agenda for historians, who over the last century have assessed these claims with increasing scrutiny. However, guided by the dominant framing of the 'agricultural revolution', these assessments restricted themselves to evaluating the direct contribution of agricultural publications to innovations in practice and increases in productivity through the dissemination of useful knowledge. In the most recent iteration, agricultural books have been identified explicitly as playing a significant, if limited, role in an 'agricultural enlightenment' from around 1750.[1] Somewhere along the way, the social dimension was largely excised from the historical accounts of agricultural literature.

This study has offered a correction: a new social history of agricultural books in early modern Britain that assesses the contribution of the printed word to the transformation in the social system of agricultural knowledge. It has shown that books disrupted and reordered how knowledge was produced, stored, transferred, acquired, exercised and legitimated, subordinating a labour-based system beneath a book-based system. It has shown that agricultural knowledge was not merely discovered and disseminated, but demystified, codified, appropriated and commodified. By connecting farming books to the balance of power within social relations, it has shown

---

[1] Jones, *Agricultural enlightenment.*

how the plough was subordinated to the pen as those who worked the land were increasingly subordinated to those who owned and managed it – a slow, stuttering process that was always contested and never complete.

A sociological approach allows for a more satisfying explanation of features of early modern farming books that appear puzzling within the enlightenment model of knowledge diffusion. When viewed as a tool of appropriation of a customary art by a learned elite, it is not surprising to find that many authors were relative amateurs with little practical experience and that their books mostly circulated among the gentry and professionals. When viewed as largely the product of the codification of an existing practical art, it is not surprising to find that many books simply re-packaged earlier texts adding little new knowledge. More significantly, however, a sociological approach highlights significant aspects of agricultural literature that were previously neglected, most of which are inexplicable within a model of books as neutral disseminators of useful knowledge: the trope of revealing the mystery of husbandry to a literate audience; the campaign to place cultivation in the hands of educated men; the attacks by authors on unlearned husbandmen; the resistance gentlemen encountered when attempting to record the knowledge of experienced practitioners; the over-dependence of gentlemen farmers on learning from books; the reimagining of the ideal farmer as a man of learning who organises the labours of others; the consolidation of local customs into a system of knowledge for managers of large farms and estates; the desire to establish a class of agricultural professionals, distinguished from common farmers through formal education and the possession of theoretical knowledge; and the reported hostility towards 'book-farming' and opposition to the authority of writers.

All of these were the signs and symptoms generated by the enclosure of customary knowledge within books. In summary, the embodied knowledge of husbandry held widely in customary practice and oral tradition by a semi-literate population was gradually codified, enabling the partial appropriation of the art by learned men, who sought to monopolise agricultural book knowledge to exert greater control over the labour process in managerial positions as landowners, stewards and large farmers. Of course, the full range of social causes and effects of agricultural publishing over centuries is not reducible to such a tidy narrative, but there can be no doubt that agricultural literature contributed to a social differentiation of knowledge that paralleled the differentiation in landholdings. No single book had any great effect, but the sustained effort to codify and adapt customary knowledge over generations created a new system of knowledge more conducive to the newly dominant systems of land management and its accompanying occupational structure. It is analogous to the enclosure of land because it had a similarly profound effect on how knowledge was accessed, how it was managed as a resource and who controlled it. Further, it was complementary to enclosure and other processes that concentrated landownership because codification helped concentrate knowledge in the hands of owners and managers of land and labour. Book knowledge did not spread evenly, but congealed around improving landlords and entre-preneurial farmers, helping to shape a new agrarian class structure based on the division between mental and manual labour – those who make decisions and those who enact them. The form of knowledge was individu-alised along with land management, as the site of expertise shifted from the community in possession of the experience of generations to the individual experimental improver. The enclosure of land and knowledge were linked as part of a wider campaign of improvement and attack on custom in all its forms, epitomised by the two great schemes of the Board of Agriculture: a General Enclosure Bill and a national survey of agricultural practice.[2] The consolidation of knowledge and landholdings were twinned in the minds of agricultural improvers, who sought to bring the cultivation of land under the close supervision of enlightened men.

Customary knowledge could not be extinguished like common rights, but it could be made increasingly redundant as it was subordinated under new ways of knowing, and begin to erode as its social foundation fractured. A life-long farm labourer working for wages under the direction of a man-ager extracting from them a limited range of manual tasks will never acquire the full 'mystery of husbandry' possessed by generations of farming com-munities. The enclosure of customary knowledge was also clearly resisted, as manifested in the suspicions of common farmers about enquiring gentle-men or the reluctance of servants to follow the new methods of their master. While we have no direct evidence of the purposeful destruction of books, the hostility towards book-farming in rural communities sits loosely on a time-line of labour struggles between hedge-breaking and machine-breaking. Yet customary knowledge did not disappear. As apparent in George Ewart Evans' oral history of the rural community in Blaxhall, a village in East Suffolk, even the progressive introduction of chemical fertilisers and combine harvesters had not eradicated old ways of knowing by the mid-twentieth century. Farming was 'still very much an art', in which general

---

[2] Two main concerns of the first President, Sir John Sinclair: Mitchison, *Agricultural Sir John*, 154, 205.

rules were applied to particular farms 'with the sympathetic understanding born of long experience'. This 'accumulated wisdom of generations of practical farmers', in his opinion, had 'by no means been supplanted'.[3]

A distinctive chronology emerges in the social history of agricultural books. While books on husbandry had limited use in the sixteenth century, by the end of the eighteenth century, there was a substantial stratum of educated men (and some women) who were directly involved in the management of farms and who could make use of books as an alternative to acquiring knowledge through practice and direct experience. The crucial phase runs from the mid-seventeenth century, when Samuel Hartlib's circle first explicitly discussed the need for a systematic body of codified knowledge, to the 1790s, when this vision of reform was institutionalised with the Board of Agriculture. This period was characterised by an almost continuous drive to record and systematise the art of husbandry. But there were changes too. From around 1660 to 1750, the driving force behind agricultural literature was the desire to produce a complete system for country gentlemen, which led to many encyclopaedic, speculative treatises. But these books remained largely derivative of customary knowledge. From the 1730s, there were a series of reactions and innovations, all of which aimed to replace custom, labour and experience as the foundations of knowledge, subordinating these to scientific theories, field experiments and systematic observations. A key motive was to reform agricultural writing to be a more effective management tool and establish the authority of writing over labour, and therefore the manager over the worker.

The gradual economic and cultural changes in England occurred more rapidly and deliberately in Scotland after 1746, as Scottish landowners were stripped of their juridical powers and forced to commercialise their estates, adapting and developing English ideas of improvement. The rapid imposition of new structures of landholding and class relations, combined with the flourishing of political economy in the universities, provided fertile conditions for agricultural literature, leading to a flourishing of new authors in the decades when both cultural and economic conditions in England and Scotland were converging. The overall argument, therefore, applies most neatly to the case of Scotland, in which a landlord-driven 'revolution from above' imposed a new system of knowledge inspired and aided by the development of book knowledge.[4]

---

[3] George Ewart Evans, *Ask the fellows who cut the hay* (London, 1956), 108–9.
[4] See Davidson, 'Scottish path 2', 414–17.

Towards a New Social History of Agricultural Knowledge

This study of farming books opens up a new field of research: the social history of agricultural knowledge in early modern Britain. The core analysis here views this history through the limited lens of farming books, but there are three ways to go further: first, extend the approach; second, test the argument; third, explore alternative methods.

Firstly, keeping the focus on books, the temporal scope should be expanded. Early printed husbandry books have only been touched on briefly, but a fuller investigation requires greater attention to the relationship between manuscript and print in the sixteenth and seventeenth centuries, from the first English edition of the thirteenth-century treatise by Walter of Henley in 1508.[5] Similarly, the study of book-based expertise and debates around book-farming could continue by tracking the life of new institutions, from the formation of the Board of Agriculture in 1793 to the establishment of the Royal Agricultural Society in 1838 and Agricultural College in 1845, up to the 1851 census when a quarter of the nation's workforce remained in agriculture.[6] The geographical scope should also be expanded. The circulation of agricultural literature did not respect the boundaries of England and Scotland and a fuller exploration must follow the movements of books around Ireland, the European continent and across the Atlantic to the colonies in North America and the Caribbean.[7] Particular attention should also be given to the interactions between French, German and English language agricultural writing and thought. Notably, almost half the books listed by Walter Harte in 1770 as the source of his ideas on agriculture were Latin or foreign-language texts.[8]

Secondly, key aspects of the argument need to be tested. A wealth of indirect and circumstantial evidence suggests that farming books were filled with customary knowledge, but how much information came from talking with or watching farmers or farm workers, and how much from the author's personal experience, experiments or reading other books? How can the various sources of knowledge be traced, measured and evaluated? This could be investigated through individual case studies where we have

---

[5] The starting point is Ambrosoli, *Wild and the sown.* See Henley, *Boke of husbandry.*
[6] Verdon, *Working the land,* 10.
[7] Alan E. Fusonie, 'The agricultural literature of the gentleman farmer in the colonies', in Alan E. Fusonie and Leila Moran (eds), *Agricultural literature: Proud heritage – Future promise: A bicentennial symposium September 24–26 1975* (Washington, 1977).
[8] In front matter to Walter Harte, *Essays on husbandry* (2nd edn; London, 1770).

surviving commonplace books or manuscript drafts. For example, the thirty-four unpublished volumes of Arthur Young's 'Elements and Practice of Agriculture' held in the British Library, which show the painstaking compilation of agricultural information over decades and the construction of a system of knowledge (materially as well as intellectually, as sections of printed books and journals were cut and pasted, giving the appearance of a scrap book).[9]

The current consensus that agricultural books were mostly owned and read by the gentry, with only minimal circulation among middling or small farmers, was accepted rather than systematically tested here, as the focus was on their content, form and authorship. A more detailed understanding about who owned, read and used these books is, therefore, needed to verify the broader claims about social impact. This initially requires an in-depth study of the production, sale, circulation and ownership of books, using available bookseller ledgers, subscription lists, sale catalogues and the records of private and circulating libraries.[10] But we also need to learn how agricultural books were actually used and read.[11] This requires consolidating existing studies that discuss the use of books on estates and the annotations of individual copies, along with systematic analyses of the incidental mentions of books in surviving correspondence and diaries of known agriculturalists, farmers and other gentlemen.[12] This would undoubtedly take the research into new and perhaps surprising areas: for example, on 3 February 1803 Anne Lister, then an 11-year-old heiress of a small Yorkshire estate, described her delight in reading Hunter's *Georgical Essays* (1770–2) after a 'ramble in the fields'.[13]

The argument here is primarily about the general cumulative impact of books, only partly evidenced by particular examples, and therefore the use of book knowledge must be tested at the regional and local level, and especially on individual farms and estates. One hypothesis is that the use of farming books would have spread sooner in regions where the tripartite structure of landlord-tenant-labourer emerged first (south-east England), and perhaps slower in areas in which smallholders and servants in husbandry

---

[9] 'Young', 'Elements'.
[10] Good examples in Scotland at the end of our period: Holmes, 'Circulation'; Towsey, 'Store their minds'.
[11] Raven, 'New reading histories'.
[12] For example, use of books discussed in Griffiths, 'Sir Hamon Le Strange'; annotated copies discussed in Ambrosoli, *Wild and the sown*.
[13] M. Green, *A spirited Yorkshirewoman* (1939), 4: www.open.ac.uk/Arts/reading/UK/record_details .php?id=3039, accessed 18 March 2016.

persisted (north-west England). At the micro-level, we would expect books to be linked to small conflicts at every level of the occupational hierarchy in agriculture, between ploughman and farmer as well as estate steward and landowner. A few existing studies of estates offer hints of tensions between books and custom: for example, the landowner Sir Ralph Verney wanted to follow farming books that advised 'digging the potash deep into the clay with mould to improve the soil', but his bailiff was 'sceptical because the technique was unknown locally'.[14] As we move from the abstract to the concrete, the argument here would no doubt be subject to many qualifications, nuances and limitations. Micro-studies would allow us to move beyond the binaries of learned/unlearned and amateur/practical farmer, giving a more finely grained analysis of how agricultural literature interacted with shifting 'grids of power', especially the amphibious role of increasing numbers of middling farmers who were both bred to husbandry from youth and participants in the literary world.[15] This would not only allow a more accurate assessment of how books entered into the management of farms but also a broader examination of how divisions of knowledge mapped onto divisions of labour.

The overall argument about the relation between agricultural literature and socio-economic change requires testing through a comparative account of other European countries, especially France, Germany and Scandinavia. Is there any correlation between the development and use of written agricultural knowledge and agrarian capitalism in other contexts? If not, how did the codification of agricultural knowledge serve the needs of distinct class structures?

Thirdly, there are two significant topics that have only been touched upon here that require new approaches beyond a focus on books. The focus here has been on class rather than gender dynamics. Hence the role of women and the gendered effects of agricultural book knowledge have only been briefly sketched. Agricultural books were mostly published by and for men, but a great deal of agricultural knowledge and skill was possessed and exercised by women. Hence the gendered dimension of appropriation was significant and merits particular investigation, which raises new questions. On the one hand, elements of the art of housewifery were subordinated

---

[14] Broad, *Transforming English rural society*, 134.
[15] Theoretically informed by: Michael J. Braddick and John Walter, 'Introduction: Grids of power: Order, hierarchy and subordination in early modern society', in Michael J. Braddick and John Walter (eds), *Negotiating power in early modern society: Order, hierarchy and subordination in Britain and Ireland* (Cambridge, 2001).

under a masculine discipline of agriculture, and, as Valenze has detailed in the case of dairying, male agriculturalists could challenge and undermine women's authority directly.[16] On the other hand, male authors often felt obliged to admit when their advice was clearly based on the experience of women in female-dominated activities, and women could be both readers and even authors of agriculture in the late eighteenth century.[17] As non-elite women were less likely to be literate than men throughout this period, the discrepancy in the value of textual knowledge was even more marked. As publishing, in particular, was predominantly a male domain, printed books provide limited insight as sources into the relative knowledge and authority held by women of different ranks, for example between a gentle-woman managing a dairy and the experienced female servants upon whom she relied. In general, since housewifery was an almost universal female occupation, whereas husbandry was class-specific, the social history of women's agricultural knowledge will have a distinctive profile.[18]

The other area that needs fresh exploration rather than direct testing is customary knowledge, the uncodified arts of husbandry and housewif-ery, which have been variously described here as practical or experiential knowledge, situated expertise or peasant epistemology. The detailed analy-sis of book-based knowledge has relied on a general characterisation of its opposite: customary, labour-based knowledge. While printed literature is obviously of limited use, manuscripts could offer a bridge between custom and print, especially the farming notebooks, accounts and memoirs that survive from the seventeenth and eighteenth centuries. Unlike print, they are directly linked to local practice and therefore have a different relation-ship to customary knowledge. A more ambitious project to reconstruct the knowledge of husbandmen, housewives, servants and labourers, as it was acquired and stored outside of texts, would require a fundamentally differ-ent approach, but is ultimately necessary to understand the social system of agricultural knowledge.[19] Similar questions about the balance of power must be asked about the exercise of customary knowledge, especially between male household heads and their wives, servants and children, or between larger and smaller farmers and their use of common fields.

---

[16] The changing sexual division of eighteenth-century agricultural work is still debated. Sharpe, *Adapting to capitalism*, see ch. 4 'Agriculture: The sexual division of labour'.
[17] A few articles were written by women for the *Annals of agriculture*, see McDonagh, *Elite women*, 145.
[18] I owe this observation to Professor Jane Whittle.
[19] A possible approach to imitate is being pioneered by The Making and Knowing Project at Columbia University that explores pre-industrial conceptions of natural knowledge: www.makingandknowing.org.

Implications for the History of Knowledge and Capitalism

The argument here about agricultural literature has immediate implications for key areas of historiography. Social historians concerned with power and conflict in rural society should consider how the dimension of knowledge and expertise may add a new layer of complexity. Economic historians of agriculture should incorporate knowledge – especially the division of knowledge – as a key aspect of labour relations, not simply a technological input. Those concerned with issues such as professionalisation, education and expertise in modern agriculture should consider their long-term roots in early modern society. Historians of knowledge studying the mechanical arts and crafts should consider the extent to which farming can be included in their enquiries. Historians of the book should consider how this case study of didactic literature, with particular attention to the balance of power between writers, readers and practitioners, compares with other areas of economic and social life. In general, this re-assessment of agricultural literature demonstrates how the histories of knowledge and economic power are intimately intertwined.

This study's primary significance, however, is that it reveals an important and neglected dimension of the development of agrarian capitalism. Existing histories of agrarian capitalism have almost nothing to say about knowledge, and relatively little to say about labour management, beyond the basic point that work is mostly performed by landless wage labourers in specialised roles under large farmers producing for the market. Conversely, histories of knowledge under capitalism have almost nothing to say about agriculture before the nineteenth century. The implications for general histories of knowledge and capitalism can be illuminated through three key concepts: the real subsumption of labour, deskilling and commodification.

The increasing centrality of knowledge to the modern economy has prompted a revival of interest in Marx's contribution to the historical role of knowledge in the capitalist division of labour.[20] A key distinction is between the 'formal' and 'real' subsumption of labour under capital.[21] Formal subsumption is when labour comes under the general command of the employer, through wage labour, without the labour process itself undergoing any substantial change. The employer is limited to ensuring that normal quality standards are maintained, or attempting to increase the

---

[20] See Moulier-Boutang, *Cognitive capitalism*.
[21] In an unpublished section of volume 1 of *Capital*, included as an Appendix in Karl Marx, *Capital: A critique of political economy: Volume I*, trans. Ben Fowkes (I; London, 1990), 1019–38.

overall duration, intensity or orderliness of labour. But since the employer
has only taken command of an established labour process, the worker who
possesses the requisite knowledge and skills (and perhaps tools) retains relative autonomy in the actual performance of their labour. The nature of
the work only changes significantly at increasing scales of production. Real
subsumption, in contrast, is when the employer takes control and reorga-
nises the labour process itself, through the introduction of machinery and
application of science. The division of labour is taken to a new degree, by
separating mental and manual tasks and transforming workers into mere
operators, as the knowledge of their task is now incorporated into fixed capital, that is, embedded in machines. Although the theory has become more
sophisticated, its underlying historical account is still extremely crude, and
primarily limited to the nineteenth and twentieth centuries.[22] The standard chronology identifies two stages; formal subsumption between the sixteenth and eighteenth centuries, based on the putting-out system, in which
the merchant controls the commodity but the craftsman maintains control
over knowledge; and real subsumption beginning with industrialisation at
the end of the eighteenth century, based on the factory system, in which
machinery dictates the labour process.[23] Agriculture is not usually a part of
this story. Marx briefly used the example of the peasant who becomes a day
labourer to explain the formal subsumption of labour, but gave no equivalent for real subsumption. However, the distinction is useful in describing
the nature of the shift in farm management from the sixteenth to the eighteenth centuries; from expecting servants and labourers to be industrious in
applying their knowledge and skills, to expecting them to follow detailed
instructions to implement new farming techniques.[24]

While the real subsumption of labour is understood as the result of
introducing machinery, fundamentally it must be based upon 'the expropriation of traditional knowledges'.[25] This is the sense in which printed
books can be understood to have assisted a shift from the formal to the real
subsumption of labour, forming a transitional phase between the expansion of wage labour and the introduction of machinery and chemistry in
the nineteenth century, which established the basis for industrial farming. From the perspective of the agricultural wage labourer, their time is

---

[22] For example, Renault, 'Work and domination'; Ali Rattansi, *Marx and the division of labour*
(London, 1982), 443–50.
[23] Vercellone, 'From formal subsumption', 15–16.
[24] See argument that accounting was the key step in farm management: Rob Bryer, 'Accounting and
control of the labour process', *Critical Perspectives on Accounting*, 17 (2006).
[25] Vercellone, 'From formal subsumption', 20–21.

nominally under the control of their employer, but the degree to which their labour is directed depends on the degree of knowledge held by their manager(s). Consider the following two situations. In one, a small husbandman works occasionally for wages on a neighbouring farm following the local customary methods, carrying out similar tasks in similar ways as on their own land, albeit under the direction of another. In the other, a labourer on a large farm is directed to carry out 'improved' methods not established locally, in which they may have to learn new tasks, or the use of new implements, and be instructed in detail on the order and manner in which they are performed. Both involve wage labour, but the degree to which the labourer has been subordinated differs enormously. A brief illustration of the latter tendency is provided by William Marshall, who detailed his forensic farm management in the 1770s. It was full of the traditional complaints that his servants were lazy cheats, arising from his efforts to enforce work intensity and orderly behaviour. However, he went further, analysing the labour process in detail in search of efficiencies, stating that to be a successful farmer required 'strict attention, to analyse each process', since 'without the help of ANALYSIS, it is difficult to get rid of customs ever so absurd'.[26] In other words, he had to impose his own knowledge and reorganise the production process, rather than rely on the customary habits of his workers. In summary, therefore, if farm labour was formally subsumed when it became wage labour, then the first step in its real subsumption – the extension of managerial control – consisted in the progressive separation of mental and manual labour on the farm and the substitution of customary for improved farming methods. Before knowledge was objectified as fixed capital in machines, it was codified in books.

An associated concept, originating in Braverman's development of Marx's analysis of the labour process, has become known as 'deskilling'. The deskilling thesis claims that capitalist production tends to divide and organise labour in ways that reduce workers' skill. It is usually applied to manufacturing and primarily seen as an effect of the introduction of new technology, but Braverman's argument about the destruction of craft skills was based on the breaking down of the unity of conception and execution in the labour process. Only a few historians have applied the concept to farming, but Robert Allen suggested that the rise of large farms and specialised wage labour in the eighteenth century amounted not only to deskilling but also specifically that enclosure led to a 'narrowing of the mental life' of the rural community due to the disappearance of cooperative

[26] Entry for 2 October 1775. Marshall, *Minutes*.

management of open fields.[27] This claim can be expanded and seen as key to the process of rural proletarianisation during the long shift from peasant to capitalist farming. Before machines were introduced in the nineteenth century, the humble farming manual acted, in certain contexts, as an agent of deskilling, by extracting workers' knowledge and packaging it for managers, thereby reducing their reliance on the experience of their workers. Yet in using the term 'deskilling' we should be careful not to understate the scale of transformation; early modern husbandmen and housewives did not merely possess manual dexterity over a diverse range of tasks, but distinctive ways of knowing.[28]

Lastly, a corollary to deskilling is the commodification of knowledge. Again, economic theory treats this as a distinctly modern phenomenon, primarily through the creation of intellectual property rights that protect private ownership of knowledge – although it has been observed that the eighteenth century saw new opportunities to sell or hire expertise in the market.[29] However, Bob Jessop offers a more instructive account with historical implications of how knowledge can become a 'fictitious commodity' (fictitious because it can be bought and sold, even though this was not the purpose for which it was produced). Since knowledge is a non-rival good, in which possession or use by one person does not preclude use by another, it is only commodified under certain conditions. If practical knowledge is viewed as an initially inseparable part of labour, it must first be detached through the 'enclosure of knowledge', or the 'private expropriation of the collectively produced knowledge handed down from previous generations'.[30] This sense of enclosing knowledge has particular significance in studies of 'biopiracy' or 'biocolonialism' in the modern world, in which multi-national companies appropriate indigenous knowledge for profit through the use of intellectual property rights.[31] Such cases

---

[27] Allen, *Enclosure and the yeoman*, 219, 289. See also Deborah Fitzgerald, 'Farmers deskilled: Hybrid corn and farmers' work', *Technology and Culture*, 34 (1993); de Pleijt and Weisdorf, 'Human capital formation'.

[28] For vivid explanations of farmers' knowledge see Wendell Berry, *The unsettling of America: Culture and agriculture* (2nd edn; Berkeley, 1986).

[29] Mokyr traces the 'knowledge-economy' to enlightenment: Mokyr, 'Intellectual origins', 318; Mokyr, *Enlightened economy*, ch. 11; Joel Mokyr, *The gifts of Athena: Historical origins of the knowledge economy* (Princeton, 2002), ch. 1. On natural knowledge as commodity in eighteenth century, see Fissell and Cooter, 'Natural knowledge', 157.

[30] Bob Jessop, 'Knowledge as a fictitious commodity: Insights and limits of a Polanyian analysis', in A. Buğra and K. Ağartan (eds), *Reading Karl Polanyi for the 21st century: Market economy as a political project* (Basingstoke, 2007), 120, 126.

[31] Shiva, *Biopiracy*; Whitt, 'Biocolonialism'.

of commodification arise from the direct encounter between a peasant and a capitalist society, but a similar process, more extenuated and uneven, can be seen in the historical transition to a capitalist society. In particular, a recognised feature of peasant knowledge is that due to being embedded within the cultural practices of a local community it can be difficult for outsiders to access.[32] In such contexts, writing is a key tool to gain access to knowledge and render it amenable to commodification, which is impossible while it remains bound within labour, custom and memory. Hence, in the early modern period, the progressive extraction of customary knowledge from its roots in daily labour and codification into an abstract form made it possible for agricultural knowledge to be bought and sold as an independent commodity, most immediately in the form of books for sale and expertise for hire. Therefore, early printed farming books were a preliminary but necessary stage for the more extensive commodification of agricultural knowledge from the nineteenth century onwards.[33]

The history of early modern farming books, therefore, has profound significance for our understanding of how modern capitalism developed. Trends understood as key to capitalist society in the last two centuries can be traced back into the seventeenth and eighteenth centuries, and dynamics considered key to labour in manufacturing or services can be identified in agriculture. If, as many have argued, capitalist relations developed early in the English countryside, and if, as argued here, this required the enclosure of customary knowledge in books, then this story of agricultural literature is not merely relevant but foundational to the history of capitalism in general.[34]

---

[32] Victoria Reyes-García et al., 'Traditional agricultural knowledge as a commons', in Jose Luis Vivero-Pol et al. (eds), *Routledge handbook of food as a commons* (London, 2018), 175–76.
[33] Fitzgerald, *Every farm a factory*.
[34] Ellen Meiksins Wood, *The origin of capitalism: A longer view* (London, 2002).

Appendix

A   Select Agricultural Corpus 1669–1792

The following is a chronological list of all new publications in England and Scotland between 1669 and 1792 that aimed to inform or instruct on the practice of farming, as defined on page 20. Compiled using the *English Short Title Catalogue* (ESTC) and the bibliographies of W. Frank Perkins (1929, 1932, 1939) and G.E. Fussell (1947, 1950), with further publications identified through additional research. Titles have been abbreviated. It is arranged in order of first publication, with dates of further editions or reprints listed below. Reprints or editions after 1792 have been excluded. 'London' is the place of publication unless stated otherwise. Items cited or used directly are also listed in the Bibliography.

i   Books and Pamphlets

1669	Blagrave, Joseph, *The epitome of the art of husbandry.*
	— 1670 (2nd ed.); 1675 (3rd ed.); 1685; 1719 (4th ed.).
1669	Worlidge, John, *Systema agriculturae: the mystery of husbandry discovered.*
	— 1675 (2nd ed.); 1681 (3rd ed.); 1687 (4th ed.) 1689 (*The second parts of systema agriculturæ… Vinetum Britannicum, or, a treatise of cider.*); 1694 (*Mr. Worlidge's two treatises*); 1697; 1698; 1716; 1718.
1684	S., J., *Profit and pleasure united, or, the husbandman's magazene.*
	— 1704; 1715 (reprinted as *The country man's treasure … By J. Lambert*).
1684	Tryon, Thomas, *The country-man's companion.*
1697	Moore, Jonas, Sir, *Englands improvement.*
	— 1703 (2nd ed.); 1705 (3rd ed.); 1707 (4th ed.); 1721.

1697   S., A., *The husbandman, farmer and grasier's compleat instructor.*
       — 1707.
1697   Donaldson, James, *Husbandry anatomized* (Edinburgh).
1697   Meager, Leonard, *The mystery of husbandry.*
1699   Belhaven, John Hamilton, Lord, *The country-mans rudiments* (Edinburgh).
       — 1713; 1723.
1700   Nourse, Timothy, *Campania foelix.*
       — 1706 (2nd ed.); 1708 (3rd ed.).
1704   *Dictionarium rusticum & urbanicum.*
       — 1717 (2nd ed.); 1726 (3rd ed.).
1707   Mortimer, John, *The whole art of husbandry.*
       — 1708 (2nd ed.); 1712; 3rd ed., 2 Vols); 1716 (4th ed.); 1721 (5th ed.); 1761 (6th ed.).
1707   Vallemont, abbé de (Pierre Le Lorrain), *Curiosities of nature and art in husbandry and gardening.*
1714   Laurence, John, *The clergy-man's recreation.*
       — 1715 (2nd ed.); 1716 (3rd ed.); 1716 (4th ed.); 1717 (5th ed.); 1718 (*Gardening improv'd.*); 1726 (6th ed.).
1715   Switzer, Stephen, *The nobleman, gentleman, and gardener's recreation.*
       — 1718 (*Ichnographia rustica*).
1717   Bradley, Richard, *New improvements of planting and gardening.*
       — 1718 (2nd ed.); 1720 (3rd ed.); 1724 (4th ed.); 1726 (5th ed.); 1731 (6th ed.); 1739 (7th ed).
1717   Jacob, Giles, *The country gentleman's vade mecum.*
1721   Agricola, Georg Andreas, *A philosophical treatise of husbandry and gardening* … [Revised by Richard Bradley].
1721   Bradley, Richard, *A general treatise of husbandry and gardening* [Vol.1: April-September, Vol.2: October-March].
       — 1721–1723; 1724; 1726.
1724   *A treatise concerning the manner of fallowing of ground* (Edinburgh).
1724   Bradley, Richard, *New experiments and observations.*
1725   Bradley, Richard, *A survey of the ancient husbandry and gardening.*
1726   Bradley, Richard, *The country gentleman and farmer's monthly director.*
       — 1727 (2nd ed.); 1727 (3rd ed.); 1732 (6th ed.); 1736.

1726   Laurence, John, *A new system of agriculture.*
1726   [Weston, Sir Richard], *The gentleman farmer.*
1727   Bradley, Richard, *The science of good husbandry: Or, the Oeconomics of Xenophon.*
1727   Bradley, Richard, *A complete body of husbandry.*
1727   Laurence, Edward, *The duty of a steward to his Lord.*
        — 1731 (2nd ed.); 1743 (3rd ed.).
1729   Mackintosh, William, *An essay on ways and means for inclosing, fallowing, planting, &c. Scotland* (Edinburgh).
1731   Tull, Jethro, *The new horse-houghing husbandry.*
1732   Dalrymple, Sir John, *An essay on the husbandry of Scotland* (Edinburgh).
1732   Ellis, William, *The practical farmer: Or, The Hertfordshire husbandman.*
        — 1732 (Part 2); 1732 (2nd ed); 1738 (3rd ed); 1741 (4th ed.); 1742; 1759 (5th ed).
1732   Switzer, Stephen, *The country gentleman's companion.*
1733   Ellis, William, *Chiltern and vale farming explained.*
        1745.
1733   Tull, Jethro, *The horse-hoing husbandry.*
        1743 (2nd ed.); 1751 (3rd ed.); 1762 (4th ed.).
1735   *A True method of treating light hazely ground … By a small Society of Farmers in Buchan* (Edinburgh).
1736   Ellis, William, *New experiments in husbandry, for the month of April.*
1736   Tull, Jethro, *A supplement to the essay on horse-hoing husbandry.*
        — 1740 (2nd ed.).
1738   Trowell, Samuel, *A new treatise of husbandry, gardening, and other matters relating to rural affairs.*
        — 1739.
1743   James, Robert, *The rational farmer, and practical husbandman.*
        — 1747.
1747   Trowell, Samuel and Ellis, William, *The farmer's instructor.*
        — 1750 (2nd ed.).
1747   Vallavine, Peter, *An abstract of an essay on tillage and vegetation.*
1750   Ellis, William, *The modern husbandman*, 8 Vols [first published serially 1742–1745].
1755   *A new system of agriculture.*

1756	Hale, Thomas, *A compleat body of husbandry.* 1758–59 (2nd ed.).
1756	Home, Francis, *The principles of agriculture and vegetation* (Edinburgh).
	— 1757; 1759 (2nd ed.); 1759 (3rd ed.); 1762; 1776.
1757	Bradley, Richard, *A general treatise of agriculture.*
1757	Lisle, Edward, *Observations in husbandry.*
	— 1757 (2nd ed., 2 Vols).
1757	Grant, Archibald, Sir, *The farmer's new-years gift* (Aberdeen).
1757	Maxwell, Robert, *The practical husbandman* (Edinburgh).
1759	Duhamel du Monceau, *A practical treatise of husbandry.*
	— 1762 (2nd ed.).
1760	*The farmer's compleat guide.*
1760	*An essay on the theory of agriculture.*
1760	Hitt, Thomas, *A treatise of husbandry on the improvement of dry and barren lands.*
1761	Mordant, John, *The complete steward: Or, the duty of a steward to his Lord.*
1762	Dickson, Adam, *A treatise of agriculture* (Edinburgh).
	— 1765 (2nd ed.); 1769 (Vol 2); 1770 (3rd ed.); 1785.
1764	Duhamel du Monceau, M., *The elements of agriculture,* translated and revised by Philip Miller, 2 vols.
1764	Harte, Walter, *Essays on husbandry.*
	— 1770 (2nd ed).
1764	Randall, Joseph, *The semi-Virgilian husbandry.*
1764	Randall, Joseph, *The farmer's new guide for raising excellent crops.*
1765	Billing, Robert, *An account of the culture of carrots.*
1765	Fordyce, George *Elements of agriculture* (Edinburgh).
	— 1771 (2nd ed.); 1779 (3rd ed.); 1789 (4th ed.).
1766	*The complete farmer: Or, a general dictionary of husbandry.*
	— 1767; 1769 (2nd ed.); 1777 (3rd ed.).
1766	Grant, Sir Archibald, *The practical farmer's pocket-companion* (Aberdeen).
1767	*The complete grazier.*
	— 1767 (2nd ed.); 1775 (3rd ed.); 1776 (4th ed.).
1767	Mills, John, *A new system of practical husbandry,* 5 vols.
1767	Young, Arthur, *The farmer's letters to the people of England.*
	— 1768 (2nd ed.); 1771 (3rd ed.).

1768   Varlo, Charles, *The modern farmers guide* (Edinburgh, Glasgow).

1768   Young, Arthur, *A six weeks tour, through the southern counties of England and Wales.*
        — 1769 (2nd ed.); 1772 (3rd ed.).

1769   Weston, Richard, *Tracts on practical agriculture and gardening.*
        — 1773 (2nd ed.).

1769   Hunter, Alexander, *Georgical essays.*
        — 1770 (Vol 1); 1771 (Vol 2); 1772 (Vol 3–4); 1773 (2nd ed., 4 Vols); 1777 (York).

1770   Cooke, George, *The complete English farmer.*
        — 1772.

1770   Dove, John, *Strictures on agriculture.*

1770   Gyllenborg, Gustaf Adolph, *The natural and chemical elements of agriculture*, translated by John Mills.

1770   Varlo, Charles, *A new system of husbandry*, 3 vols (York).
        — 1771 (2nd ed.); 1772 (3rd ed., Winchester); 1774 (4th ed.).

1770   Peters, Matthew, *The rational farmer* (Newport).
        — 1771 (2nd ed., London)

1770   Young, Arthur, *Rural oeconomy: Or, essays on the practical parts of husbandry.*
        — 1773 (2nd ed.); 1776; 1792 (3rd ed.).

1770   Young, Arthur, *The farmer's guide in hiring and stocking farms.*

1770   Young, Arthur, *A course of experimental agriculture*, 2 vols.

1770   Young, Arthur, *A six months tour through the North of England*, 4 vols.
        — 1770 (2nd ed.); 1771.

1771   Henry, David, *The complete English farmer.*

1771   Peters, Matthew, *Winter riches.*

1771   Young, Arthur, *The farmer's calendar.*
        — 1778 (2nd ed.).

1771   Young, Arthur, *The farmer's tour through the East of England*, 4 vols.

1772   Comber, Thomas, *Real improvements in agriculture.*

1772   *Ellis's husbandry, abridged and methodized*, 2 vols.

1774   Forbes, Francis, *The modern improvements in agriculture.*
        — 1784.

1775	Anderson, James, *Essays relating to agriculture and rural affairs* (Edinburgh).
	— 1777 (2nd ed.); 1777 (Vol 2); 1784 (3rd ed.).
1775	Kent, Nathaniel, *Hints to gentlemen of landed property.*
	— 1776 (2nd ed.).
1775	Forbes, Francis, *Miscellaneous dissertations on rural subjects.*
1775	Harrison, Gustavus, *Agriculture delineated.*
1775	Hogg, William, *The complete English farmer.*
	— 1780 (2nd ed.).
1775	Wimpey, Joseph, *Rural improvements.*
	— 1775 (2nd ed.)
1775	*Cabbage and clover husbandry.*
1776	Beardé de l'Abbaye, *Essays in agriculture.*
1776	Bowden, Thomas, *The farmer's director.*
1776	Kames, Henry Home, Lord, *The gentleman farmer* (Edinburgh).
	— 1779 (2nd ed.); 1788 (3rd ed.).
1776	Peters, Matthew, *Agricultura: Or the good husbandman.*
1777	Black, James, *Observations on the tillage of the earth.*
1777	Clarke, Cuthbert, *The true theory and practice of husbandry.*
	— 1781.
1778	Broad, John, *The Worcestershire farmer* (Birmingham).
1778	Forbes, Francis, *The extensive practice of the new husbandry.*
	— 1786 (2nd ed.).
1778	Marshall, William, *Minutes of agriculture.*
	— 1783 (*With experiments and observations concerning agriculture and the weather*).
1778	Wight, Andrew, *Present state of husbandry in Scotland,* 2 vols (Edinburgh).
	— 1784.
1779	Marshall, William, *Experiments and observations.*
1779	*A general dictionary of husbandry, planting, gardening* (Bath).
1780	Trusler, John, *Practical husbandry.*
	— 1785 (2nd ed.); 1790 (3rd ed.).
1780	Young, Arthur, *A tour in Ireland.*
	— 1780 (2nd ed., 2 Vols).
1781	Ringsted, Josiah, *The farmer.*
	— 1781 (2nd ed.).
1781	*Directions for ploughing, harrowing, sowing, pulling, watering, grassing* (Hartford).

1783   *Useful and practical observations on agriculture.*
1784   Twamley, Josiah, *Dairying exemplified* (Warwick).
1785   Young, David, *National improvements upon agriculture* (Edinburgh).
1785   Stone, Thomas, *An essay on agriculture* (Lynn).
1786   Varlo, Charles, *The essence of agriculture.*
1786   Culley, George, *Observations on live stock.*
1786   Ley, Charles, *The nobleman, gentleman, land steward, and surveyor's compleat guide.*
1787   Marshall, William, *The rural economy of Norfolk*, 2 vols.
1787   Winter, George, *A new and compendious system of husbandry* (Bristol).
1788   Dickson, Adam, *The husbandry of the ancients* (Edinburgh).
1788   *The gentleman farmer's pocket companion.*
1788   Marshall, William, *The rural economy of Yorkshire*, 2 vols.
1788   Young, David, *The farmers account-book of expenditure and produce* (Edinburgh)
1789   Adam, James, *Practical essays on agriculture*, 2 vols.
1789   Marshall, William, *The rural economy of Glocestershire*, 2 vols (Gloucester).
1790   Macmillan, Anthony, *A treatise on pasturage* (Edinburgh).
1790   Marshall, William, *The rural economy of the midland counties*, 2 vols.
1792   Skirving, William, *The husbandman's assistant* (Edinburgh).

ii   Periodicals

1681–1683 &   *Collections for improvement of husbandry and trade*, edited by
1692–1702   John Houghton.
1726–1727   *Weekly miscellany for the improvement of the husbandry, trade, arts, and sciences*, edited by Richard Bradley.
1733–34   *The practical husbandman and planter ...By a society of husbandmen and planters*, edited by Stephen Switzer.
1743   *Select transactions of the honourable the society of improvers in the knowledge of agriculture in Scotland*, edited by Robert Maxwell (Edinburgh).
1764–6   *Museum rusticum et commerciale: Or, select papers on agriculture, commerce, arts, and manufactures,* by the Society for the Encouragement of Arts, Manufactures and Commerce.

1768–1782	*Memoirs of agriculture and other oeconomical arts, by R. Dossie* (Society for the Encouragement of Arts, Manufactures and Commerce).
1769–70	*De Re Rustica: Or, the repository for select papers on agriculture, arts, and manufacturers.*
1772–4	*Scots Farmer: Or, select essays on agriculture, adapted to the soil and climate of Scotland* (Edinburgh).
1776–1780	*The farmer's magazine, and useful family companion. By Agricola Sylvan, gentleman.*
1776	*Transactions of the Society for the Encouragement of Agriculture in Dumfries, Wigton, and Kirkcudbright.*
1780–1816	*Letters and papers on agriculture, planting, &c. selected from the correspondence of the Bath and West of England Society for the Encouragement of Agriculture, Arts, Manufactures and Commerce* (Bath).
1783–1848	*Transactions of the Society instituted at London, for the Encouragement of Arts, Manufactures and Commerce.*
1784–1808	*Annals of agriculture, and other useful arts. Collected and published by Arthur Young.*

B   Agricultural Authors 1669–1792

The following is a chronological list with available biographical information of all new English and Scottish agricultural authors whose first publication appeared 1669–1792, selected using the same criteria as Appendix A. Compiled primarily from the Oxford *Dictionary of National Biography* and G. E. Fussell's descriptive surveys (1947, 1950), with additional information gleaned elsewhere. It excludes foreign authors, translators of foreign works, editors of collected works, contributors to periodicals, and the publications of societies. See discussion in the Introduction.

Table B.1 *British agricultural writers whose first publication appeared 1669–1792.*

Date of First Book	Author Name	Date of Birth & Death	Age	Father's Occupation	Education and Training	Occupations (a) *Non-Agricultural*	Occupations (b): *Agricultural*	Non-agricultural Book Topics
1669	John Worlidge*	d.1693				Town Mayor	Landowner, Steward	Gardening, Bees, Cider
1669	Joseph Blagrave	1610–1682	59		Astronomy	Astrologer		Almanacs, Medicine
1670	John Smith				Apprenticed in Skinners' Company (shipping trade)	Tradesman, Fishery		Trade
1676	James Lambert^							
1681	John Houghton	1645–1705	36	Embroiderer (royal residence)	Cambridge University; Apprentice apothecary	Apothecary, Shopkeeper, Trader in luxuries		Trade
1697	Sir Jonas Moore	1617–1679	n/a	Farmer (yeoman)	Grammar school	Mathematics, Astronomy	Surveyor	Mathematics, Astronomy, Almanacs
1697	Leonard Meager	c.1624–1704	79			Gardener		Gardening
1697	James Donaldson	d.1719		Landowner		Merchant, Military, Publisher		Poetry, Economics, Crafts, Newspaper

1699	John Hamilton, Lord Belhaven	1656–1708	43	Judge (court session)		Politician, Military	Landowner	Politics
1700	Timothy Nourse	c.1636–1699	64	Knight	Oxford University (BA 1658, MA 1660)	Clergyman (ordained priest 1664; Catholic conversion 1672)	Landowner	Religion
1707	John Mortimer	1656?–1736	51	Landowner	Commercial	Merchant	Landowner	
1714	John Laurence	1668–1732	46	Clergyman (vicar)	Cambridge University (BA 1689, MA 1692)	Clergyman (rector 1700–1721), Gardening		Gardening, Religion
1715	Stephen Switzer	bap.1682–1745	33	Farmer, Landowner	Apprenticeship	Landscape Gardener, Seedsman		Gardening, Landscape Design
1715	George Clerke^							
1717	Richard Bradley	1688?–1732	29			Academic (botany), Hired to supervise plantings in Middlesex		Gardening
1717	Giles Jacob	bap.1686–1744	31	Maltster	Law?	Secretary to Politician, Legal Author	Steward	Law, Literature
1727	Edward Laurence	bap.1674–1739	53	Clergyman (vicar)			Surveyor, Steward	Surveying

Table B.1 (cont.)

Date of First Book	Author Name	Date of Birth & Death	Age	Father's Occupation	Education and Training	Occupations (a) *Non-Agricultural*	Occupations (b): *Agricultural*	Non-agricultural Book Topics
1728	Batty Langley	bap.1696–1751	32	Gardener	Gardening (trained in father's profession)	Landscape Design, Architecture	Surveyor	Gardening, Landscape Design, Architecture, Masonry
1730	George Rye^							
1731	Jethro Tull	bap.1674–1741	57	Landowner	Oxford University; Gray's Inn	Law	Landowner, Farmer	
1732	William Ellis	c.1700–1758	32			Customs Officer, Brewing industry	Farmer, Salesman, Advisor	
1732	Sir John Dalrymple	1673–1747	59	Viscount & Earl	Leiden University	Military, Politician, Diplomat	Landowner	
1733	Thomas Jarvis^							
1738	Samuel Trowel	d.1747				Law?	Steward	
1738	William Plunkett^							
1741	Alexander Blackwell	1709–1747	32	Professor of Theology	Edinburgh University, Physic at Leiden University	Printer, Physician	Projector	

1743	Robert Maxwell	1695–1765	48	Landowner		Public Lecturer	Landowner, Farmer, Consultant, Land Valuer	Beekeeping
1743	Robert James	bap.1703–1776	40	Military Officer (army major)	Grammar school; Oxford University; Medicine	Physician		Medicine
1756	Sir Archibald Grant of Monymusk, second baronet	1696–1778	61	First Baronet, Lord of Session	Lincoln's Inn; Law	Politician	Estate Landowner	
1756	Francis Home	1719–1813	37	Lawyer (advocate)	Edinburgh University (medicine); Apprenticed to Surgeon	Physician		Medicine
1757	Edward Lisle*	c.1666–1722	n/a			Clergyman	Landowner, Farmer	
1757	Thomas Hale^							
1759	Benjamin Stillingfleet	1702–1771	57	Clergyman, Physician	Norwich school; Cambridge University (BA 1724)	Tutor; Surveyor of Savoy Barracks		Natural history; botany
1759	Richard North*	d.1766				Nursery gardener		
1759	Robert Brown^							

Table B.1 (cont.)

Date of First Book	Author Name	Date of Birth & Death	Age	Father's Occupation	Education and Training	Occupations (a) Non-Agricultural	Occupations (b): Agricultural	Non-agricultural Book Topics
1760	Thomas Hitt*				Apprentice at Belvoir Castle, Duke of Rutland	Nurseryman, Garden Designer		Gardening
1761	Bartholomew Rocque*					Market Gardener, Landscape Designer		
1761	John Mordant^							
1762	Adam Dickson	bap.1721–1776	41	Clergyman (minister), Farmer	Edinburgh University (MA 1744)	Clergyman (minister)		
1762	John Mills	c.1717–1786/96	45					Weather, Natural Philosophy
1764	Walter Harte	1708/9–1774	58	Clergyman (vicar, canon of Bristol)	Grammar school; Oxford University (BA 1728, MA 1731)	Clergyman (chaplain), Tutor, Writer		Poetry, Essay, Religion
1764	Henry Rowlands	1655–1723	49		Classics	Clergyman (vicar 1756–1781), Antiquary		Antiquities
1764	John Randall	d.1789				Schoolmaster		Education, Geography

1765	George Fordyce	1736–1802	29	Landowner	Edinburgh University (MD 1758)	Physician		Medicine
1765	Robert Billing*						"Farmer"	
1765	Charles Varlo	c.1725–1795	40	Farmer	Boarding school, Tutor		Servant, Consultant, Livestock Farmer, Salesman	Politics
1767	Arthur Young	1741–1820	26	Clergyman (rector)	School; Apprentice to wine merchants	Reporter (Morning Post)	Farmer, Publicist, Political Reformer, Land agent (Ireland, 1 year)	Politics, Trade
1769	Richard Weston	bap.1732–1806	37			Thread-hosier		Local History, Botany, Gardening
1770	George Cooke*						"Farmer"	
1770	Matthew Peters*	1711–	59		Educated as Civil Engineer			
1770	Alexander Hunter	1729?–1809	41	Druggist	Grammar school, Edinburgh University (MD 1753)	Physician		Medical, York Lunatic Asylum
1770	John Dove*	d.1772		Farmer			Shepherd (youth)	Religion
1770	Francis Miller^							

Table B.1 (cont.)

Date of First Book	Author Name	Date of Birth & Death	Age	Father's Occupation	Education and Training	Occupations (a) Non-Agricultural	Occupations (b): Agricultural	Non-agricultural Book Topics
1771	David Henry (?)	1709–1792	62		College of Aberdeen (intended for clergy)	Printer (London)	Farmer	History, London Guidebooks
1772	Thomas Comber*	d.1778?			Cambridge University (BA, LLB)	Clergyman (rector 1770–1778)		
1773	Paisley^							
1774	William Barron*	d.1803				Clergyman, Historian		History
1774	Josiah Ringsted^							
1775	James Anderson	1739–1808	36	Farmer (large tenant)	Edinburgh University	Political Economist, Book Reviewer	Landowner, Farmer	Political Economy, Fisheries, Poor Law, Trade
1775	Nathaniel Kent	1737–1810	38			Clerk, Secretary (Diplomatic service)	Land Agent	
1775	Joseph Wimpey^						Landowner	

1775	Francis Forbes^	c.1740–1814?	35					
1775	Gustavus Harrison^							
1775	William Hogg^							
1776	Henry Home, Lord Kames	1696–1782	80	Landowner (border laird)	Tutors, apprenticed to writer, Civil Law college	Law, Judge	Landowner	Law, Morality, Religion
1776	Thomas Bowden^							
1777	Cuthbert Clarke	1728/9–1790	49			Public Lecturer	Machine design	Natural Philosophy, Mechanics
1777	James Black*							
1777	W. Perryman^							
1778	William Marshall	bap.1745–1818	33	Farmer (yeomen)	Linen trade apprentice	Insurance, Commerce (West Indies)	Tenant Farmer, Land Agent and Steward, Landscaper, Consultant	Landscape design
1780	George Boswell*						Landowner	

Table B.1 *(cont.)*

Date of First Book	Author Name	Date of Birth & Death	Age	Father's Occupation	Education and Training	Occupations (a) *Non-Agricultural*	Occupations (b): *Agricultural*	Non-agricultural Book Topics
1780	John Trusler	1735–1820	45	Shopkeeper (mother clothier)	Westminster school; Cambridge University (BA 1757)	Clergyman (curate), 'medical gentleman'		Medicine, History, Politeness, Law, Religion, Travel, and Gardening
1782	William Raley*					Physician, Botany		
1784	James Small	bap.1740–1793	44	Farmer	Apprentice to carpenter & plough maker	Blacksmith, Carpenter	Farmer, Plough & Cart-wright	
1784	Nicholas Turner*							
1784	James Cooke*					Clergyman ('Rev'), Inventor		
1784	Josiah Twamley*						Cheese Factor	
1785	David Young*					Merchant		

1785	Thomas Stone	bap.1753–1815	32	Draper (prosperous), Landowner		East Indies?	Farmer, Land surveyor, Landowner, Enclosure Commissioner, Estate manager, Land valuer	Enclosures
1786	George Culley	bap.1735–1806	51	Farmer, Landowner	Farming (with Robert Bakewell)		Farmer (tenant)	
1786	Charles Ley*						Land surveyor	
1787	George Winter*						Patented drill machine	
1789	James Adam	1732–1794	57	Architect	Edinburgh University	Architect	Landowner	Architecture
1789	Thomas Wright*					Clergyman		
1790	Anthony Macmillan^							
1791	Thomas Martyn	1735–1825	56	Professor of botany	Tutored; Cambridge University (MA 1758)	Professor of Botany		Botany
1792	William Skirving	d.1796		Farmer	Edinburgh University; trained for ministry	Private Tutor, Political Reformer	Farmer, Landowner	

* = Authors with no DNB entry, but some information known

^ = No information available

Bibliography

A Primary

i Manuscripts

British Library
Add MS 56378, 'Agriculture; or drill-husbandry' by Edward King (1738–44).
Add 35126–35133, 'Original letters addressed to Arthur Young, F.R.S., Secretary to the Board of Agriculture [d 1820], with a few holograph draft replies; 1743–1820', 8 vols.
Add MS 34821–34854, 'Elements and practice of agriculture' by Arthur Young (1818).

Somerset Record Office
MS DD/SAS C/1193/4, 'Memoirs of the birth, education, life and death of: Mr John Cannon. Sometime Officer of the Excise & Writing Master at Mere Glastenbury & West Lydford in the County of Somerset' (1684–1743).

ii Printed Sources

A. S., *The husbandman, farmer and grasier's compleat instructor* (London, 1697).
Adam, James, *Practical essays on agriculture*, 2 vols (London, 1789).
Agricola, Georg Andreas, *A philosophical treatise of husbandry and gardening* (London, 1721).
Anderson, James, *Essays relating to agriculture and rural affairs* (Edinburgh, 1775).
Anderson, James, *An inquiry into the causes that have hitherto retarded the advancement of agriculture in Europe* (Edinburgh, 1779).
Anderson, James (ed.), *The bee: Or literary weekly intelligencer* (Edinburgh, 22 December 1790 [Vol. 1]–21 January 1794 [Vol. 18]).
Anderson, James, *Recreations in agriculture, natural history, arts, and miscellaneous literature* (London, 1797–1802).
Bacon, Francis, *The two books of Francis Bacon* (London, 1605).
Bacon, Francis, *Natural history* (London, 1658).
Baker, John Wynn, *Some hints for the better improvement of husbandry* (Dublin, 1762).

Baker, John Wynn, *Plan for instructing youths in the knowledge of husbandry* (London, 1765).

Baker, John Wynn, *Experiments in agriculture* (Dublin, 1772).

Baker, Thomas, *Tunbridge-Walks: Or, the yeoman of Kent* (London, 1703).

Baxter, John and Ellman, John, *The library of agricultural and horticultural knowledge* (Lewes, 1830).

Belhaven, John Hamilton, Lord, *The country-man's rudiments: Or, an advice to the farmers in East-Lothian how to labour and improve their ground* (Edinburgh, 1713).

Billing, Robert, *An account of the culture of carrots* (London, 1765).

Blagrave, Joseph, *The epitome of the art of husbandry* (London, 1669).

Blith, Walter, *The English improver* (London, 1649).

Blith, Walter, *The English improver improved* (London, 1652).

Blome, Richard, *The gentleman's recreation* (London, 1686).

The book of knowledge: treating of the wisdom of the ancients in four parts (London, 1720).

Bowden, Thomas, *The farmer's director: Or, a compendium of English husbandry* (London, 1776).

Bradley, Richard, *New improvements of planting and gardening* (London, 1717).

Bradley, Richard, *A general treatise of husbandry and gardening, for the month of April* (London, 1721–1722).

Bradley, Richard, *New experiments and observations* (London, 1724).

Bradley, Richard, *A survey of the ancient husbandry and gardening* (London, 1725).

Bradley, Richard, *The country gentleman and farmer's monthly director* (London, 1726).

Bradley, Richard, *A complete body of husbandry* (London, 1727).

Bradley, Richard, *The science of good husbandry: Or, the oeconomics of Xenophon* (London, 1727).

Bradley, Richard, *Ten practical discourses* (London, 1727).

Bradley, Richard, *The weekly miscellany for the improvement of husbandry, trade, arts, and sciences* (London, 1727).

Bradley, Richard, *The country housewife and lady's director* (3rd edn; London, 1728).

Bradley, Richard, *General treatise of husbandry and gardening* (London, 1757).

Breton, Nicholas, *The court and country* (London, 1618).

Cabbage and clover husbandry (London, 1775).

Cato and Varro, *On agriculture*, trans. W. D. Hooper and Harrison Boyd Ash (Cambridge, MA, 1934).

Chambers, Ephraim, *Cyclopædia*, 2 vols (London, 1728).

Chomel, Noel and Bradley, Richard, *Dictionaire oeconomique: Or, the family dictionary* (London, 1725).

Clarke, Cuthbert, *The true theory and practice of husbandry* (London, 1777).

Clerke, George, *The landed-man's assistant: Or, steward's vade mecum* (London, 1712).

Cochrane, Archibald, *A treatise, shewing the intimate connection that subsists between agriculture and chemistry* (London, 1795).

Columella, L. Junius Moderatus, *Columella of husbandry* (London, 1745).

Columella, L. Junius Moderatus, *On agriculture*, trans. Harrison Boyd Ash (Cambridge, MA, 1941).

The commercial and agricultural magazine, 6 vols (London, 1799–1802).

The complete farmer: Or, a general dictionary of husbandry (London, 1766).

Cooke, George, *The complete English farmer: Or, husbandry made perfectly easy* (London, 1770).

The country gentleman's companion; or, the farmer's complete accompt-book, for the pocket or desk, for the year 1795 (Bath, 1794).

Coventry, Andrew, *Discourses explanatory of the object and plan of the course of lectures on agriculture and rural economy* (Edinburgh, 1808).

Cowley, Abraham, 'Of agriculture', *The works of Mr. Abraham Cowley vol. 2* (London, 1707), 704–31.

Critical review, or annals of literature (London, 1 January 1756 (Vol. 1, no. 1) to June 1817 (Vol. 5, no. 6)).

The chronicles of John Cannon, excise officer and writing master: Pt. 1, 1684–1733 (Somerset, Oxfordshire, Berkshire), ed. John Money (Oxford, 2009).

Culley, George, *Observations in livestock* (London, 1786).

Cyuile and uncyuile life (London, 1579).

Dalrymple, Sir John, *An essay on the husbandry of Scotland* (Edinburgh, 1732).

Davy, Humphry, *Elements of agricultural chemistry* (London, 1815).

Defoe, Daniel, *A tour thro' the whole island of Great Britain* (London, 1724).

Dickson, Adam, *Treatise of agriculture* (Edinburgh, 1762).

Dickson, Adam, *Small farms destructive to the country in its present situation* (Edinburgh, 1764).

Dickson, Adam, *The husbandry of the ancients* (Edinburgh, 1788).

Dictionarium rusticum & urbanicum (London, 1704).

Dodsley, Robert, *Public virtue: A poem* (London, 1753).

Donaldson, James, *Husbandry anatomized, or, an enquiry into the present manner of teiling and manuring the ground in Scotland* (Edinburgh, 1697).

Donaldson, James, *Modern agriculture; or, the present state of husbandry in Great Britain*, 4 vols (Edinburgh, 1795).

Donaldson, William, *Agriculture considered as a moral and political duty* (London, 1775).

Dowe, Bartholomew, 'A dairie booke for all good huswiues' in Torquato Tasso, *The housholders philosophie* (London, 1588).

Doyle, Martin, *A cyclopædia of practical husbandry and rural affairs in general* (Dublin, 1839).

Drown, William and Drown, Solomon, *Compendium of agriculture; or, the farmer's guide* (Providence, RI, 1824).

Duhamel, M. and Miller, Philip, *The elements of agriculture*, 2 vols (London, 1764).

Dymock, Cressy, *An essay for the advancement of husbandry-learning: Or propositions for the er recting college of husbandry* (London, 1651).

Dymock, Cressy, *The new and better art of agriculture* (London, 1668)

Edwards, George, *Some observations for assisting farmers and others to acquire the knowledge of their business* (London?, 1779).

Edwards, George, *A plan of an undertaking intended for the improvement of husbandry* (Newcastle, 1783).

Ellis, William, *The practical farmer: Or, the Hertfordshire husbandman* (London, 1732).

Ellis, William, *Chiltern and vale farming explained* (London, 1733).

Ellis, William, *New experiments in husbandry, for the month of April* (London, 1736).

Ellis, William, *The modern husbandman*, 8 vols (London, 1750).

Ellis, William, *The country housewife's family companion* (London, 1750).

Ellis's husbandry, abridged and methodized (London, 1772).

Elyot, Thomas, *The dictionary of Syr Thomas Eliot knyght* (London, 1538).

English review (London, January 1783 (Vol. 1) to December 1796 (Vol. 28)).

Essay on the theory of agriculture (London, 1760).

Estienne, Charles, Liébault, Jean, and Surflet, Richard, *Maison rustique, or the countrie farme* (London, 1600).

Evelyn, John, *Sylva, or a discourse of forest-trees* (London, 1664).

Evelyn, John, *A philosophical discourse of earth* (London, 1676).

A familiar dialogue betwixt one Physiologus a gentleman student of Athens and his country friend Geoponus (Oxford, 1612).

'The farmer', Bodleian Harding collection, Roud Number: V20791 (London, 1736–63). *Broadside Ballads Online* <http://ballads.bodleian.ox.ac.uk/search/roud/V20791>[accessed 3 April 2018].

The farmer convinced; or, the reviewers of the monthly review anatomized (London, 1788).

The farmer's compleat guide (London, 1760).

The farmer's magazine (Edinburgh, January 1800 (no. 1) to November 1825 (Vol. 26, no. 104)).

The farmer's wife; or complete country housewife (London, 1780).

Fielding, Henry, *The history of Tom Jones, a foundling* (London, 1749).

Fiennes, Celia, *Through England on a side saddle in the time of William and Mary* (London, 1888).

Fitzherbert, John, *Here begynneth a newe tracte or treatyse moost profytable for all husbandmen* (London, 1523).

Fitzherbert, John, *Here begynneth a ryght frutefull mater: And hath to name the boke of surueyeng and improumentes* (London, 1523).

Fitzherbert, John, *Fitzharberts booke of husbandrie deuided into foure seuerall bookes* (London, 1598).

Fothergill, Anthony, 'On the application of chemistry to agriculture, and rural oeconomy', *Letters and papers on agriculture, planting, &c. selected from the correspondence-book of the Society instituted at Bath*, 3 (1786), 59–67.

Fordyce, George, *Elements of agriculture* (Edinburgh, 1765).

A general dictionary of husbandry, planting, gardening (Bath, 1779).

The gentleman farmer: Or, certain observations made by an English gentleman, upon the husbandry of Flanders (London, 1726).

'Gentlemen farmers; for the year 1783', Roud Number: V27994 (Nottingham, 1797–1807). *Broadside Ballads Online* <http://ballads.bodleian.ox.ac.uk/search/roud/V27994>[accessed 3 April 2018].

The gentleman farmer's pocket companion (London, 1788).

Gentleman's magazine (London, January 1731 (Vol. 1, no. 1) to September 1907 (Vol. 303, no. 2121).

Grant, Sir Archibald, *Political observations occasioned by the state of agriculture in the North of Scotland* (Aberdeen, 1756).

Grant, Sir Archibald, *Memorandum to the tenants of Monymusk, January 1756* (Edinburgh?, 1756).

Grant, Sir Archibald, *A dissertation on the chief obstacles to the improvement of land* (Aberdeen, 1760).

Grant, Sir Archibald, *The practical farmer's pocket-companion* (Aberdeen, 1766).

Graves, Richard, *Columella; or, the distressed anchoret* (London, 1779).

Graves, Richard, *The spiritual Quixote, 3 vols* (London, 1783).

Hale, Thomas, *A compleat body of husbandry* (London, 1756).

Harrison, Gustavus, *Agriculture delineated* (London, 1775).

Harte, Walter, *Essays on husbandry* (London, 1764).

Harte, Walter, *Essays on husbandry* (2nd edn; London, 1770).

Hartlib, Samuel, *Samuel Hartlib his legacie: Or an enlargement of the discourse of husbandry used in Brabant and Flaunders* (London, 1651).

Hartlib, Samuel, *The compleat husband-man* (London, 1659).

Hartlib, Samuel and Dymock, Cressy, *The reformfd [sic] husband-man* (London, 1651)

Henley, Walter, *Boke of husbandry* (London, 1508).

Henley, Walter, *The booke of thrift* (London, 1589).

Henry, David, *The complete English farmer* (London, 1771).

Heresbach, Conrad and Googe, Barnaby, *Foure bookes of husbandry* (London, 1577).

Hodgkinson, Joseph, *Plain and useful instructions to farmers* (London, 1794).

Home, Francis, *The principles of agriculture and vegetation* (Edinburgh, 1756).

Hoskyns, Chandos, *A short inquiry into the history of agriculture, in ancient, medieval, and modern times* (London, 1849).

Houghton, John, *A collection for improvement of husbandry and trade* (London, 1681).

Houghton, John, *A proposal for improvement of husbandry and trade* (London, 1691).

Houghton, John, *A collection for improvement of husbandry and trade, edited by Richard Bradley* (London, 1727).

Howell, John, *Epistolae ho-elianae* (London, 1650).

Howlett, John, *Enclosures, a cause of improved agriculture* (London, 1787).

Hunter, Alexander, *Georgical essays*, 4 vols (London, 1770–72).

The husbandmans plea against tithes (London, 1647).

Jacob, Giles, *The compleat court-keeper: Or, land-steward's assistant* (London, 1713).

Jacob, Giles, *The country gentleman's vade mecum* (London, 1717).

Jacob, Giles, *A new law-dictionary* (London, 1729).

James, Robert, *The rational farmer, and practical husbandman* (London, 1743).

Johnson, Cuthbert William, *The farmer's encyclopædia, and dictionary of rural affairs* (London, 1842).

Johnson, Samuel, *A dictionary of the English language*, 2 vols (London, 1755).

Kames, Lord (Henry Home), *The gentleman farmer* (Edinburgh, 1776).

Kent, Nathaniel, *Hints to gentlemen of landed property* (London, 1775).

Lamport, William, 'A proposal for the further improvement of agriculture', *Letters and papers on agriculture, planting, &c. selected from the correspondence-book of the Society instituted at Bath*, 1 (1780), 'Appendix'.

Lamport, William, *Cursory remarks on the importance of agriculture* (London, 1784).

Laurence, Edward, *The duty of a steward to his lord* (London, 1727).

Laurence, John, *The clergy-man's recreation: Shewing the pleasure and profit of the art of gardening* (London, 1714).

Laurence, John, *A new system of agriculture* (London, 1726).

Lawrence, John, *The new farmer's calendar* (London, 1800).

Lawrence, John, *The modern land steward* (London, 1801).

Lee, Joseph, *Considerations concerning common fields and inclosures* (London, 1654).

Ley, Charles, *The nobleman, gentleman, land steward, and surveyor's compleat guide* (London, 1786).

Lisle, Edward, *Observations in husbandry*, 2 vols (London, 1757).

Loudon, John, *An encyclopædia of agriculture* (London, 1825).

Loudon, John, *Self-instruction for young gardeners, foresters, bailiffs, land-stewards, and farmers: With a memoir of the author* (1845, repr. Cambridge, 2013).

Macmillan, Anthony, *A treatise on pasturage* (Edinburgh, 1790).

Markham, Gervase, *The English husbandman* (London, 1613).

Markham, Gervase, *The second booke of the English husbandman* (London, 1614).

Markham, Gervase, *Countrey contentments, in two bookes … the second intituled, the English husvvife* (London, 1615).

Markham, Gervase, *Maison rustique, or the countrey farme* (London, 1616).

Markham, Gervase, *Markhams farwell to husbandry* (London, 1620).

Markham, Gervase, *The English husbandman* (London, 1635).

Marshall, William, *Minutes of agriculture* (London, 1778).

Marshall, William, *Experiments and observations concerning agriculture* (London, 1779).

Marshall, William, *Rural economy of Norfolk*, 2 vols (London, 1787).

Marshall, William, *Rural economy of Yorkshire*, 2 vols (London, 1788).

Marshall, William, *Rural economy of Glocestershire*, 2 vols (London, 1789).

Marshall, William, *Rural economy of the Midland counties*, 2 vols (London, 1790).

Marshall, William, *Rural economy of the southern counties*, 2 vols (London, 1796).

Marshall, William, *Proposals for a rural institute, or college of agriculture* (London, 1799).

Marshall, William, *On the landed property of England* (London, 1804).

Marshall, William, *The review and abstract of the county reports to the Board of Agriculture*, 5 vols (York, 1818).

Mascall, Leonard, *A booke of the arte and maner, howe to plant and graffe all sortes of trees* (London, 1572).

Mascall, Leonard, *The husbandlye ordring and gouernmente of poultrie* (London, 1581).

Mascall, Leonard, *The first booke of cattell* (London, 1587).

Maxey, Edward, *A nevv instuction [sic] of plowing and setting of corne, handled in manner of a dialogue betweene a ploughman and a scholler* (London, 1601).

Maxwell, Robert, *The practical husbandman: Being a collection of miscellaneous papers on husbandry* (Edinburgh, 1757).

Meager, Leonard, *The mystery of husbandry* (London, 1697).

Millar, John, *An historical view of the English government*, 4 vols (London, 1803).

Mills, John, *A new system of practical husbandry*, 5 vols (London, 1767).

Molesworth, Robert, *Some considerations for the promoting of agriculture and employing the poor* (Dublin, 1723).

Mordant, John, *The complete steward: Or, the duty of a steward to his lord*, 2 vols (London, 1761).

Morning chronicle (London, 1789–1865).

Monthly review (London, May 1749 (Vol. 1) to December 1844).

Mortimer, John, *The whole art of husbandry* (London, 1707).

Morton, John Chalmers, *A cyclopedia of agriculture, practical and scientific* (Glasgow, 1856).

Morton, John Chalmers, 'Agricultural education', *Journal of the Royal Agricultural Society of England*, 1 (1865), 436–57.

Museum rusticum et commerciale: Or, select papers on agriculture, commerce, arts, and manufactures, by the Society for the Encouragement of Arts, Manufactures and Commerce (London, 1764–6).

N. H., *The compleat tradesman* (London, 1684).

A new system of agriculture (London, 1755).

Norden, John, *The surveiors dialogue* (London, 1610).

The northern farmer: Or select essays on agriculture (London, 1778).

Nourse, Timothy, *Campania felix, or a discourse of the benefits and improvements of husbandry* (London, 1700).

Perryman, William, *An essay on the education of youth intended for the profession of agriculture* (London, 1777).

Peters, Matthew, *The rational farmer* (2nd edn; London, 1771).

Peters, Matthew, *Winter riches* (London, 1771).

Peters, Matthew, *Agricultura: Or the good husbandman* (London, 1776).

Plat, Sir Hugh, *The jewel house of art and nature* (London, 1594).

Plat, Sir Hugh, *The newe and admirable arte of setting of corne* (London, 1600).

Plattes, Gabriel, *A discovery of infinite treasure* (London, 1639).

Plattes, Gabriel, *A description of the famous Kingdome of Macaria* (London, 1641).

Plattes, Gabriel, *The profitable intelligencer* (London, 1644).

Plunkett, William, *A new method of farming* (Dublin, 1738).

A political enquiry into the consequences of enclosing waste lands (London, 1785).

Parliamentary Papers 1852–3, LXXXVIII, '1851 Census. Population Tables, vol. I. part II. Ages and occupations'.

Postlethwayt, Malachy, *The universal dictionary of trade and commerce* (London, 1757).

Potts, Thomas, *The British farmer's cyclopædia* (London, 1807).

The papers of George Washington digital edition (Charlottesville, 2008). Original source: Presidential Series (24 September 1788–3 March 1797 [in progress]), Vol. 15 (1 January–30 April 1794).

Philosophical transactions (London, 1665–present).

Pursuits of agriculture: a satirical poem (London, 1808).

R. T., *The art of good husbandry, or, the improvement of time being a sure way to get and keep money* (London, 1675).

Randall, Joseph, *The semi-virgilian husbandry* (London, 1764).

Richardson, Samuel, *Clarissa*, 7 vols (London, 1748).

Robert Furse: A Devon family memoir of 1593, ed. Anita Travers (Exeter, 2012).

Robertson, Thomas, *General report upon the size of farms, and upon the persons who cultivate farms* (Edinburgh, 1796).

Rochefoucauld, François de La, *The Frenchman's year in Suffolk: French impressions of Suffolk life in 1784*, trans. Norman Scarfe (1988).

Rowlands, Henry, *Idea agriculturæ* (Dublin, 1764).

Rye, George, *Considerations on agriculture* (Dublin, 1730).

S., J., *Profit and pleasure united, or the husbandman's magazine* (London, 1684).

The satirist (London, July 1807 (Vol. 2) to August 1814 (Vol. 15, no. 2)).

Shaw, John, *How to order any land* (London, 1637).

Sinclair, John, *Code of agriculture* (2nd edn; London, 1819).

Sinclair, John, *Substance of Sir John Sinclair's address to the Board of Agriculture* (London, 1793).

Sinclair, John, *Plan for establishing a Board of Agriculture and Internal Improvement* (London, 1793).

Skirving, William, *The husbandman's assistant* (Edinburgh, 1792).

Small, James, *Treatise on ploughs and wheel carriages* (Edinburgh, 1784).

Smellie, William (ed.), *Encyclopædia Britannica*, 3 vols (Edinburgh, 1771).

Smith, Adam, *An inquiry into the nature and causes of the wealth of nations* (London, 1776).

Smollett, Tobias, *The expedition of Humphry Clinker*, 3 vols (London, 1771).

Somerville, John, *The system followed during the two last years by the Board of Agriculture* (London, 1800).

Spedding, James, Ellis, Robert, and Heath, Douglas (eds), *The works of Francis Bacon vol. VIII* (Boston, 1861–79).

Steele, Richard, *The trades-man's calling* (London, 1684).

Stevenson, Matthew, *The twelve moneths* (London, 1661).

Stone, Thomas, *Suggestions for rendering the inclosure of common fields and waste lands a source of population and riches* (London, 1787).

Sturtevant, Simon, *Metallica; or the treatise of metallica* (London, 1612).

Switzer, Stephen, *The nobleman, gentleman, and gardener's recreation* (London, 1715).

Switzer, Stephen, *Iconographia rustica: The nobleman, gentleman, and gardener's recreation, 3 vols* (London, 1718).

Switzer, Stephen, *The practical husbandman and planter*, 2 vols (London, 1733–34).

Thompson, William, *The new gardener's calendar* (London, 1779).

Trowell, Samuel, *A new treatise of husbandry, gardening, and other matters relating to rural affairs* (London, 1739).

A true method of treating light hazely ground (Edinburgh, 1735).

Trusler, John, *Practical husbandry* (London, 1780).

Trusler, John, *On the importance, utility, and duty of a farmer's life* (London, 1792).

Tryon, Thomas, *The country-man's companion* (London, 1684).

Tull, Jethro, *The new horse-houghing husbandry* (London, 1731).

Tull, Jethro, *The horse-hoing husbandry* (London, 1733).

Tull, Jethro, *A supplement to the essay on horse-hoing husbandry* (2nd edn; London, 1740).

Tull, Jethro, *The horse-hoeing husbandry… introduction by William Cobbett* (London, 1822).

Tusser, Thomas, *A hundreth good pointes of husbandrie* (London, 1557).

Tusser, Thomas, *Five hundreth good pointes of husbandry, united to as many of good huswifery* (London, 1573).

Tusser, Thomas, *Five hundred points of good husbandry: Together with a book of huswifery*, ed. William Fordyce Mavor (Cambridge, 2013).

Twamley, Josiah, *Dairying exemplified, or the business of cheese-making* (Warwick, 1784).

Vallavine, Peter, *An abstract of an essay on tillage and vegetation* (London, 1747).

Vallemont, Pierre Le Lorrain, *Curiosities of nature and art in husbandry and gardening* (London, 1707).

Varlo, Charles, *A treatise on agriculture, intitled the Yorkshire farmer* (Dublin, 1765).

Varlo, Charles, *The modern farmers guide*, 2 vols (Glasgow, 1768).

Varlo, Charles, *A new system of husbandry*, 3 vols (York, 1770).

Varlo, Charles, *Nature display'd, a new work* (London, 1794).

Wade, Edward, *A proposal for improving and adorning the island of Great Britain* (London, 1755).

[Walkden, Peter], *A diary, from January 1733 to March 1734, written by the Reverend Peter Walkden… Transcribed and with an introduction, indexes and notes by members of Chipping Local History Society* (Smith Settle, Otley, West Yorkshire, 2000).

Ward, Edward, *The wooden world dissected* (London, 1707).

Westminster magazine (London, January 1773 (Vol. 1, no. 1) to December 1785).

Weston, Richard, *Tracts on practical agriculture and gardening* (2nd edn; London, 1773).

Weston, Sir Richard, *A discours of husbandrie used in Brabant and Flanders* (London, 1650).

Wight, Andrew, *Present state of husbandry in Scotland*, 2 vols (Edinburgh, 1778).

Wimpey, Joseph, *Rural improvements* (London, 1775).

Winter, George, *A new and compendious system of husbandry* (Bristol, 1787).

Woodward, Donald (ed.), *The farming and memorandum books of Henry Best of Elmswell, 1642* (Oxford, 1984).

Woolley, Hannah, *The cook's guide* (London, 1664).

Woolley, Hannah, *The compleat servant-maid* (London, 1677).

Worlidge, John, *Systema agriculturæ; the mystery of husbandry discovered* (London, 1669).

Wright, Thomas, *The art of floating land* (London, 1799).

Xenophon, *Treatise of housholde*, trans. Gentian Hervet (London, 1532).

Young, Arthur, *The farmer's letters to the people of England* (London, 1767).

Young, Arthur, *A letter to Lord Clive* (London, 1767).

Young, Arthur, *A six weeks tour, through the southern counties of England and Wales* (London, 1768).

Young, Arthur, *Rural oeconomy: Or, essays on the practical parts of husbandry* (London, 1770).

Young, Arthur, *The farmer's guide in hiring and stocking farms* (London, 1770).

Young, Arthur, *A course of experimental agriculture*, 2 vols (London, 1770).

Young, Arthur, *A six months tour through the North of England*, 4 vols (London, 1770).

Young, Arthur, *The farmer's kalendar* (London, 1771).

Young, Arthur, *The farmer's tour through the East of England*, 4 vols (London, 1771).

Young, Arthur, *A tour in Ireland* (London, 1780).

Young, Arthur, 'How far is agriculture capable of being made one of the pursuits, in which men of a certain rank may educate their children, as at present in commerce and manufactures?', *Annals of Agriculture*, 21 (1793), 229–79.

Young, Arthur, *The autobiography of Arthur Young with selections from his correspondence*, ed. Matilda Betham-Edwards (London, 1898).

B   Secondary

i   Online Databases

Eighteenth-Century Borrowing from the University of Glasgow (https://18c-borrowing .glasgow.ac.uk).

Oxford Dictionary of National Biography (www.oxforddnb.com).

Oxford English Dictionary (www.oed.com).

ii   Printed Material

Abbott, Andrew, *The system of professions: An essay on the division of expert labor* (London, 1988).

Adams, Ian H., 'The agents of agricultural change', in Martin L. Parry and Terry R. Slater (eds), *The making of the Scottish countryside* (London, 1980), 155–75.

Adams, J. R. R., 'Agricultural literature for the common reader in eighteenth-century Ulster', *Folk Life*, 26:1 (1987), 103–8.

Ågren, Maria (ed.), *Making a living, making a difference: Gender and work in early modern European society* (Oxford, 2017).

Albritton, Robert, 'Did agrarian capitalism exist?', *The Journal of Peasant Studies*, 20:3 (1993), 419–41.

Allan, David, *Commonplace books and reading in Georgian England* (Cambridge, 2010).

Allen, Robert C., 'The growth of labor productivity in early modern English agriculture', *Explorations in Economic History*, 25:2 (1988), 117–46.

Allen, Robert C., *Enclosure and the yeoman: The agricultural development of the south midlands, 1450–1850* (Oxford, 1992).

Allen, Robert C., 'Tracking the agricultural revolution in England', *EcHR*, 52:2 (1999), 209–35.

Ambrosoli, Mauro, *The wild and the sown: Botany and agriculture in Western Europe, 1350–1850* (Cambridge, 1997).

Armstrong, W. A., 'Labour I: Rural population growth, systems of employment, and incomes', in G. E. Mingay (ed.), *AHEW: 1750–1850 Vol 6* (Cambridge, 1989), 641–728.

Armytage, W. H. G., 'Education for social change in England 1600–1660', *The Vocational Aspect of Education*, 4:9 (1952), 85–101.

Ash, Eric H., *Power, knowledge, and expertise in Elizabethan England* (Baltimore, 2004).

Ash, Eric H., 'Amending nature: Draining the English fens', in Lissa Roberts, Simon Schaffer, and Peter Dear (eds), *The mindful hand: Inquiry and invention from the late renaissance to industrialization* (Chicago, 2007), 117–44.

Ash, Eric H., 'Introduction: Expertise and the early modern state', *Osiris*, 25:1 (2010), 1–24.

Aston, T. H. and Philpin, C. H. E. (eds), *The Brenner debate: Agrarian class structure and economic development in pre-industrial Europe* (Cambridge, 1985).

Barker, Joseph, 'The emergence of agrarian capitalism in early modern England: A reconsideration of farm sizes', PhD thesis (University of Cambridge, 2013).

Beckett, John, 'The pattern of landownership in England and Wales, 1660–1880', *EcHR*, 37:1 (1984), 1–22.

Beckett, John, 'Estate management in eighteenth-century England: The Lowther-Spedding relationship in Cumberland', in John Chartres and David Hey (eds), *English rural society 1500–1800: Essays in honour of Joan Thirsk* (Cambridge, 1990), 55–72.

Beckett, John, 'The decline of the small landowner in England and Wales 1660–1900', in F. M. L.Thompson (ed.), *Landowners, capitalists and entrepreneurs: Essays for Sir John Habakkuk* (Oxford, 1994), 89–112.

Beckett, J. V., Turner, M. E., and Cowell, Ben, 'Farming through enclosure', *Rural History*, 9:2 (1998), 141–55.

Bell, Vicars, *To meet Mr Ellis: Little Gaddesden in the eighteenth century* (London, 1956).

Ben-Amos, Ilana Krausman, *Adolescence and youth in early modern England* (London, 1994).

Benedict, Barbara M., 'Writing on writing: Representations of the book in eighteenth-century literature', in Laura L. Runge and Pat Rogers (eds), *Producing the eighteenth-century book: Writers and publishers in England, 1650–1800* (Newark, 2009), 274–90.

Bennett, H. S., *English books & readers 1457 to 1557: Being a study in the history of the book trade from Caxton to the incorporation of the Stationers' Company* (London, 1952).

Bennett, H. S., *English books & readers 1558 to 1603: Being a study in the history of the book trade in the reign of Elizabeth I* (Cambridge, 1965).

Bennett, H. S., *English books & readers 1603 to 1640: Being a study in the history of the book trade in the reigns of James I and Charles I* (Cambridge, 1970).

Bennett, Jim, 'The mechanical arts', in Katharine Park and Lorraine Daston (eds), *Cambridge history of science, Vol 3: Early modern science* (Cambridge, 2006), 673–95.

Berens, E. M., *Myths and legends of ancient Greece and Rome* (Luton, 2011).

Berry, Wendell, *The unsettling of America: Culture and agriculture* (3rd edn; Berkeley, 1996).

Bertucci, Paolo and Courcelle, Olivier, 'Artisanal knowledge, expertise, and patronage in early eighteenth-century Paris: The Société Des Arts (1728–36)', *Eighteenth-Century Studies*, 48:2 (2015), 159–79.

Beutler, Corinne, 'Un chapitre de la sensibilité collective: la littérature agricole en Europe continentale au XVIe siècle', *Annales*, 28:5 (1973), 1280–301.

Bowen, J. P. and Brown, A. T. (eds), *Custom and commercialisation in English rural society: Revisiting Tawney and Postan* (Hertfordshire, 2016).

Braddick, Michael J. and Walter, John, 'Introduction: Grids of power: Order, hierarchy and subordination in early modern society', in Michael J. Braddick and John Walter (eds), *Negotiating power in early modern society: Order, hierarchy and subordination in Britain and Ireland* (Cambridge, 2001), 1–42.

Brassley, Paul, 'Agricultural science and education', in E. J. T. Collins (ed.), *AHEW: 1850–1914 Vol. 7* (Cambridge, 2000), 594–649.

Brassley, Paul, 'The professionalisation of English agriculture?', *Rural History*, 16:2 (2005), 235–51.

Brassley, Paul, 'Agricultural education, training and advice in the UK, 1850–2000', in Nadine Viver (ed.), *The state and rural societies: Policy and education in Europe 1750–2000* (Turnhout, 2008), 259–78.

Braverman, Harry, *Labor and monopoly capital: The degradation of work in the twentieth century* (London, 1974).

Brenner, Robert, 'Agrarian class structure and economic development in pre-industrial Europe', *Past & Present*, 70:1 (1976), 30–75.

Brenner, Robert, 'The agrarian roots of European capitalism', *Past & Present*, 97:1 (1982), 16–113.

Britten, James, 'Proverbs and folk-lore from William Ellis's "Modern Husbandman" (1750)', *The Folk-Lore Record*, 3:1 (1880), 80–86.

Broad, John, *Transforming English rural society: The Verneys and the Claydons, 1600–1820* (Cambridge, 2004).

Broad, John, 'Farmers and improvement, 1780–1840', in Richard W. Hoyle (ed.), *The farmer in England, 1650–1980* (Farnham, 2013), 165–92.

Broadberry, Stephen, Campbell, Bruce, Klein, Alexander, Overton, Mark, and van Leeuwen, Bas, *British economic growth, 1270–1870* (Cambridge, 2015).

Bryer, Rob, 'The history of accounting and the transition to capitalism in England. Part two: evidence', *Accounting, Organizations and Society*, 25:4 (2000), 327–81.

Bryer, Rob, 'The genesis of the capitalist farmer: Towards a Marxist accounting history of the origins of the English agricultural revolution', *Critical Perspectives on Accounting*, 17:4 (2006), 367–97.

Bryer, Rob, 'Accounting and control of the labour process', *Critical Perspectives on Accounting*, 17:5 (2006), 551–98.

Bucknell, Clare, 'The mid-eighteenth-century georgic and agricultural improvement', *Journal for Eighteenth-Century Studies*, 36:3 (2013), 335–52.

Burke, Peter, *Social history of knowledge: From Gutenberg to Diderot* (Cambridge, 2000).

Burke, Peter, *What is the history of knowledge?* (Cambridge, 2016).

Burnette, Joyce, 'Agriculture, 1700–1870', in Roderick Floud, Jane Humphries, and Paul Johnson (eds), *The Cambridge economic history of modern Britain: Volume I: 1700–1870* (Cambridge, 2014), 89–117.

Bushnell, Rebecca, *Green desire: Imagining early modern English gardens* (London, 2003).

Bushnell, Rebecca, 'The gardener and the book', in Natasha Glaisyer and Sara Pennell (eds), *Didactic literature in England, 1500–1800: Expertise constructed* (Aldershot, 2003), 118–36.

Büttner, Jochen, 'Shooting with ink', in Matteo Valleriani (ed.), *The structures of practical knowledge* (Switzerland, 2017), 116–66.

Buttress, F. A., *Agricultural periodicals of the British Isles, 1681–1900, and their location* (Cambridge, 1950).

Campbell, Mildred, *The English yeomen under Elizabeth and the Stuarts* (London, 1942).

Carolan, Michael S., 'Sustainable agriculture, science and the co-production of "expert" knowledge: The value of interactional expertise', *Local Environment*, 11:4 (2006), 421–31.

Carpenter, Christopher, *Locality and polity: A study of Warwickshire landed society, 1401–1499* (Cambridge, 1992).

Caunce, Stephen, 'Farm servants and the development of capitalism in English agriculture', *AgHR*, 45:1 (1997), 49–60.

Chambers, J. D. and Mingay, G. E., *The agricultural revolution 1750–1880* (New York, 1966).

Chartier, Roger, *The order of books: Readers, authors, and libraries in Europe between the fourteenth and eighteenth centuries* (Cambridge, 1994).

Clarke, Desmond and Varlo, Charles, *The unfortunate husbandman: An account of the life and travels of a real farmer in Ireland, Scotland, England and America* (London, 1964).

Clay, Christopher, 'Landlords and estate management in England', in Joan Thirsk (ed.), *AHEW: 1640–1750 Vol. 5 / 2. Agrarian change* (Cambridge, 1985), 119–251.

Clow, Archibald and Clow, Nan L., *The chemical revolution: A contribution to social technology* (London, 1952).

Colclough, Stephen, *Consuming texts: Readers and reading communities, 1695–1870* (London, 2007).

Collins, E. J. T., 'Harvest technology and labour supply in Britain, 1790-1870', *EcHR*, 22:3 (1969), 453–73.

Collins, Harry and Evans, Robert, *Rethinking expertise* (Chicago, 2007).

Cooke, Kathy J., 'Expertise, book farming, and government agriculture: The origins of agricultural seed certification in the United States', *Agricultural History*, 76:3 (2002), 524–45.

Cooper, J. P., 'Ideas of gentility in early modern England', in G. E. Aylmer and J. S. Morrill (eds), *Land, men and beliefs: Studies in early-modern history* (London, 1983), 43–77.

Córdoba, Ricardo (ed.), *Craft treatises and handbooks: The dissemination of technical knowledge in the middle ages* (Turnhout, 2013).

Corfield, Penelope J., 'Class by name and number in eighteenth-century Britain', *History*, 72:234 (1987), 38–61.

Corfield, Penelope J., *Power and the professions in Britain 1700–1850* (London, 1995).

Corse, Taylor, 'Husbandry in Humphry Clinker, Tobias Smollett's georgic novel', *SEL Studies in English Literature 1500–1900*, 57:3 (2017), 583–603.

Crane, Mary Thomas, *Framing authority: Sayings, self, and society in sixteenth-century England* (Princeton, 1993).

Crawford, Rachel, 'English Georgic and British nationhood', *ELH*, 65:1 (1998), 123–58.

Cressy, David, *Literacy and the social order: Reading and writing in Tudor and Stuart England* (Cambridge, 2006).

Croot, Patricia, *The world of the small farmer: Tenure, profit and politics in the early modern somerset levels*, ed. Jane Whittle (Hertfordshire, 2017).

Curth, Louise Hill, 'The medical content of English almanacs 1640–1700', *Journal of the History of Medicine and Allied Sciences*, 60:3 (2005), 255–82.

Curth, Louise Hill, *English almanacs, astrology and popular medicine, 1550–1700* (Manchester, 2007).

Darnton, Robert, 'What is the history of books?', *Daedalus*, 111:3 (1982), 65–83.

Davids, Karel, 'Craft secrecy in Europe in the early modern period: A comparative view', *Early Science and Medicine*, 10:3 *Openness and secrecy in early modern science* (2005), 341–48.

Davidson, Neil, 'The Scottish path to capitalist agriculture 1: From the crisis of feudalism to the origins of agrarian transformation (1688–1746)', *Journal of Agrarian Change*, 4:3 (2004), 227–68.

Davidson, Neil, 'The Scottish path to capitalist agriculture 2: The capitalist offensive (1747–1815)', *Journal of Agrarian Change*, 4:4 (2004), 411–60.

Davidson, Neil, 'The Scottish path to capitalist agriculture 3: The enlightenment as the theory and practice of improvement', *Journal of Agrarian Change*, 5:1 (2005), 1–72.

Davies, Margaret, 'Country gentry and falling rents in the 1660s and 1670s', *Midland History*, 4:2 (1977), 86–96.

Davis, Natalie Zemon, 'Printing and the people', *Society and culture in early modern France: Eight essays* (Cambridge, 1975), 189–226.

De Bruyn, Frans, 'From Virgilian georgic to agricultural science: an instance in the transvaluation of literature in eighteenth-century Britain', in Albert J. Rivero (ed.), *Augustan subjects: Essays in honor of Martin C. Battestin* (London, 1997), 47–67.

De Bruyn, Frans, 'Reading Virgil's Georgics as a scientific text: The eighteenth-century debate between Jethro Tull and Stephen Switzer', *ELH*, 71:3 (2004), 661–89.

De Munck, Bert, 'Corpses, live models, and nature: assessing skills and knowledge before the industrial revolution (Case: Antwerp)', *Technology and Culture*, 51:2 (2010), 332–56.

De Pleijt, Alexandra M. and Weisdorf, Jacob L., 'Human capital formation from occupations: The "deskilling hypothesis" revisited', *Cliometrica*, 11:1 (2017), 1–30.

Dear, Peter, 'Mysteries of state, mysteries of nature: Authority, knowledge and expertise in the seventeenth century', in Sheila Jasanoff (ed.), *States of knowledge: The co-production of science and social order* (London, 2004), 206–24.

Dear, Peter, 'The meanings of experience', in Katharine Park and Lorraine Daston (eds), *Cambridge history of science: Vol 3: Early modern science* (Cambridge, 2006), 106–31.

Devine, Tom, *The transformation of rural Scotland: Social change and the agrarian economy, 1660–1815* (Edinburgh, 1994).

Dolan, Francis, *Digging the past: How and why to imagine seventeenth-century agriculture* (Philadelphia, 2019).

Donaldson, John, *Agricultural biography* (London, 1854).

Doody, Aude, 'Virgil the farmer? Critiques of the Georgics in Columella and Pliny', *Classical Philology*, 102:2 (2007), 180–97.

Doody, Aude, 'The authority of writing in Varro's *De Re Rustica*', in Jason König and Greg Woolf (eds), *Authority and expertise in ancient scientific culture* (Cambridge, 2017), 182–202.

Drayton, Richard, *Nature's government: Science, imperial Britain, and the 'improvement' of the world* (London, 2000).

Dreyfus, Hubert L. and Dreyfus, Stuart E., 'Peripheral vision expertise in real world contexts', *Organization studies*, 26:5 (2005), 779–92.

Driver, Martha W., 'When is a miscellany not miscellaneous? Making sense of the "Kalender of Shepherds"', *The Yearbook of English Studies*, 33: Medieval and Early Modern Miscellanies and Anthologies (2003), 199–214.

Dupré, Sven, 'Doing it wrong: The translation of artisanal knowledge and the codification of error', in Matteo Valleriani (ed.), *The structures of practical knowledge* (Switzerland, 2017), 167–88.

Dyer, Christopher, *Making a living in the middle ages: The people of Britain 850–1520* (New Haven, 2002).

Eamon, William, *Science and the secrets of nature: Books of secrets in medieval and early modern culture* (Princeton, 1994).

Eamon, William, 'How to read a book of secrets', in Elaine Leong and Alisha Rankin (eds), *Secrets and knowledge in medicine and science, 1500–1800* (Farnham, 2011), 23–46.

Eddy, M. D., 'Tools for reordering: Commonplacing and the space of words in Linnaeus's Philosophia Botanica', *Intellectual History Review*, 20:2 (2010), 227–52.

Eisenstein, Elizabeth, *The printing press as an agent of change* (Cambridge, 1979).

Eisinger, Chester E., 'The farmer in the eighteenth century almanac', *Agricultural History*, 28:3 (1954), 107–12.

Evans, George Ewart, *Ask the fellows who cut the hay* (London, 1956).

Everitt, Alan, 'Farm labourers', in Joan Thirsk (ed.), *AHEW: 1500–1640 Vol. 4* (Cambridge, 1967), 396–465.

Farr, James R., *Artisans in Europe, 1300–1914* (Cambridge, 2000).

Feingold, Richard, *Nature and society: Later eighteenth-century uses of the pastoral and georgic* (Hassocks, Sussex, 1978).

Fenton, Alexander, 'Skene of Hallyard's manuscript of Husbandrie', *AgHR*, 11:2 (1963), 65–81.

Filipiak, Jeffrey, 'The work of local culture: Wendell Berry and communities as the source of farming knowledge', *Agricultural History*, 85:2 (2011), 174–94.

Fissell, Mary and Cooter, Roger, 'Exploring natural knowledge: Science and the popular', in Roy Porter (ed.), *Cambridge history of science: Vol 4: Eighteenth-century science* (Cambridge, 2003), 129–58.

Fissell, Mary E., 'Readers, texts, and contexts: Vernacular medical works in early modern England', in Roy Porter (ed.), *The popularization of medicine 1650–1850* (London, 1992), 72–96.

Fitzgerald, Deborah Kay, 'Farmers deskilled: Hybrid corn and farmers' work', *Technology and Culture*, 34:2 (1993), 324–43.

Fitzgerald, Deborah Kay, *Every farm a factory: The industrial ideal in American agriculture* (New Haven, 2003).

Fitzherbert, H. C., Reginald, 'The authorship of the "Book of Husbandry" and the "Book of Surveying"', *English Historical Review*, 12:46 (1897), 225–36.

Fitzpatrick, Siobhán, 'Science, 1550–1800', in Raymond Gillespie and Andrew Hadfield (eds), *Oxford history of the Irish book, Vol III: The Irish book in English, 1550–1800* (Oxford, 2006), 335–46.

Flather, Amanda J., 'Space, place, and gender: the sexual and spatial division of labor in the early modern household', *History and Theory*, 52:3 (2013), 344–60.

Fox, Adam, *Oral and literate culture in England, 1500–1700* (Oxford, 2000).

Fox, Adam, 'Words, words, words: Education, literacy and print', in Keith Wrightson (ed.), *A social history of England, 1500–1750* (Cambridge, 2017), 129–51.

French, Henry and Hoyle, R. W., *The character of English rural society: Earls Colne, 1550–1750* (Manchester, 2007).

French, Henry R., 'The search for the "middle sort of people" in England, 1600–1800', *Historical Journal*, 43:1 (2000), 277–93.

French, Henry R., '"Gentlemen": Remaking the English ruling class', in Keith Wrightson (ed.), *A social history of England, 1500–1750* (Cambridge, 2017), 269–89.

Fusonie, Alan E., 'The agricultural literature of the gentleman farmer in the colonies', in Alan E. Fusonie and Leila Moran (eds), *Agricultural literature: Proud heritage – Future promise: A bicentennial symposium September 24–26 1975* (Washington, 1977), 33–55.

Fussell, G. E., 'Cuthbert Clark, an eighteenth-century book-farmer', *Journal of the Ministry of Agriculture*, 37 (1930), 571–74.

Fussell, G. E., 'John Wynn Baker: An "improver" in eighteenth century Ireland', *Agricultural History*, 5:4 (1931), 151–61.

Fussell, G. E., 'Early farming journals', *EcHR*, 3:3 (1932), 417–22.

Fussell, G. E., 'Farmers' calendars from Tusser to Arthur Young', *Economic History*, 2:8 (1933), 521–35.

Fussell, G. E., '"A Real Farmer" of eighteenth-century England and his book, "The Modern Farmers Guide"', *Agricultural History*, 17:4 (1943), 211–15.

Fussell, G. E., *The old English farming books from Fitzherbert to Tull 1523 to 1730* (London, 1947).

Fussell, G. E., 'Who was the "celebrated Thomas Hale"?', *Notes and Queries*, 192:17 (1947), 366–67.

Fussell, G. E., *More old English farming books from Tull to the Board of Agriculture, 1731 to 1793* (London, 1950).

Fussell, G. E., 'Rural reading in old time England', *Library Review*, 19:6 (1964), 405–8.

Fussell, G. E., *The classical tradition in West European farming* (Fairleigh, 1972).

Fussell, G. E., 'Agricultural science and experiment in the eighteenth century: An attempt at a definition', *AgHR*, 24:1 (1976), 44–47.

Fussell, G. E., 'Nineteenth-century farming encyclopedias: A note', *Agricultural History*, 55:1 (1981), 16–20.

Fussell, G. E., *The old English farming books, Vol III 1793–1839* (London, 1983).

Fussell, G. E., *The old English farming books, Vol IV 1840–1860* (London, 1984).

Fussell, G. E. and Fyrth, H., 'Eighteenth-century Scottish agricultural writings', *History*, 35:123–4 (1950), 49–63.

Gazley, John, *The life of Arthur Young, 1741–1820* (Philadelphia, 1973).

Glaisyer, Natasha, 'Readers, correspondents, and communities: John Houghton's "A Collection for Improvement of Husbandry and Trade" (1692–1703)', in Alexandra Shepard and Phil Withington (eds), *Communities in early modern England: Networks, place, rhetoric* (Manchester, 2000), 235–51.

Glaisyer, Natasha and Pennell, Sara, 'Introduction', in Natasha Glaisyer and Sara Pennell (eds), *Didactic literature in England, 1500–1800: Expertise constructed* (Aldershot, 2003), 1–18.

Goddard, Nicholas, 'The development and influence of agricultural periodicals and newspapers, 1780–1880', *AgHR*, 31:2 (1983), 116–31.

Goddard, Nicholas, *Harvests of change: The Royal Agricultural Society of England, 1838–1988* (London, 1988).

Goddard, Nicholas, 'Agricultural literature and societies', in G. E.Mingay (ed.), *AHEW: 1750–1850 Vol. 6* (Cambridge, 1989), 361–83.

Goddard, Nicholas, '"Not a reading class": The development of the Victorian agricultural textbook', *Paradigm*, 1:23 (1997), 12–21.

Goody, Jack and Watt, Ian, 'Consequences of literacy', *Comparative Studies in Society and History*, 5:3 (1963), 304–45.

Goodyear, F. R. D., 'Technical writing', in E. J. Kenney and W. V. Clausen (eds), *Cambridge history of classical literature Vol 2* (Cambridge, 1982), 667–73.

Griffiths, Elizabeth, 'Responses to adversity: The changing strategies of two Norfolk landowning families, c.1665–1700', in R. W. Hoyle (ed.), *People, landscape and alternative agriculture: Essays for Joan Thirsk* (Oxford, 2004), 74–92.

Griffiths, Elizabeth, '"A country life": Sir Hamon Le Strange of Hunstanton in Norfolk, 1583–1654', in R. W.Hoyle (ed.), *Custom, improvement and the landscape in early modern Britain* (Farnham, 2011), 203–34.

Gritt, A. J., 'The "survival" of service in the English agricultural labour force: Lessons from Lancashire, c.1650–1851', *AgHR*, 50:1 (2002), 25–50.

Gritt, A. J., 'The farming and domestic economy of a Lancashire smallholder: Richard Latham and the agricultural revolution, 1724–67', in Richard W.Hoyle (ed.), *The farmer in England, 1650–1980* (Farnham, 2013), 101–34.

Guéry, François and Deleule, Didier, *The productive body*, trans. Philip Barnard and Stephen Shapiro (Alresford, Hants, 2014).

Guichard, Charlotte, 'Connoisseurship and artistic expertise: London and Paris, 1600–1800', in Christelle Rabier (ed.), *Fields of expertise: A comparative history of expert procedures in Paris and London, 1600 to present* (Newcastle, 2007), 173–92.

Hainsworth, D. R., *Stewards, lords and people: The estate steward and his world in later Stuart England* (Cambridge, 1992).

Håkanson, L., 'Creating knowledge: The power and logic of articulation', *Industrial and Corporate Change*, 16:1 (2007), 51–88.

Harvey, Karen, *The little republic: Masculinity and domestic authority in eighteenth-century Britain* (Oxford, 2012).

Harvey, P. D. A., 'Agricultural treatises and manorial accounting in medieval England', *AgHR*, 20:2 (1972), 170–82.

Hasbach, Wilhelm, *A history of the English agricultural labourer*, trans. R. Kenyon (London, 1908).

Haslam, C. S. and Young, Arthur, *The biography of Arthur Young: From his birth until 1787* (Rugby, 1930).

Heal, Felicity and Holmes, Clive, *The gentry in England and Wales, 1500–1700* (London, 1994).

Hedrick, Ulysses P., 'What farmers read in western New York, 1800–1850', *New York History*, 17:3 (1936), 281–89.

Heinzelman, Kurt, 'The last georgic: Wealth of Nations and the scene of writing', in Stephen Copley and Kathryn Sutherland (eds), *Adam Smith's Wealth of Nations: New interdisciplinary essays* (Manchester, 1995), 171–94.

Hellawell, Philippa, '"The best and most practical philosophers": Seamen and the authority of experience in early modern science', *History of Science*, 58:1 (2019), 28–50.

Henrey, Blanche, *British botanical and horticultural literature before 1800*, 3 vols. (London, 1975).

Hindle, Steve, 'Work, reward and labour discipline in late seventeenth-century England', in A. Shepard, J. Walter, and S. Hindle (eds), *Remaking English society: Social relations and social change in early modern England* (Woodbridge, 2013), 255–80.

Hipkin, Stephen, 'Tenant farming and short-term leasing on Romney Marsh, 1587–1705', *EcHR*, 53:4 (2000), 646–76.

Hipkin, Stephen, 'The structure of landownership and land occupation in the Romney Marsh region, 1646–1834', *AgHR*, 51:1 (2003), 69–94.

Hobsbawm, E. J., 'Scottish reformers of the eighteenth century and capitalist agriculture', in E. J. Hobsbawm, Witold Kula, Ashok Mitra, K. N. Raj, and Ignacy Sachs (eds), *Peasants in history: Essays in honour of Daniel Thorner* (Oxford, 1980), 3–29.

Hodge, Joseph Morgan, *Triumph of the expert: Agrarian doctrines of development and the legacies of British colonialism* (Athens, 2007).

Hoffmann, Volker, Probst, Kirsten, and Christinck, Anja, 'Farmers and researchers: How can collaborative advantages be created in participatory research and technology development?', *Agriculture and Human values*, 24:3 (2007), 355–68.

Holmes, Heather, 'Scottish agricultural newspapers and journals and the industrialisation of agriculture, 1800–1880', *Folk Life*, 40:1 (2001), 25–38.

Holmes, Heather, 'Scottish agricultural writers and the creation of their personal identities between 1697 and 1790', *Folk Life*, 44:1 (2005), 87–109.

Holmes, Heather, 'The circulation of Scottish agricultural books during the eighteenth century', *AgHR*, 54:1 (2006), 45–78.

Holmes, Heather, 'Analysing a source of evidence for the purchase and ownership of Scottish books in the late eighteenth century: A comparison of three subscription lists in the agricultural books of David Young of Perth published in 1785, 1788 and 1790', *Folk Life*, 47:1 (2009), 32–50.

Holmes, Heather, 'The dissemination of agricultural knowledge 1700–1850', in Alexander Fenton and Kenneth Veitch (eds), *Scottish life and society: A compendium of Scottish ethnology: Vol 2 Farming and the land* (Edinburgh, 2011), 867–93.

Holmes, Heather, 'Agricultural pamphlets' & 'Agricultural publishing', in Stephen W.Brown and Warren McDougall (eds), *Enlightenment and expansion 1707–1800 (The Edinburgh history of the book in Scotland*, Vol. 2; (Edinburgh, 2012), 399–406, 503–9.

Holmes, Heather, 'Sir John Sinclair, the county agricultural surveys, and the collection and dissemination of knowledge 1793–1817, with a bibliography of the surveys: Part 1', *Journal of the Edinburgh Bibliographical Society*, 7 (2012), 29–63.

Holmes, Heather, 'Sir John Sinclair, the county agricultural surveys, and the collection and dissemination of knowledge 1793–1817, with a bibliography of the surveys: Part 2', *Journal of the Edinburgh Bibliographical Society*, 8 (2013), 67–136.

Hoppit, Julian (ed.), *Nehemiah Grew and England's economic development: The means of a most ample increase of the wealth and strength of England 1706–7* (Oxford, 2012).

Horn, Pamela, 'The contribution of the propagandist to eighteenth-century agricultural improvement', *Historical Journal*, 25:2 (1982), 313–29.

Horn, Pamela, 'An eighteenth-century land agent: The career of Nathaniel Kent (1737–1810)', *AgHR*, 30:1 (1982), 1–16.

Horn, Pamela, *William Marshall (1745–1818) and the Georgian countryside* (Abingdon, 1982).

Houghton, Walter E., 'The history of trades: Its relation to seventeenth-century thought: As seen in Bacon, Petty, Evelyn, and Boyle', *Journal of the History of Ideas*, 2:1 (1941), 33–60.

Houston, R. A., *Scottish literacy and the Scottish identity: Illiteracy and society in Scotland and Northern England, 1600–1800* (Cambridge, 1985), 43–61.

Howard, Emily Nichole, 'Grounds of knowledge: Unofficial epistemologies of British environmental writing, 1745–1835', PhD thesis (University of Michigan, 2015).

Howsam, Leslie, *Old books and new histories: An orientation to studies in book and print culture* (London, 2006).

Hoyle, R. W., 'Tenure and the land market in early modern England: Or a late contribution to the Brenner debate', *EcHR*, 43:1 (1990), 1–20.

Hoyle, R. W., 'Introduction: Custom, improvement and anti-improvement', in Richard W.Hoyle (ed.), *Custom, improvement and the landscape in early modern Britain* (Farnham, 2011), 1–38.

Hoyle, R. W., 'Rural economies under stress: "A world so altered"', in Susan Doran and Norman Jones (eds), *The Elizabethan world* (Abingdon, Oxfordshire, 2011), 439–57.

Hoyle, R. W., 'Introduction: Recovering the farmer', in Richard W.Hoyle (ed.), *The farmer in England, 1650–1980* (Farnham, 2013), 1–42.

Hoyles, Martin, *Gardeners delight: Gardening books from 1560 to 1960* (London, 1994).

Hudson, Kenneth, *Patriotism with profit: British agricultural societies in the eighteenth and nineteenth centuries* (London, 1972).

Hughes, E., 'The eighteenth century estate agent', in Henry Alfred Cronne, T. W. Moody, and D. B. Quinn (eds), *Essays in British and Irish History: In honour of James Eadie Todd* (London, 1949), 185–99.

Humphries, Jane, 'Enclosures, common rights, and women: The proletarianization of families in the late eighteenth and early nineteenth centuries', *The Journal of Economic History*, 50:1 (1990), 17–42.

Hunter, Lynette, 'Books for daily life: Household, husbandry, behaviour', in John Barnard and D. F. McKenzie (eds), *Cambridge history of the book in Britain Vol 4: 1557–1695* (Cambridge, 2002), 514–32.

Iliffe, Rob, 'Capitalizing expertise: Philosophical and artisanal expertise in early modern London', in Christelle Rabier (ed.), *Fields of expertise: A comparative history of expert procedures in Paris and London, 1600 to present* (Newcastle, 2007), 55–84.

Jackson, I. A. N., 'Approaches to the history of readers and reading in eighteenth-century Britain', *Historical Journal*, 47:4 (2004), 1041–54.

James, Frank A. J. L. '"Agricultural Chymistry is at present in it's infancy": The Board of Agriculture, The Royal Institution and Humphry Davy', *Ambix*, 62:4 (2015), 363–85.

Jessop, Bob, 'Knowledge as a fictitious commodity: Insights and limits of a Polanyian analysis', in A. Buğra and K. Ağartan (eds), *Reading Karl Polanyi for the 21st century: Market economy as a political project* (Basingstoke, 2007), 115–34.

Johns, Adrian, *The nature of the book: Print and knowledge in the making* (Chicago, 1998).

Johns, Adrian, 'Print and public science', in Roy Porter (ed.), *Cambridge history of science: Vol 4: Eighteenth-century science* (Cambridge, 2003), 536–60.

Johnson, Edgar Augustus J., 'The place of learning, science, vocational training, and "art" in pre-Smithian economic thought', *Journal of Economic History*, 24:2 (1964), 129–44.

Jones, E. L., 'Agriculture and economic growth in England, 1660–1750: Agricultural change', *Journal of Economic History*, 25:1 (1965), 1–18.

Jones, Jean, 'James Hutton's agricultural research and his life as a farmer', *Annals of Science*, 42:6 (1985), 573–601.

Jones, Peter M., *Agricultural enlightenment: Knowledge, technology, and nature, 1750–1840* (Oxford, 2016).

Kaufman, Paul, *Borrowings from the Bristol Library, 1773–1784, a unique record of reading vogues* (Charlottesville, 1960).

Kavey, Allison, *Books of secrets: Natural philosophy in England, 1550–1600* (Chicago, 2007).

Kaye, Barrington, *The development of the architectural profession in England: A sociological study* (London, 1960).

Keibek, S. A. J., 'By-employments in early modern England and their significance for estimating historical male occupational structures', *Cambridge Working Papers in Economic and Social History*, 29 (2017).

Keibek, S. A. J., 'The male occupational structure of England and Wales, 1600–1850', PhD thesis (University of Cambridge, 2017).

Keibek, S. A. J. and Shaw-Taylor, Leigh, 'Early modern rural by-employments: A re-examination of the probate inventory evidence', *AgHR*, 61:2 (2013), 244–81.

Keiser, George R., 'Practical books for the gentleman', in Lotte Hellinga and J. B. Trapp (eds), *Cambridge history of the book in Britain Vol 3: 1400–1557* (Cambridge, 1999), 470–94.

Kennedy, Máire, 'Botany in print: Books and their readers in eighteenth century Dublin', *Dublin Historical Record*, 68:2 (2015), 193–205.

Kerridge, Eric, *The agricultural revolution* (New York, 1967).

King, Peter, 'Customary rights and women's earnings: The importance of gleaning to the rural labouring poor, 1750–1850', *EcHR*, 44:3 (1991), 461–76.

Klein, Ursula, 'Artisanal-scientific experts in eighteenth-century France and Germany', *Annals of Science*, 69:3 (2012), 303–6.

Klein, Ursula, 'Hybrid experts', in Matteo Valleriani (ed.), *The structures of practical knowledge* (Switzerland, 2017), 287–306.

Klein, Ursula and Spary, Emma C. (eds), *Materials and expertise in early modern Europe: Between market and laboratory* (Chicago, 2010).

Koepp, Cynthia J., 'The alphabetical order: Work in Diderot's Encyclopédie', in Steven Laurence Kaplan and Cynthia J Koepp (eds), *Work in France: Representations, meaning, organization, and practice* (London, 1986), 229–57.

Krzywoszynska, Anna, 'What farmers know: Experiential knowledge and care in vine growing', *Sociologia Ruralis*, 56:2 (2016), 289–310.

Kussmaul, Ann, *Servants in husbandry in early modern England* (Cambridge, 1981).

Kusukawa, Sachiko and Maclean, Ian, *Transmitting knowledge: Words, images, and instruments in early modern Europe* (Oxford, 2006).

Lane, Joan, *Apprenticeship in England, 1600–1914* (London, 1996).

Langford, Paul, *A polite and commercial people: England, 1727–1783* (Oxford, 1989).

Lehmann, William C., *Henry Home, Lord Kames, and the Scottish Enlightenment: A study in national character and in the history of ideas* (The Hague, 1971).

Lennard, Reginald, 'English agriculture under Charles II: The evidence of the Royal Society's "Enquiries"', *EcHR*, 4:1 (1932), 23–45.

Leong, Elaine and Rankin (eds), *Secrets and knowledge in medicine and science, 1500–1800* (Farnham, 2011).

Leslie, Michael and Raylor, Timothy, 'Introduction', in Michael Leslie and Timothy Raylor (eds), *Culture and cultivation in early modern England: Writing and the land* (Leicester, 1992), 1–12.

Lis, Catharina and Soly, Hugo, *Worthy efforts: Attitudes to work and workers in pre-industrial Europe* (Leiden, 2012).

Long, Pamela O., 'Power, patronage, and the authorship of *ars*: From mechanical know-how to mechanical knowledge in the last scribal age', *Isis*, 88:1 (1997), 1–41.

Long, Pamela O., *Openness, secrecy, authorship: Technical arts and the culture of knowledge from antiquity to the renaissance* (Baltimore, 2001).

Long, Pamela O., *Artisans/practitioners and the rise of the new sciences 1400–1600* (Oregon, 2011).

Low, Anthony, *The georgic revolution* (Princeton, 1985).

Lowry, S. Todd, 'The agricultural foundation of the seventeenth-century English oeconomy', *History of Political Economy*, 35:5 (2003), 74–100.

Lundström, Christina and Lindblom, Jessica, 'Considering farmers' situated expertise in using AgriDSS to fostering sustainable farming practices in precision agriculture', *Proceedings of the 13th International Conference on Precision Agriculture* (31 July–3 August 2016, St. Louis, MO, USA).

Lyon, Fergus, 'How farmers research and learn: The case of arable farmers of East Anglia, UK', *Agriculture and Human values*, 13:4 (1996), 39–47.

MacDonald, Stuart, 'Agricultural improvement and the neglected labourer', *AgHR*, 31:2 (1983), 81–90.

Maddern, Philippa, 'Gentility', in Raluca Radulescu and Alison Truelove (eds), *Gentry Culture in Late Medieval England* (Manchester, 2005), 18–34.

Marglin, Stephen A., 'What do bosses do?: The origins and functions of hierarchy in capitalist production', *Review of Radical Political Economics*, 6:2 (1974), 60–112.

Marglin, Stephen A., 'Knowledge and power', in Frank H.Stephen (ed.), *Firms, organization and labour: Approaches to the economics of work organization* (London, 1984), 146–64.

Marglin, Stephen A., 'Losing touch: The cultural conditions of worker accommodation and resistance', in Frédérique Apffel-Marglin and Stephen A. Marglin (eds), *Dominating knowledge: Development, culture and resistance* (Oxford, 1990), 217–82.

Marglin, Stephen A., 'Farmers, seedsmen, and scientists: Systems of agriculture and systems of knowledge', in Frédérique Apffel-Marglin and Stephen A. Marglin (eds), *Decolonizing knowledge: From development to dialogue* (Oxford, 1996), 185–248.

Matei, Oana, 'Husbanding creation and the technology of amelioration in the works of Gabriel Plattes', *Society and Politics*, 7:1 (2013), 84–102.

Marx, Karl, *Capital: A critique of political economy: Volume I*, trans. Ben Fowkes (London, 1990).

McDonagh, Briony, '"All towards the improvements of the estate": Mrs Elizabeth Prowse at Wicken (Northamptonshire), 1764–1810', in Richard W. Hoyle (ed.), *Custom, improvement and the landscape in early modern Britain* (Farnham, 2011), 263–88.

McDonagh, Briony, *Elite women and the agricultural landscape, 1700–1830* (London, 2018).

McDonagh, Briony and Daniels, Stephen, 'Enclosure stories: Narratives from Northamptonshire', *Cultural Geographies*, 19:1 (2012), 107–21.

McDonald, Donald, *Agricultural writers, from Sir Walter of Henley to Arthur Young, 1200–1800* (London, 1908).

McKenzie, Donald Francis, *Bibliography and the sociology of texts* (Cambridge, 1999).

McLaren, Dorothy Kathleen, 'By the book? Farming manuals, animal breeding and "agricultural revolution"', MA thesis (University of British Columbia, 1991).

McLean, Tom, 'The measurement and management of human performance in seventeenth century English farming: The case of Henry Best', *Accounting Forum*, 33:1 (2009), 62–73.

McRae, Andrew, *God speed the plough: The representation of agrarian England, 1500–1660* (Cambridge, 1996).

Merrett, Robert James, 'The gentleman farmer in Emma: Agrarian writing and Jane Austen's cultural idealism', *University of Toronto Quarterly*, 77:2 (2008), 711–37.

Mingay, G. E., *English landed society in the eighteenth century* (London, 1963).

Mingay, G. E., 'The eighteenth-century land steward', in E. L. Jones and G. E. Mingay (eds), *Land, labour and population in the industrial revolution: Essays presented to J. D. Chambers* (London, 1967), 3–27.

Mingay, G. E., *The gentry: The rise and fall of a ruling class* (London, 1976).

Mingay, G. E., *The agricultural revolution: Changes in agriculture, 1650–1880* (London, 1977).

Mingay, G. E. and Young, Arthur, *Arthur Young and his times* (London, 1975).

Minkler, Alanson, 'Knowledge and internal organization', *Journal of Economic Behaviour and Organisation*, 21:1 (1993), 17–30.

Mitch, David, 'Learning by doing among Victorian farmworkers: A case study in the biological and cognitive foundations of skill acquisition', *LSE Working Papers in Economic History*, No. 16 (February 1994).

Mitchison, Rosalind, *Agricultural Sir John: The life of Sir John Sinclair of Ulbster 1754–1835* (London, 1962).

Mokyr, Joel, *The gifts of Athena: Historical origins of the knowledge economy* (Princeton, 2002).

Mokyr, Joel, 'The intellectual origins of modern economic growth', *Journal of Economic History*, 65:2 (2005), 285–351.

Mokyr, Joel, *The enlightened economy: Britain and the industrial revolution 1700–1850* (London, 2009).

Moss, Ann, *Printed commonplace-books and the structuring of Renaissance thought* (Oxford, 1996).

Moulier-Boutang, Yann, *Cognitive capitalism* (Cambridge, 2011).

Mukherjee, Ayesha, '*Floræs Paradise*: Hugh Platt and the economy of early modern gardening', *Seventeenth Century*, 25:1 (2010), 1–26.

Mukherjee, Ayesha, 'The secrets of Sir Hugh Plat', in Elaine Leong and Alisha Rankin (eds), *Secrets and knowledge in medicine and science, 1500–1800* (Farnham, 2011), 69–86.

Muldrew, Craig, *Food, energy and the creation of industriousness: Work and material culture in agrarian England, 1550–1780* (Cambridge, 2011).

Munroe, Jennifer, 'Gender, class, and the art of gardening: Gardening manuals in early modern England', *Prose Studies*, 28:2 (2006), 197–210.

Myrdal, Janken, 'Agricultural literature in Scandinavia and Anglo-Saxon countries, 1700–1800 as indicator of changed mentality', *Knowledge networks in rural Europe since 1700* (University of Leuven, Belgium, 27–29 August 2014), unpublished conference paper.

Myrdal, Janken, 'Agricultural literature in Eurasia circa 200 BCE – 1500 CE', *Stockholm Papers in Economic History No. 15* (2014).

Nangle, Benjamin Christie, *The monthly review: First series 1749–1789: Indexes of contributors and articles* (Oxford, 1934).

Neeson, Jeanette M., 'The opponents of enclosure in eighteenth-century Northamptonshire', *Past & Present*, 105:1 (1984), 114–39.

Neeson, Jeanette M., *Commoners: Common right, enclosure and social change in England, 1700–1820* (Cambridge, 1996).

Ochs, Kathleen H., 'The Royal Society of London's history of trades programme: An early episode in applied science', *Notes and Records*, 39:2 (1985), 129–58.

O'Day, Rosemary, *The professions in early modern England, 1450–1800: Servants of the commonweal* (Harlow, 2000).

Ong, Walter, *Ramus, method, and the decay of dialogue: From the art of discourse to the art of reason* (Cambridge, MA, 2004).

Orde, Anne (ed.), *Matthew and George Culley: Travel journals and letters, 1765–1798* (Oxford, 2002).

Ormrod, David, 'Agrarian capitalism and merchant capitalism: Tawney, Dobb, Brenner and beyond', in Jane Whittle (ed.), *Landlords and tenants in Britain, 1440–1660: Tawney's Agrarian Problem revisited* (Woodbridge, 2013), 200–15.

Oschinsky, Dorothea, *Walter of Henley and other treatises on estate management and accounting* (Oxford, 1971).

Overton, Mark, 'The diffusion of agricultural innovations in early modern England: Turnips and clover in Norfolk and Suffolk, 1580–1740', *Transactions of the Institute of British Geographers*, 10:2 (1985), 205–21.

Overton, Mark, *Agricultural revolution in England: The transformation of the agrarian economy, 1500–1850* (Cambridge, 1996).

Ovitt, George, 'The status of the mechanical arts in medieval classifications of learning', *Viator*, 14:1 (1983), 89–105.

Pagano, Ugo, 'The crisis of intellectual monopoly capitalism', *Cambridge Journal of Economics*, 38:6 (2014), 1409–29.

Pannabecker, John R., 'Diderot, the mechanical arts, and the *Encyclopédie*: In search of the heritage of technology education', *Journal of Technology Education*, 6:1 (1994), 45–57.

Pennell, Sara, 'Perfecting practice? Women, manuscript recipes and knowledge in early modern England', in Victoria E. Burke and Jonathan Gibson (eds), *Early modern women's manuscript writing: Selected papers from the Trinity/Trent colloquium* (Abingdon, Oxfordshire, 2004), 237–58.

Perkins, W. Frank, *British and Irish writers on agriculture* (3rd edn; Lymington, 1939).

Perry, Ruth, *Novel relations: The transformation of kinship in English literature and culture, 1748–1818* (Cambridge, 2009).

Peters, Scott J., '"Every farmer should be awakened": Liberty Hyde Bailey's vision of agricultural extension work', *Agricultural History*, 80:2 (2006), 190–219.

Picciotto, Joanna, *Labors of innocence in early modern England* (Cambridge, MA, 2010).

Pickstone, John, 'Science in nineteenth-century England: Plural configurations and singular politics', in Martin Daunton (ed.), *The organisation of knowledge in Victorian Britain* (Oxford, 2005), 29–60.

Polanyi, Michael, *The tacit dimension* (London, 1983).

Popplow, Marcus, 'Economizing agricultural resources in the German economic enlightenment', in Ursula Klein and Emma C. Spary (eds), *Materials and expertise in early modern Europe: Between market and laboratory* (Chicago, 2010), 261–87.

Popplow, Marcus, 'Knowledge management to exploit agrarian resources as part of late-eighteenth-century cultures of innovation: Friedrich Casimir Medicus and Franz von Paula Schrank', *Annals of Science*, 69:3 (2012), 413–33.

Porter, J. H., 'The development of rural society', in G. E. Mingay (ed.), *AHEW: 1750–1850 Vol. 6* (Cambridge, 1989), 836–65.

Porter, Roy, *Health for sale: Quackery in England, 1660–1850* (Manchester, 1989).

Porter, Roy, *Enlightenment: Britain and the creation of the modern world* (London, 2001).

Pretty, Jules N., 'Farmers' extension practice and technology adaptation: Agricultural revolution in 17–19th century Britain', *Agriculture and Human Values*, 8:1 (1991), 132–48.

Prothero, Rowland Edmund (Baron Ernle), *English farming, past and present* (London, 1912).

Purcell, Mark, 'Books and readers in eighteenth-century Westmorland: The Brownes of Townend', *Library History*, 17:2 (2013), 91–106.

Rabier, Christelle (ed.), *Fields of expertise: A comparative history of expert procedures in Paris and London, 1600 to present* (Newcastle, 2007).

Rattansi, Ali, *Marx and the division of labour* (London, 1982).

Raven, James, 'New reading histories, print culture and the identification of change: The case of eighteenth-century England', *Social History*, 23:3 (1998), 268–87.

Raven, James, *The business of books: Booksellers and the English book trade 1450–1850* (London, 2007).

Raven, James, 'Debating bibliomania and the collection of books in the eighteenth century', *Library & Information History*, 29 (2013).

Raven, James, *Publishing business in eighteenth-century England* (Woodbridge, 2014).

Raven, James, *What is the history of the book?* (Cambridge, 2018).

Renault, Emmanuel, 'Work and Domination in Marx', *Critical Horizons*, 15:2 (2014), 179–93.

Reyes-García, Victoria, Benyei, Petra, and Calvet-Mir, Laura, 'Traditional agricultural knowledge as a commons', in Jose Luis Vivero-Pol, Tomaso Ferrando, Olivier De Schutter, and Ugo Mattei (eds), *Routledge handbook of food as a commons* (London, 2018), 173–84.

Reynolds, Melissa, '"Here is a good boke to lerne": Practical books, the coming of the press, and the search for knowledge, ca. 1400–1560', *Journal of British Studies*, 58:2 (2019), 259–88.

Rhodes, Joshua, 'Subletting in eighteenth-century England: A new methodological approach', *AgHR*, 66:1 (2018), 67–92.

Richards, Paul, *Indigenous agricultural revolution: Ecology and food production in West Africa* (London, 1985).

Richards, Stewart, '"Masters of Arts and Bachelors of Barley": The struggle for agricultural education in mid-nineteenth-century Britain', *History of Education*, 12:3 (1983), 161–75.

Roberts, Lissa, Schaffer, Simon, and Dear, Peter (eds), *The mindful hand: Inquiry and invention from the late renaissance to industrialization* (Chicago, 2007).

Roberts, Michael, 'Sickles and scythes: Women's work and men's work at harvest time', *History Workshop*, 7:1 (1979), 3–28.

Roberts, Michael, '"Waiting upon chance": English hiring fairs and their meanings from the 14th to the 20th century', *Journal of Historical Sociology*, 1:2 (1988), 119–60.

Robson, Elly, 'Improvement and epistemologies of landscape in seventeenth-century English forest enclosure', *Historical Journal*, 60:3 (2016), 597–632.

Rosenheim, James M., *The emergence of a ruling order: English landed society 1650–1750* (London, 1998).

Rule, John, 'The property of skill in the period of manufacture', in Patrick Joyce (ed.), *The history meanings of work* (Cambridge, 1989), 99–118.

Russell, John, *A history of agricultural science in Great Britain 1620–1954* (London, 1966).

Sapoznik, Alexandra, 'Resource allocation and peasant decision making: Oakington, Cambridgeshire, 1360–99', *AgHR*, 61:2 (2013), 187–205.

Sapoznik, Alexandra, 'Britain, 1000–1750', in Erik Thoen and Tim Soens (eds), *Struggling with the environment: Land use and productivity* (Rural Economy and Society in North-western Europe, 500–2000; Turnhout, 2016), 71–108.

Savoia, Paolo, 'Cheesemaking in the scientific revolution: A seventeenth-century Royal Society report on dairy products and the history of European knowledge', *Nuncius*, 34:2 (2019), 427–55.

Sayce, Roger, *The history of the Royal Agricultural College, Cirencester* (Gloucestershire, 1992).

Sayre, Laura B., 'Farming by the book: British georgic in prose and practice, 1697–1820', PhD thesis (Princeton University, 2002).

Sayre, Laura B., 'The pre-history of soil science: Jethro Tull, the invention of the seed drill, and the foundations of modern agriculture', *Physics and Chemistry of the Earth*, 35:15 (2010), 851–59.

Schaffer, Simon, 'The earth's fertility as a social fact in early modern England', in Mikulas Teich, Roy Porter, and Bo Gustafsson (eds), *Nature and society in historical context* (Cambridge, 1997), 124–47.

Schaffer, Simon, 'Enlightenment brought down to earth', *History of Science*, 41:3 (2003), 257–68.

Schotte, Margaret E., *Sailing school: Navigating science and skill, 1550–1800* (Baltimore, 2019).

Scott, James C., *Weapons of the weak: Everyday forms of peasant resistance* (London, 1985).

Scott, James C., *Domination and the arts of resistance: Hidden transcripts* (London, 1990).

Scott, James C., *Seeing like a state: How certain schemes to improve the human condition have failed* (London, 1998).

Segers, Yves and Van Molle, Leen, 'Introduction: Knowledge networks in rural Europe. Theories, concepts and historiographies', *Knowledge networks in rural Europe since 1700* (University of Leuven, Belgium, 27–29 August 2014), unpublished conference paper.

Shapin, Steven, 'The invisible technician', *American scientist*, 77:6 (1989), 554–63.

Shapin, Steven, '"A scholar and a gentleman": The problematic identity of the scientific practitioner in early modern England', *History of Science*, 29:3 (1991), 279–327.

Shapin, Steven, *A social history of truth: Civility and science in seventeenth-century England* (Chicago, 1994).

Shapin, Steven, 'Trusting George Cheyne: Scientific expertise, common sense, and moral authority in early eighteenth-century dietetic medicine', *Bulletin of the History of Medicine*, 77:2 (2003), 263–97.

Sharpe, Pamela, *Adapting to capitalism: Working women in the English economy, 1700–1850* (London, 1996).

Shaw-Taylor, Leigh, 'Labourers, cows, common rights and Parliamentary Enclosure: The evidence of contemporary comment c.1760–1810', *Past & Present*, 171:1 (2001), 95–126.

Shaw-Taylor, Leigh, 'Parliamentary enclosure and the emergence of an English agricultural proletariat', *The Journal of Economic History*, 61:3 (2001), 640–62.

Shaw-Taylor, Leigh, 'The rise of agrarian capitalism and the decline of family farming in England', *EcHR*, 65:1 (2012), 26–60.

Shaw-Taylor, Leigh and Wrigley, E. A., 'Occupational structure and population change', in Roderick Floud, Jane Humphries, and Paul Johnson (eds), *The Cambridge economic history of modern Britain: Volume I: 1700–1870* (Cambridge, 2014), 53–88.

Shepard, Alexandra, *Accounting for oneself: Worth, status, and the social order in early modern England* (Oxford, 2015).

Shiva, Vandana, *Biopiracy: The plunder of nature and knowledge* (Berkeley, 1998).

Slack, Paul, *The invention of improvement: Information and material progress in seventeenth-century England* (Oxford, 2015).

Smith, Pamela H., *The body of the artisan: Art and experience in the scientific revolution* (Chicago, 2004).

Smith, Pamela H., 'Craft techniques and how-to books', in Mark Clarke, Bert de Munck, and Sven Dupré (eds), *Transmission of artists' knowledge* (Belgium, 2011), 75–84.

Smith, Pamela H., 'Secrets and craft knowledge in early modern Europe', in Elaine Leong and Alisha Rankin (eds), *Secrets and knowledge in medicine and science, 1500–1800* (Farnham, 2011).

Smith, Pamela H. and Schmidt, Benjamin (eds), *Making knowledge in early modern Europe: Practices, objects, and texts, 1400–1800* (Chicago, 2007).

Smith, P. H., Meyers, A. R. W., and Cook, H. J. (eds), *Ways of making and knowing: The material culture of empirical knowledge* (Ann Arbor, US, 2014).

Smout, T. C., 'A new look at the Scottish improvers', *Scottish Historical Review*, 91:1 (2012), 125–49.

Snell, Keith, *Annals of the labouring poor: Social change and agrarian England, 1660–1900* (Cambridge, 1987).

Sohn-Rethal, Alfred, *Intellectual and manual labour: A critique of epistemology* (New Jersey, 1978).

Somers, Margaret R., 'The "misteries" of property: Relationality, rural industrialization, and community in Chartist narratives of political rights', in John Brewer and Susan Staves (eds), *Early modern conceptions of property* (London, 1995), 63–92.

Sørensen, Esben Bøgh, 'To be bold of one's own: Agrarian capitalism and household management in Thomas Tusser's Five Hundred points of good husbandry', *Cultural and Social History*, 18:2 (2021), 133–61.

Spaeth, Barbette Stanley, *The Roman goddess Ceres* (Austin, 1996).

Spedding, Patrick, '"The new machine": Discovering the limits of ECCO', *Eighteenth-Century Studies*, 44:4 (2011), 437–53.

Spencer, David, 'Braverman and the contribution of labour process analysis to the critique of capitalist production – Twenty-five years on', *Work, Employment & Society*, 14:2 (2000), 223–43.

Spufford, Margaret, *Small books and pleasant histories: Popular fiction and its readership in seventeenth-century England* (Cambridge, 1985).

Spurr, M. S., 'Agriculture and the Georgics', *Greece and Rome*, 33:2 (1986), 164–87.

Stafford, William, 'Representations of the social order in *The Gentleman's Magazine*, 1785–1815', *Eighteenth-Century Life*, 33:2 (2009), 64–91.

Stehr, Nico, 'Experts, counsellors and advisers', in Nico Stehr and Richard V. Ericson (eds), *The culture and power of knowledge in modern society: Inquiries into contemporary societies* (Berlin, 1992), 107–55.

Suarez, Michael, 'Towards a bibliometric analysis of the surviving record, 1701–1800', in Michael F. Suarez and Michael L. Turner (eds), *Cambridge history of the book in Britain Vol 5: 1695–1830* (Cambridge, 2014), 514–32.

Sullivan, Richard J., 'Measurement of English farming technological change, 1523–1900', *Explorations in economic history*, 21:3 (1984), 270–89.

Sullivan, Richard J., 'The timing and pattern of technological development in English agriculture, 1611–1850', *Journal of Economic History*, 45:2 (1985), 305–14.

Symon, J. A., 'Diffusion of agricultural knowledge', *Transactions of the Highland and Agricultural Society of Scotland*, 5th series, 1 (1956), 1–19.

Tarlow, Sarah, *The archaeology of improvement in Britain, 1750–1850* (Cambridge, 2007).

Tawney, R. H., *The agrarian problem in the sixteenth century* (London, 1912).

Tawney, R. H., 'The rise of the gentry, 1558–1640', *EcHR*, 11:1 (1941), 1–38.

Taylor, Frederick, *The principles of scientific management* (London, 1914).

Tebeaux, Elizabeth, *The emergence of a tradition: Technical writing in the English Renaissance, 1475–1640* (New York, 1997).

Tebeaux, Elizabeth, 'English agriculture and estate management instructions, 1200–1700: From orality to textuality to modern instructions', *Technical Communication Quarterly*, 19:4 (2010), 352–78.

Thaczyk, Viktoria, '"Which cannot be sufficiently described by my pen." The codification of knowledge in theater engineering, 1480–1680', in Matteo Valleriani (ed.), *The structures of practical knowledge* (Switzerland, 2017), 77–114.

Thirsk, Joan, 'Younger sons in the seventeenth century', *History*, 54:182 (1969), 358–77.

Thirsk, Joan, 'Plough and pen: Agricultural writers in the seventeenth century', in T. H.Aston, P. R.Cross, Christopher Dyer, and Joan Thirsk (eds), *Social relations and ideas: Essays in honour of R.H. Hilton* (Cambridge, 1983), 295–318.

Thirsk, Joan, *The rural economy of England: Collected essays* (London, 1984).

Thirsk, Joan, 'Agricultural innovations and their diffusion', in Joan Thirsk (ed.), *AHEW: 1640–1750 Vol 5 / 2. Agrarian change* (Cambridge, 1985), 533–89.

Thirsk, Joan, 'Making a fresh start: Sixteenth-century agriculture and the classical inspiration', in Michael Leslie and Timothy Raylor (eds), *Culture and cultivation in early modern England: Writing and the land* (Leicester, 1992), 15–34.

Thirsk, Joan, 'The world-wide farming web, 1500–1800', in John Broad (ed.), *A common agricultural heritage? Revising French and British rural divergence* (Exeter, 2009), 13–22.

Thomas, Keith, *Man and the natural world: Changing attitudes in England 1500–1800* (London, 1983).

Thompson, E. P., *Customs in common* (New York, 1991).

Thompson, F. M. L., *English landed society in the nineteenth century* (London, 1963).

Thompson, F. M. L., 'The social distribution of landed property in England since the sixteenth century', *EcHR*, 19:3 (1966), 505–17.

Thompson, F. M. L., 'The second agricultural revolution, 1815–1880', *EcHR*, 21:1 (1968), 62–77.

Tinel, Bruno, 'Why and how do capitalists divide labour? From Marglin and back again through Babbage and Marx', *Review of Political Economy*, 25:2 (2013), 254–72.

Towsey, Mark, '"Store their minds with much valuable knowledge": Agricultural improvement at the Selkirk Subscription Library, 1799–1814', *Journal for Eighteenth-Century Studies*, 38:4 (2015), 569–84.

Tribe, Keith, *Land, labour and economic discourse* (London, 1978).

Tribe, Keith, *Genealogies of capitalism* (Atlantic Highlands, NJ, 1981).

Turner, Michael, 'The demise of the yeoman, c.1750–1940', in John Broad (ed.), *A common agricultural heritage? Revising French and British rural divergence* (Exeter, 2009), 55–67.

Turner, M. E., Beckett, J. V., and Afton, B., *Farm production in England, 1700–1914* (Oxford, 2001).

Turner, M. E., Beckett, J. V., and Afton, B., *Agricultural rent in England, 1690–1914* (Cambridge, 2004).

Valenze, Deborah, 'The art of women and the business of men: Women's work and the dairy industry c.1740–1840', *Past & Present*, 130:1 (1991), 142–69.

Valenze, Deborah, *The first industrial woman* (Oxford, 1995).

Valleriani, Matteo, 'The epistemology of practical knowledge', in Matteo Valleriani (ed.), *The structures of practical knowledge* (Switzerland, 2017), 1–19.

Van Trijp, Didi, 'Fresh fish: Observation up close in late seventeenth-century England', *Notes and Records*, 75:3 (2020), 311–32.

Vercellone, Carlo, 'From formal subsumption to general intellect: Elements for a Marxist reading of the thesis of cognitive capitalism', *Historical Materialism*, 15:1 (2007), 13–36.

Verdon, Nicola, *Rural women workers in nineteenth-century England: Gender, work and wages* (Woodbridge, 2002).

Verdon, Nicola, '"… Subjects deserving of the highest praise": Farmers' wives and the farm economy in England, c.1700–1850', *AgHR*, 51:1 (2003), 23–39.

Verdon, Nicola, *Working the land: A history of the farmworker in England from 1850 to the present day* (London, 2017).

Wade-Martins, Susanna, *Farmers, landlords and landscapes: Rural Britain, 1720 to 1870* (Macclesfield, 2004).

Wall, Wendy, 'Renaissance national husbandry: Gervase Markham and the publication of England', *Sixteenth Century Journal*, 27:3 (1996), 767–85.

Wallace, Andrew, 'Virgil and Bacon in the schoolroom', *ELH*, 73:1 (2006), 161–85.

Wallis, Patrick, Colson, Justin, and Chilosi, David, 'Structural change and economic growth in the British economy before the Industrial Revolution, 1500–1800', *Journal of Economic History*, 78:3 (2018), 862–903.

Warde, Paul, 'The idea of improvement, c.1520–1700', in R. W. Hoyle (ed.), *Custom, improvement and the landscape in early modern Britain* (Farnham, 2011).

Warde, Paul, 'The invention of sustainability', *Modern Intellectual History*, 8:1 (2011), 153–70.

Warde, Paul, *The invention of sustainability: Nature, human action, and destiny, 1500–1870* (Cambridge, 2018).

Warren, Dennis M., Slikkerveer, L. Jan, and Brokensha, David (eds), *The cultural dimension of development: Indigenous knowledge systems* (London, 1995).

Watson, J. A. S. and Amery, G. D., 'Early Scottish agricultural writers', *Transactions of the Highland and Agricultural Society of Scotland*, 43 (1931), 60–85.

Wear, Andrew, *Knowledge and practice in English medicine, 1550–1680* (Cambridge, 2000).

Weatherill, Lorna (ed.), *Account book of Richard Latham, 1724–1767* (Oxford, 1990).

Webster, Charles, *The great instauration: Science, medicine and reform, 1626–1660* (London, 1975).

Webster, Sarah, 'Estate improvement and the professionalisation of land agents on the Egremont estates in Sussex and Yorkshire, 1770–1835', *Rural History*, 18:1 (2007), 47–69.

Whitney, Elspeth, 'Paradise restored. The mechanical arts from antiquity through the thirteenth century', *Transactions of the American Philosophical Society*, 80:1 (1990), 1–169.

Whitt, Laurie Anne, 'Biocolonialism and the commodification of knowledge', *Science as Culture*, 7:1 (1998), 33–67.

Whittle, Jane, *The development of agrarian capitalism: Land and labour in Norfolk 1440–1580* (Oxford, 2000).

Whittle, Jane, 'Housewives and servants in rural England, 1440–1650: Evidence of women's work from probate documents', *Transactions of the Royal Historical Society*, 15 (2005), 51–74.

Whittle, Jane (ed.), *Landlords and tenants in Britain, 1440–1660: Tawney's Agrarian Problem revisited* (Woodbridge, 2013).

Whittle, Jane, 'Land and people', in Keith Wrightson (ed.), *A social history of England, 1500–1750* (Cambridge, 2017), 152–73.

Whittle, Jane, 'A different pattern of employment: Servants in rural England c.1500–1660', in Jane Whittle (ed.), *Rural servants in Europe 1400–1900* (Woodbridge, 2017), 57–76.

Whittle, Jane and Griffiths, Elizabeth, *Consumption and gender in the early seventeenth-century household: The world of Alice Le Strange* (Oxford, 2012).

Whittle, Jane and Hailwood, Mark, 'The gender division of labour in early modern England', *EcHR*, 73:1 (2020), 3–32.

Whyman, Susan, *The pen and the people: English letter writers 1660–1800* (Oxford, 2009).

Willes, Margaret, *The making of the English gardener: Plants, books and inspiration, 1560–1660* (London, 2011).

Williams, Raymond, *The country and the city* (New York, 1973).

Williamson, Tom, 'Understanding enclosure', *Landscapes*, 1:1 (2000), 56–79.

Wilmot, Sarah, '*The business of improvement*: Agriculture and scientific culture in Britain, c.1770–c.1870* (Bristol, 1990).

Withers, Charles W. J., 'William Cullen's agricultural lectures and writings and the development of agricultural science in eighteenth-century Scotland', *AgHR*, 37:2 (1989), 144–56.

Withers, Charles W. J., 'On georgics and geology: James Hutton's "Elements of Agriculture" and agricultural science in eighteenth-century Scotland', *AgHR*, 42:1 (1994), 38–48.

Wood, Andy, *The memory of the people: Custom and popular senses of the past in early modern England* (Cambridge, 2013).

Wood, Ellen Meiksins, *The origin of capitalism: A longer view* (London, 2002).

Woodward, S. J. R., Romera, A. J., Beskow, W. B., and Lovatt, S. J., 'Better simulation modelling to support farming systems innovation: Review and synthesis', *New Zealand Journal of Agricultural Research*, 51:3 (2008), 235–52.

Woolf, Daniel, *The social circulation of the past: English historical culture 1500–1730* (Oxford, 2003).

Wordie, J. Ross, *Estate management in eighteenth-century England: The building of the Leveson-Gower fortune* (London, 1982).

Wordie, J. Ross, 'The chronology of English enclosure, 1500–1914', *EcHR*, 36:4 (1983), 483–505.

Wright, Erik Olin, *Class counts: Student edition* (Cambridge, 2000).

Wrightson, Keith, *English society, 1580–1680* (London, 1982).

Wrightson, Keith, *Earthly necessities: Economic lives in early modern Britain, 1470–1750* (London, 2000).

Wrigley, E. A., 'Urban growth and agricultural change: England and the continent in the early modern period', *Journal of Interdisciplinary History*, 15:4 (1985), 683–728.

Wrigley, E. A., 'Men on the land and men in the countryside: Employment in agriculture in early-nineteenth-century England', in Lloyd Bonfield, Richard M. Smith, and Keith Wrightson (eds), *The world we have gained: Histories of population and social structure: Essays presented to Peter Laslett on his seventieth birthday* (Oxford, 1986), 295–336.

Wrigley, Julia, 'The division between mental and manual labor: Artisan education in science in nineteenth-century Britain', *American Journal of Sociology*, 88: Supplement: Marxist Inquiries: Studies of Labor, Class, and States (1982), S31–S51.

Yeo, Richard, *Encyclopaedic visions: Scientific dictionaries and enlightenment culture* (Cambridge, 2001).

Index

For EU product safety concerns, contact us at Calle de José Abascal, 56–1°,
28003 Madrid, Spain or eugpsr@cambridge.org.

www.ingramcontent.com/pod-product-compliance
Ingram Content Group UK Ltd.
Pitfield, Milton Keynes, MK11 3LW, UK
UKHW020400140625
459647UK00020B/2575